ON THE COVER: Just a few of the sample documents from this book, printed on predesigned laser papers with a standard black-and-white laser printer.

For every kind of computer user, there is a SYBEX book.

All computer users learn in their own way. Some need straightforward and methodical explanations. Others are just too busy for this approach. But no matter what camp you fall into, SYBEX has a book that can help you get the most out of your computer and computer software while learning at your own pace.

Beginners generally want to start at the beginning. The **ABC's** series, with its step-by-step lessons in plain language, helps you build basic skills quickly. Or you might try our **Quick & Easy** series, the friendly, full-color guide.

The **Mastering** and **Understanding** series will tell you everything you need to know about a subject. They're perfect for intermediate and advanced computer users, yet they don't make the mistake of leaving beginners behind.

If you're a busy person and are already comfortable with computers, you can choose from two SYBEX series—**Up & Running** and **Running Start**. The **Up & Running** series gets you started in just 20 lessons. Or you can get two books in one, a step-by-step tutorial and an alphabetical reference, with our **Running Start** series.

Everyone who uses computer software can also use a computer software reference. SYBEX offers the gamut—from portable **Instant References** to comprehensive **Encyclopedias**, **Desktop References**, and **Bibles**.

SYBEX even offers special titles on subjects that don't neatly fit a category—like **Tips & Tricks**, the **Shareware Treasure Chests**, and a wide range of books for Macintosh computers and software.

SYBEX books are written by authors who are expert in their subjects. In fact, many make their living as professionals, consultants, or teachers in the field of computer software. And their manuscripts are thoroughly reviewed by our technical and editorial staff for accuracy and ease-of-use.

So when you want answers about computers or any popular software package, just help yourself to SYBEX.

For a complete catalog of our publications, please write:

SYBEX Inc.
2021 Challenger Drive
Alameda, CA 94501
Tel: (510) 523-8233/(800) 227-2346 Telex: 336311
Fax: (510) 523-2373

SYBEX is committed to using natural resources wisely to preserve and improve our environment. As a leader in the computer book publishing industry, we are aware that over 40% of America's solid waste is paper. This is why we have been printing the text of books like this one on recycled paper since 1982.

This year our use of recycled paper will result in the saving of more than 15,300 trees. We will lower air pollution effluents by 54,000 pounds, save 6,300,000 gallons of water, and reduce landfill by 2,700 cubic yards.

In choosing a SYBEX book you are not only making a choice for the best in skills and information, you are also choosing to enhance the quality of life for all of us.

The Instant Office for Microsoft® Office

Alan Simpson

San Francisco • Paris • Düsseldorf • Soest

Acquisitions Editor: Joanne Cuthbertson
Developmental Editor: Sarah Wadsworth
Editor: Guy Hart-Davis
Technical Editors: Elizabeth Shannon, Jessica A. Obando
Book Design and Composition: Seventeenth Street Studios
Proofreader/Production Assistant: Kate Westrich
Indexer: Ted Laux
Cover Designer: Joanna Gladden
Cover Photographer: David Bishop

Screen reproductions produced with Collage Complete.
Collage Complete is a trademark of Inner Media Inc.

Library of Congress Card Number: 94-67202
ISBN: 0-7821-1556-X

Manufactured in the United States of America

10 9 8 7 6 5 4 3 2 1

Dedication

To Susita, Zashley, Niño, Snowball, Clifford, Tigger, Babs, Cleo, Leo, and Tiny Tim

Acknowledgments

Like any book, this one was a team effort. My thanks to all these folks for their time, skills, talent, and many important contributions to this book:

At SYBEX: Sarah Wadsworth, the developmental editor; Guy Hart-Davis, the editor; Beth Shannon and Jessica Obando, the technical editors; Lorrie Fink, the typesetter and book designer; and Kate Westrich, the proofreader.

Many thanks to Rodnay, Alan, and Rudy for this opportunity to try something radically new and different.

Thanks to Martha Mellor for her reviews, criticisms, and technical support.

Many thanks to everyone at Waterside Productions, my literary agents, for keeping me busy and happy.

Thanks to my family for their patience, support, and encouragement.

Contents at a Glance

Table of Contents

Appendix A: Absolute "How To" Basics 259

Appendix B: Universal Office Skills Quick Reference 284

Introduction (Read Me First)

Welcome to *The Instant Office for Microsoft Office*, the quickest and easiest way to take care of everyday business using your PC, Windows, and Microsoft Office. I wrote this book for "normal" PC users—the kind of people who ask questions like:

- "What's the quickest way to print a fax cover sheet?" or
- "How do I figure out the payment on a loan?" or
- "What's the best way to manage a list of names and addresses?"

Now you might be thinking, "Big deal—doesn't *every* computer book answer questions like that?" No, they don't. Not directly, anyway. If you look through the table of contents or index to most computer books, you see that everything centers around general features of a particular application. You'll find topics like "fonts" and "tables" and "functions."

Such books assume that you already know what features of an application you'll need in order to reach your goal. You're just looking up instructions on how to use a particular feature.

But the truth of the matter is, most PC users *don't* know which features, or even which *application*, to use to get a particular job done.

And in this book, you don't have to know. Just look up whatever you want to create on the inside covers or in the index. Then flip to the appropriate page in my *Do-It-Now Encyclopedia*. There you'll find the easiest way to create the document or manage the data.

How to Use This Book

How you use this book depends, first, on how much experience you already have with PCs, Windows, and Office.

You're New to PCs

If you're new to PCs, I suggest you start off by taking this path through the book:

- *Visual Dictionary*, pages 364–379: For starters, take a quick tour through my Visual Dictionary to start learning the names of things and buzzwords you'll need to contend with.
- *English–Computerese Dictionary*, page 363: Then maybe take a quick look at my English–Computerese Dictionary, to get a feel for words we use to describe actions like "get into" (*open*) or "get out of" (*exit*).
- *Absolute "How To" Basics*, pages 259–283: Finally, read Appendix A to learn how to start your PC and get into Windows. Windows will be your "home base" for all your Microsoft Office applications.

Once you've completed that, you'll be caught up with the people in the next category of users—those with PC experience but little or no Windows experience.

You're Familiar with PCs and Have Some Windows Experience

If you already know how to work a mouse and keyboard, but your Windows skills are just so-so and you often feel lost, then I'd suggest you start off by tightening up those Windows skills. Try this tour through the book:

- *Take Control of Windows*, pages 269–276: This section in Appendix A will teach you the most important skills to know to be in charge of Windows.
- *Arrange Windows and Icons*, pages 285–289: This reference section reinforces, and expands somewhat upon, the information at the end of Appendix A.

Once you've read those two sections, consider yourself an experienced Windows user. Move yourself into the next category of user, which is...

You Know Windows but Are New to Office

Once you can get along with your PC and Windows reasonably well, it's time to start exploring Microsoft Office. Read the opening sections:

- *Keys to the Office* explains what Office is all about, as well as basic concepts like applications and documents.
- *Instant Office* introduces each application in Office and provides instructions on starting, using, and exiting those applications.

With that under your belt, you'll be ready to start being productive with your PC, which puts you in this category...

You're Ready to Get to Work

When you're ready to get to work, you can use the reference sections of this book in whatever manner best suits your needs at the moment.

- *Do-It-Now Encyclopedia* (pages 33–258): The main reference section of this book is the *Do-It-Now Encyclopedia,* which has blue thumb-tabs so you can flip right to it in an instant. There, you just look up whatever it is you want to make or manage, and follow the simple instructions.
- Endpapers (inside the front and back cover): Inside the front and back covers of this book you'll find a list of all kinds of common, everyday business documents you can create in minutes. Use those lists, or the more traditional index at the back of the book, to find whatever it is you're trying to create.
- *Universal Office Skills* (pages 284–354): If, while using the *Do-It-Now Encyclopedia,* you come across an instruction that you don't understand, try looking it up in Appendix B. There you'll find references to actions, such as "choose" and "select," as well as tools you'll use, like "menus," "dialog boxes," and "Help."

Back by the index you'll find a couple of other brief sections that you might need to refer to occasionally:

- Appendix C: *Sources* (pages 355–360) lists products mentioned in this book, along with names and addresses of the vendors or publishers of those products.

- *Glossary* (pages 379–385) provides a standard glossary of common computer terms used in this book. There, you'll also find instructions on how to use the glossary that's built into Windows and your Office applications.

Installing Microsoft Office

If you purchased this book before buying Microsoft Office, you'll need to make sure your PC can handle Office before you buy the product. That's what the rest of this *Introduction* covers. (Skip it if Office is already on your PC.)

What You Need to Run Microsoft Office

If you're reading this book because you're considering purchasing Microsoft Office, do be aware that Office is a modern software package that requires a modern PC to run. To use Microsoft Office, your PC must meet the requirements listed under "Minimum" in Table I.1. For top performance, however, you should purchase a system that matches the requirements listed under "Recommended" in that table or upgrade your current PC to that level.

TABLE I.1

Minimum and Recommended Hardware and Software Requirements for Using Microsoft Office

HARDWARE/SOFTWARE	MINIMUM	RECOMMENDED
Processor	386SX	486 or Pentium
Memory (RAM)	4 megabytes (MB)	8 or more megabytes (MB)
Hard Disk Space	25–62 megabytes (MB)	65–100 megabytes (MB)
Monitor	EGA or higher	VGA, SVGA, or higher
DOS/Windows	DOS 3.1, Windows 3.1	DOS 6.x, Windows 3.1 or later
Printer	Any	Laser

How to Install Microsoft Office

Like any software product, you need to purchase and install Microsoft Office before you can use it. (It's not "built-in" to anyone's computer.) Of course, you only need to install Office once, not every time you want to use it. So if you, or somebody else, has already installed Office on your PC, then you don't need to worry about any of that.

Once you have the Microsoft Office floppy disks in hand, you need to install their files to your hard disk. Just follow the installation instructions that came with your Office package. Or, if you're an experienced Windows guru, you can just go through the standard installation procedure that most Windows applications require:

1. Start your PC and get to the Windows Program Manager.
2. Insert the disk labeled *Disk 1 - Setup* in floppy drive A: or B:.
3. Choose File ➢ Run from Program Manager's menu bar.
4. If you put the floppy disk in drive A:, type **a:\setup.exe,** or if you put the floppy in drive B:, type **b:\setup.exe;** then press ↵ or choose OK.
5. Follow all instructions that appear on the screen, until you've completed the installation.

The whole installation procedure takes about 15 or 20 minutes. If you're an absolute beginner, please remember that you should read Appendix A before you try to do *anything* with your PC. And don't install Office if it's already been installed on your PC.

Where to Get Microsoft Office

You can purchase Microsoft Office at just about any computer store or "warehouse" store that carries computer supplies. You can also order Office through any of the mail-order services that advertise in computer magazines.

Version Numbers of Applications in This Book

PCs are an evolving technology, which means they keep getting more powerful and easier to use. As the PC evolves into a more friendly machine, so do the applications that make the PC run.

Each time a software company releases a new-and-improved version of an application, they don't change its name. Rather, they increase its version number. Simply stated, the higher the version number, the more recent the product.

In this book, I'll be covering the most recent versions of Microsoft Office's applications, as summarized below:

PRODUCT	VERSION
Microsoft Office Manager	4.3
Microsoft Word	6.0a
Microsoft Excel	5.0
Microsoft PowerPoint	4.0
Microsoft Mail	3.2
Microsoft Access	2.0

Microsoft Access comes with Microsoft Office Professional Edition only, but you can purchase it separately should you decide to add it to your current collection of applications.

Upgrading Your Version

If you need to upgrade to a newer version of an Office application, check with your computer dealer for availability and pricing. Or contact Microsoft Corporation at the address and phone number listed in Appendix C.

Instant Office

Keys to the Office

WELCOME TO *The Instant Office for Microsoft Office*—the book that's designed to help you put that PC to work right now. Before you start pounding the keyboard, let's take a moment to talk about Office in general, get our bearings, and figure out where would be your best starting point, based on your past PC experience.

What Is Microsoft Office?

Microsoft Office is sort of a complete office in a box. It offers the *applications* (tools) you need to take care of everyday business. You can use Office to do simple things like type a letter or calculate the payment on a loan. And you can use it for bigger jobs, such as sending out form letters or invitations, as well.

When you first buy Microsoft Office, it looks much like any other software package—a collection of manuals and software on floppy disks, as in Figure KO.1.

FIGURE KO.1

When you first purchase Microsoft Office, it looks like most other computer software products: a collection of manuals and software.

After you (or somebody else) installs Office on your computer, it becomes more like an office on a desktop, rather than in a box. When you start Windows on your PC, Office initially appears as an application icon in the Windows Program Manager, and perhaps as the Office Manager toolbar, as shown in Figure KO.2.

Let's take a moment to talk about applications and documents, for those of you who are new to PCs.

FIGURE KO.2

After you've installed Office, its application icon appears in the Windows Program Manager. You might also see the Office Manager toolbar somewhere on the screen.

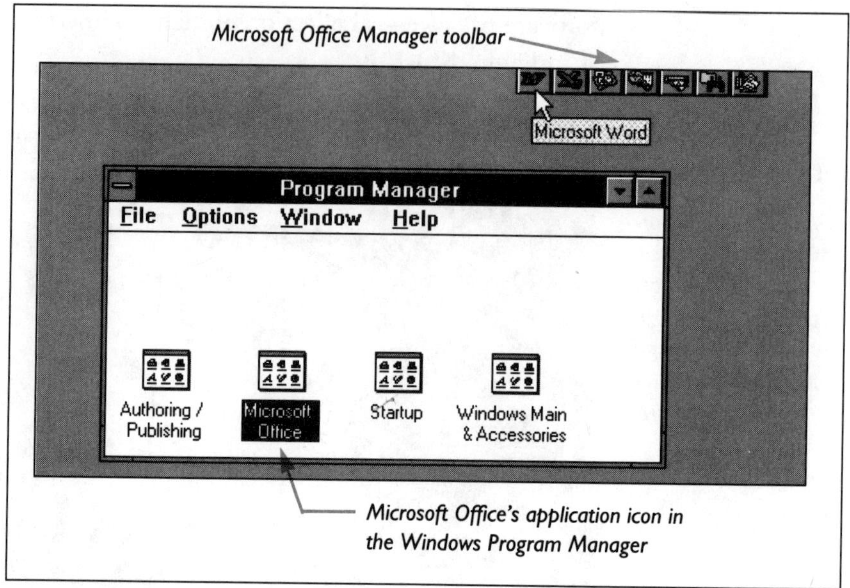

What Is an Application?

When you use a computer to do work, everything centers around using an *application* to create a *document.* To help you keep these two terms straight, here are a couple of definitions:

Application: A software program that you purchase, and install on your computer, to help with certain types of work. For example, you use a word-processing application to help with typing and writing.

Document: Anything that you create using an application. For example, letters, memos, envelopes, mailing labels, and newsletters are a few examples of the types of document you can create using a word-processing application.

Microsoft Office is a collection of four main applications—five main applications if you buy the Professional Edition, which includes Microsoft Access. Each application is designed to help you with a particular type of business task, as summarized in Table KO.1.

TABLE KO.1

Major Applications in Microsoft Office

APPLICATION NAME	STARTUP BUTTON	TYPE	BEST USED FOR	EXAMPLES
Word		Word Processing	Typing, writing	Letters, memos, stories, envelopes, labels, newsletters
Excel		Spreadsheet	Math, charting	Financial analyses, pie charts, statistics
PowerPoint		Presentation	Visual aids	Slides, overheads, any visual aids for a presentation
Access[1]		Database	Record keeping	Names and addresses, inventory, library, bookkeeping
Mail[2]		E-Mail	Local E-Mail	Send a document to another user on the network

1. Access is included in Microsoft Office Professional Edition only, but it can be purchased separately from Microsoft.

2. Each Office package contains one Microsoft Mail Workstation license. Microsoft Mail must be purchased and installed separately.

Easy Mix-and-Match

Not only does Microsoft Office give you a lot of great applications at a low price; it also offers excellent integrations of applications, making it easy to mix-and-match things from different applications. If you're new to PCs, let me just say that this is a big improvement over the way we did things in the past.

In the dark ages of PCs, when DOS was king, you could create a decent-looking chart in your spreadsheet application. And you could create a beautifully formatted report using your word processor. But putting a copy of the chart into your report tended to be like trying to drill teeth on an angry alligator—neither easy nor pleasant.

Office solves this lack of integration using a new technology dubbed *OLE 2.0* (OLE stands for Object Linking and Embedding). For example, Figure KO.3 shows two Office applications open on the screen simultaneously: Microsoft Excel, which I used to create a chart, and Microsoft Word, which I used to type up some text.

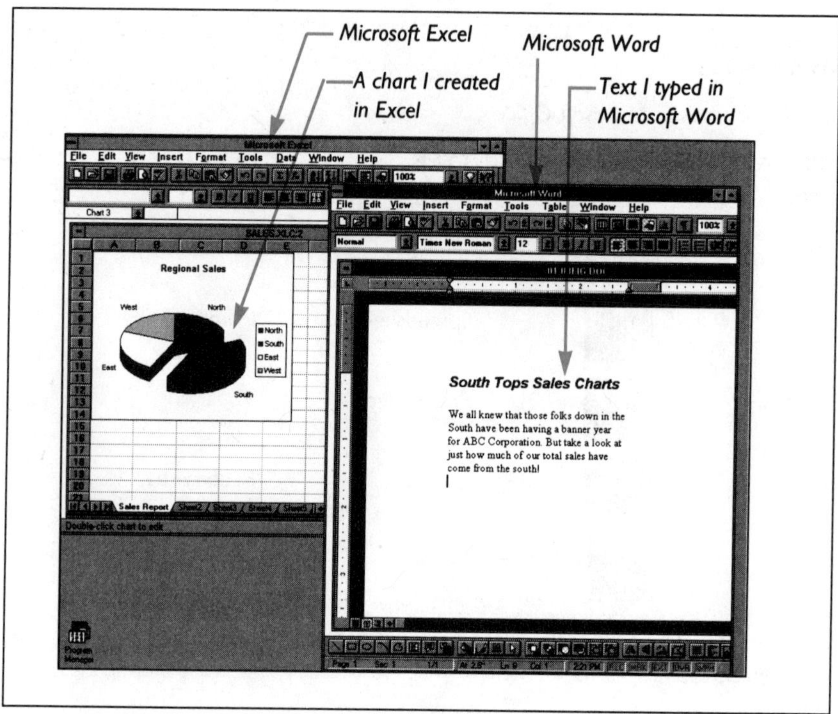

FIGURE KO.3

A chart I created using Microsoft Excel and a report I typed up using Microsoft Word, both on the screen.

Because Office is so flexible, I can easily put a copy of that Excel chart right into my Word document, as in Figure KO.4.

There are many more many ways to mix-and-match in Office, as I'll explain in the *Instant Office* section (next).

Where to Go from Here

Where you turn to next in this book depends on how much you understand of what's been covered in this section.

- **If you're new to PCs or Windows**, you might understand very little of what's been said in this first section. Antidote: Read Appendix A, *Absolute "How To" Basics* for a quick crash course in PC and Windows basic skills. You might also want to browse through

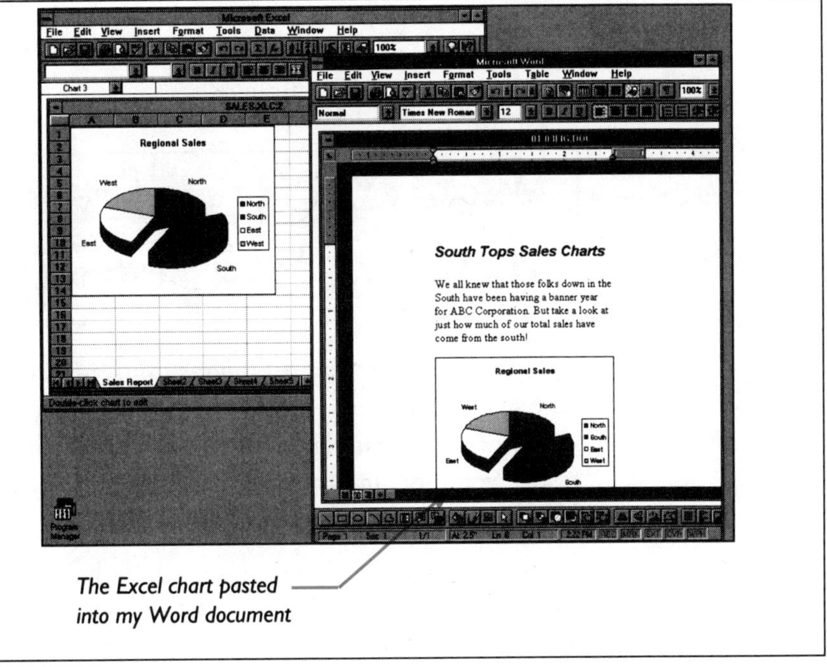

FIGURE KO.4

Office lets me easily take a copy of the chart in my Excel worksheet and plop it right into my Word document.

the Visual Dictionary near the end of the book to start familiarizing yourself with the names of things. Then proceed to the *Instant Office* section.

- **If you're an experienced Windows user**, and already know about menus, mouse clicks, and such, go on ahead to the *Instant Office* section now.

Extra Goodies: Fonts, Clip Art, Colored Paper

Occasionally I'll use fonts (print styles), clip art (pictures), and precolored papers (like on the front cover) in this book. I'm not going to limit myself to items that come with Microsoft Office. Instead, I prefer to show you lots of different examples, so you can get a feel for just how creative Microsoft Office will allow you to be.

If an item isn't part of Office, I'll try to include its name and manufacturer in text. For example, here's a font named Motion that I purchased from a company named Emigre.

Motion Light from Emigre
Motion Bold from Emigre

To find out more about Emigre's fonts, just check your local computer store or contact Emigre directly. Refer to Appendix C for a names and addresses of the manufacturers. If you contact them, I'm sure they'd gladly send you more information about their products.

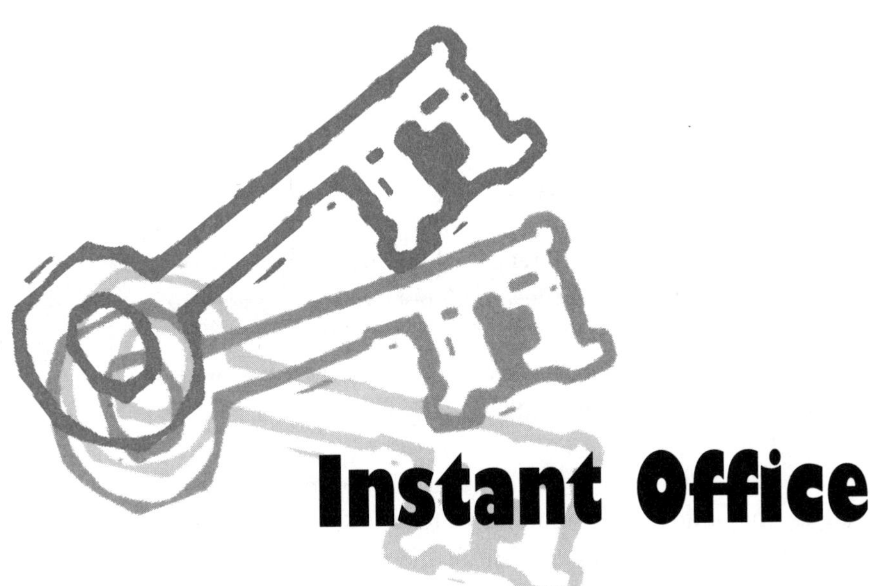

Instant Office

IN THIS SECTION, I'll show you how to take yourself through a quick tour of each application in Microsoft Office. That tour will teach you the basic concepts of the application and will show you the basic skills and techniques you need to use that application.

Of course, you don't need to learn, or even tour, *every* application right off the bat. You might want to start off with just Office Manager, which you can learn in about five minutes flat.

Then try one of the applications—perhaps Microsoft Word. That's the application you'll probably use the most, and it's probably the easiest to learn as well. Once you get a feel for what Word is in this section, try creating some of the sample Word documents in the *Do-It-Now Encyclopedia.* You'll start to get the hang of it with the practice the *Encyclopedia* gives you.

Please keep in mind that we're not shooting for professional-level mastery of each application in this chapter. Rather, the information presented here is really just enough to get your proverbial feet wet. But chances are, once you've completed the tour of each application, you'll be on your way to creating your own documents—especially with some help from the *Do-It-Now Encyclopedia.*

Learn by Discovery

In this book, I won't even try to repeat all the information that's in the "official" manuals and help screens. Why not? There's no need to. Modern applications are specifically designed to help you "learn by discovery," to learn what you need to learn as the need arises—which is the most natural and expedient way to learn anything.

The initial tour or "Quick Preview" that each application will present on your screen will tell you all you need to know to get started. Then you can use the built-in help and Cue Cards to fill in the blanks, to learn as you go. The Help system *is* your official User's Manual and offers everything a manual offers—index, glossary, step-by-step instructions—and much, much more.

So whenever you find yourself wondering "How do I...?" or "What is...?" don't start flipping through the manuals. Don't call tech support. And don't call upon cranky colleagues. Just press F1 instead. Or choose Help from the application's menu bar.

The Office Manager

Office Manager isn't really an application—it's a toolbar on your screen that offers quick access to your Office applications. Typically, the Office Manager toolbar appears automatically when you first start Windows. It will either be docked near the upper-right corner of the screen or perhaps free-floating (as shown below).

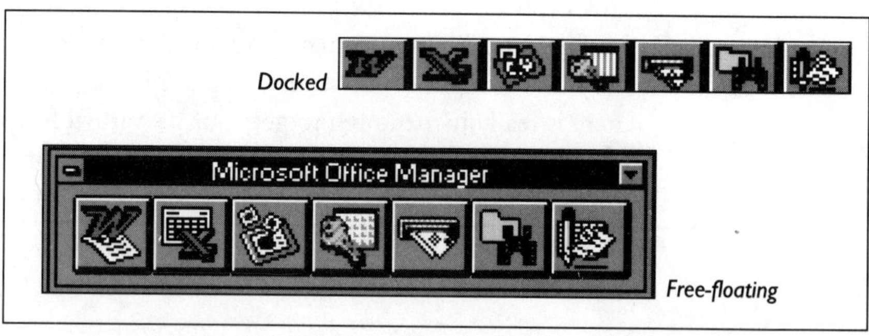

To Start Office Manager

If the Office Manager toolbar isn't on your screen (when you're in Windows), just follow these steps to start it:

1. Starting from the Windows Program Manager, open the Microsoft Office group window by double-clicking on it.
2. Double-click the Microsoft Office application icon.

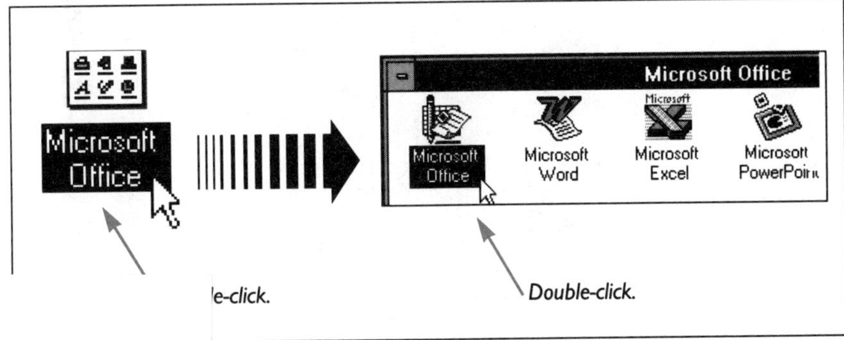

...nager at a Glance

...kills for using Office Manager, just read this section, ...wse through the *Toolbars* entry in Appendix B. ...our of Office Manager, right-click the Office Manager ...ue Cards, and choose the first option.

...nager Tips

...name of the application that a button will start, move ...pointer to that button, and wait a second for the ... appear. To run the application, just click the button.

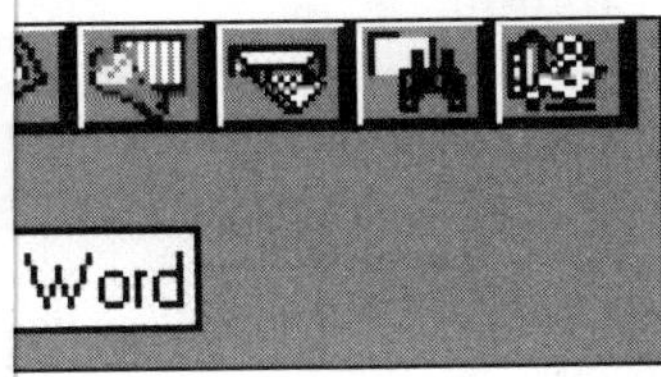

- To move, customize, or get help with Office Manager, first right-click anywhere on the toolbar. Then choose an option from the pop-up menu that appears. The Customize option lets you add, delete, and rearrange buttons. Use the Small, Regular, and Large Buttons commands to switch between a docked and a free-floating toolbar.

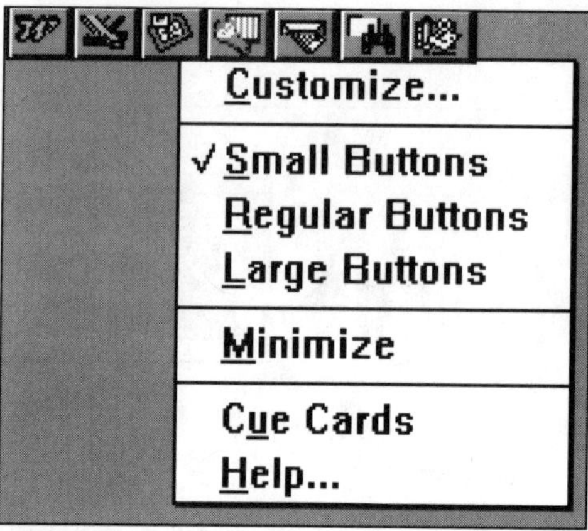

- You can also get to Office Manager features by clicking (with the left mouse button) the Microsoft Office button in the toolbar.

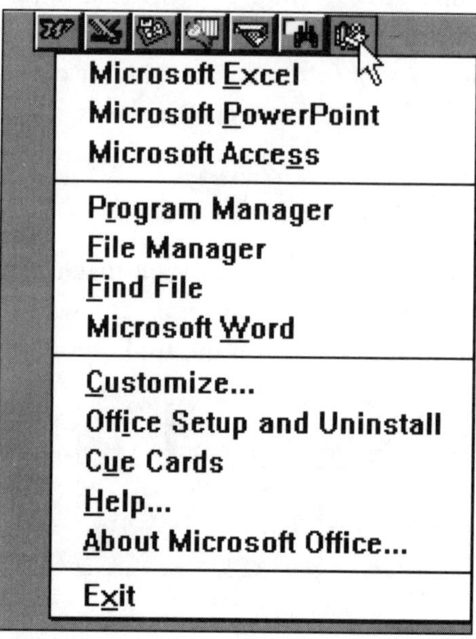

Office Manager Help

To get help with Office Manager, right-click the toolbar and choose Help or Cue Cards.

Exiting Office Manager

It's not necessary to exit Office Manager before exiting Windows. However, if you do want to turn off the toolbar, perhaps to conserve memory for other applications, just click the Microsoft Office button in the toolbar and choose Exit.

Microsoft Word

Microsoft Word is the word-processing application in Office. Whenever you think "typewriter," think Word instead. You can use Word to easily create any written document, from a single mailing label or labels on up to a book. For example, I wrote this book using Microsoft Word.

To Start Microsoft Word

1. Use either of these techniques to start Word:

   - Click this icon in the Office Manager toolbar.

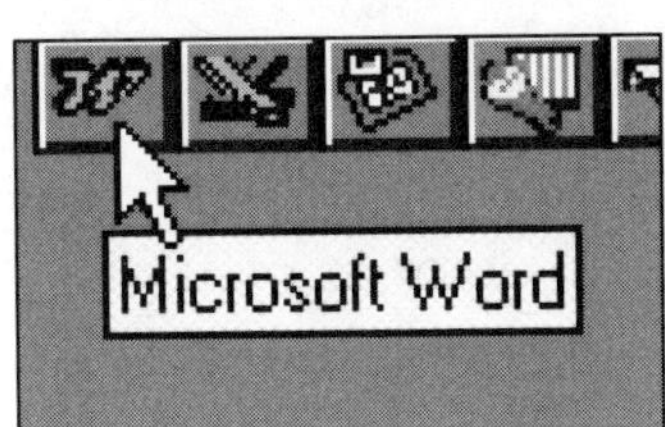

   - Or, from Program Manager, double-click on the Microsoft Office group icon, then double-click the Microsoft Word application icon.

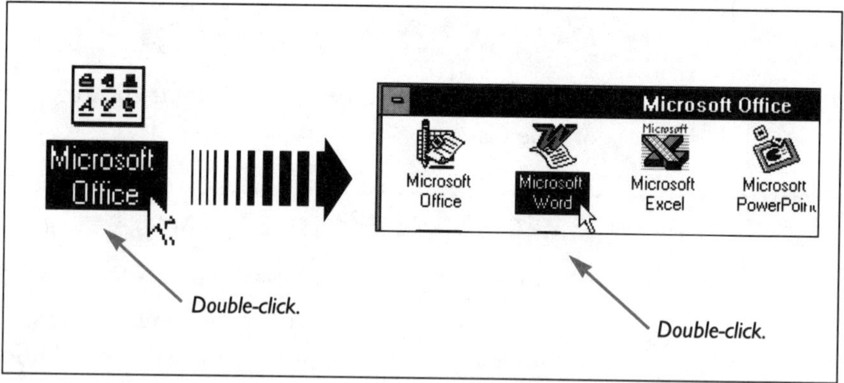

2. If the Tip of the Day appears, choose OK to leave that dialog box and get to work.

3. Remember that if Word doesn't start up in full-screen size, you can double-click its title bar or click its Maximize button to expand it to full-screen.

Word at a Glance

Figure IO.1 shows what Word looks like.

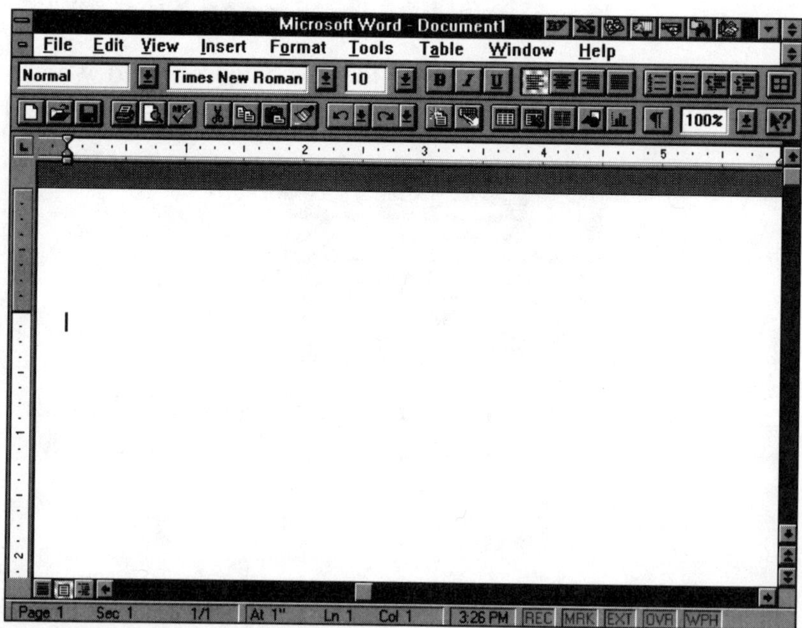

FIGURE IO.1

This is how Microsoft Word looks when it's running at full-screen size on your screen. As usual, the title bar shows you the name of the application, Microsoft Word.

To learn basic skills for using Word, see the following sections of Appendix B: *Menus; Help; Wizards; Toolbars; Typing Text and Numbers; Select, Then Do; Save Your Work; Open (Retrieve) Saved Work.*

For a guided tour of Word, choose Help ➢ Quick Preview from Word's menu bar. You might also want to explore Help ➢ Examples and Demos.

To exit Word, choose File ➢ Exit from Word's menu bar and respond to any prompts.

Word Tips

- If Word's menu bar presents only the two commands File and Help, as shown below, you'll need to open a document window before you can start typing, Choose File ➢ New ➢ OK.

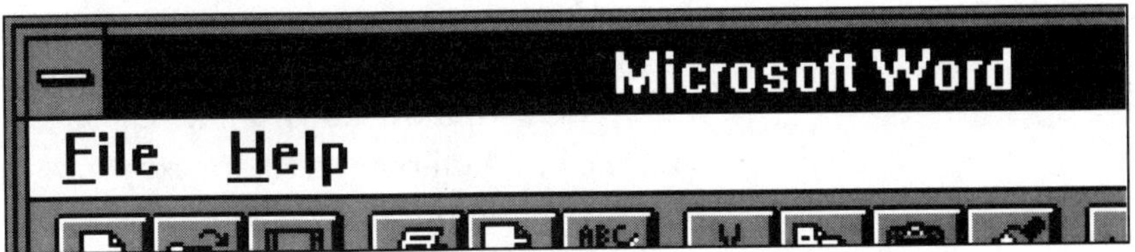

- When typing a paragraph in Word, don't press ↵ at the end of each line. Rather, press ↵ only at the end of each paragraph, to insert blank lines, or to end a short line. For example, in Figure IO.2 I've put an [Enter] symbol to show where you would press ↵ while typing the start of a letter. (That [Enter] symbol never appears on your screen or printed document.)

FIGURE 10.2

When typing in Word, press the ↵ key only to end short lines, insert blank lines, and to end a complete paragraph. Don't press ↵ at the end of every line.

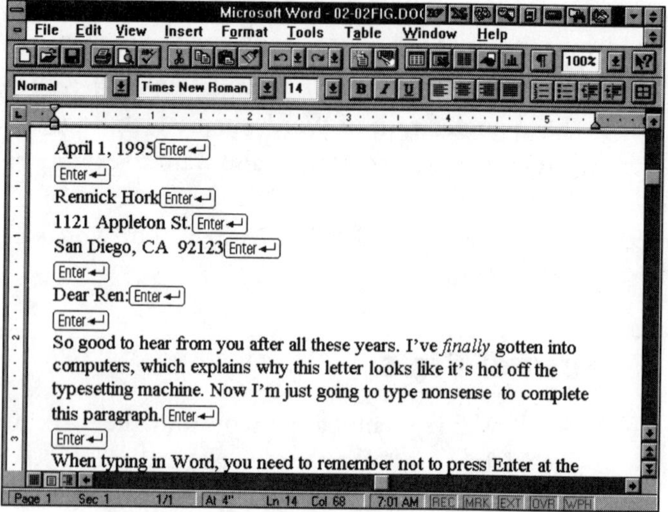

- The blinking insertion point indicates where the next text you type will appear. To move the insertion point past the end of the document, press ↵ to move down a line. Or press Tab to indent. To move the insertion point back to text you've already typed to make corrections, insertions, or deletions, just click wherever you want to put the insertion point. Or use the cursor-movement keys (←, →, ↑, ↓) to position the insertion point.

To move the insertion point back to existing text, click or use the cursor keys to move the cursor to wherever you want to make a change.

oint back, through text you've already typed.
land the insertion point. Or use the cursor
nt. To move down past the end of your typed
move to a new line. Right now, the insertion
sentence.

The insertion point blinks.

To move down past the end of the document, press Enter (↵).

The mouse pointer has an I-beam shape when it's over a Word document.

- To make simple corrections, press Backspace to delete the character to the left of the insertion point. Or press Delete (Del) to delete the character to the right of the insertion point.
- To delete, move, or *format* (change the appearance of) a large chunk of text, use the standard techniques described under *Select, Then Do* in Appendix B.
- Word often presents instructions and useful information in the status bar, near the lower-left corner of the Word window. Glance down there when you're wondering what to do next.
- For a quick overview of commonly used Word features, see *Word Document* in the *Visual Dictionary* near the back of this book.

Word Help

Word offers the standard Windows help system. Press F1 for immediate help. Or, from Word's menu bar, choose Help and then any option from the menu that appears.

Exiting Word

Always remember to exit Word, and save your document, before turning off the computer. Choose File ➢ Exit from Word's menu bar, and respond to any prompts that appear.

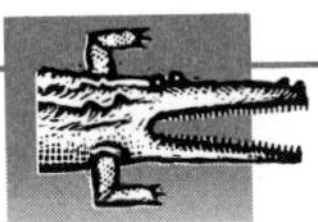

WARNING: *You should always exit an application when you've finished with it, even if you don't care about saving your work. Shutting down a PC with applications still running leads to lost work, corrupted files, and other unpleasantnesses.*

When you save a document, you must give it a valid DOS file name (eight characters maximum length, no spaces or punctuation). If you don't include an extension in the filename that you use to save a Word document, Word automatically adds the extension .DOC. For example, if you save your work as **myletter**, Word will actually store that document on disk as MYLETTER.DOC. You should always allow Word to add that .DOC extension, rather than making up your own. That way, whenever you see .DOC at the end of a file name, you'll know it's a Microsoft Word document.

For more information on exiting applications and saving documents, see *Exit an Application* in Appendix B.

Microsoft Excel

Microsoft Excel is designed to help you with math. It's especially good for "what-if" scenarios, and also has powerful capabilities for creating pie charts, bar graphs, line graphs, and other business graphics.

To Start Microsoft Excel

1. Use either of these techniques to start Excel:

   - Click the Microsoft Excel button the Office Manager toolbar.

   - Or, from Program Manager, double click on the Microsoft Office group icon, then double-click the Microsoft Excel application icon.

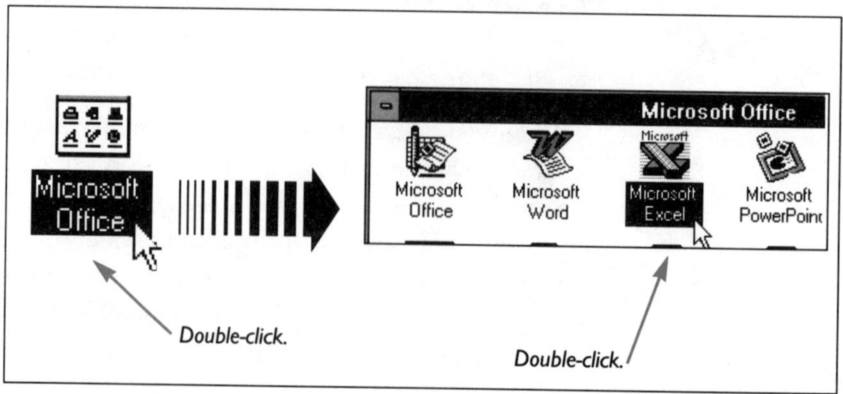

2. If Excel doesn't start up in full-screen size, you can double-click its title bar or click its Maximize button to expand it to full-screen.

Excel at a Glance

Figure IO.3 shows what Excel looks like.

FIGURE IO.3

This is how Microsoft Excel looks when it's running at full-screen size on your screen. The title bar shows you the name of the application.

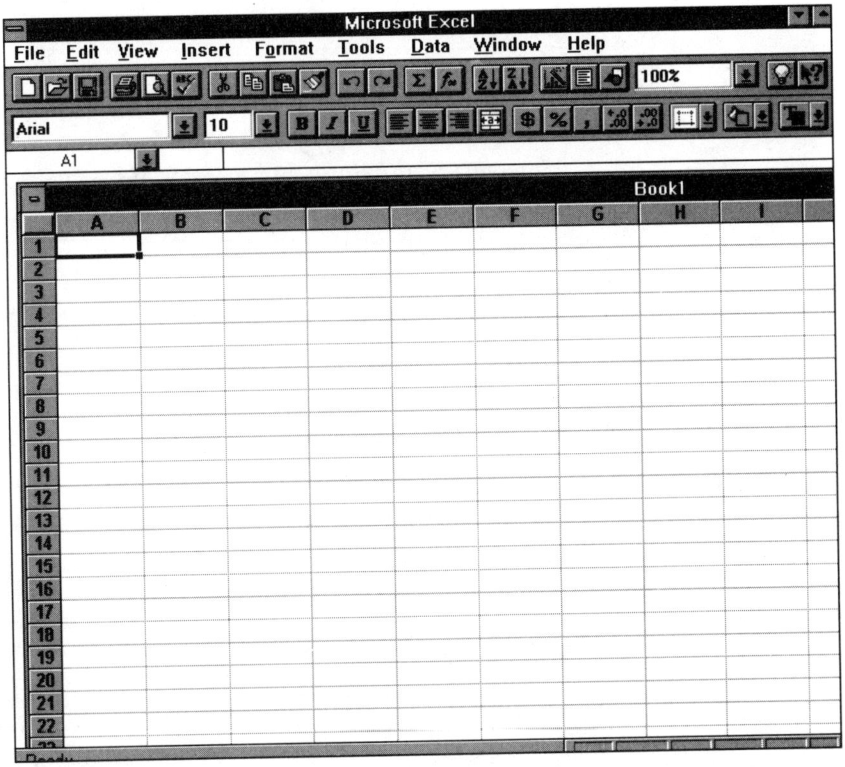

To learn basic startup skills for working in Excel, see the following sections in Appendix B: *Menus; Help; Typing Text and Numbers; Select, Then Do; Save Your Work;* and *Open (Retrieve) Saved Work.*

For a guided tour of Excel, choose Help ➢ Quick Preview from Excel's menu bar.

To exit Excel, choose File ➢ Exit from Excel's menu bar and respond to any prompts.

Excel Tips

- For a hands-on introduction to Excel features and basic skills, choose Help ➢ Quick Preview. Then choose Getting Started and follow the instructions on the screen.
- In a nutshell, here's how Excel works. You click any cell, then type in text, a number, or a formula. To type in a formula, first type an equal sign (=). Use cell addresses in your formulas. For example, suppose you type the number **10** into cell A1 and then type **15** into cell A2. Then you type **=A1+A2** into cell A3. Cell A3 would show **25**, the sum of 10 and 15. When you change the number in cell A1 or cell A2, cell A3 instantly shows you the sum of the new numbers.
- Excel often presents instructions and useful information in the status bar, near the lower-left corner of the Excel window. Glance down there once in a while for instructions on what to do next.
- Excel offers hundreds of *functions* to help with everything from business math to trigonometry. To explore the possibilities, search Excel's help for *functions* and *worksheet.*
- Press F1 whenever you need help in Excel.

Excel Help

Press F1 for immediate help, or choose an option from the Help command in Excel's menu bar. For help in choosing or using a function, choose Insert ➢ Function to get to the Function Wizard.

Exiting Excel

Always remember to exit Excel and, optionally, save your work before turning off the computer. Choose File ➢ Exit from Excel's menu bar, and respond to any prompts that appear. (See *Exit an Application* in Appendix B if you need help.)

When you save a file in Excel and omit the file name extension Excel automatically adds .XLS to your name. For example, if you save your work as **myloan**, then Word will actually store that document on disk as MYLOAN.XLS.

Microsoft PowerPoint

Microsoft PowerPoint helps you create a presentation with slides or overheads.

To Start Microsoft PowerPoint

1. Use either of these techniques to start PowerPoint:
   - Click the Microsoft PowerPoint button in the Office Manager toolbar.

   - Or, from Program Manager, double-click on the Microsoft Office group icon, then double-click the Microsoft PowerPoint application icon.

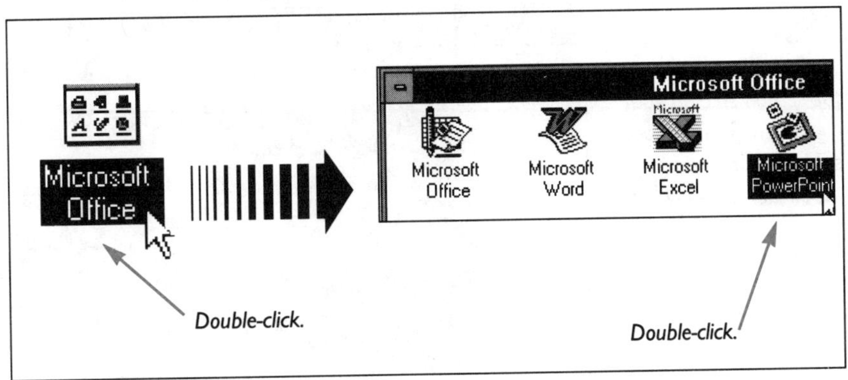

2. If the Tip of the Day appears, choose OK to move on to the PowerPoint opening screen, shown at the top of the next page.

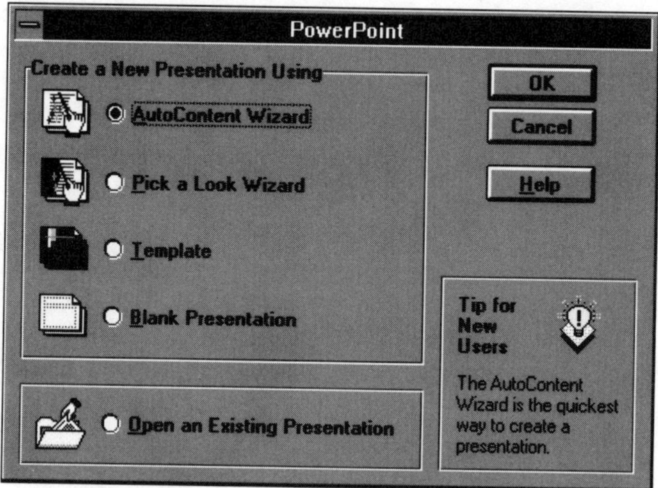

3. If this is the first time you've used PowerPoint, try the guided tour. Choose Cancel from the startup dialog box. Then choose Help Quick Preview from PowerPoint's menu bar. When you've completed the tour, you can choose File ➢ New from PowerPoint's menu bar to start your own presentation.

PowerPoint at a Glance

Figure IO.4 shows what PowerPoint looks like.

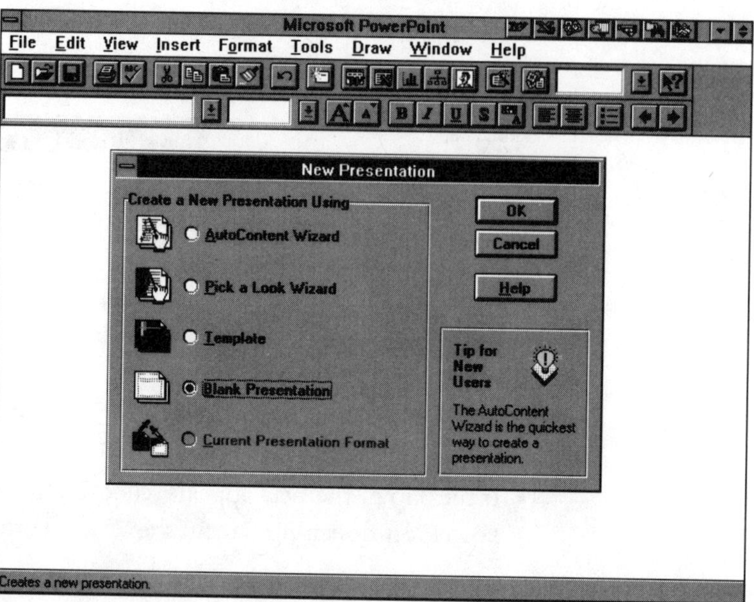

FIGURE IO.4

This is how Microsoft PowerPoint looks at full-screen size on your screen. The title bar shows the name of the application, as always.

To learn startup skills for using PowerPoint, see the following sections in Appendix B: *Wizards*, *Menus*, and *Help*.

For a guided tour of PowerPoint, choose Help ➢ Quick Preview from PowerPoint's menu bar.

To exit PowerPoint, choose File ➢ Exit from PowerPoint's menu bar and respond to any prompts.

PowerPoint Tips

- The AutoContent Wizard is the easiest way to create a new presentation. If you don't see an option for that on the screen, choose File New from PowerPoint's menu bar to get to the New Presentation dialog box.
- PowerPoint also occasionally presents instructions and useful information in the status bar near the lower-left corner of the PowerPoint window. Glance down there when you're not sure what to do next.

PowerPoint Help

Press F1 for immediate help. Or choose Help from PowerPoint's menu bar and choose an option from the pull-down menu. You can also get some coaching by choosing Help ➢ Cue Cards from PowerPoint's menu bar.

Exiting PowerPoint

Always remember to exit PowerPoint and save your work before turning off the computer. Just choose File ➢ Exit from PowerPoint's menu bar and respond to any messages that appear. (See *Exit an Application* in Appendix B if you need help with that.)

When you save a presentation and don't include a filename extension PowerPoint automatically adds the extension .PPT. For example, if you save your work as **myprsnt**, then Word will actually store that document on disk as MYPRSNT.PPT.

Microsoft Access

Microsoft Access helps you manage large volumes of data (information). You can use it to do simple things, like manage a list of names and addresses. Or you can take it to an extreme and create a complete custom application for managing all the data in a business.

To Start Microsoft Access

1. Use either of these techniques to start Access:
   - Click the Microsoft Access button in the Office Manager toolbar.

   - Or, from Program Manager, double-click on the Microsoft Office group icon, then double-click the Microsoft Access application icon.

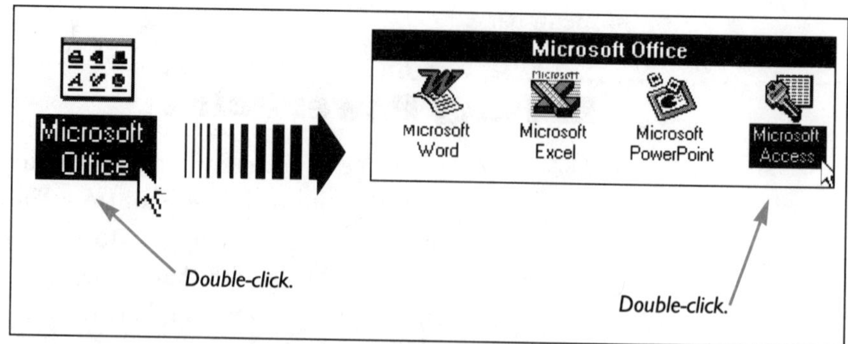

2. If the MSAccess Cue Cards window (Figure IO.5) appears, you can take a quick tour by choosing the first option, Get a quick introduction. If that window *doesn't* appear, you can still take the quick tour. Just choose Help ➢ Cue Cards, then choose See a quick overview. Follow the instructions on the screen.

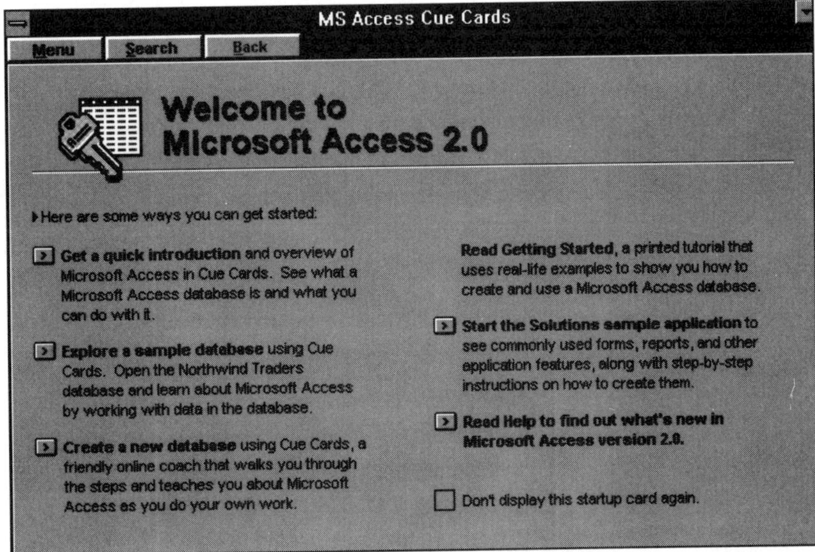

FIGURE 10.5

If Access displays this screen at startup, choose Get a quick introduction and overview *to take the tour. If this screen doesn't appear, you can choose Help ➢ Cue Cards to get to the tour.*

3. When you're ready to leave the Cue Cards, double-click the control-menu box in the upper-left corner of the Cue Card window.

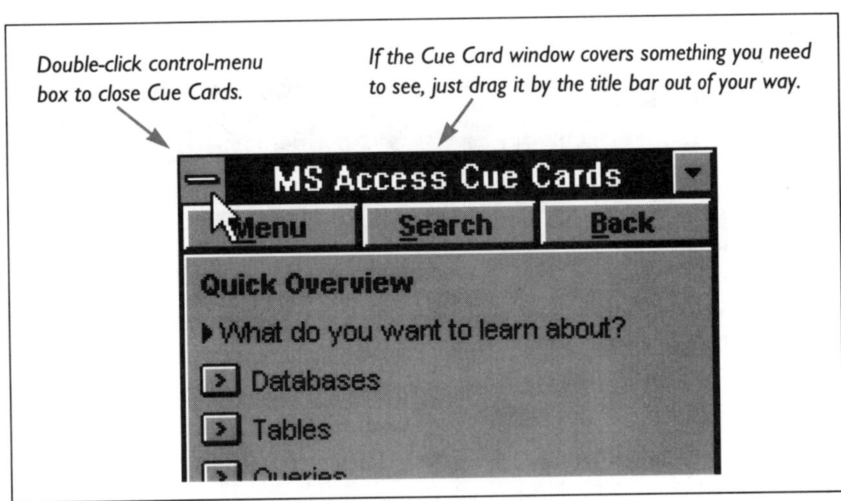

Access at a Glance

To learn startup skills for using Access, see the following sections in Appendix B: *Menus, Wizards, Help, and Cue Cards.*

For a guided tour of Access, choose Help ➢ Cue Cards from Access's menu bar, then choose *See a quick overview.*

To exit Access, choose File ➢ Exit from Access's menu bar.

Figure 10.6 shows what Access looks like.

Access Tips

- As with most applications, you can double-click Access's title bar to switch between partial- and full-screen view.
- Access is by far the biggest and most feature-laden application in Office. It can take *months* to fully master Access. Be patient, and don't be too hard on yourself if learning seems a little slow at first.
- Access often presents instructions and useful information in the status bar, near the lower-left corner of the Access window. Glance down there once in a while for instructions on what to do next.

FIGURE 10.6

Before you can do anything in Access, you must either open an existing database, or create a new one. An open database initially appears as a database window.

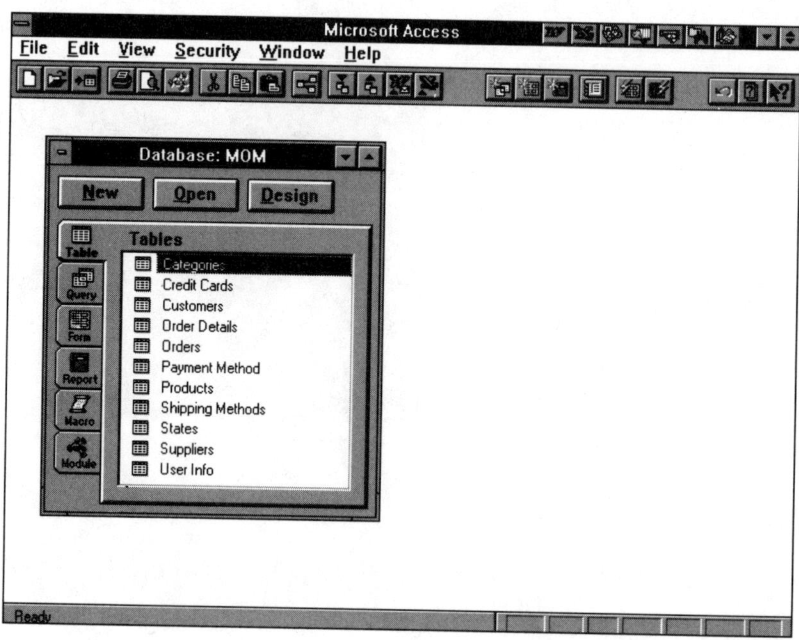

- When you first start Access, you might only see the File and Help commands. That means no database is open. Before you can start to work, you must either create a new database (choose File ➢New Database from Access's menu bar), or open an existing database (choose File ➢ Open Database from Access's menu bar). Once a database is open and ready for use, its *database window* appears on the desktop (as shown in Figure IO.6).
- Before you can store data in a database, you must create a *table* to hold that data. The easiest way to do so (once you have the database window on the screen) is to choose File ➢ New ➢ Table ➢ Table Wizards, and then follow the instructions on the screen.

Access Help

To get help in Access, press F1 or choose an option from Access's Help menu. For coaching as you work, try choosing Help ➢ Cue Cards from Access's menu bar.

Exiting Access

Always remember to exit Access and save your work before turning off the computer. Just choose File ➢ Exit from Access's menu bar. (See *Exit an Application* in Appendix B if you need help with that.)

When you create a new Access database (File ➢ New Database), you're prompted for a file name immediately. If you omit the extension, Access adds .MDB to your file name. For example, if you save your work as **mynames**, then Access will store that database as MYNAMES.MDB.

Don't be alarmed if Access doesn't prompt you to save your work when you exit. Access tends to save things automatically as you go along, and saves all of the objects for a database in one file. So there's a good chance that when you exit Access, all your work will have already been saved.

Microsoft Mail

Microsoft Mail lets you send electronic mail to other users on your local area network (LAN). You cannot use Mail unless your network administrator has installed the Mail "Post Office" on your network server and has given you a password to use Mail.

NOTE: *Mail is strictly for electronic mail. For standard paper mail (letters, envelopes, mailing labels), use Microsoft Word.*

To Start Microsoft Mail

1. Use either of these techniques to start Mail:
   - Click the Microsoft Mail button in the Office Manager toolbar:

   - Or, from Program Manager, double-click on the Microsoft Office group icon, then double-click the Microsoft Mail application icon.

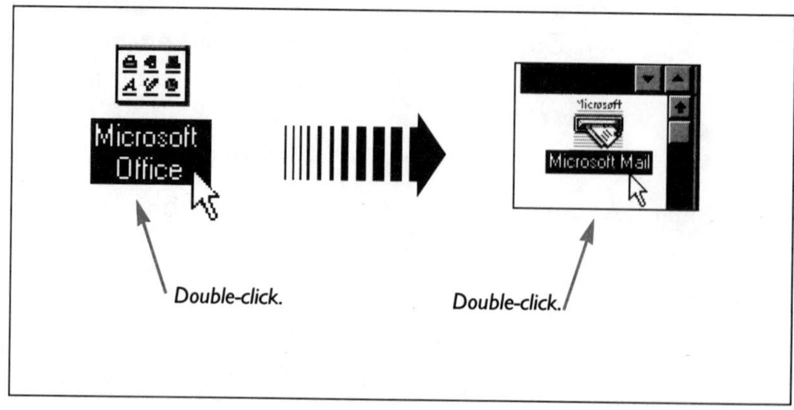

2. You'll see a dialog box like the one below. You must enter your password and then choose OK to proceed.

3. You'll be taken to the dialog box shown in Figure 10.7. For a quick overview and instructions on using Mail, choose Help ➢ Demos from the Mail menu bar.

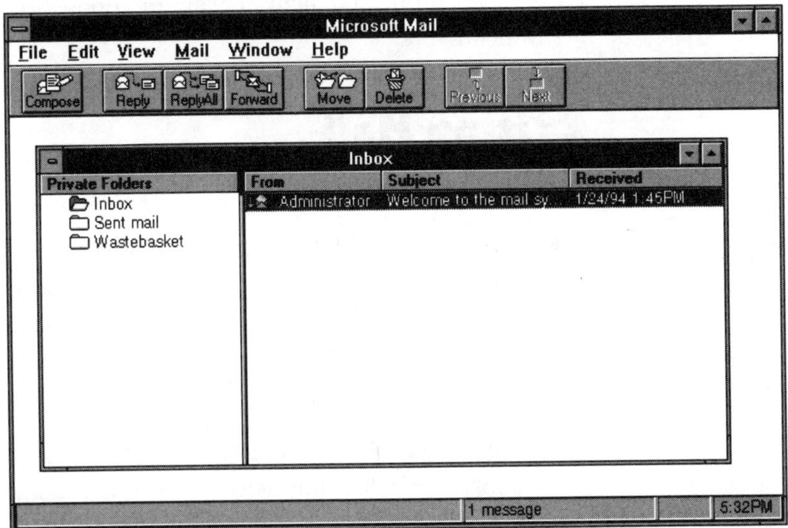

FIGURE 10.7

The Microsoft Mail dialog box gives you access to electronic mail in your workgroup.

Mail at a Glance

To learn startup skills for using Mail, see the following sections in Appendix B: *Menus* and *Help*.

For a guided tour of Mail, choose Help ➢ Demos from Mail's menu bar.

To exit Mail, choose File ➢ Exit from Mail's menu bar. Respond to any prompts that Mail throws at you.

Mail Tips

- To send the document that's currently on your screen in Word, Excel, or PowerPoint, first save that document using File ➢ Save from the application's menu bar. Then choose File ➢ Send or File ➢ Add Routing Slip from that application's menu bar.
- Mail often presents instructions and useful information in the status bar, near the lower-left corner of the Mail window. Glance down there once in a while for instructions on what to do next.

Mail Help

Press F1 for immediate help in Mail, or choose an option from Mail's Help menu.

Exiting Mail

There are two ways to exit Mail:

- Choose File ➢ Exit from Mail's menu bar. This deletes messages in your wastebasket and prompts you to send any outstanding mail, but it does not sign you out if you have other Mail-enabled applications running. So you won't need to re-enter your password if you decide to send more mail later.
- Choose File ➢ Exit and Sign Out—sort of the opposite of the above. This does not delete or send mail, but it does close all Mail-enabled applications and sign you out. Use this method when you're going to be away from your computer and want to prevent unauthorized access to your mail.

Application Mix-and-Match

After you're proficient with two or more Office applications, you may want to start mixing-and-matching documents from those applications. For example, you might want to plop an Excel chart into your Word document. Or you might want to use Word to print form letters and envelopes for everyone in an Access database.

The best way to explore the possibilities, as well as to get step-by-step instructions when you need them, is through Office Manager's Cue Cards. Here's how:

1. If the Office Manager toolbar isn't visible on your screen, display it (as described at the beginning of this section).
2. Right-click the Office Manager toolbar and choose Cue Cards. You'll see a dialog box like the one in Figure IO.8.

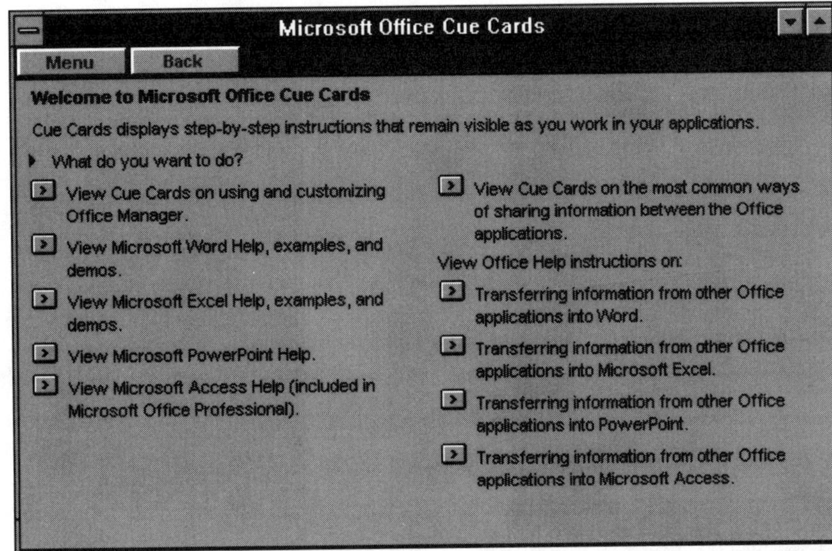

FIGURE IO.8

The Microsoft Office Cue Cards offer a quick and easy way to explore application integration. To get here, right-click the Office Manager toolbar, then choose Cue Cards.

3. For an overview of application integration, choose *View Cue Cards on the most common ways of sharing information....* Then choose the last option, *I'm not sure. Show me....*

As usual, you can leave the Cue Cards at any time by double-clicking the control-menu box in the upper-left corner of the Cue Card window.

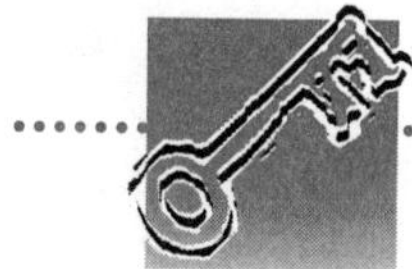

Closing Pep Talk

Learning to use a PC, Windows, and Microsoft Office is exactly like learning anything else, from riding a bike to reading and writing. You always start off feeling like a complete knucklehead. (Which reminds me of the first time I went golfing, and didn't think to bring my golf clubs or any golf balls with me. Brilliant, no?)

You just have to be willing to invest a little time, and use the built-in demos, previews, cue cards, and help to get into the swing of things. As you gain experience, it will all become more familiar, easier, and even routine. Once you start realizing how quickly you can take care of everyday business with your PC and Microsoft Office, you'll wonder how you ever got along without them.

Do-It-Now Encyclopedia

Agenda	Sales Meeting 05/26/94 9:00 AM to 12:00 PM Building 1, Conference Room	
Meeting called by:	Wanda Bea Granolabar	
Type of meeting:	Sales Staff	
Please read:	Minutes of last week's meeting, if you were absent	
Please bring:	Your own coffee cup	
	Agenda topics	
9:00-9:10 AM	Meeting Overview	Wanda Granolabar
9:10-9:40 AM	Last week's sales	Martha Mellor
9:40-10:10 AM	New sales strategies	Malcom Sheepdip
10:10-11:40 AM	Upcoming Product Launch	Wilma Shedskin
11:40-12:00 PM	Current Sales Projections	Malcom Sheepdip
Resource persons:	Wanda and Martha	

AGENDA

5 min.

Microsoft Word includes a handy Agenda Wizard that will let you type up a polished meeting schedule in a flash. You can choose a general style for the agenda: Boxes, Modern (shown here), or Standard. You'll also be given an option to print blank forms for taking minutes.

STEPS

1. Start Microsoft Word.
2. Choose File ➢ New from the Word menu bar.
3. Double-click on Agenda Wizard.

4. Read the Wizard window that appears and make your choices from the options provided. The small sample document changes to reflect your current choice.

5. Click on the button labeled Next.

6. Repeat Steps 4 and 5 until you get to the checkered flag. Then choose a help option and choose Finish.

After a brief delay, the agenda appears on your screen as a Word table. If you asked for forms for taking minutes, they'll be on separate pages under the agenda.

You'll probably need to fill in the blanks on some sections of the agenda. To do so, just click wherever you want to add text, or press the Tab and Shift+Tab keys until the cursor gets to where you want to type. Then type your text. Where a single table row contains two or more lines of text you need to press ↵ to move down to the next line before you start typing new text.

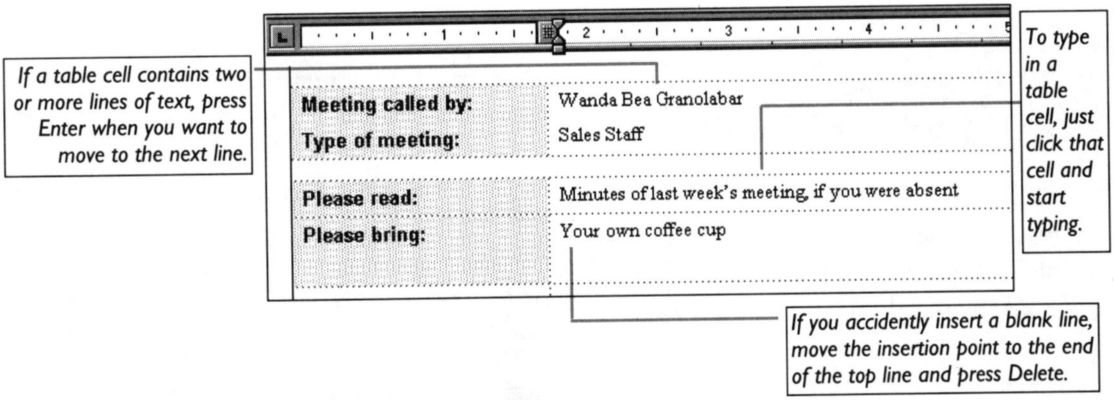

If a table cell contains two or more lines of text, press Enter when you want to move to the next line.

Meeting called by:	Wanda Bea Granolabar
Type of meeting:	Sales Staff
Please read:	Minutes of last week's meeting, if you were absent
Please bring:	Your own coffee cup

To type in a table cell, just click that cell and start typing.

If you accidently insert a blank line, move the insertion point to the end of the top line and press Delete.

TIPS

- **To change the magnification** of the document, choose View ➢ Zoom, a Zoom To option, then OK.
- **To add or change text** in the agenda, just click wherever you want to type, and then start typing.
- **To delete or change text**, use the standard select-then-do techniques (see Appendix B).

- **To print the agenda,** press Ctrl+P or choose File ➢ Print from the Word menu bar. Indicate the number of copies to print, and then choose OK.
- **To exit Word** and return to Windows, choose File ➢ Exit and follow the usual procedure (described under *Exit an Application* in Appendix B) to decide if you want to save this particular agenda or not.

RELATED SKILLS AND TOPICS

TOPIC	WHERE TO FIND IT
Save Your Work	Appendix B
Select, Then Do	Appendix B
Wizards	Appendix B

AWARD

5 min.

If you need to type up an award or certificate, use the Microsoft Word Award Wizard. You'll have your choice of four styles: Formal, Modern, Decorative, or Jazzy (shown).

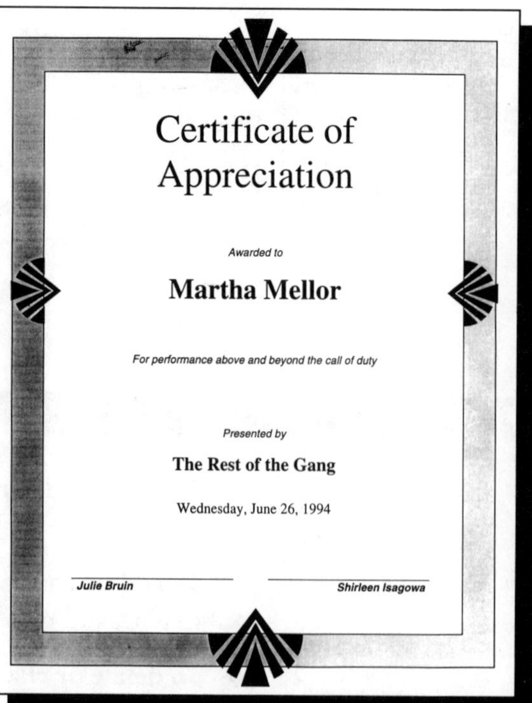
Certificate of Appreciation

Awarded to

Martha Mellor

For performance above and beyond the call of duty

Presented by

The Rest of the Gang

Wednesday, June 26, 1994

Julie Bruin

Shirleen Isagowa

STEPS

1. Start Microsoft Word.
2. Choose File ➢ New from the Word menu bar.
3. Double-click on Award Wizard.
4. Read the Wizard window that appears and make your choices from the options provided. The sample document changes to reflect your current choice.
5. Choose Next.
6. Repeat Steps 4 and 5 until you get to the checkered flag. Then choose a help option, and choose Finish.

It might take the Wizard a couple of minutes to get the job done. But after a brief delay, the award appears on the screen as a Word document. You can choose View ➢ Zoom from the Word menu bar to change the magnification.

Most of the text on the award is in text boxes. This means that when you first click on a piece of text, you may see a frame surrounding that text. Don't worry about that. You can still make changes and corrections using the standard select-then-do techniques (explained in Appendix B).

TIPS

- To add or change text, click wherever you want to make changes, and then type and edit normally.
- To print the award, choose File ➢ Print from the Word menu bar, or press Ctrl+P. Then choose OK or press ↵.
- To exit Word, choose File ➢ Exit from the Word menu bar, or press Alt+F4. As usual, you'll be given the option to save a copy of the award for editing and printing later.
- To print a more official-looking award, use paper with preprinted borders from your local office supply store. Or contact Queblo, Paper Direct, or Premier Papers (you'll find the addresses in Appendix C) for a catalog of preprinted papers.

RELATED SKILLS AND TOPICS

TOPIC	WHERE TO FIND IT
Save Your Work	Appendix B
Select, Then Do	Appendix B
Wizards	Appendix B

BOOKLET

45 min.

Booklets are great for menus, in-house directories, employee handbooks, theater programs, and much more. You can use standard 8.5 x 11" paper, folded in half, to create booklets. You'll just need two extra items that aren't terribly expensive: Clickbook (also distributed under the name "Make-A-Booklet") and a stapler with a long reach. You can order both from Paper Direct (Appendix C).

STEPS

WARNING: This entire section assumes that you have already purchased and installed Paper Direct's Make-A-Booklet software, and have gone through the "Printer Setup" procedure described in that product's manual. If you're worried about the installation, don't. It's easy and you only have to do it once.

1. Start Microsoft Word.
2. If you want to number the pages in your booklet, choose Insert ➢ Page Numbers ➢ a Position [such as *Bottom of Page (Footer)*], and an Alignment (such as Center). Then choose OK.
3. Start your typing with the first inside page (we'll do the cover separately later). Keep in mind that the booklet software will scale down each page to fit on half a page. So start by choosing a font that's about twice the size that you really want. For example, to print most body text in Times Roman 12 pt, choose Format ➢ Font, and Times Roman *24 pt.*
4. Type the text of your document normally. (I gave this document a guru rating, because I'm assuming you can create a document by now. Here, I just want to focus on getting your text into booklet format.)
5. If you want to add headings or any other formatting features, do so. But don't forget to double the point size of any fonts you choose. Keep in mind that any pictures you insert will also be scaled down to about half size.
6. When you're ready to print your booklet, first save it (File ➢ Save). Then choose File ➢ Print a Clickbook from Word's menu bar. (That command will be available *only* if you've properly installed the Clickbook software.)
7. Follow all the instructions on the screen to print your booklet.
8. When you've finished printing the entire booklet, you can close the current document (File ➢ Close). If you're *not* ready to create the booklet's cover, you can exit Word now (File ➢ Exit) in the usual manner.

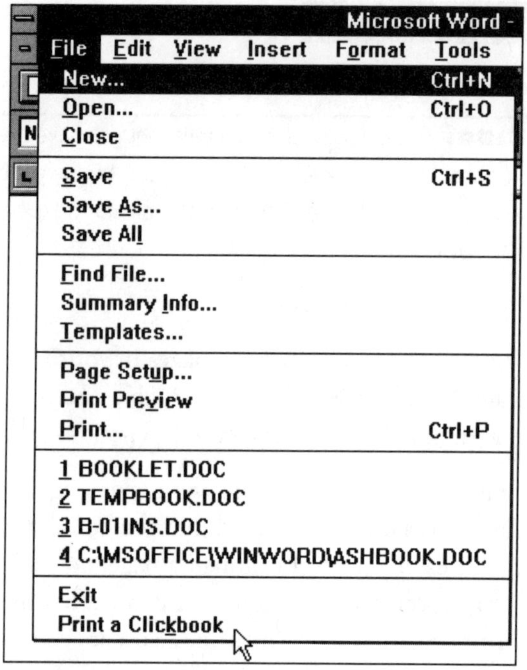

STEPS

Printing a Booklet Cover

You might want to use a heavy paper for your booklet cover, so I recommend that you create it separately, following the steps presented here. You should also check your printer manual to see just how stiff a paper it can handle. Most printers can handle up to 38-lb paper, which is sufficient weight for a booklet cover.

1. If you exited Word in the preceding steps, restart it. If you don't have an empty document window on your screen, choose File ➢ New ➢ OK to get to a new, blank document window. For the best view of your document, choose View ➢ Page Layout from Word's menu bar.

2. If you want to center the text vertically on the cover, choose File ➢ Page Setup, and click the Layout tab. Set the Vertical Alignment option to Center, then choose OK.

3. Type your booklet title, keeping in mind that the font you use will be reduced to about half its actual size. For example, if you want a 36-pt title, use a 72-pt font. You can also use the Center button on the formatting toolbar to horizontally center the title, if you wish. Figure B.1 shows an example.

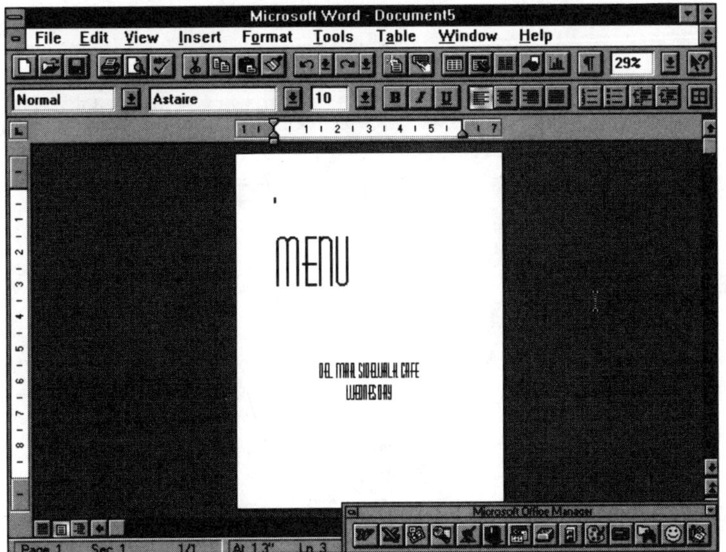

FIGURE B.1

The cover for a sample booklet in Microsoft Word. Shown here in "whole page" view (View ➢ Zoom ➢ Whole Page ➢ OK).

4. Before using expensive paper to print the cover, first do a dry run with regular paper to see if you'll need any blank sheets. That is, choose File ➢ Print a Clickbook, and follow all the instructions on the screen until the cover is printed.

5. If you're happy with the appearance of the cover, insert your actual cover paper into the printer. If you have Clickbook configured to print assembly instructions, put a blank sheet or two of regular paper over the better cover paper so as not to waste your cover paper.

6. Again, choose File ➢ Print a Clickbook, and follow all the instructions on the screen until the cover is printed.

7. Staple the printed pages in the middle and fold them in half, as per Clickbook's assembly instructions.

8. As usual, you can exit Word and save your cover (File ➢ Exit) when you're done.

TIPS

- To preview multiple pages of your document before printing, first go to Page Layout view (View ➢ Page Layout). Then choose View ➢ Zoom ➢ Many Pages, and use the little button under that option to specify how many pages you want to be able to see on the screen, as in the example below.

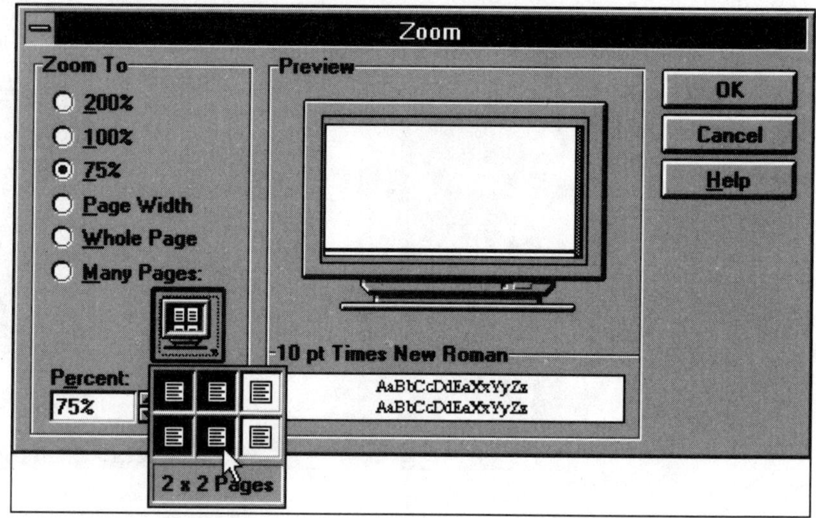

- You can print a blank page by inserting a page break in your document. Just position the insertion point and press Ctrl+↵ or choose Insert ➢ Break ➢ Page Break ➢ OK.
- If your printed pages don't come out in proper order for binding as a booklet, repeat Clickbook's printer-setup procedure to make sure it knows how to print your document.

RELATED SKILLS AND TOPICS

TOPIC	WHERE TO FIND IT
Typing Text and Numbers	Appendix B
Select, Then Do	Appendix B

Golf Supplies

Nonsense text here just for illustration. Ya know what I mean?. Nonsense text here just for illustration. Ya know what I mean? Nonsense text here just for illustration. Ya know what I mean? Nonsense text here just for illustration. Ya know what I mean?

Tennis Supplies

Nonsense text here just for illustration. Ya know what I mean?. Nonsense text here just for illustration. Ya know what I mean? Nonsense text here just for illustration

Swim Wear

Nonsense text here just for illustration. Ya know what I mean?. Nonsense text here just for illustration. Ya know what I mean? Nonsense text here just for illustration. Ya know what I mean? Nonsense text here just for illustration. Ya know what I mean?

Sports Bongo
123 West Eighty Second St.
Watchamacallit, MA 54321
555-1234

Spring has Sprung

Better stock up on your warm-weather sporting goods.

Today!

B

BROCHURE

45 min.

Here's a three-panel brochure that you can use as a tri-fold mailer (also called a "gatefold" mailer). It takes some Word skill to create the brochure, so I wouldn't recommend this project for the absolute beginner. For an alternative method of creating brochures on your own PC, contact Nebs (see Appendix C) and ask for information on their Brochure Express application and services.

STEPS

1. Start Microsoft Word.
2. Choose File ➢ New from the Word menu.
3. Double-click on Brochur1.

4. To maximize your viewing area of the page, first choose View ➢ Page Layout. Then choose View ➢ Zoom ➢ Whole Page ➢ OK. The screen should show a blank sheet of paper in landscape (sideways).

5. To define the columns for the brochure, choose Format ➢ Columns ➢ Three. If you want Word to draw a line between columns, choose Line Between.

6. Choose OK to exit the Columns dialog box. (Even if you asked for lines between columns, they won't be visible yet.)

7. Press ↵ five times to insert some blank lines.

8. Choose Insert ➢ Break ➢ Column Break ➢ OK to insert the first column break.

9. Repeat steps 7 and 8 to insert a second column break. If you selected Line Between back in step 5, you can now see the tops of the lines between the columns, which gives you a better view of how the page is laid out.

10. Now, if have not already done so, turn on the Formatting toolbar. (Choose View ➢ Toolbars and if Formatting *isn't* already selected, select it. Choose OK.)

At this point, the page layout is all set up for your brochure. From here on out, creating the brochure is basically a matter of creating a Word document from scratch. Here are some pointers to help you along:

- To add text, click wherever you want to insert the text, and then start typing. If you can't get the cursor down far enough, press ↵ to move to the next line.
- To apply styles to text, select that text and choose formatting options, in the usual manner. Or, experiment with some of the predefined styles on the Formatting toolbar or under Format ➢ Style.

In my sample brochure, the fancy "Sports Bongo "title is printed in a font named Remedy from Emigre Graphics (see Appendix C). The pictures are GOLF.WMF and TENNIS.WMF from the Microsoft Office clip-art collection.

- To decrease the top and bottom margins, choose File ➢ Page Setup, click the Margins tab, and decrease the Top and Bottom margin measurements. Then choose OK.
- To center text in the column, select that text and then click the Center button on the Formatting toolbar.
- If text accidentally bumps to the next column or the next page, or even if it's just too far down the page, delete blank lines or text above that line to pull text back to the current column.
- To force text to the next column, move the cursor above that text and insert blank lines by pressing ↵.
- To insert a picture, move the insertion point to wherever you want to place the picture. Then choose Insert ➢ Picture and select the name of the file that contains the picture you want. Then choose OK. Click the picture to select it, then right-click the picture and choose Frame Picture. Now you can move the picture by dragging its frame, and size the picture by dragging its sizing handles. For online info, search Word's help for *pictures* (*graphics*).

TIPS

- To print the brochure, choose File ➢ Print, specify the number of copies you want, then choose OK.
- To save the brochure and exit Word, choose File ➢ Exit from the Word menu bar. Choose Yes and enter a valid file name (see Appendix B).

RELATED SKILLS AND TOPICS

TOPIC	WHERE TO FIND IT
Save Your Work	Appendix B
Select, Then Do	Appendix B

CALCULATOR

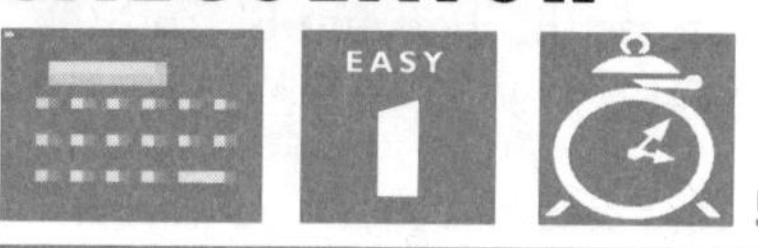

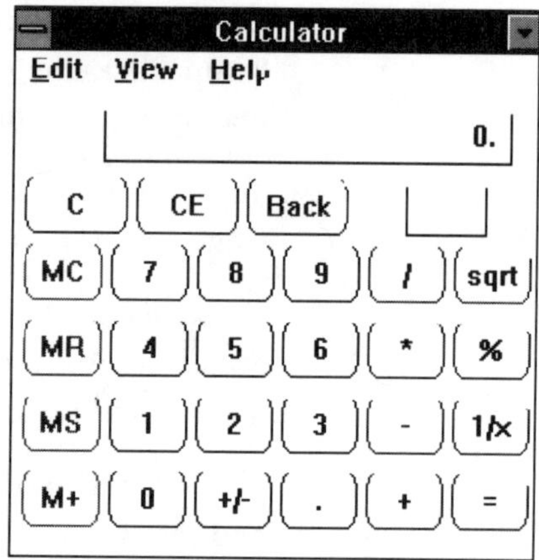

No need to go hunting for your calculator every time you need to do a little arithmetic. Just pop the Windows Calculator up on your screen.

STEPS

1. If you've already added the Calculator to your set of Office buttons, just click that button and skip the rest of these steps.
2. Right-click the Office Manager toolbar and choose Customize.
3. Click on the Toolbar tab.
4. Scroll down to Calculator (the names are *not* in alphabetical order). Select Calculator so that it's marked with an X.
5. Choose OK. Now you can open the calculator at any time just by clicking its button in the Office Manager toolbar.

You can work the on-screen calculator as you would any pocket calculator. For example, to multiply 25 by 16 you would:

1. Type **25** (or click on the **2** then the **5**).
2. Type * or click on the * button to multiply.
3. Type **16** (or click on the **1** and **6** buttons).
4. Click on = or type = or just press ↵. The answer appears.

TIPS

- While the calculator is displayed, you can press F1 for help.
- When you click outside the calculator, it may disappear. To bring it

back, click the Calculator button in the Office Manager toolbar again. Or press Alt+Tab until Calculator reappears.

- To copy the number from the calculator display into a document, choose Edit ➢ Copy from the calculator's menu bar. Move the insertion point to wherever you want to put that number, and choose Edit ➢ Paste from that application's menu bar.
- To clear the calculator and start from scratch, click the Clear button (C) or press Esc.
- To close the calculator, double-click its control menu box (in the upper-left corner of the calculator window).
- The Calculator is a Windows accessory, not a part of Microsoft Office. So you can use the calculator on any Windows PC, whether Office is installed or not.

RELATED SKILLS AND TOPICS

TOPIC	WHERE TO FIND IT
Arrange Windows and Icons	Appendix B

CALENDAR

5 min.

Use the Microsoft Word Calendar Wizard to blast out a quick calendar for any month of any year. Choose from among three styles: Boxed, Banner, or Jazzy (shown here).

C

STEPS

1. Start Microsoft Word.
2. Choose File ➢ New from the Word menu bar.
3. Double-click on **Calendar Wizard** and wait a few seconds.

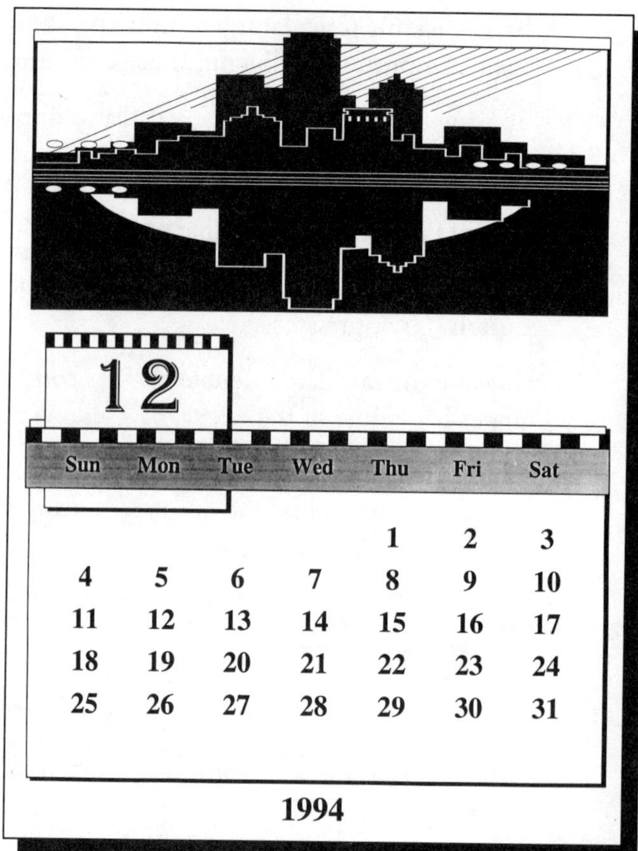

4. When the Wizard window appears, read and answer every question and keep an eye on the Wizard window for a preview of your selection. Then choose Next.

5. Repeat Step 4 until you get to the checkered flag. Then choose a help option, and choose Finish.

It might take a few minutes, but eventually you'll see the completed calendar on your screen.

TIPS

- **To zoom in or out** on the calendar, choose View ➢ Zoom, a Zoom To magnification, then OK. Or choose a magnification from the Zoom Control on the Formatting toolbar.

- **To change the picture in the calendar,** click the picture once, then press Delete (Del) or click the Cut button on the Standard toolbar to delete it. Click the picture's empty frame to select it, so that sizing handles appear. Then choose Insert ➢ Picture from the Word menu bar. Choose the filename of the picture you want to insert, then choose OK.
- **To print** choose File ➢ Print (or press Ctrl+P), then choose OK. It may take a while to print, especially if you've included a picture.
- **To exit** Word, choose File ➢ Exit from the Word menu bar, or press Alt+F4. Follow the standard procedure (see Appendix B) to decide whether you want to save this copy of the calendar.

RELATED SKILLS AND TOPICS

TOPIC	WHERE TO FIND IT
Type Text and Numbers	Appendix B
Wizards	Appendix B

C

CHECKS.XLS

	A	B	C	D	E	F
1	Check No	Date	Transactions	Debit	Credit	Balance
2			Starting Balance		$ 1,000.00	$ 1,000.00
3	1001	12/1/94	Utilities	$ 150.00		$ 850.00
4	1002	12/1/94	Rent	$ 500.00		$ 350.00
5	1003	12/5/94	Tonya Skates	$ 150.00		$ 200.00
6		12/15/94	Deposit		$ 1,000.00	$ 1,200.00
7	1004	12/15/94	Good Luck Insurance	$ 250.00		$ 950.00
8	1005	12/20/94	Macy's	$ 435.55		$ 514.45
9	1006	12/20/94	Junker Automotive	$ 150.00		$ 364.45
10	1007	12/20/94	Dr. Lawson	$ 50.00		$ 314.45
11		12/21/94	Deposit		$ 500.00	$ 814.45
12		12/21/94	Bank Charge	$ 10.00		$ 804.45
13		12/21/94	Interest earned		$ 4.50	$ 808.95
14	1008	12/30/94	ABC Party Supply	$ 275.00		$ 533.95

Sheet1 Sheet2 Sheet3 Sheet4 Sheet5

Keeps track of account balance for you.

CHECK REGISTER

30 min.

Here's a simple check register to keep track of deposits, withdrawals, and a current balance in a bank account. It might take a few minutes to create the initial worksheet. But once you've created the sheet, you can use it over and over again just like a paper check register or bank book.

STEPS

Create the Check Register

1. Start Microsoft Excel.

2. Open the Formatting toolbar (choose View ➢ Toolbars, and select Formatting by clicking to put an X in its check box if it isn't already selected. Choose OK).

3. Type the column labels shown below into cells A1 through F1, simply by clicking whatever cell you want to type in, and then typing. (You can also press Tab and Shift+Tab to move from cell to cell.) Then widen each column to your tastes by dragging the right edge of the column heading, as indicated below.

Drag the edge of the column heading to widen or narrow the column.

	A	B	C	D	E	F
1	Check No.	Date	Transaction	Debit	Credit	Balance

4. Click the row heading at the left of column 1 to select that row. Then choose Boldface and Center from the Formatting toolbar, as indicated below.

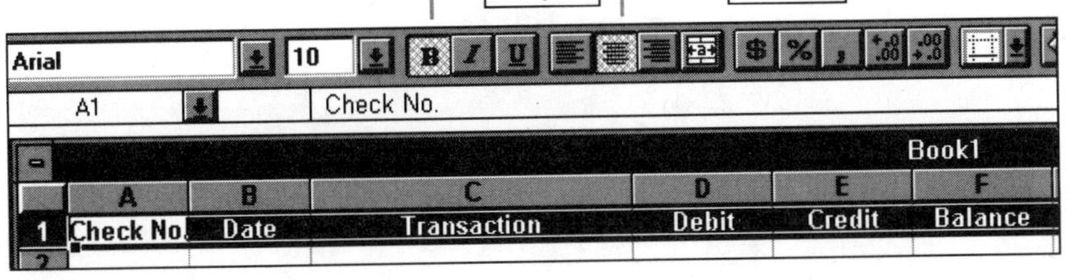

First, click the row heading to select the entire row.

5. Into row 2, type the information for the starting balance for the account. Make sure you type the starting balance into cell E2, as shown in the example below.

Book1

	A	B	C	D	E	F
1	**Check No.**	**Date**	**Transaction**	**Debit**	**Credit**	**Balance**
2		12/1/94	Beginning Balance		1500	
3						

6. Select columns D through F by dragging the mouse pointer through the column headings, as shown below. Then click the Currency Style button in the toolbar. Numbers in those columns

C

will be displayed in currency style. If 1500 appears as ####, the column is too narrow. Drag the right edge of column E's column heading to widen the column.

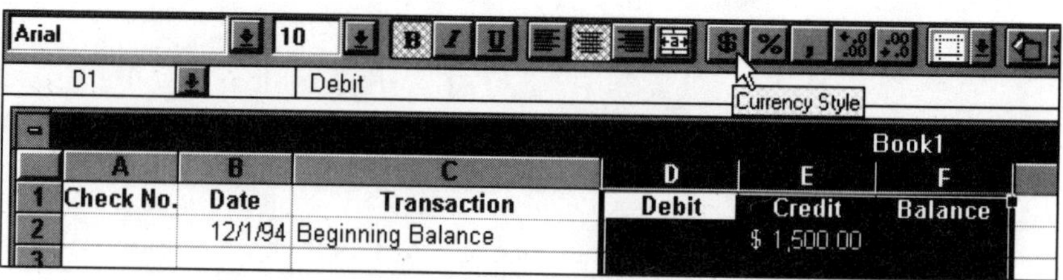

7. Click on cell F2, and type *exactly* the formula shown below into that cell. Be sure to press ↵ or click on the check mark after you've typed in the formula. After you do, cell F2 should reflect the starting balance in the cell to the left, cell E2.

```
=IF(OR(E2>0,D2>0),SUM($E$2:E2)-SUM($D$2:D2),"")
```

8. Copy the formula in cell F2 down as many rows as you wish. To do so, click on cell F2, move the mouse pointer to the little square *fill handle* in the lower right corner of the frame until it changes to a black + sign, as shown below. Then drag the mouse pointer down to row 100 or so.

	A	B	C	D	E	F
1	Check No.	Date	Transaction	Debit	Credit	Balance
2		12/1/94	Beginning Balance		$ 1,500.00	$ 1,500.00
3						
4						
5						
6						
7						

Drag fill handle down to copy the formula

9. Press Ctrl+Home to move back to the top of the spreadsheet.

10. To freeze the column labels in row 1, so they don't disappear off the top of the screen when you scroll farther down the sheet, first select row 2 (the row under your labels) by clicking its row heading, as shown below. Then choose Window ➢ Freeze Panes from the Excel menu bar.

	A	B	C	D	E	F
1	Check No	Date	Transaction	Debit	Credit	Balance
2		12/1/94	Beginning Balance		$ 1,500.00	

11. To protect the formulas in column F from accidental deletion, select columns A through E by dragging the mouse pointer through the column headings, as shown below. Then choose Format ➢ Cells and click the Protection tab. Clear the Locked option then choose OK. Next, choose Tools ➢ Protection ➢ Protect Sheet ➢ OK (the password is optional). You've just protected the spreadsheet from being changed, except for columns A–E. You can edit columns A–E as usual.

	A	B	C	D	E	F
1	Check No	Date	Transaction	Debit	Credit	Balance
2		12/1/94	Beginning Balance		$ 1,500.00	
3						
4						
5						
6						
7						
8						
9						

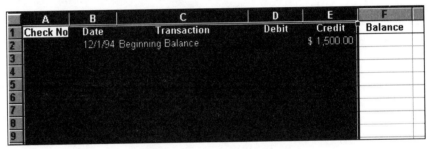

12. Save the completed worksheet (choose File ➢ Save, type in a valid file name, such as **Checks**, then choose OK).

Your check-register worksheet is done and saved, so you can use it at any time in the future to record transactions and calculate the balance. The next section describes how to use the check register.

STEPS

Using the Check Register

1. If you've exited Excel since last using the check register, start Excel. Then open your check register worksheet (choose File ➢ Open and double-click the name you gave your worksheet, e.g., **CHECKS.XLS**).

2. Click on the next available blank row in the worksheet. You can use the scroll bar, PgUp, and PgDn keys to scroll around.

3. Type in the check number (if any), date, and description of the transaction.
4. If the transaction amount is to be subtracted from the balance, type the amount into the Debit column. Otherwise, to add the amount to the balance, type the amount into the Credit column.
5. Repeat steps 2 through 4 to add as many transactions as you wish.
6. To print the check register, choose File ➢ Print ➢ OK as usual. When you're finished, choose File ➢ Exit ➢ Yes to save your new transactions and exit Excel back to Windows.

TIPS

- **To enter today's date** into the Date column, place the insertion point in the appropriate cell and press Ctrl+; then press →.
- **When typing an amount** into the Debit or Credit column, you need not include the dollar sign or commas. For example, when you type **1000** into a cell, the cell shows **$1,000.00**.
- **To print** the check register, press Ctrl+P or choose File ➢ Print from the Excel menu bar. Then choose OK.
- **If column F doesn't show the balance** after you type a number in the Debit or Credit column, it's probably because you're past the last copy of the formula. Select the cell that contains the last balance, and then copy its formula down through as many rows as you wish. You can use the fill handle, as in Step 8 under *Steps: Create the Check Register* above.

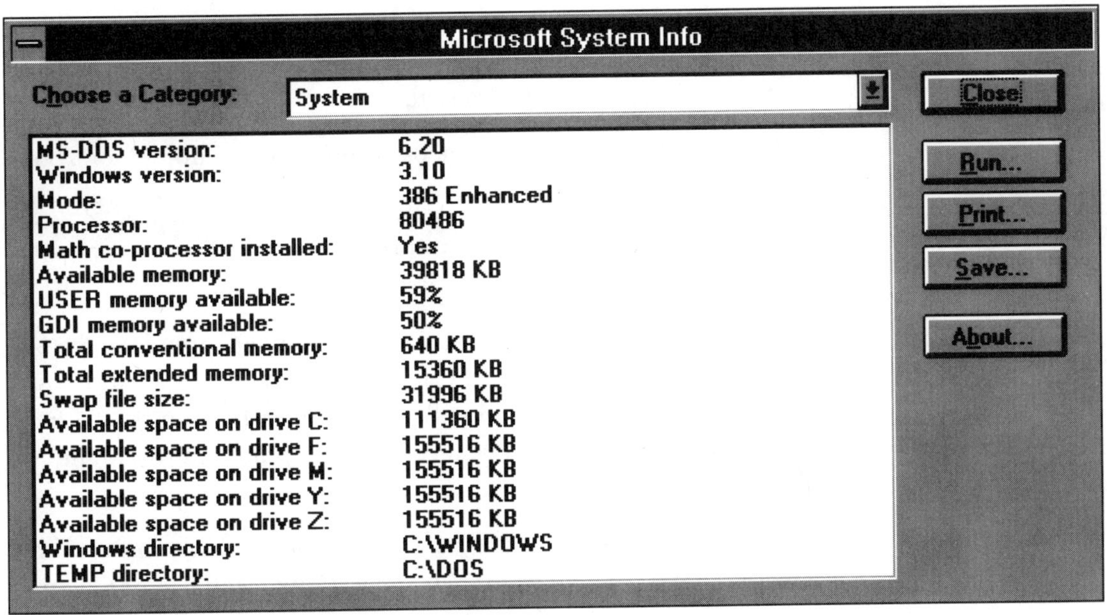

COMPUTER SPEC SHEET

1 min.

Don't you hate it when you call a Tech Support line and get questions rather than answers from the person on the other end? For instance, they might ask for version numbers, serial numbers, how much conventional and extended memory your system has, and so forth. Here are a couple of techniques you can use to find all that information about your system. The first technique is the quicker of the two, since you perform it from within an Office application in Windows. For the second technique, which gives you more information, you need to be in DOS.

STEPS

From Windows

1. Start Microsoft Word, Excel, PowerPoint, or Access.
2. Choose Help ➢ About from that application's menu bar. On the first screen, you'll (usually) see the version number, and serial number, for that product.

3. For more information about your system, click the System Info button. You'll be taken to the System Info dialog box, like the one shown at the start of this section.
4. From the System Info box, choose Print to print information about your system.
5. Choose OK and Close, as appropriate, to work your way back to the application you started in Step 1.
6. If you want to format the system information you printed in Step 4, first start Microsoft Word (if you aren't already there.) Then choose File ➢ Open, type **c:\windows\msinfo.txt**, and then press ↵. Once the document is in Word, you can edit and print it as you would any other document.
7. To return to Program Manager, exit any applications you started by choosing File ➢ Exit from each application's menu bar, until you get to Program Manager.

STEPS

From DOS

You can get even more detailed information about your system using the Microsoft Systems Diagnostics program, MSD.EXE. Microsoft ships that program with many of its products, so chances are that program is already at your disposal. If in doubt, just try it out. Follow these steps:

1. If you're currently using an Office application, save your work and exit (by choosing File ➢ Exit from the application's menu bar), until you get to the Windows Program Manager.
2. If you're in Windows, choose File ➢ Exit Windows from Program Manager's menu bar. When prompted about ending your Windows session, choose OK to get to the DOS command prompt (C:\>).
3. At the DOS command prompt, type **msd** and press ↵. After MSD analyses your system, you'll come to a screen like the one shown in Figure C.1.

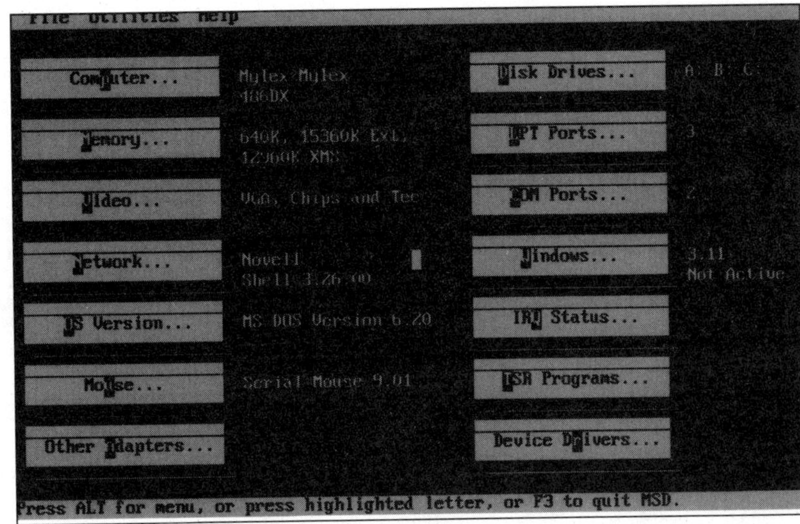

FIGURE C1

MSD displays lots of information about your system, including computer (and processor) type, total and available memory, information about drives, and so forth.

4. For more detail on any topic, just click on the appropriate button. Or press whatever letter is highlighted on the button (e.g., press **p** for more information about your Com**p**uter). Choose OK or press ↵ after reviewing the information that appears. If you *don't* want to print any of the information, skip to step 8.

5. To print information about your system, choose File ➢ Print Report from MSD's menu bar.

6. You can choose which items to print, or not print, by clicking the check box next to each option. (Or, if your mouse doesn't work in DOS, type the highlighted letter in any option, then use the space bar to choose or clear the check box. Only reports with an X in the check box will be printed.

7. Choose OK when you're ready to print. If prompted for customer information, you can either fill in the blanks or just choose OK to proceed.

8. When you've finished with the MSD program, choose File ➢ Exit from its menu bar or just press F3. You'll be returned to the DOS command prompt (C:\>).

9. To return to Windows, type **win** and then press ↵.

C

RELATED SKILLS AND TOPICS

TOPIC	WHERE TO FIND IT
Version (Determine)	Appendix B

Table: Mailing List

Ma	Prefix	First Name	Middle	Last Name	Title	Organization Name	Addres
1	Mr.	Andy	Albert	Zeeborp	President	ABC Corporation	1121 El Verd
2	Ms.	Sally		Rambunctuous			P.O. Box 44
4	Mr.	Andy	Arnie	Adams	President	ABC Corporation	123 A St.
5	Miss	Marie	Melissa	Miller	Software Consultant		P.O. Box 12
6	Dr.	Robert	K.	Baker	Radiology Dep't	St. Elsewhere Hospital	1234 Washi
7	Mr.	Robert	J.	Miller	Botanist	Evergreen Nursery	11711 Repo
8	Miss	Maria	Ann	Adams	Author		4323 Moong
9	Mr.	John	Jeff	Newell	President	Newell Construction	212 Riversic
10	Dr.	Susita	Marie	Schumack	Neurosurgeon	Reese Clinic	3313 Park A
11	Mr.	Richard	R.	Rosiello	President	Rickdontic Labs	P.O. Box 11
12	Mr.	Frank	R.	Watson	Greenskeeper	Whispering Palms Golf Cl	8771 Conch
13	Miss	Anita		Smith	Accounts Payable	Sunshine Gardens	3221 Encinit
14	Ms.	Thelma	T.	Gillis	Author		P.O. Box 33
15	Mr.	Henry	Keith	Smythe		Zodiac Gardens	91 Delaware
16	Mrs.	Helga		Königer		Königer-Verlag GmbH	Von-Erckert
17	Mr.	Gören		Janulf		CITES Uitgeverij B.V.	Birkstraat 95
18	Dr.	Sandra		Davis, Jr.	Botanist	Florália	P.O. Box 11
19	Ms.	Rita	R.	Wilson	President	High Tech Applications	1101 West

Record: 1 of 18

DATABASE (CREATE)

30 min.

A database is a collection of data (information). The data you store can be information about anything—from an address list to a wine collection. A database can be a complicated thing. But here in the Do-It-Now Encyclopedia, *I'll be encouraging you to get your feet wet with Access by creating a relatively simple single-table database for storing people's names and addresses. After you've had a little experience with your name-and-address database, you may want to come back to this section and try creating a different database of your own. Table D.1 lists the single-table databases that the Access Wizards will help you create.*

TABLE D.1

Single-table databases that you can create in minutes using Microsoft Access Wizards

USE THIS WIZARD...	...TO MANAGE	CATEGORY
Accounts	Chart of accounts	Personal
Artists	Artist biographies	Personal
Authors	Author biographies	Personal
Book Collection	Personal or business library	Personal
Classes	Courses offered in a school	Business
Contacts	Names and addresses of business contacts	Business
Customers	Customer names and addresses	Business
Deliveries	Any type of deliveries	Business
Diet Log	Foods/calories consumed	Personal
Employees	Personnel information	Business
Events	Seminars and other events	Business
Exercise Log	Fitness progress	Personal
Expenses	Business expense	Business
Fixed Assets	Assets and depreciation	Business
Friends	Friend names and addresses	Personal
Guests	Hotel or house guests	Personal
Household Inventory	Value of various items in the house	Personal
Investments	Personal investments	Personal
Mailing List	General-purpose mailing list and name and addess book.	Business
Music Collection	Personal music library	Personal
Payments	Payments received from customers	Business
Photographs	Photograph collection	Personal
Plants	Indoor/outdoor plants	Personal
Products	Products carried in an inventory	Business
Projects	General information about upcoming/ongoing projects	Business
Recipes	Food recipes	Personal
Reservations	Reservations at hotels, seminars, etc.	Business
Rolls of Film	Photographic	Personal
Service Records	Services performed on equipment	Business
Students	Student names and addresses	Business

D

TABLE D.1 continued

USE THIS WIZARD...	...TO MANAGE	CATEGORY
Suppliers	Companies from which you purchase supplies	Business
Tasks	Time frame and description of a task	Business
Time Billed	Billable hours	Business
Transactions	Bank transactions	Business
Video Collection	Videotape library	Personal
Wine list	Wine collection	Personal

STEPS

Create an Empty Database

The first step to creating a new Access database is simply to give that database a name. Here's how:

1. Start Microsoft Access.
2. Choose File ➢ New Database from the Access menu bar.
3. Enter a file name that will be easy for you to remember, such as **People** if you plan on storing people's names and addresses in this database.
4. Choose OK.

An empty *database window* appears. Notice that the name you chose appears in the database window's title bar. This little database window will be your home base when you're working with your Access database. As you'll see, the object buttons and command buttons let you create, change, and use various types of items that will help you manage your data.

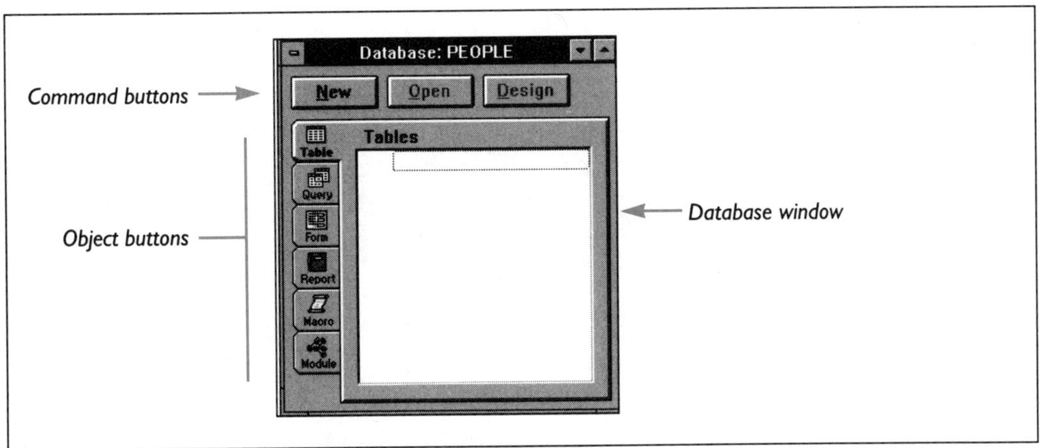

D

STEPS

Create a Table to Hold Info

Once you've created an empty database, your next step will be to create a table for storing your data. Here you'll just be telling Access what *kinds* of information you want to store. You won't start typing in people's names and addresses until later. So follow these steps:

1. Click the New button in the database window, or choose File ➢ New ➢ Table from the Access menu bar.
2. Choose Table Wizards.
3. If this is your first database, I suggest you choose **Mailing List** under Sample Tables. Though, as mentioned, the Wizard can create a table for many different kinds of data collections, as was summarized in Table D.1.
4. Double-click on any fields (types of information) you're interested in storing. When you double-click a field name, it's copied to the list titled *Fields in my new table.* If you're following my example, I suggest you choose the field names listed in Table D.2—though you can certainly choose additional fields if you wish. (Note that you can click the < and > buttons to move field names from one list to the other.)

TABLE D.2

Suggested fields to put into your database table of names and addresses

FIELD NAME	WHAT YOU'LL PUT THERE LATER
MailingListID	An automatically assigned number (1, 2, 3, and so on)
Prefix	Mr., Ms., Dr., etc.
FirstName	First names (Mary, John, etc.)
MiddleName	A person's middle name or initial
LastName	A person's surname
Title	A job title (Attorney at Law) or maybe a Department (Department of Biology)
OrganizationName	Business affiliation (e.g., University of Iowa)
Address	Street address or mailing address
City	City the person lives in
State	State the person lives in
PostalCode	Zip code or postal code
Country	Country (can leave this blank or enter **USA**)
HomePhone	Home phone number
WorkPhone	Work phone number
MobilePhone	Car phone number
FaxNumber	Fax phone number
Note	Miscellaneous notes

5. When the *Fields in my new table list* includes all the types of information you want your table to contain, choose Next.

6. In the next Wizard window, you can just choose Next to accept the Wizard's suggestions.

7. In the third Wizard window, choose the first option, Modify the Table Design, then choose Finish.

8. To improve compatibility with Microsoft Word (which you might want to use to print envelopes, mailing labels, and so forth), you need to remove some *input masks* that the Wizard has provided.

To do so, scroll down to the PostalCode field name, and click that name. Under Field Properties in the lower half of the window, you should see this Input Mask:

9. Drag the cursor through the input mask (**00000\-9999**) and then press Delete (Del) to delete it. You want that to be completely empty.

10. Now scroll down to HomePhone and click on it. The Input Mask for the phone number looks like this:

11. Drag the cursor through the input mask (**!\(999")"000\-0000**) and press Delete (Del) to delete it.

12. Repeat steps 10 and 11 to delete the input mask from the fields named WorkPhone, MobilePhone, and FaxNumber.

13. Choose File ➢ Close ➢ Yes to save your changes and close the table design window.

STEPS

Create a Fill-in-the-Blank Form

As you'll see, Access lets you work with data in two ways—either in a tabular list format, or in a fill-in-the-blank form format. To illustrate, first we need to create a fill-in-the-blank form. Follow these steps:

1. With the Mailing List table name still highlighted in the database window, click on the AutoForm button in the toolbar:

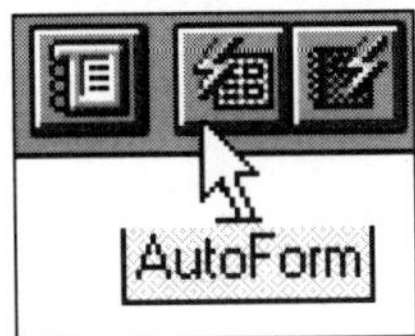

D

2. When the blank form appears on the screen, just choose File ➢ Close ➢ Yes, type in a name up to 64 characters in length (e.g., **Address Form**) and then choose OK. We'll reopen and use the form later.

STEPS

Create a Simple Report

You'll probably want to print information from your database from time to time. In this section we'll create an instant report format to make it easy to print a quick list of names and addresses.

1. With the table name Mailing List still highlighted in the database window, click the AutoReport button in the Access toolbar (shown at left). Or choose File ➢ New ➢ Report ➢ Report Wizards ➢ AutoReport ➢ OK.

2. After a brief delay, you'll see the report format on your screen. That'll come in handy later, after you put some names and addresses into your table. But for now, you can just close and save it for future use. Choose File ➢ Close ➢ Yes, and type in **Address List** or any other name of your choosing (up to 64 characters in length).
3. Choose OK.

You've finished creating your database. To illustrate how you can *use* this new database at any time in the future, let's exit Access right now. Choose File ➢ Exit from the Access menu bar.

You are now returned to the Windows Program Manager. In the next section, I'll show you how to open and use your database.

RELATED SKILLS AND TOPICS

TOPIC	WHERE TO FIND IT
Microsoft Access	*Instant Office*
Wizards	Appendix B

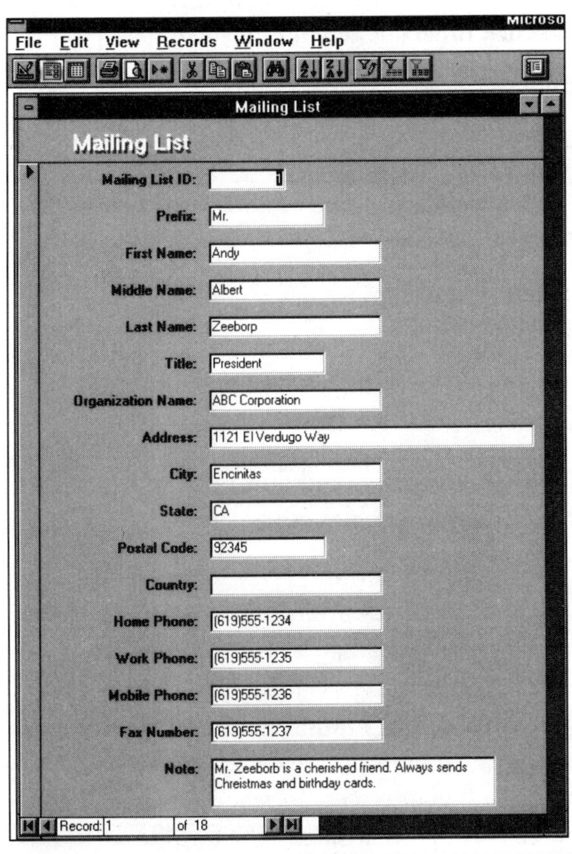

DATABASE (USE)

15 min.

After you've created your Access database, you can use techniques described here to open it and add, change, delete, view, and print data.

STEPS

1. Start Microsoft Access.
2. Choose File. Chances are, the name of your database will appear near the bottom of the File menu. Just click its name (e.g., PEOPLE.MDB) and skip the rest of this step. If the name of your data base doesn't appear at the bottom of the File menu, choose Open Database and double-click the name of your database.

The Access database window appears.

STEPS

Adding, Changing, and Deleting Access Data

When you want to store, change, or remove data:

1. Click the Form button in the database window, then click the Open button in that same window. An empty fill-in-the-blank form appears on your screen.
2. Use any of the techniques listed below and illustrated in Figure D.1 to add, edit, delete, and scroll through existing data.
    - To add new data, click the New button (➢*) in the toolbar, if it's available. If you don't see that button, choose Records ➢ Go To ➢ New from the menu bar. Then, starting with Prefix, just click on any "blank" on the form, and type in an item of information. If you don't know the information for a field, just leave it blank. For example, below I typed in one person's name and address. If your screen does not show the entire form, use the scroll bar at the right side of the form to scroll up and down through fields.

NOTE: *One field in your table might contain the text (Counter), which will change to a number once you start filling in other fields in the form. You need not, and cannot, change or delete the contents of that Counter field.*

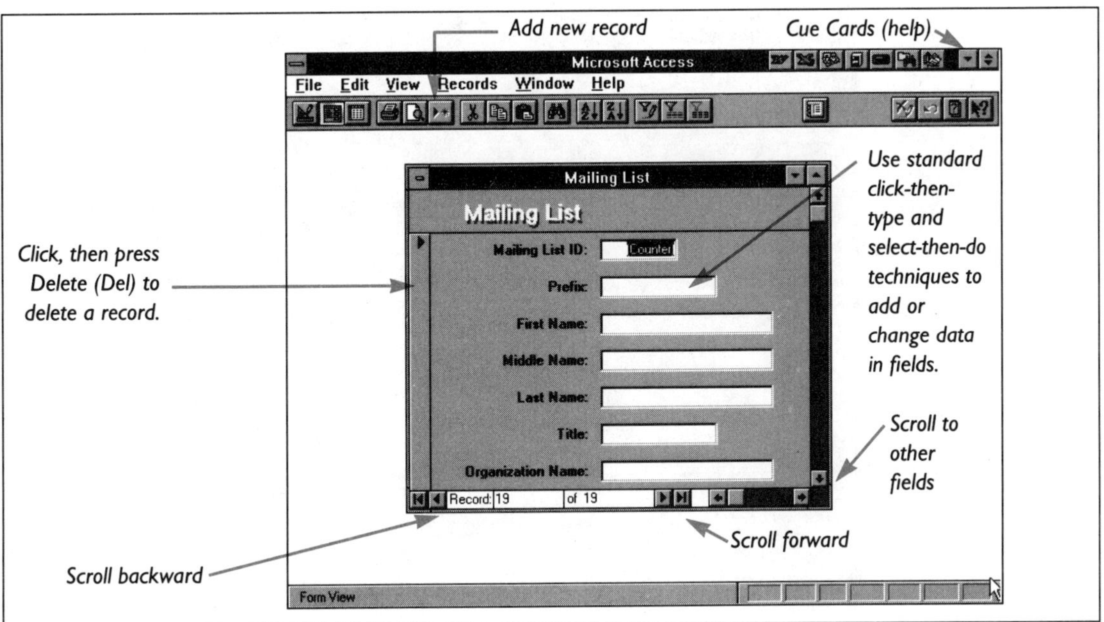

FIGURE D.1

Access tools for adding, editing, and scrolling through your data

- To scroll through existing data (if any), use the scroll buttons at the bottom of the form.
- You can size the form's window using the standard techniques (by dragging a corner or a side).
- To change existing data, click wherever you want to make a change, and then edit normally.
- To delete an entire record, click the record selector at the left edge of the form, or choose Edit ➢ Select Record. Then press Delete (Del) and respond to the warning. (A record is all the information on the form at the moment. In this example, one person's name, address, and other information form one record.)
- To switch to *datasheet view,* click the Datasheet View button or choose View ➢ Datasheet. Your data (if any) appears as a list, rather than as a fill-in-the-blank form. To switch back to the form view, click the Form View button or choose View ➢ Form.

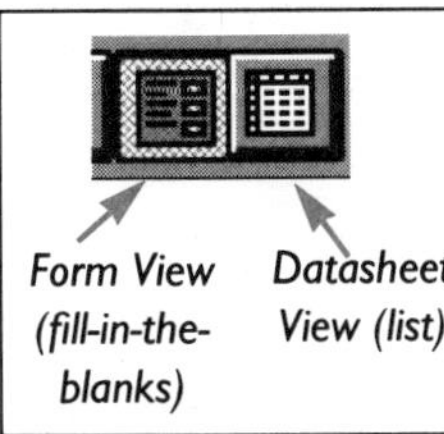

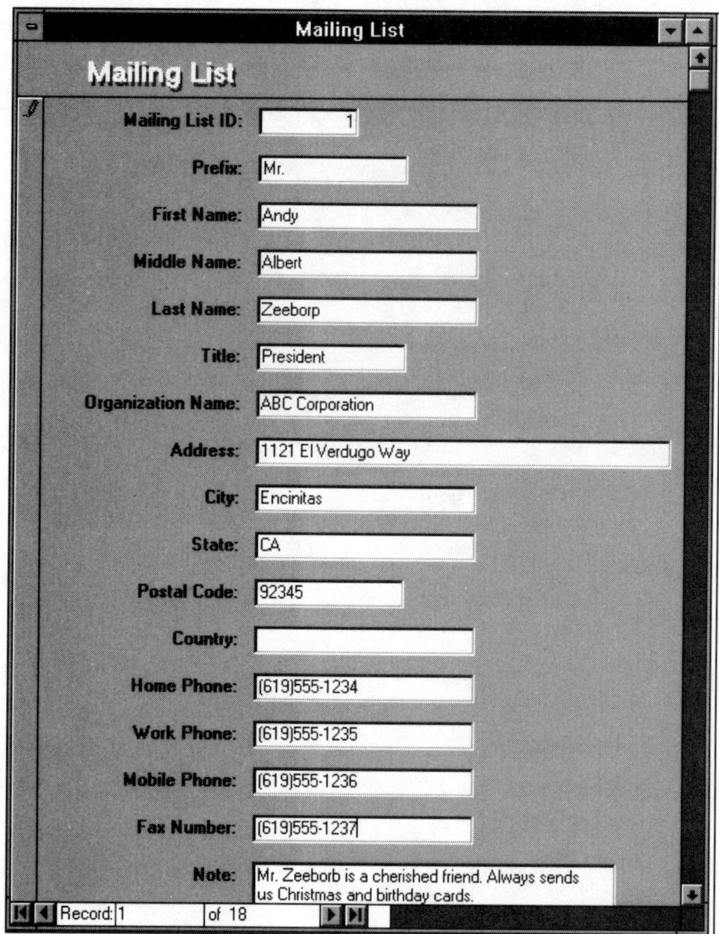

- When you've finished adding/viewing/changing data for the time being, close the form. Choose File ➢ Close. Your work is saved automatically, so you won't be asked for permission to save it.

STEPS

Printing Your Access Data

To print data from your database:

1. If you haven't already done so, start Access and open your database.
2. In the database window, click the Report object button.

3. Click the name of the report you want to print (e.g., Address List). Then click the Print button in the toolbar, or choose File ➢ Print. Then choose OK.

Using Your Database for Mass Mailings

If you've followed my example and created a mailing-list database, you can use Microsoft Word to print form letters, mailing labels, envelopes, and a directory from that database. See the following entries in this *Do-It-Now Encyclopedia*:

Directory

Envelopes (Many)

Form Letters

Mailing Labels (Many)

TIPS

- **To sort (or alphabetize) data in your printed report,** click the Report button in the database window, click the name of the report, then click the Design button in the database window. From the menu bar, choose View ➢ Sorting and Grouping. Click the blank cell under Field/Expression, click the drop-down list button that appears, then choose whichever field(s) you want to base the sort on. For example, here I've opted to base the sort on the

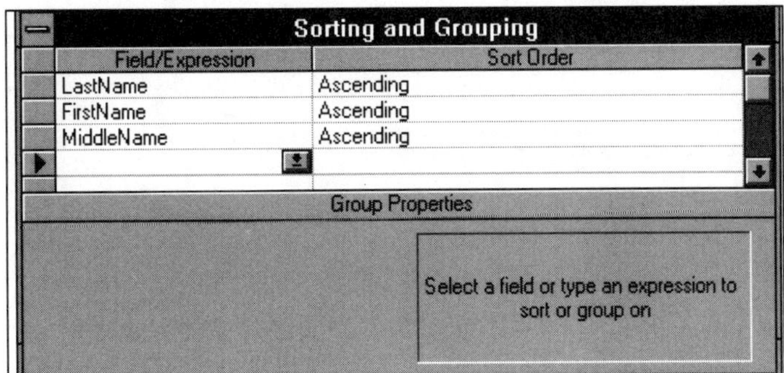

Double-click here to close Cue Cards

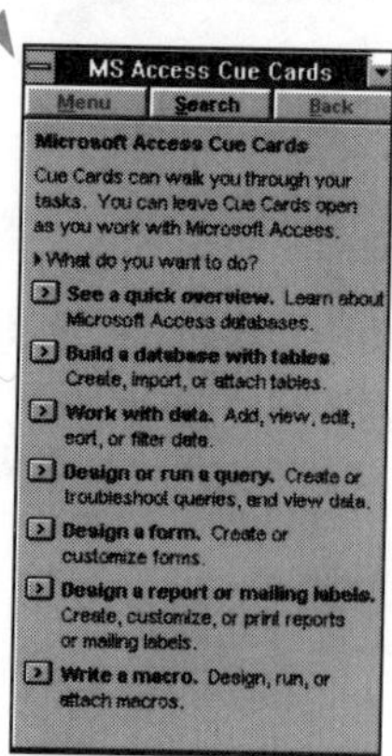

LastName and FirstName fields, like the White Pages in the telephone directory. Choose File ➢ Close ➢ Yes to save your selection, then print the report normally.

- **After you're comfortable with Access basics,** you might want to try creating a custom form. Or maybe just rearrange fields on the form you're already created. To learn to do this, you'll need to refer to your Access documentation or the Access help screens.
- **To learn more about Access,** try its Cue Cards by choosing Help ➢ Cue Cards from the Access menu bar. Answer questions and follow instructions as they appear on the screen. To close the Cue Cards, double-click the control-menu box in the upper-left corner of the Cue Cards window, as shown below.
- **To exit Microsoft Access** and save your work, choose File ➢ Exit from the Access menu bar. Don't be alarmed if you're not asked about saving your work—Access automatically saves much of your work as you go along. You'll be returned to Windows.
- **If you like Access,** and want to aspire towards guru-hood, you might want to check out my book *Understanding Microsoft Access,* also published by SYBEX.

RELATED SKILLS AND TOPICS

TOPIC	WHERE TO FIND IT
Microsoft Access	*Instant Office*

DATE ARITHMETIC

30 min.

Here's a handy little Excel worksheet that will tell you how many days, hours, minutes, etc. there are between two dates and/or times. You can also use this worksheet to determine the date x days from now. Very handy if you need to figure out when a payment is due, or how many days past due a particular bill is

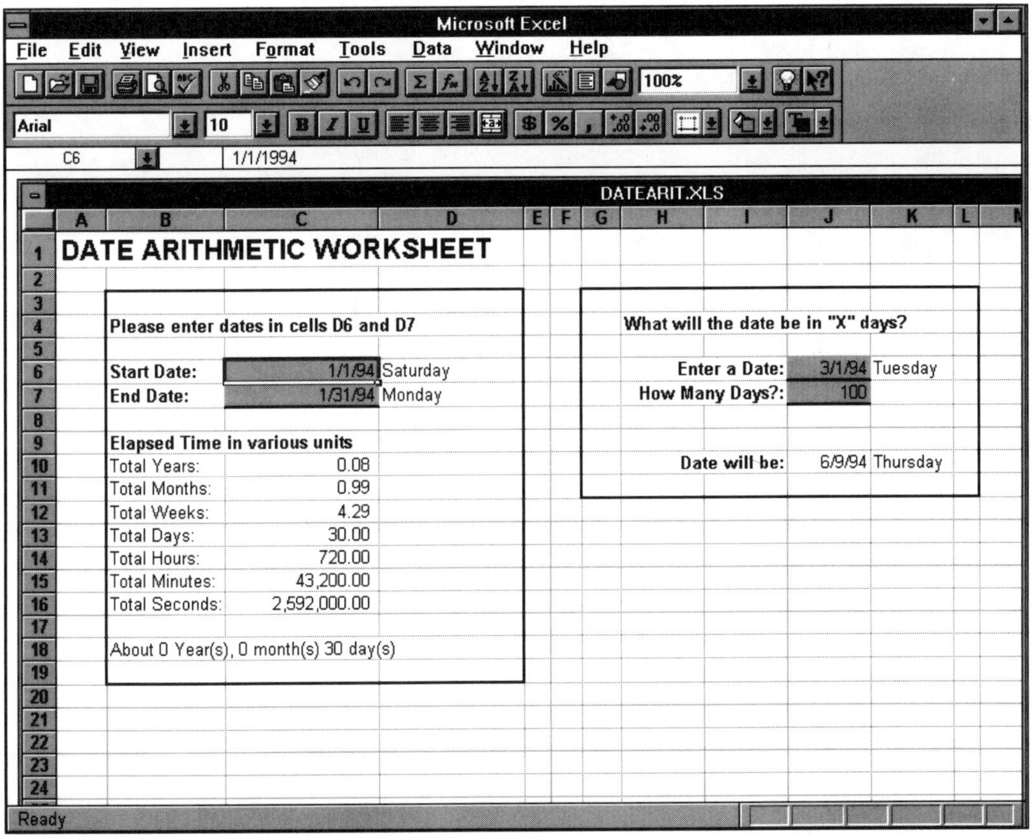

Microsoft Excel

File Edit View Insert Format Tools Data Window Help

C6 1/1/1994

DATEARIT.XLS

	A	B	C	D	E	F	G	H	I	J	K
1	DATE ARITHMETIC WORKSHEET										
2											
3											
4		Please enter dates in cells D6 and D7						What will the date be in "X" days?			
5											
6		Start Date:	1/1/94	Saturday					Enter a Date:	3/1/94	Tuesday
7		End Date:	1/31/94	Monday					How Many Days?:	100	
8											
9		Elapsed Time in various units									
10		Total Years:	0.08						Date will be:	6/9/94	Thursday
11		Total Months:	0.99								
12		Total Weeks:	4.29								
13		Total Days:	30.00								
14		Total Hours:	720.00								
15		Total Minutes:	43,200.00								
16		Total Seconds:	2,592,000.00								
17											
18		About 0 Year(s), 0 month(s) 30 day(s)									

Ready

STEPS

To Create the Worksheet

NOTE: See the (Almost) Free Companion Disk *coupon near the back of this book for alternatives to typing in this worksheet yourself.*

1. Start Microsoft Excel.
2. Table D.3 shows you the contents of each cell in the spreadsheet. To create this worksheet, click on the cell listed in the first column, and type the text or formula in the second column *exactly* as shown. For example, after you click on cell B4, type these words, exactly:

```
Please enter dates in cells D6 and D7
```

TABLE D.3:

The exact contents of each non-blank cell in the Date Arithmetic worksheet

THIS CELL	CONTAINS (LITERALLY) THIS TEXT OR FORMULA
A1	Date Arithmetic
B4	Please enter dates in cells D6 and D7
B6	Start Date:
B7	End Date:
B9	Elapsed Time in various units
B10	Total Years:
B11	Total Months:
B12	Total Weeks:
B13	Total Days:
B14	Total Hours:
B15	Total Minutes:
B16	Total Seconds:
B18	="About "&INT($C$10)&" Year(s), "&INT($C$11-12*INT($C$10))&" month(s) "&INT(($C$11-INT($C$11))*30.455)&" day(s)"
C10	=($C$7-$C$6)/365.25
C11	=($C$7-$C$6)/30.455
C12	=($C$7-$C$6)/7
C13	=$C$7-$C$6
C14	=($C$7-$C$6)*24
C15	=($C$7-$C$6)*1440
C16	=($C$7-$C$6)*86400
D6	=CHOOSE(WEEKDAY($C$6),"Sunday","Monday","Tuesday","Wednesday", "Thursday","Friday","Saturday")
D7	=CHOOSE(WEEKDAY($C$7),"Sunday","Monday","Tuesday","Wednesday","Thursday","Friday", "Saturday")
H4	What will the date be in "X" days?
I6	Enter a Date:
I7	How Many Days?:
I10	Date will be:
J10	=J6+J7
K6	=CHOOSE(WEEKDAY($J$6),"Sunday","Monday","Tuesday","Wednesday","Thursday", "Friday","Saturday")
K10	=CHOOSE(WEEKDAY($J$10),"Sunday","Monday","Tuesday","Wednesday","Thursday", "Friday","Saturday")

3. After you've typed in all the text and formulas, use the standard select-then-do technique, and the Formatting toolbar to choose fonts, add boldface, shading, borders, and align numbers as you like (see Appendix B if you need more info).

4. To protect text and formulas, first select cells C6 and C7. Choose Format ➢ Cells and click the Protection tab. Then clear the Locked check box, and choose OK.

5. Repeat the above procedure, but this time clear the locks on cells I6 and I7 (select those two cells before you choose Format from the menu bar).

6. To protect the cells you've left locked, choose Tools ➢ Protection ➢ Protect Sheet ➢ OK.

7. To save the completed worksheet, choose File ➢ Save, type a valid file name (e.g., **DateArit**) and then choose OK.

STEPS

To Use the Worksheet

Whenever you want to use the worksheet:

1. If the worksheet isn't currently on your screen, start Excel and use File ➢ Open to open the DATEARIT.XLS worksheet.

2. To calculate the amount of time between two dates, first click on cell C6 and then type a starting date into that cell. Use *mm/dd/yy* format (e.g., 1/1/95 or 12/31/95).

3. Then click on cell C7, and type an ending date into that cell, again using the *mm/dd/yy* format. Rows 10 through 18 will show the amount of time elapsed in various units of measure.

4. To calculate the date *x* days in the past or future, click on cell I6 and type a date into that cell, again using the *mm/dd/yy* format. Then click on cell C17, type a positive or negative number into that cell I7, and press ↵. Cells I10 and I11 will show the date and day of week.

TIPS

- To learn more about Excel's date and time functions, search Excel's help for date functions.
- Some date and time functions, such as NETWORKDAYS and YEARFRAC, require the extra set of analysis functions. Otherwise, the cell containing the function just shows #NAME?. To install that tool pack, choose Tools ➢ Add-Ins, select Analysis Functions, then choose OK. Then double-click any cell that shows #NAME? and then press ↵.

RELATED SKILLS AND TOPICS

TOPIC	WHERE TO FIND IT
Microsoft Excel	*Instant Office*
Typing Text and Numbers	Appendix B
Select, Then Do	Appendix B

DEPRECIATION ALLOWANCE

15 min.

Here's a fairly easy Excel worksheet for calculating and comparing different types of depreciation. A handy thing to have around a tax time, if you depreciate assets. Or when you want to experiment with different depreciation methods for a new asset.

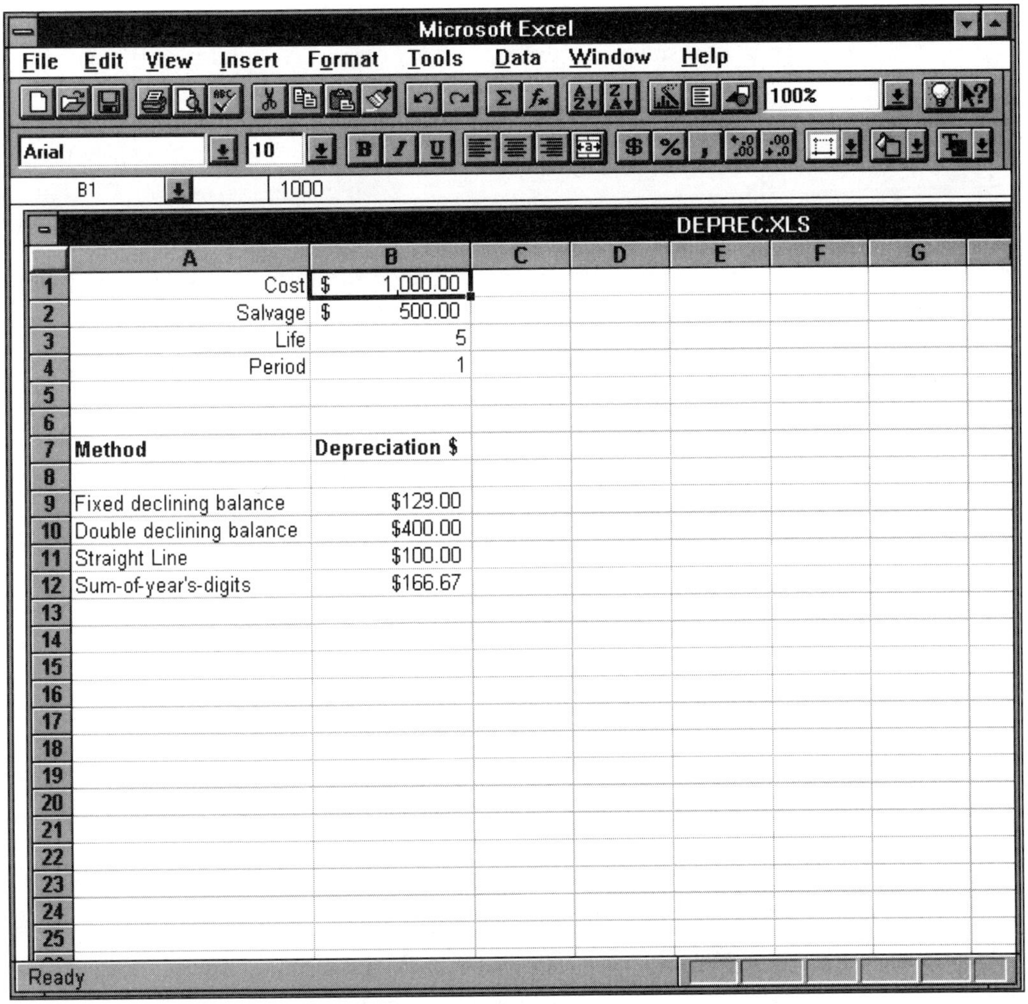

Microsoft Excel

File Edit View Insert Format Tools Data Window Help

B1 1000

DEPREC.XLS

	A	B
1	Cost	$ 1,000.00
2	Salvage	$ 500.00
3	Life	5
4	Period	1
5		
6		
7	**Method**	**Depreciation $**
8		
9	Fixed declining balance	$129.00
10	Double declining balance	$400.00
11	Straight Line	$100.00
12	Sum-of-year's-digits	$166.67

Ready

D

STEPS

Creating the Worksheet

NOTE: *See the* (Almost) Free Companion Disk *coupon near the back of this book for alternatives to typing in this worksheet yourself.*

1. Start Microsoft Excel. If a blank worksheet does *not* appear on the screen, choose File ➢ New from Excel's menu bar.

2. Use Table D.4 as your guide to typing the contents of each cell in this worksheet. For example, click on cell A1 then type the words

   Depreciation Allowance

   Then click on cell A3 and type the words

   Initial Cost

   and so on until you've typed in everything that's listed in that table.

3. Widen the columns, as necessary, to ensure that data fits within its cell. To widen a column, just drag the right edge of the column heading to the right. (The column heading is the gray cell at the top of the column.)

4. To make the worksheet a little prettier, first open the Formatting toolbar (View ➢ Toolbars ➢ Formatting ➢ OK).

5. To shade the cells where you can type in assumptions, select those cells (B3:B6) and use the Color button on the Formatting toolbar to choose a color. Use the neighboring Borders button to add borders if you like. You can also select text to display in boldface and then click the Bold button in the Formatting toolbar.

6. To display the initial cost and salvage values in currency format, select those cells (B3:B4) and click the Currency button in the Formatting toolbar. You can format the results in cells B10:B13 in a similar manner.

7. To protect the formulas, select cells (B3:B6), then choose Format ➢ Cells and click the Protection tab. Clear the Locked checkbox, then choose OK. Then choose Tools ➢ Protection ➢ Protect Sheet and choose OK.

8. To save the completed worksheet for future use, choose File ➢ Save and enter a valid file name, such as **deprec**, then choose OK.

STEPS

To Use the Depreciation Worksheet

1. If the Depreciation worksheet isn't on your screen, start Excel and choose File ➢ Open to open the worksheet (DEPREC.XLS).

TABLE D.4:

Text, Numbers, and Formulas used in the Depreciation worksheet

THIS CELL	CONTAINS (LITERALLY) THIS TEXT, NUMBER, OR FORMULA
A1	Depreciation Allowance
A3	Initial Cost
A4	Salvage Value
A5	Life Expectancy
A6	Period
A8	Method
A10	Declining Balance
A11	Double-Declining Balance
A12	Straight Line
A13	Sum-of-Years'-Digits
B3	10000
B4	1000
B5	5
B6	1
B8	Results
B10	=DB($B$3,$B$4,$B$5,$B$6)
B11	=DDB($B$3,$B$4,$B$5,$B$6)
B12	=SLN(B3,B4,B5)
B13	=SYD(B3,B4,B5,B6)

2. Click on cell B3, and type in an initial cost, Then click on, and type into cells B3, B4, B5, and B6 the salvage value, life expectancy, and period of the asset you're depreciating.

The results in rows B10 through B13 are recalculated to reflect the proper depreciation amount as soon as you change an assumption in cells B3:B6.

TIPS

- For more information and examples of calculating depreciation, search Excel's help for topics under **depreciation**.

RELATED SKILLS AND TOPICS

TOPIC	WHERE TO FIND IT
Microsoft Excel	*Instant Office*
Select, Then Do	Appendix B
Typing Text and Numbers	Appendix B

DIRECTORY (NAME AND ADDRESS LIST)

15 min.

If you want to type up a list of names and addresses, your best starting point will be to create an Access database to store that information. That way, you'll only need to type each name and address once. From then on, you can reuse that list to print new directories, envelopes, mailing labels, form letters . . . whatever. If you have not already done so, create your Access "People" database, as discussed under Database (Create) *here in the* Do-It-Now Encyclopedia. *Then follow the instructions under* Database (Use) *to add some names and addresses to the database table. After you've typed in all (or at least some) of your names and addresses, exit Access. Then follow the steps below to format and print the directory.*

STEPS

Creating the Directory Format

To accomplish these steps, you must have already created your People database and added at least one person's name and address to it. Then:

1. Start Microsoft Word.
2. Choose Tools ➢ Mail Merge ➢ Create ➢ Catalog ➢ Active Window.

Adams, Miss Maria Ann
Author
4323 Moonglow Rd.
Wyandotte, OK 74370
Home: (505)555-3438
Work:
Car:
Fax:

Adams, Mr. Andy Arnie
President
ABC Corporation
123 A St.
San Diego, CA 91234
Home: (619)556-9320
Work:
Car:
Fax:

Baker, Dr. Robert K.
Radiology Dep't
St. Elsewhere Hospital
1234 Washington Lane
New York, NY 12345-1232
Home: (212)555-1023
Work:
Car:
Fax:

Davis, Jr., Dr. Sandra
Botanist
Florália
P.O. Box 110.123
Niterói, Rio de Janeiro 24.001
Brasil
Home: (021)7178500
Work:
Car:
Fax:

Gillis, Ms. Thelma T.
Author
P.O. Box 3384
Rancho Santa Fe, CA 92067
Home: (619)555-9583
Work:
Car:
Fax:

Janulf, Mr. Gören
CITES Uitgeverij B.V.
Birkstraat 95
Soest, CJ-3487
The Netherlands
Home: (31)1 534437
Work:
Car:
Fax:

Königer, Mrs. Helga
Königer-Verlag GmbH
Von-Erckert Str. 36
München, D-8000
West Germany
Home: (49) 211 9739
Work:
Car:
Fax:

Miller, Mr. Robert J.
Botanist
Evergreen Nursery
11711 Reposo Alto
Encinitas, CA 92026
Home: (619)555-4938
Work:
Car:
Fax:

Miller, Miss Marie Melissa
Software Consultant
P.O. Box 1234
Encinitas, CA 92024
Home: (619)555-1234
Work:
Car:
Fax:

Newell, Mr. John Jeff
President
Newell Construction
212 Riverside Dr.
Bernalillo, NM 88004
Home: (414)555-4049
Work:
Car:
Fax:

3. Under Data Source, choose Get Data.
4. Choose Open Data Source.
5. Under List Files of Type choose **MS Access Databases (*.mdb).**
6. Switch to the directory your Access database is stored in. In most cases, you'll want to double-click on **c:** near the top of the directory list, then double-click on **access**. Finally, under File Name, double-click on the name of your Access database (e.g., **PEOPLE.MDB**). It might take a minute for Access to load.
7. When the Microsoft Access dialog box appears, click on the name of the table that contains names and addresses (e.g., **Mailing List**), then choose OK.
8. Wait a few seconds then, when prompted, choose Edit Main Document.
9. Now you need to use the Insert Merge Field button to choose a field from your database to display on the page. You can choose whatever fields you wish, and arrange them however you wish. But it's important to understand that Word *won't* insert blank spaces and punctuation automatically. You need to type those things, yourself, while inserting the merge fields. Here are some pointers:
    - If you want to follow the field with a blank space, be sure to press the spacebar after you insert the field.
    - If you want to follow a field with a comma, text, or anything else, type that text or character right after the field.
    - To move to the next line, press ↵ as usual.
    - If you want to apply attributes, such as boldface or a particular font to a portion of the text, select the merge fields and attributes as you would in any "normal" Word document.

Figure D.2 shows how I arranged merge fields from the sample directory shown at the start of this section. Notice that I inserted a comma and space after the «LastName» field, a space after Prefix, and a space after FirstName. I selected that line, and made it boldface. I also typed in the headings for the phone numbers, (Home Phone, Work Phone, etc.).

FIGURE D.2

How I arranged merge fields to print the directory shown near the beginning of this section

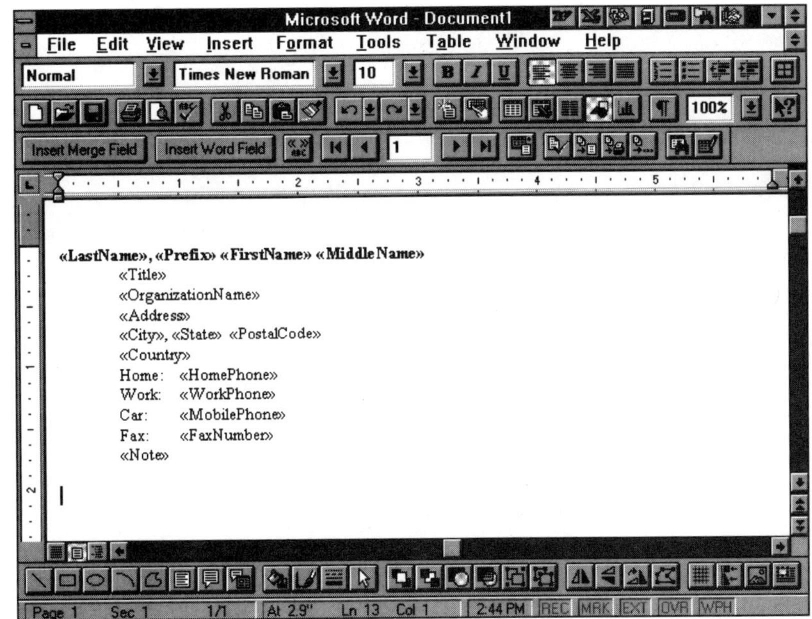

I also used the Tab key to indent text under the first line and to align the phone numbers. After inserting the last merge, named <<Note>> in this example, I pressed ↵ twice to ensure that there'd be a blank line after each entry.

10. If you want to print in a two-column format, as in my example, first move the insertion point to the top of the document (press Ctrl+Home). Then choose Format ➢ Columns ➢ Two. If you want a printed line between the columns, choose Line Between. Choose OK. (Don't worry if the Middle Name field jumps down to the next line.)

11. When you're happy with the organization of your merge fields, close and save this document (choose File ➢ Close ➢ Yes, type in a file name (such as **MrgDirec**) and choose OK.

You won't need to repeat all those steps in the future. From now on, whenever you want to print an updated directory of names and addresses, just follow the steps in the next section.

STEPS

Printing the Directory

Now that you've created your Access database and directory format, printing the directory will be a snap. Just follow these steps:

1. If you haven't done so yet, start Microsoft Word.
2. Choose File ➢ Open, and double-click the name of your directory format document (e.g., **MRGDIREC.DOC**).
3. When the merge fields appear on the screen, click the Mail Merge button on the Mail Merge button bar, shown here. You'll be taken to the Merge dialog box:

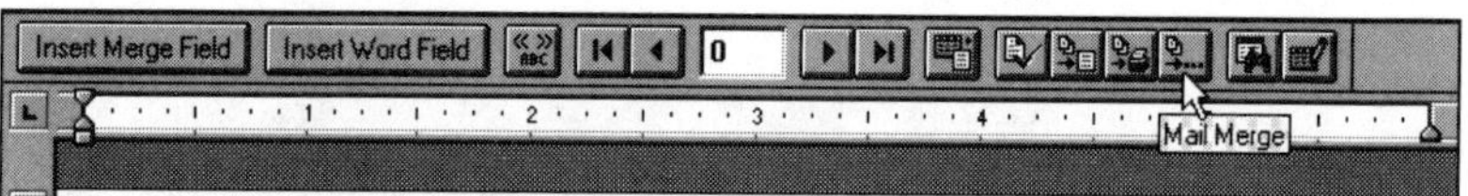

4. Choose Query Options.
5. Click the Sort Records tab, and then choose fields to sort by. In Figure D.3, I've opted to sort by LastName, then FirstName, then

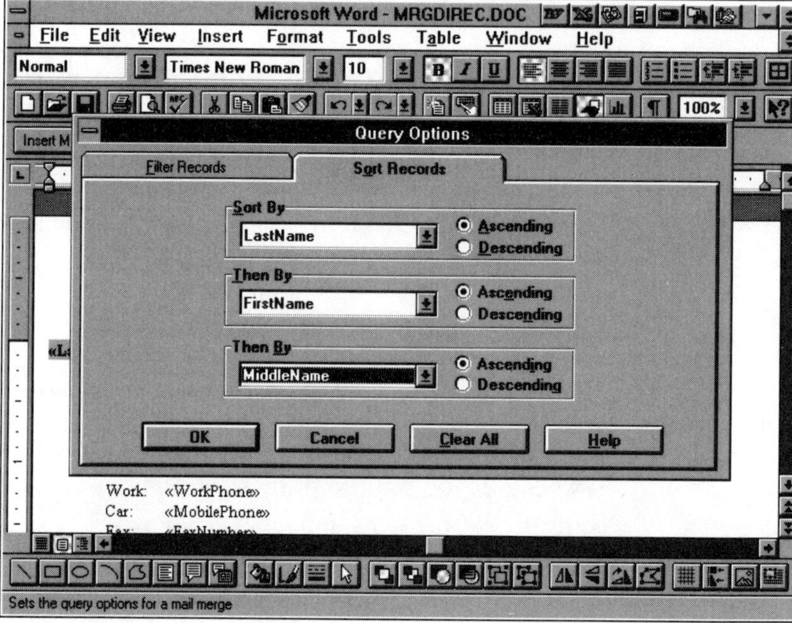

FIGURE D.3

The Query Options dialog box set up to alphabetize names and addresses by peoples' names.

MiddleName, which is the same alphabetizing scheme as the phone book (the White Pages, that is).

6. Choose OK, then choose Merge.

7. To print the directory, choose File ➢ Print ➢ OK.

8. When the printer has finished, you can exit Word without saving anything. Choose File ➢ Exit ➢ No (twice). You'll be returned to your home base, the Windows Program Manager.

TIPS

- In step 8 above, you can exit Word without saving anything because your names and addresses and directory format are still stored on disk. Neither has changed—the two have just been merged together.
- See also the entries titled *Envelopes (Many), Form Letters, and Mailing Labels (Many)* for other things you can do with your Access database and Word.
- If you don't want a person's name and address to be split across two columns, or two pages, start Microsoft Word and open MRGDIREC.DOC. Select all the merge fields *except the last one*, by dragging the mouse pointer through them. Then choose Format ➢ Paragraph and click the Text Flow tab. Choose Keep with Next ➢ OK. Then choose File ➢ Close ➢ Yes. From now on, whenever you print the directory (as discussed above under *Steps: Printing the Directory*), one person's data will never be split across columns or pages.

RELATED SKILLS AND TOPICS

TOPIC	WHERE TO FIND IT
Microsoft Access	*Instant Office*
Microsoft Word	*Instant Office*
Typing Text and Numbers	Appendix B

Need Some Help?

Having troubles getting started?
I can help you:

- Choose A System
- Find the Right Software
- Learn New Programs

Friendly, personal service
At your site: $30.00/hr
Call Wanda Bea Starr
At 555-0123

DISPLAY AD

30 min.

Suppose you want to create a small display advertisement to promote your business in a local newsletter or magazine. Rather than just stick your business card in the ad, why not go for something with a little more pizzazz? Here's a quick-and-dirty technique you can use to create a simple but effective ad with a picture.

D

STEPS

1. Start Microsoft PowerPoint.
2. If you come to the Tip of the Day, just choose OK to move on.
3. If you *don't* get the dialog box shown in Figure D.4, choose File ➢ New from PowerPoint's menu bar.

FIGURE D.4:

The New Presentation dialog box in PowerPoint (which might also be titled just PowerPoint), lets you start a new presentation using any of several techniques.

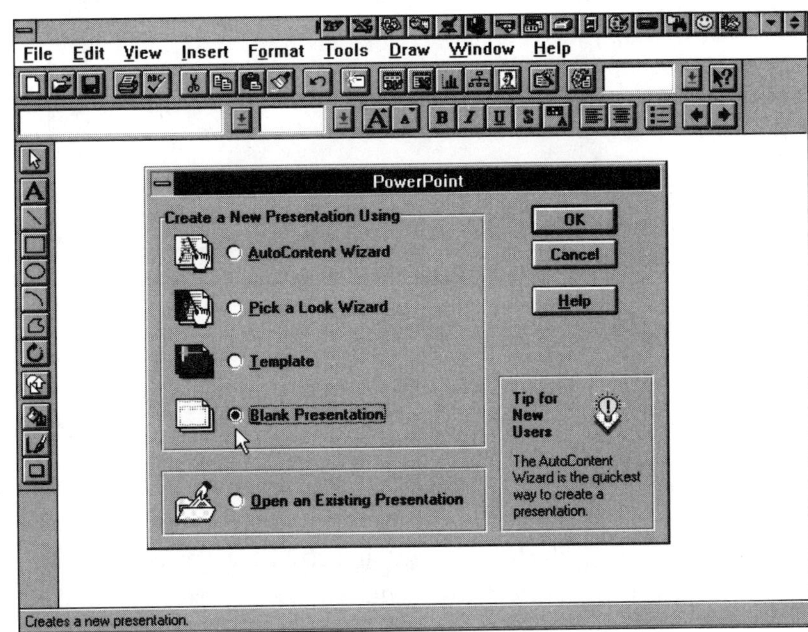

4. Choose Blank Presentation, then choose OK.
5. You can use any AutoLayout that you want, but I suggest you use the Text & Clip Art layout. Click that layout (the mouse pointer in the picture below is touching it).

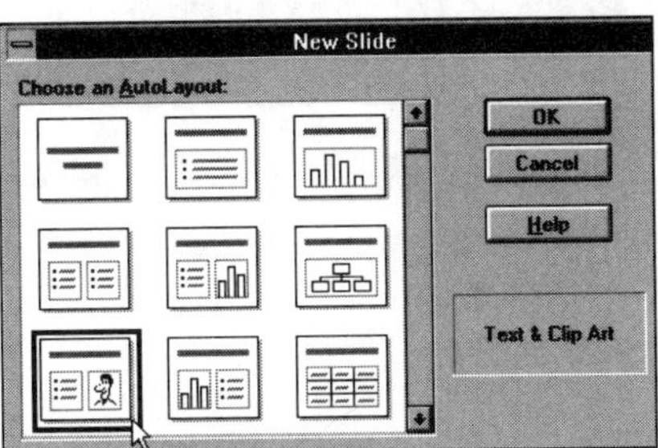

6. Choose OK. After a brief delay, you should see the presentation window shown in Figure D.5.

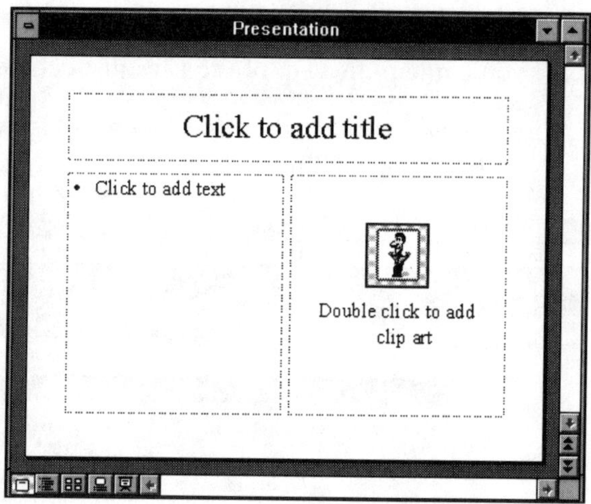

FIGURE D.5

Ready to create a display ad using PowerPoint's Text & Clip Art layout

7. Click where it says *Click to add title*, and type the title for your ad. (This will likely be the first thing the potential customer reads, so try to make your message short and sweet, but meaningful.)

8. If you want to use a unique font, first select the text that you just typed (by dragging the mouse pointer through it). Then choose a font and size from PowerPoint's Formatting toolbar, or from the menus via the Format ➢ Font commands. For example, below I chose Remedy Double at 72 points (I purchased that font from Émigré).

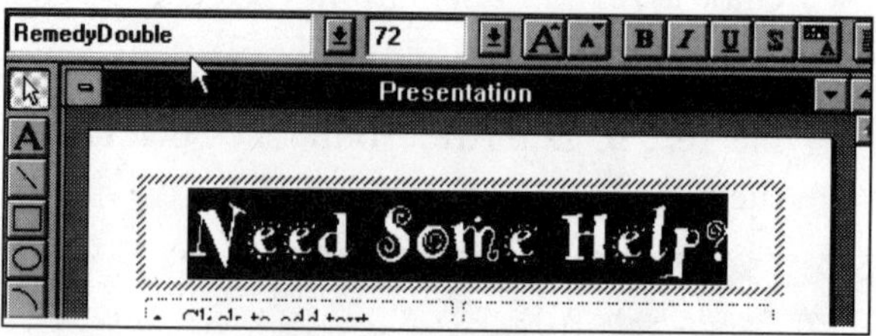

9. If you want to add a drop shadow to your text, as in my example, select the text to shadow. Then click on the Text Shadow button in the Formatting toolbar.

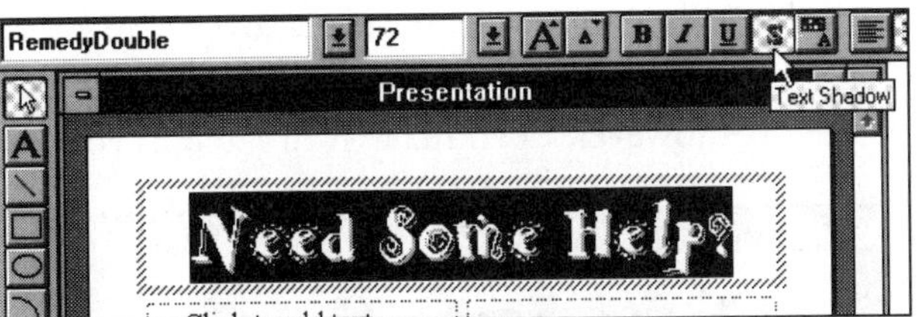

10. We'll do a picture next. Double-click the little picture above the prompt that says *Double click to add clip art.*

11. If asked about adding clip art, I suggest you choose OK from each prompt. It takes a while, but you only have to go through that procedure once.

12. When you get to the Microsoft Clip Art Gallery dialog box shown, shown in Figure D.6, choose a category (I chose Cartoons), then click on the picture of your choice.

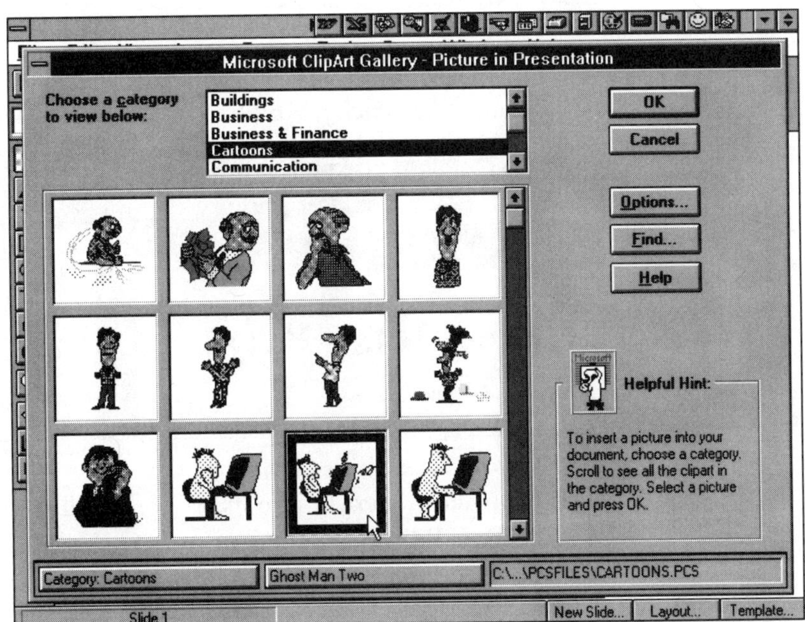

FIGURE D.6

The Microsoft Clip Art Gallery dialog box lets you choose a category and a and specific picture.

13. Choose OK. The clip-art image comes into your ad.

14. Finally, we'll add some text. Click where it says Click to Add Text. Type each line, pressing ↵ at the end of each line. Don't worry

about the bullets—you can remove them later if you like. For example, below I typed a bunch of text, more than can even fit into the box. However, I can make it fit later, as you'll see.

15. To delete bullets, click the line that you want to remove the bullet from. Then click the Bullet On/Off button in the toolbar, as below.

16. To make the text fit into its box, select all the text in the box (choose Edit ➢ Select All or press Ctrl+A). Then choose a font and size from the Formatting toolbar or by choosing Format ➢ Font.

17. Optionally, use any of the techniques listed under *Tips* below to spruce up your text and bullets.

18. When you're happy with your ad, choose File ➢ Print ➢ OK to print it.

19. When the printing is done, you can exit PowerPoint and save your ad. From PowerPoint's menu bar, choose File ➢ Exit ➢ Yes. Type in a file name, such as **dsplayad**, and then choose OK until you get back to your home base, the Windows Program Manager.

TIPS

D

When you're typing the text portion of your display ad, you can use any of the buttons in the Formatting toolbar, as well as menu commands, to format the text to your liking. Some especially useful techniques include:

- To center text, select the text you want to center, then click the Center alignment button in the Formatting toolbar.
- To indent text, select the text you want to indent, then click the Demote (Indent More) button in the toolbar. (The bullet on bulleted text might change, but don't worry about that.)
- To change the character used for bullets, first select the bulleted text. Then choose Format ➢ Bullet from PowerPoint's menu bar. Under Bullets From, choose a font for the bullet. You can click on any bullet, or drag the cursor through bullets, to get a magnified view. When you find the character you want to use as a bullet, click on it. Then choose OK.
- If you make a change, and don't like the results, choose Edit ➢ Undo or press Ctrl+Z to undo the most recent change.

RELATED SKILLS AND TOPICS

TOPIC	WHERE TO FIND IT
Fonts	Appendix B
Microsoft PowerPoint	*Instant Office*
Picture	*Do-It-Now Encyclopedia*
Photo	*Do-It-Now Encyclopedia*
Select, Then Do	Appendix B
Sign	*Do-It-Now Encyclopedia*
Signature	*Do-It-Now Encyclopedia*

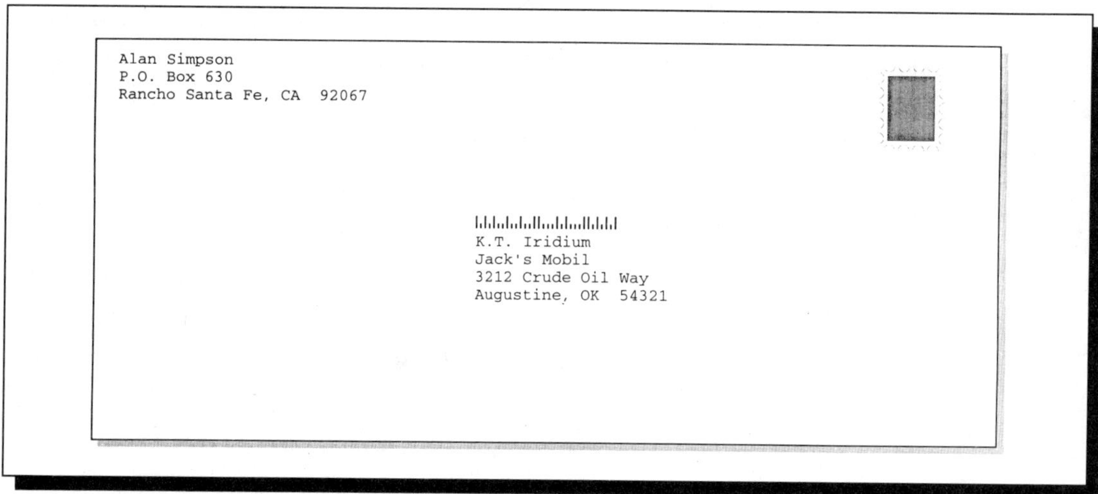

Alan Simpson
P.O. Box 630
Rancho Santa Fe, CA 92067
K.T. Iridium
Jack's Mobil
3212 Crude Oil Way
Augustine, OK 54321

ENVELOPE (ONE)

 5 min.

Use this technique to type up a single envelope. If you want to type up a letter and envelope at the same time, try the techniques described under Letters (Business and Personal) here in the Do-It-Now Encyclopedia. *If you need to type up lots of envelopes for mass mailing, see the entry Envelopes (Many) that follows this one.*

STEPS

1. Start Microsoft Word.
2. Choose Tools ➢ Envelopes and Labels.
3. Click on the Envelopes tab near the top of the dialog box.
4. In the space provided under Delivery Address, type the complete name and mailing address that you want to put on the envelope. Press ↵ after typing each line.
5. If you've never done so before, type the return address where indicated, or choose Omit to omit the return address (as when you're using pre-printed envelopes).

6. Choose Options and then choose your envelope size (standard business envelopes are Size 10). Choose any other options that appeal to you, such as Delivery Point Bar Code if the delivery address is within the United States. Then choose OK.

7. Put the envelope into the printer, in whatever direction is indicated under Feed on your screen. Then choose Print.

If the envelope isn't printed within a few seconds, check to make sure that you've inserted the envelope far enough into the printer for the printer to sense its presence.

If you've finished with Word for the time being, you can choose File ➢ Exit ➢ No to exit and return to your home base, the Windows Program Manager.

TIPS

- If you have any problems printing envelopes, see your printer manual for more information.
- To add a picture to an envelope, complete only steps 1–6 above. Then choose Add to Document, and use Insert ➢ Picture in the usual manner to add a picture. Then choose File ➢ Print ➢ OK from the Word menu bar to print the envelope. (Don't forget to feed the envelope into the printer!)
- If you want to print the same picture on all your envelopes, create AutoText entries named EnvelopeExtra1 and EnvelopeExtra2. For specific instructions, search Word's help for topics under *envelope,* or see Chapter 23 in the Microsoft Word *User's Guide* that came with your Microsoft Office package.

RELATED SKILLS AND TOPICS

TOPIC	WHERE TO FIND IT
Microsoft Word	*Instant Office*
Dialog boxes	Appendix B

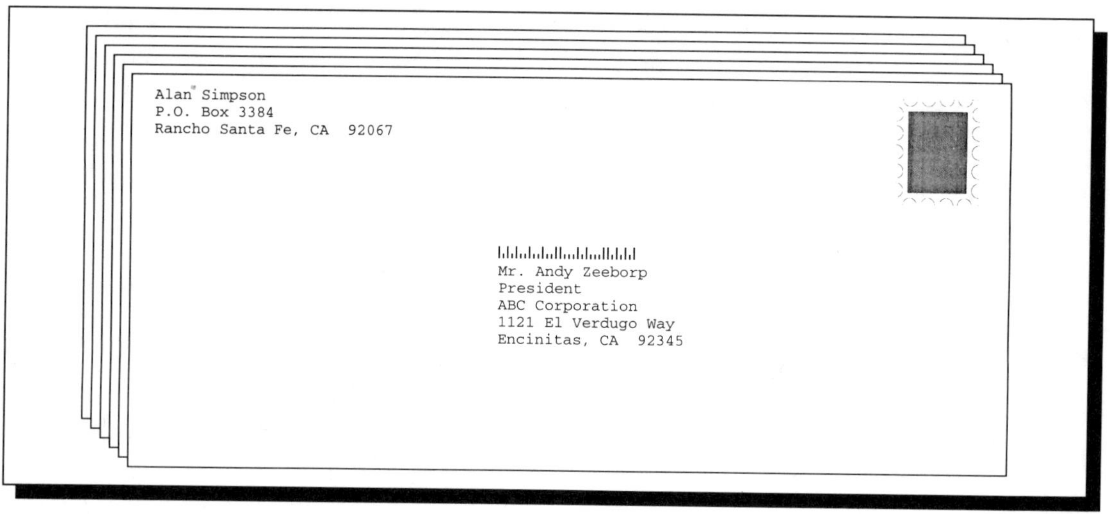

ENVELOPES (MANY)

55 min.

If you need to print up many envelopes for a mass mailing, your best starting point will be to create an Access database to store people's names and addresses, so you never have to retype the same name and address twice. See the Database (Create) *entry here in the* Do-It-Now Encyclopedia, *and create the PEOPLE.MDB database. Then follow the instructions under* Database (Use) *to add some names and addresses to the database table. After you've typed in some names and addresses, follow the steps below to create an envelope format.*

STEPS

Creating the Envelope Format

It takes several minutes to create an envelope format. But fortunately, you only need to do this once. In the future, you'll be able to reuse this format over and over again to print new envelopes at any time.

1. Start Microsoft Word.
2. Choose Tools ➢ Mail Merge. You'll be taken to the Mail Merge Helper dialog box.
3. Under Main Document, choose Create.

4. Choose Envelopes.

5. Choose Active Window.

6. Under Data Source, choose Get Data.

7. Choose Open Data Source.

8. Under List Files of Type choose **MS Access Databases (*.mdb)**.

9. Switch to your Access directory. (Assuming your database is stored on C:\ACCESS, you'll want to double-click on **c:** at the top of the Directories list, then double-click on **access**.)

10. Under File Name, click the name of your Access database (e.g., **PEOPLE.MDB**), then choose OK.

11. Wait a few seconds for the Access dialog box to appear, then click the Tables tab. Click the name of your name and address table (e.g., **Mailing List**) then choose OK.

12. Wait a few seconds, then, when given the option, choose Set Up Main Document.

13. Click the Envelope Options tab, and choose an envelope size from the Envelope Size drop-down list (the standard size is Size 10, which may already be selected for you).

14. Feel free to choose a font or any other available options.

15. Click the Printing Options tab.

16. Choose a Feed Method (or leave as set) and, a Feed From option. For example, if you need to feed envelopes one at a time, choose Manual Feed. If your printer has an envelope feeder, choose one of the other options (such as Envelope Feed).

17. Choose OK. You're taken to the Envelope Address dialog box.

18. If you want to print postal bar codes on your envelopes, choose Insert Postal Bar Code, choose the name of the Access field that contains zip codes (most likely **PostalCode**), and the field that contains the street address (most likely **Address**). Then choose OK.

FIGURE E.1

An envelope format designed from fields in a Access database table

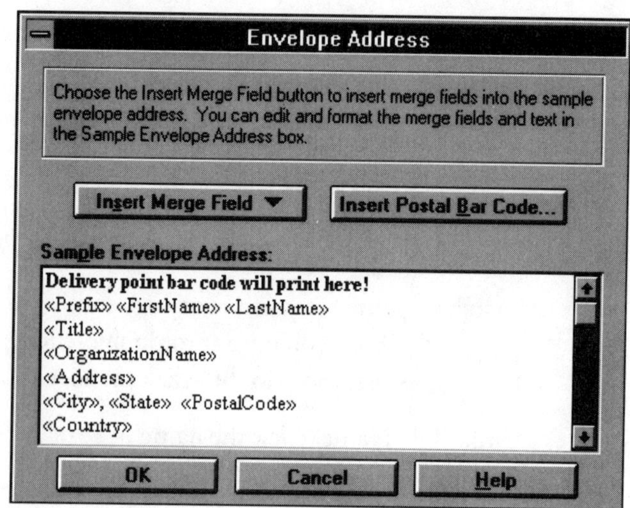

19. Press the End key, then press ↵ to move down to the next line.

20. Use the Insert Merge Field to select fields from your table in exactly the format you want them to appear on the envelope. Keep in mind that you need to insert spaces and punctuation yourself. For example, click Insert Merge Field, then click Prefix to place the prefix field first. Then:

    - If you want to type a comma or any other text after the field you just entered, type that text. For example, you'll probably want to type a comma after you place the City field, as in the example shown in Figure E.1.
    - If you want to print a blank space before the next field, press the spacebar.
    - If you want to print the next field on the next line, press ↵.
    - If you want to indent a tab stop, press Ctrl+Tab.

21. Repeat step 20 until all the fields are arranged as in the example shown in Figure E.1. Then choose OK.

22. Now, under Main Document, choose Edit, then choose the first option that appears on the menu (most likely Envelope: Document 1).

23. If your return address appears on the envelope, and you want to remove it, just select and then delete the return address. If the

return address is incorrect, correct it now using standard Word editing techniques.

24. Choose File ➢ Close ➢ Yes. Type a valid file name, such as **mrgenv** (for Merge Envelopes), then choose OK.

Whew, that was a bit of a hassle. But, as I mentioned, you'll never need to repeat those steps again. Instead, just merge MRGENV.DOC with your Access database as described in the next section.

STEPS

Printing the Envelopes

Now that you've created your Access database and envelope format, printing envelopes will be a snap. Just follow these steps:

1. If you haven't done so yet, start Microsoft Word.
2. Choose File ➢ Open, and double-click the name of your envelope format document (e.g., **MRGENV.DOC**).
3. Click the View Merged Data button in the Merge toolbar (shown here). One envelope containing information from your Access data base appears on your screen:

4. Load the envelope(s) into the printer.
5. Now you have several choices:
    - **To print one envelope**, use the First Record, Previous Record, Go to Record, Next Record, Last Record, or Find Record buttons on the Merge toolbar to isolate the envelope you want to print. Then choose File ➢ Print ➢ OK to print just that envelope.
    - **To print an envelope for everyone** in your database, click the Merge to Printer button on the Merge toolbar.
    - **To preview all the envelopes before printing,** choose the Merge to New Document button on the toolbar. You can then

scroll through, and change text using the standard Word navigating and editing techniques. When you're ready to print the envelopes, choose File ➢ Print ➢ OK.

- **To print envelopes for *some* people** in your database, click the Mail Merge button on the toolbar, and then choose Query Options. Fill out the Filter Records form to define which records you want to print envelopes for. For example, in Figure E.2 I've opted to print envelopes for California (CA) residents only. (You can also choose Sort Records to define a sort order for printing.) Choose OK, then choose Merge. Then choose File ➢ Print ➢ OK to print the envelopes.

FIGURE E.2

A query set up to print envelopes for California (CA) residents only

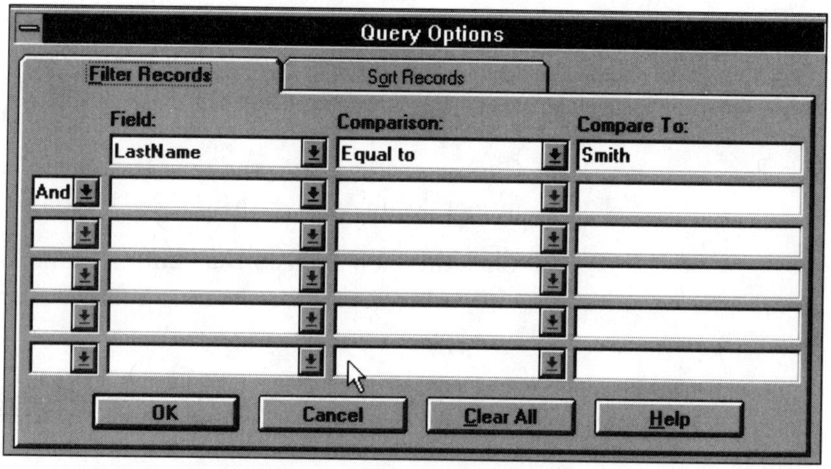

6. After the envelopes are printed, you can exit Word without saving anything. Choose File ➢ Exit ➢ No. You'll be returned to your home base, the Windows Program Manager.

TIPS

- You can exit Word without saving anything in step 6 above because your names and addresses and envelope format are still stored on disk. Neither has been changed—the two have just been merged together.

- If your return address shows up incorrectly on all the new documents you create, start Microsoft Word. Then choose Tools ➢ Options, click on the User Info tab, and type your complete return address (including your name) under Mailing Address. Choose OK.
- See also the entries titled *Mailing Labels (Many), Form Letters,* and *Directory (Name and Address List)* for other things you can do with your Access database and Word.

RELATED SKILLS AND TOPICS

TOPIC	WHERE TO FIND IT
Microsoft Access	*Instant Office*
Microsoft Word	*Instant Office*

FAX COVER SHEET

5 min.

Microsoft Word's Fax Wizard will give you an instant fax cover sheet. You can either print a bunch of blank cover sheets to fill in by hand later or type up each fax cover sheet as needed. If you have a fax modem, you can even send the cover sheet right from your computer, without printing it first.

STEPS

1. Start Microsoft Word.
2. Choose File ➢ New from Word's menu bar.
3. Double-click on Fax Wizard.
4. Read, and answer, the questions that appear in the Wizard window. The sample in the window changes to reflect your current choice. Click on the button labeled Next after answering the question(s).

F

Alan's Electron Studio P.O. Box 630, Rancho Santa Fe, CA 92067

FAX

Date: **03/28/94**

Number of pages including cover sheet: ______

To:

Phone:

Fax phone:

CC:

From:

Alan Simpson

Phone: (619)555-1212

Fax phone: (619)756-0159

REMARKS: ☐ Urgent ☐ For your review ☐ Reply ASAP ☐ Please comment

5. Repeat step 4 until you get to the checkered flag, then choose Finish.

Now you have two choices. If you want to print up a bunch of empty cover sheets to fill in later when you need them, choose File ➢ Print, choose however many copies you want to print, then choose OK.

Alternatively, you can fill in the blanks on the cover sheet right on your screen. Just click wherever you want to add text, then start typing. Use the scroll bar at the right side of the cover sheet to scroll up and down through the sheet, or choose View ➢ Zoom, choose a magnification, and choose OK to change your view.

When you get to the large message area near the bottom of the sheet, type your message using standard Word techniques. But don't press Tab to indent, or you'll add a table row (the fax sheet is a Word table). Instead, press Ctrl+Tab to indent. If you press Tab by accident, just click the Undo button or choose Edit ➢ Undo. After you've filled in all the blanks on the sheet, choose File ➢ Print ➢ OK to print it.

Faxing without Printing

If you have a fax-modem board in your computer, you can just fax directly from the screen. The usual technique is to choose File ➢ Print ➢ Printer. Click the driver for your fax modem or fax board, then choose Close. Choose OK. But there are many different brands of fax boards out there, and obviously I have no idea which one you're using. If my instructions don't work for you, please refer to the manual that came with your fax board.

After sending the fax from Word, remember to return to your normal printer by choosing File ➢ Print ➢ Printer, and the appropriate printer.

TIPS

- The fax cover sheet is (mostly) a Microsoft Word table.
- To exit Word, choose File ➢ Exit from the Word menu bar, or press Alt+F4. As usual, you'll be given the option to save this copy of the fax cover sheet for editing and printing later, and then you'll be returned to the Windows Program Manager.

- The Fax Wizard remembers your answers to its questions. So, when you use the Fax Wizard again in the future, you won't need to fill in all the same information.

RELATED SKILLS AND TOPICS

TOPIC	WHERE TO FIND IT
Microsoft Word	*Instant Office*
Typing Text and Numbers	Appendix B
Wizards	*Instant Office*

FORM LETTERS

15 min.

If you want to send out personalized form letters, your best starting point will be to create an Access database to store people's names and addresses. That way, you'll have a permanent list of names and addresses you can use repeatedly to print future letters, envelopes, mailing labels, whatever. If you have not already done so, create the Access database named PEOPLE.MDB as discussed under Database (Create)*.*

Then, follow the instructions under Database (Use) *to add some names and addresses to the database table. After you've typed in all (or at least, some) of your names and addresses, follow the steps below to format and print form letters.*

STEPS

Creating the Letter

After you've stored some names and addresses in an Access database, you can type up the form letter that you want to send out. If you've already typed up the form letter and saved it, skip to the section titled

Electron Studios

P.O. Box 3384
Rancho Santa Fe, CA 92067
June 7, 1993

Mr. Andy Adams
President
ABC Corporation
123 A St.
San Diego, CA 91234

Dear Andy:

Thank you for your inquiry about Electron Studio's Encyclopedias. The enclosed material should give you a better understanding of our company and the products and services that we offer.

We are proud of our reputation for putting the customer first in every area of our operations. We feel that this attitude is one of the most important contributors to our success and to the success of the customers we serve.

I will be contacting you within the next two weeks to see if you have any questions or need any additional information. Again, thank you for your interest.

Sincerely,

Janet X. Wilson
Account Representative

F

Steps: Adding the Merge Fields now. Otherwise, to start the letter from scratch, start here at Step 1:

1. Start Microsoft Word.
2. Choose File ➢ New.
3. Now you have two choices:
   - If you want to type the letter from scratch, choose OK to get to a blank sheet of paper. Then type your letter using normal Word typing and editing techniques (Appendix B).
   - If you want to use the Word Letter Wizard to help you create the letter, double-click on Letter Wizard. Choose *Select a prewritten business letter* from the first Wizard window, then choose Next. Proceed through the Wizard by answering each question and choosing Next. When asked for the recipient's address, leave it blank or delete whatever name and address are in there from before. When you get to the checkered flag, choose *Just display the letter*, then Finish. Replace any placeholders (text in square brackets and underlined text) with the actual content you want in your letter.

TIP: *If you've need help with the Letter Wizard, refer to* Letters (Business and Personal) *here in the* Do-It-Now Encyclopedia.

4. Delete any text that will be coming from your database. For example, if you've already typed one recipient's name and address, delete that. Also, delete [*Name*] or any person's name after the word Dear. To delete text, just drag the mouse pointer through it, and then press Delete or Del.
5. Carefully review the letter, make sure it says exactly what you want it to say, and perhaps run the spelling checker on it (Tools ➢ Spelling).
6. When you're happy with the text and appearance of the letter, close and save it. That is, choose File ➢ Close ➢ Yes. Enter a valid file name such as **FormLet1**, then choose OK.

Your letter is stored on disk, and you're still in Word, with a fresh screen to work from.

STEPS

Adding Merge Fields to the Letter

Once your letter is stored on disk, you need to add *merge fields* to show where, and how, you want Word in insert people's names and addresses from your Access database. Follow these steps to do so:

1. If you're not already in Microsoft Word, start it now.
2. Choose File ➢ Open and double-click the name of your form letter file (e.g., FORMLET1.DOC)
3. Choose Tools ➢ Mail Merge ➢ Create ➢ Form Letters.
4. Choose Active Window.
5. Choose Get Data.
6. Choose Open Data Source.
7. Under List Files of Type, choose **MS Access Databases (*.mdb)**.
8. Switch to your Access directory. (Assuming your database is stored in C:\ACCESS, you'll want to double-click on **c:** at the top of the Directories list, then double-click on **access**.)
9. Under File Name, click the name of your Access database (e.g., **PEOPLE.MDB**), then choose OK. Wait half a minute or so for Word to establish a connection with Access.
10. When the Microsoft Access dialog box appears, click on the Tables tab, click the name of the Access table that contains your names and addresses (e.g., **Mailing List**), then choose OK.
11. When you see a message indicating that Word found no merge fields in your document, just choose Edit Main Document. Your letter should appear on the screen.
12. Move the blinking insertion point (cursor) to wherever you want to place an item of information from your database. Then click on the Insert Merge Field button in the Merge toolbar.

13. Click the name of the field that you want to insert (e.g., Prefix). The field name appears, enclosed in chevrons («»). Now...

- If you want to print a blank space before the next field, press the spacebar.
- If you want to type a comma or any other text after the field you just entered, type that text. For example, you'll probably want to type a comma after you place the City field, as in the example shown in Figure F.1.
- If you want to print the next field on the next line, press ↵ If you used a Wizard to create the letter, and the cursor does not move back over to the left margin, choose Format ➢ Style ➢ Inside Address ➢ Apply to return to normal indenting. You can also just choose the Inside Address style drop-down list on the Formatting toolbar, if that toolbar is open (View ➢ Toolbars ➢ Formatting ➢ OK).

14. Repeat step 13 until all the fields that you want to print are placed on the letter, as in my example in Figure F.1. Note that if the letter is casual, you can place the FirstName field next to the word Dear, as below:

```
Dear <<FirstName>>:
```

Or for a more formal letter, place the Prefix and LastName fields there, like this:

```
Dear <<Prefix>> <<LastName>>
```

Figure F.1 shows an example where I've placed the fields named Prefix, FirstName, LastName, and so forth from my mailing list table. Note the blank space between Prefix, FirstName, and LastName, the comma and space after City, and so forth. I've also placed a blank space and the <<FirstName>> merge field just after the word Dear in that example.

15. Choose File ➢ Close ➢ Yes to save this completed version of the letter.

Your form letter format is (finally) done and saved on disk. Now you need to merge your letter with your Access table of names and addresses, as discussed next.

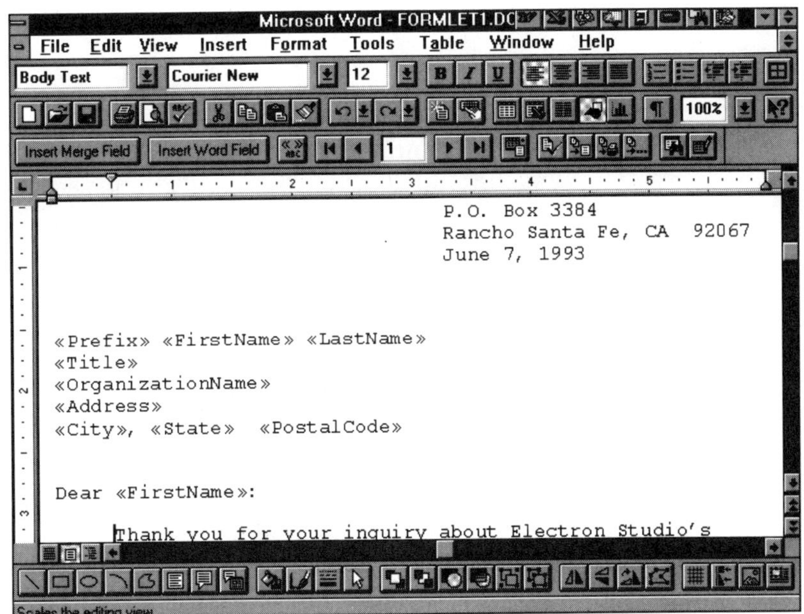

FIGURE F.1

An form letter format designed from fields in an Access database table.

STEPS

Printing the Form Letters

Follow these steps to merge your form letter with your Access names and addresses:

1. If you haven't done so yet, start Microsoft Word.
2. Choose File ➢ Open, and double-click the name of your form letter format document (e.g., FORMLET1.DOC).
3. When a letter appears on the screen, click the View Merged Data button in the Mail Merge toolbar (shown below). One letter should now show a name and addresses from your Access table.

4. If you're using preprinted letterhead stationery, make sure to put some in the printer.

5. Now you have several choices on the Merge toolbar. To determine which button is which, just touch the mouse pointer to a button, and wait a second for the ToolTip to appear on the screen.

   - **To print a letter for *one* person** in your database, use the First Record, Previous Record, GoTo Record, Next Record, and Last Record buttons to find the appropriate name and address. When the letter's inside address contains the right name and address, choose File ➢ Print ➢ OK.
   - **To print form letters for everyone in your database**, click the Merge to Printer button, and choose OK.
   - **To preview all the form letters before printing,** choose the Merge to New Document button. You can then scroll through the letters and change text using the standard Word navigating and editing techniques. When you're ready to print the form letters, choose File ➢ Print ➢ OK.
   - **To print form letters for *some* people** in your database, click the Mail Merge button, and then choose Query Options. Fill out the Filter Records form to define which records you want to print form letters for. For example, in Figure F.2 I've opted to print form letters only for people with the last name Smith. (You can also choose Sort Records to define a sort order for printing.) Choose OK, then choose Merge. Then choose File ➢ Print ➢ OK to print the form letters.

Query Options

Filter Records | Sort Records

	Field:	Comparison:	Compare To:
	LastName	Equal to	Smith
And			

OK | Cancel | Clear All | Help

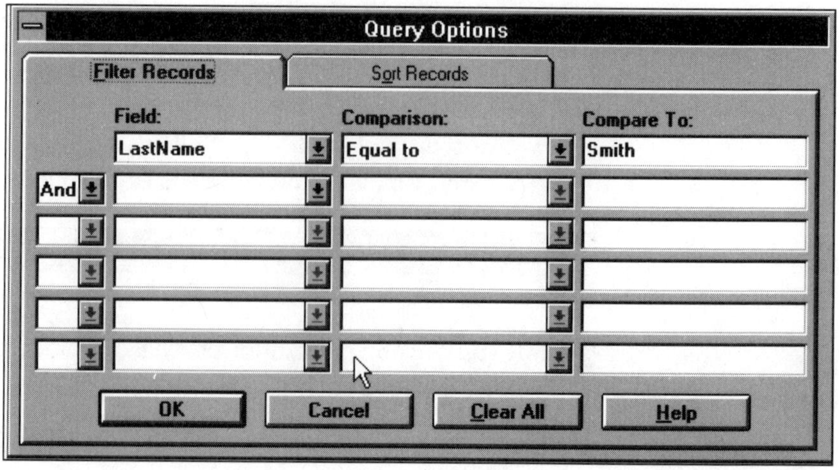

FIGURE F.2

A query set to isolate Access records that have "Smith" in the LastName field

6. After the form letters are printed, you can exit Word without saving anything. Choose File ➢ Exit ➢ No. You'll be returned to home base, the Windows Program Manager.

TIPS

- In step 6 above, you can exit Word without saving anything because your names and addresses and the form-letter format are still stored on disk. Neither has changed—the two have just been merged together.
- If you often send form letters, you can scan (digitize) your signature, and store it on disk as a picture. Then you can insert that picture onto the signature line of your form letter. Then you won't have to sign any of the form letters!
- See also, here in the *Do-It-Now Encyclopedia*, the entries titled *Envelopes (Many)*, *Directory (Names and Addresses)*, and *Mailing Labels (Many)* for other things you can do with your Access data base and Word.

RELATED SKILLS AND TOPICS

TOPIC	WHERE TO FIND IT
Microsoft Access	*Instant Office*
Microsoft Word	*Instant Office*
Wizards	Appendix B

F

FUTURE VALUE OF DEPOSITS

5 min.

Suppose you want to save up a nest egg for retirement. You have $1,000 in an account right now. That account earns 6% interest per year, compounded monthly. If you faithfully deposit $100.00 every month into that account, how much money will you have at the end of 10 years? Here's a simple worksheet that can answer that kind of question instantly.

FUTURVAL.XLS

	A	B	C	D	E	F
1	Future Value of Deposits					
2						
3	Annual Interest Rate	6%				
4	Years	10				
5	Monthly Deposit	$ 100.00				
6	Starting Balance	$ 1,000.00				
7						
8	**You will have:**	$ 18,289.27				

STEPS

1. Start Microsoft Excel.
2. Drag the cursor through the column headings at the tops of columns A and B, as below. Then choose Format ➢ Column ➢ Width, type **20** as the column width, then choose OK.

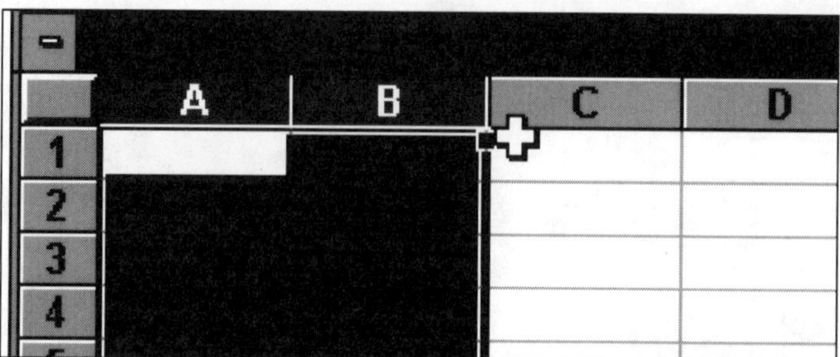

3. Type (literally) the text, numbers, and formulas shown in Table F.1 into the cell listed in the left column. For example, click on cell A1 and type **Future Value of Deposits**. Then click on cell A3 and type the words **Annual Interest Rate**.

TABLE F.1

The exact, literal contents of each cell in the Future Value of Deposits worksheet.

CELL	CONTAINS (LITERALLY)
A1	Future Value of Deposits
A3	Annual Interest Rate
A4	Years
A5	Monthly Deposit
A6	Starting Balance
A8	You will have:
B3	6%
B4	10
B5	100
B6	1000
B8	=FV(B3/12,B4*12,-B5,-B6,1)

4. After typing the contents of each cell, check to make sure the Formatting toolbar is open. If it is not, choose View ➢ Toolbars ➢ Formatting ➢ OK.

5. Now you can select the text in cell A1 and increase its size using the Formatting toolbar. Also, you can click on cell A8 and choose the Bold button from the Formatting toolbar.

6. To display dollar amounts in currency format, select cells B5:B8 by dragging the cursor through them. Then click on the Currency button ($) in the Formatting toolbar.

7. To try out different savings scenarios, change any value in cells B3, B4, B5, and B6. The Future Value calculation in cell B8 will show you the future value of those deposits instantly.

8. To print the worksheet, choose File ➢ Print ➢ OK.

9. When you're done with the worksheet, choose File ➢ Exit. If you think you might want to use this worksheet again in the future,

choose Yes, type in a valid file name (e.g., **FuturVal**) and then choose OK. If you don't want to save this worksheet, choose No when asked about saving.

You'll be returned to your home base, the Windows Program Manager.

TIPS

- For a list of other financial functions that Excel offers, search Excel's help for *financial functions.*

RELATED SKILLS AND TOPICS

TOPIC	WHERE TO FIND IT
Microsoft Excel	*Instant Office*
Typing Text and Numbers	Appendix B
Select, Then Do	Appendix B

GRAPH (BUSINESS CHART)

15 min.

Use the techniques described here to create any kind of business chart, from bar graphs to pie charts. Here I'll show you the quickest way to create a full-page stand-alone chart using Microsoft PowerPoint. Then, for those of you who want to add a business chart to some other kind of document, the Tips section will help you get started in adding graphs to Word documents, Excel worksheets, and Access databases.

STEPS

1. Start Microsoft PowerPoint. If the Tip of the Day appears, choose OK to move on.

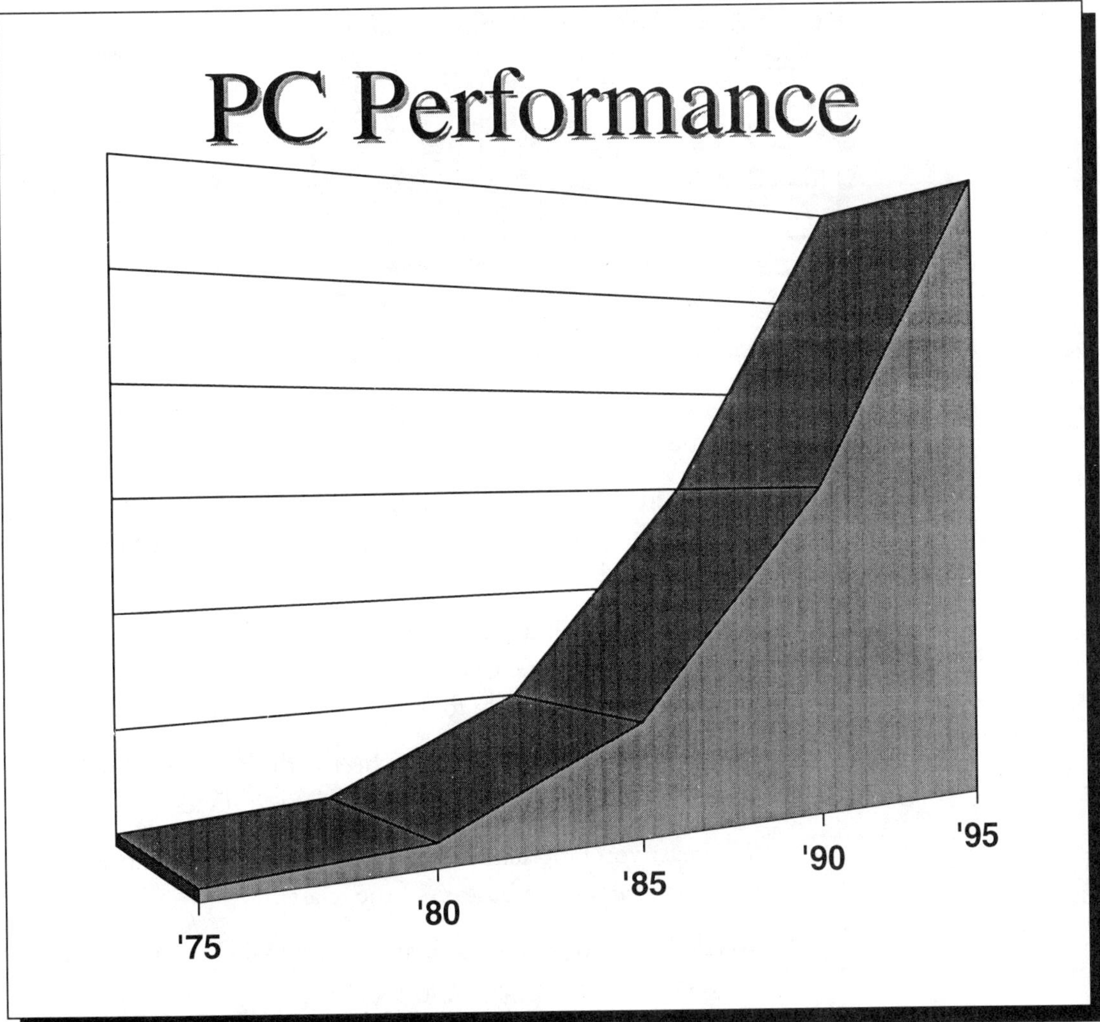

2. Choose Blank Presentation ➢ OK.
3. Choose the Graph AutoLayout (click the option in the upper-right corner, as shown below). Then choose OK.

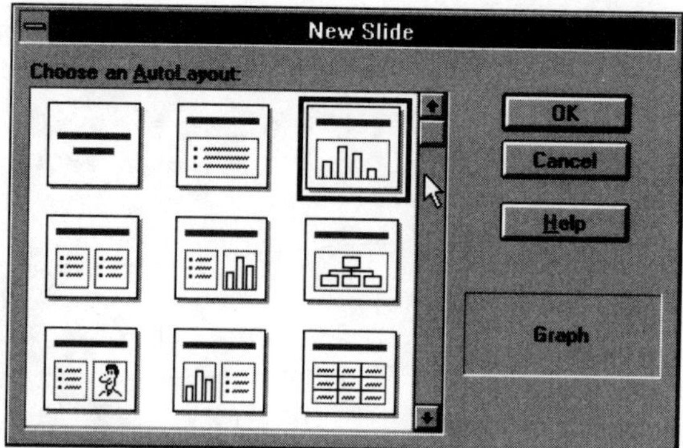

4. When the Presentation window appears, click where indicated to type a title, then type your title.

5. As instructed on the screen, double-click the chart icon. Wait a few seconds for the Presentation - Datasheet dialog box and Microsoft Graph toolbar, shown in Figure G.1, to appear.

6. Use the Chart Type button on the toolbar to choose the type of chart you want to create. Optionally, for examples and tips on picking a chart type, search help for *Choosing a chart type.*

7. Replace the sample data in the datasheet with the values you want to plot on your graph. Here are some basic techniques:

   - Whatever you type across the top row will appear as labels on the X axis (along the bottom of the chart).
   - Whatever you type down the first column will become series names that appear in the chart legend.
   - The actual numbers being plotted on the graph start in cell A1, which (unlike in a spreadsheet) is the second row down and the second column over.
   - You can size and position the Datasheet window as you need. For example, to move the datasheet, drag its title bar. To size the datasheet, drag its borders.
   - To type new data into a cell, just click that cell and type right over the sample data. Then click in another cell, or press ↵ or Tab to update the chart.

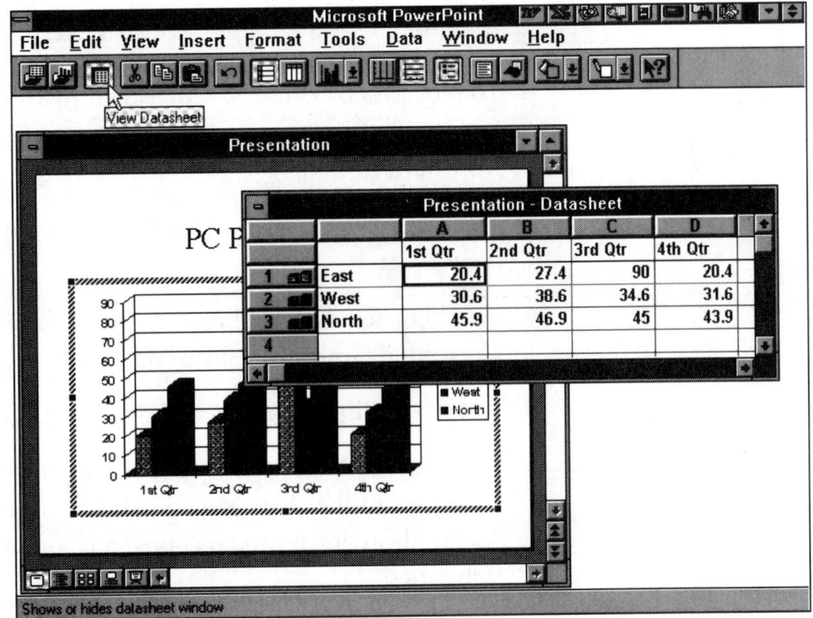

FIGURE G.1

The Presentation - Datasheet dialog box and Microsoft Graph toolbar appear on your screen.

- To clear out a row or column, click the row or column heading so that the entire row or column is selected. Then press Delete (Del) or choose Edit ➢ Delete.
- To insert cells, click wherever you want to make an insertion. Then choose Insert ➢ Cells, and make your selection from the dialog box that appears. Choose OK.
- To undo an insertion or deletion, choose Edit ➢ Undo.
- Remember, you can click the View Datasheet button in the toolbar to temporarily hide or display the datasheet to get a better look at your graph.

8. To change the appearance, angle, or other characteristics of the actual chart, first hide the datasheet (click the View Datasheet button). Then play around with some of the toolbar buttons and techniques described below. Don't worry about experimenting—you can always choose Edit ➢ Undo (right away) if you don't like a particular change. If the toolbar shown below isn't visible on your screen, try double-clicking the chart to bring these charting tools back.

- To plot data by column, rather than by row, click the By Column button. If you change your mind, just click the By Row button.
- To change the chart type, use the Chart Type drop-down list in the toolbar.
- To add or remove grid lines, click the Vertical Gridlines and Horizontal Gridlines buttons on or off.
- To hide or display the legend, click the Legend button.
- To change colors or show patterns rather than colors, click any data series in the chart (e.g., a red bar). Then use the Color and Pattern drop down lists to choose a color and/or pattern for each series.
- To change the size or shape of the chart, click the chart once so it has sizing handles. Then drag the sizing handles as you wish.
- To add drama by changing the angle, perspective, and so forth, right-click the body of the chart between any gridlines, then choose 3-D View from the instant menu. Play around with some of the buttons, and choose Apply to see their effects. When you're happy with the chart, choose OK.
- Remember, to change values being plotted, click the View Datasheet button.

9. When you're happy with the appearance of your chart, click outside the chart—for example, on the chart title.
10. You'll be taken back to the regular Power Point toolbar. From there, you can still resize and move the chart by dragging its borders and sizing handles. You can crop or recolor the chart by right-clicking and choosing an option. You can get back to the Chart tools by double-clicking the chart.
11. To print the chart, choose File ➢ Print ➢ OK as usual.

12. When you've finished with your chart, File ➢ Exit. If you want to save the chart for future use, choose Yes, type in a valid file name, and choose OK. You'll be returned to your home base, the Windows Program Manager.

TIPS

G

- **Have fun when designing your charts!** Experiment with clicking, double-clicking, right-clicking, and the various toolbar buttons and help (F1) screens. You can't do any real harm, and you can always choose Edit ➢ Undo to undo the most recent change.
- **To put a chart in a Word document**, start from Word with the insertion point at about where you want the chart to appear. Then choose Insert ➢ Object ➢ Microsoft Graph 5.0 ➢ OK. Edit the datasheet as described above. When you've finished designing the chart, click anywhere outside the chart, in your document. If you need to re-edit the chart, double-click it.

- **To put a chart in an Excel worksheet,** start Excel and open (or create) your worksheet. Select the cells that contain the numbers and titles that you want to plot on the chart. (To select, either drag the mouse pointer through the cells, or hold down the Shift key while extending the selection area with the arrow keys.) Then click the Chart Wizard button in the toolbar, drag out a frame indicating how large you want the graph to be, then answer questions posed by the Chart Wizard.
- **To create a chart from data in an Access table**, start Access and open your Access database. Choose File ➢ New ➢ Form. Select the table or query that contains the data you want to plot, than choose Form Wizards. Choose the Graph Wizard, then OK, and complete the Wizard's questions as they appear. When the chart is done, it will be stored as any other Access form, and automatically updated to reflect any changes in your data.

RELATED SKILLS AND TOPICS

TOPIC	WHERE TO FIND IT
Microsoft PowerPoint	*Instant Office*
Wizards	Appendix B

INVOICE

15 min.

If you need to type up an occasional invoice, the Microsoft Word invoice template (INVOICE.DOT) can make quick work of it. The first time you use the template, you'll want to tailor it to your own business. But from then on, typing up an invoice will just be a matter of filling in the blanks on your screen.

STEPS

Personalizing the Invoice Template

Follow these steps to modify the Word Invoice template to suit your own needs. You need only do this once—the very first time you use the Invoice template.

1. Start Microsoft Word.
2. Choose File ➢ Open from the Word menu bar.
3. Under List Files of Type, choose **Document Templates (*.dot)** (see Figure I.1).
4. Switch to the template directory. To do so, just double-click on the directory named **template** in the list of directory names (see Figure I.1). If you don't see the directory named template, first double-click on the **msoffice** directory name, then double-click on the **winword** directory name. You should then be able to double-click on the directory named **template**.
5. Double-click on the file name **INVOICE.DOT** (Figure I.1).

ABC Corporation

No Hay Problema
123 Ricky Ricardo Way
San Diego, CA 91234
213.555-1234 Fax 213.555-1235

INVOICE NO: 1001
DATE: March 29, 1994

To:
Willie Wanabee
1121 Appleton Drive
San Diego, CA 92039
(619)555-0493

Ship To:
Willie Wanabee
1121 Appleton Drive
San Diego, CA 92039
(619)555-0493

SALESPERSON	P.O. NUMBER	DATE SHIPPED	SHIPPED VIA	F.O.B. POINT	TERMS
BBG		4/1/94	UPS		Net 30

QUANTITY	DESCRIPTION	UNIT PRICE	AMOUNT
1	G.I. Josephine Action Character	$ 14.95	$ 14.95
5	G.I. Josephine Leisure Outfits	$ 4.95	$ 24.75
15	Sugar Rush Candy Bars	$ 0.59	$ 8.85
			$ 0.00
			$ 0.00
			$ 0.00
			$ 0.00
		SUBTOTAL	$ 48.55
		SALES TAX	$ 3.37
		SHIPPING & HANDLING	$ 5.00
		TOTAL DUE	$ 56.92

Make all checks payable to: ABC Corporation
If you have any questions concerning this invoice, call: Wanda Wilson, (800)555-0394

THANK YOU FOR YOUR BUSINESS!

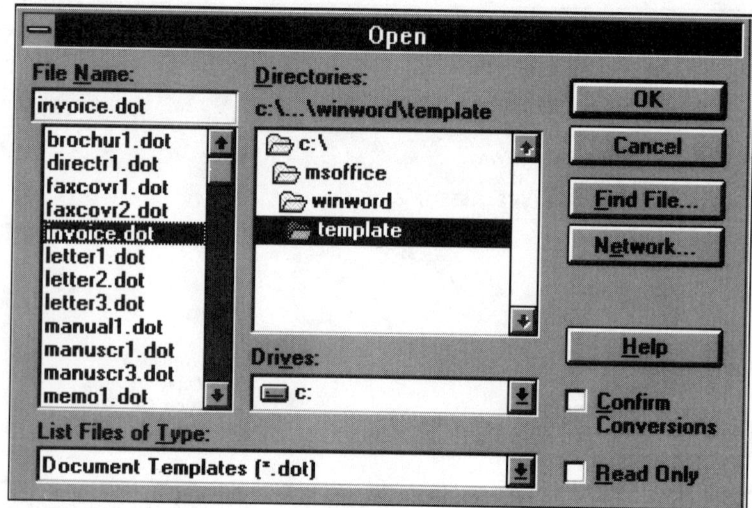

FIGURE I.1

To customize the Word invoice template, first display document template names and switch to the template directory, then double-click on INVOICE.DOT.

6. If the invoice is wider than your screen, reduce the magnification (choose View ➢ Zoom ➢ 75% ➢ OK).
7. Choose Tools ➢ Unprotect Document, so you can change some of the placeholders in the document.
8. Select the text that reads **Your Company Name** and then type in your own business name.
9. Repeat Step 8 to replace Your Company Slogan, Your Company Street Address, City, State, ZIP, and the phone numbers, as in the example shown in Figure I.2.
10. Scroll down to the bottom of the invoice (press Ctrl+End) and change the placeholders next to *Make all checks payable...* and *If you have any questions...* to the appropriate information for your business.
11. When you're done, choose Tools ➢ Protect Document ➢ Forms ➢ OK. That will prevent you from making accidental changes later.
12. Choose File ➢ Close ➢ Yes.

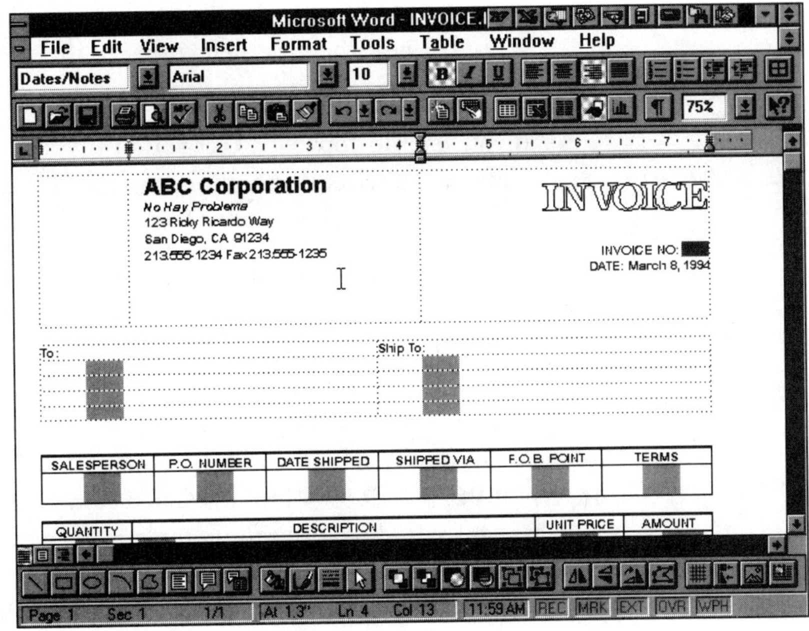

FIGURE 1.2

The Word Invoice template after changing the placeholders to a "real" company name and address.

You can now exit Microsoft Word, if you wish, by choosing File ➢ Exit. Your own company text is saved as part of the template. Remember, you only need to jump through that particular hoop once. From this point on, you can follow the steps below whenever you need to print up an invoice.

STEPS

Typing Up an Invoice

When you're ready to type up an invoice, follow these steps:

1. Start Microsoft Word (if it isn't already on your screen).
2. Choose File ➢ New from the Word menu bar.
3. Double-click on **Invoice.**
4. Now you can fill in the empty fields (gray blanks). Click whatever blank you want to fill, or press Tab and Shift+Tab to move from field to field (Tab moves you forwards; Shift+Tab moves you

backwards.) The current cell turns a darker shade of gray, and the status bar near the lower-left corner of the screen tells you what information is expected in each blank. Just click and start typing.

5. If you want to copy whatever you just typed to the next cell, press Shift+ ← to select that text, then press Ctrl+C. Move to the destination (blank) cell, and press Ctrl+V.

As you type in quantities, unit prices, sales tax, and shipping and handling, the subtotal and total due are recalculated automatically. If you need to figure out sales tax and don't have a calculator handy, try popping up the Windows Calculator (see the *Calculator* entry here in the *Do-It-Now Encyclopedia*). Then use decimal numbers to do the math. For example, to figure out how much $49.55 comes out with 6.75% sales tax added on, type **1.0675 * 49.55 =** into the Calculator.

When you're ready to print the completed invoice, just choose File ➢ Print. Set the number of copies you want to print, then choose OK. Once you've finished printing the invoice, you can close it by choosing File ➢ Close. If you want to save a copy of this particular invoice, choose Yes and give it a unique file name (such as the invoice number). If you don't want to save a copy on disk, just choose No when asked about saving.

When you want to type up another new invoice, repeat steps 2 through 5 above. (If you've exited Word, you'll need to repeat step 1 first.)

TIPS

- As an alternative to using up disk space to save a copy of each invoice, you can just print three copies of each one. Send two copies to the customer, and keep the other copy on file for your own records.

- To experiment with a more sophisticated invoicing system, start Microsoft Access, choose File ➢ Open, double-click on the SAMPAPPS directory name, then double-click on ORDERS.MDB. When the blank invoice appears, just experiment. (Look to the status bar near the lower-left corner of the screen for tips on what to type into the Prod ID cell.) When you've finished experimenting, choose File ➢ Exit to return to Windows.

RELATED SKILLS AND TOPICS

TOPIC	WHERE TO FIND IT
Drives, Directories, and Files	Appendix B
Microsoft Access	*Instant Office*
Microsoft Word	*Instant Office*

LABELS, TAGS, AND CARDS

15 min.

You can follow these steps to print up just about any kind of labels, tags, or cards. See Table L.1 for some examples of label sizes that Word supports. You can purchase Avery laser printer labels at most office supply and computer stores. Or order by mail from Paper Direct, Premier Papers, or Queblo, listed in Appendix C.

STEPS

1. Start Microsoft Word.
2. Choose Tools ➢ Envelopes and Labels from the Word menu bar.
3. Choose the Labels tab.
4. Choose Options.
5. Choose a printer type, label size, and product number from Options under the Printer Information, Label Products, and Product Number options. Then choose OK.
6. Choose New Document. Word creates a table with each cell sized as a label.
7. Type up your label. You can use the standards select-then-do techniques, and the Formatting toolbar (Tools ➢ View ➢ Formatting ➢ OK) to choose fonts, center text, copy text, and so forth.

Electron Studios

"Where Electrons Dance"

11211 Virtual Art Drive
Ozone, CA 98765

(619)555-4039 Fax: (619)555-1029

Electron Studios

"Where Electrons Dance"

11211 Virtual Art Drive
Ozone, CA 98765

(619)555-4039 Fax: (619)555-1029

Electron Studios

"Where Electrons Dance"

11211 Virtual Art Drive
Ozone, CA 98765

(619)555-4039 Fax: (619)555-1029

Electron Studios

"Where Electrons Dance"

11211 Virtual Art Drive
Ozone, CA 98765

(619)555-4039 Fax: (619)555-1029

Electron Studios

"Where Electrons Dance"

11211 Virtual Art Drive
Ozone, CA 98765

(619)555-4039 Fax: (619)555-1029

Electron Studios

"Where Electrons Dance"

11211 Virtual Art Drive
Ozone, CA 98765

(619)555-4039 Fax: (619)555-1029

Electron Studios

"Where Electrons Dance"

11211 Virtual Art Drive
Ozone, CA 98765

(619)555-4039 Fax: (619)555-1029

Electron Studios

"Where Electrons Dance"

11211 Virtual Art Drive
Ozone, CA 98765

(619)555-4039 Fax: (619)555-1029

Electron Studios

"Where Electrons Dance"

11211 Virtual Art Drive
Ozone, CA 98765

(619)555-4039 Fax: (619)555-1029

Electron Studios

"Where Electrons Dance"

11211 Virtual Art Drive
Ozone, CA 98765

(619)555-4039 Fax: (619)555-1029

TABLE L.1

Some examples of labels, cards, tags, and specialty papers you can purchase for use with laser printers.

LABEL/CARD/TAG SIZE	HEIGHT × WIDTH (INCHES)	AVERY PRODUCT NUMBER(S)
Address	many sizes	5160–5162, others
Audio tape	1.67 3.5	5198
Business cards	2 3.5	5371
Disk (3.5")	2.75 2.75	5096, 5196, 5896
Disk (5.25")	1.5 4	5097, 5197, 5897
File folder	0.67 3.44	5266
Index card	3 5	5388
Index maker®	many sizes	LSK-3–LSK-8
Name tag	2.17 3.5 or 3 4	5383, 5384, 5395
Postcard	4 6	5389
Ready index®	many sizes	RI-213-x
Return address	0.5 1.75	5267
Rotary card	2.17 4 or 3 5	5385, 5386
Shipping	many sizes	5163–5164, 8163
Sign (full sheet)	8.5 11	5165
Tab	0.33 4 or 3	Worksaver™ 5, 8
Transparency	8.5 11	5182
Videotape (front)	1.83 3.06	5199-F
Videotape (spine)	0.67 5.81	5199-S

8. If you want to print multiple copies of the same label, follow the bulleted below. If you *don't* want to print multiple copies of the same label, skip to Step 9.

   - Copy one completed label by clicking *inside* the cell's border, near the left edge of the cell, as shown below.

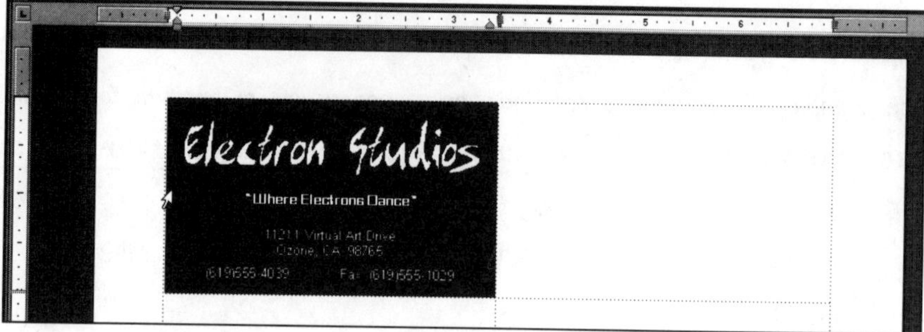

- Choose Edit ➢ Copy or press Ctrl+C to copy the selected cell to the Windows Clipboard.
- Press Tab until the insertion point gets to the next available empty cell, then choose Edit ➢ Paste Cells or press Ctrl+V. Repeat this step to make as many copies as you wish.

9. When you're ready to print, insert the label stock (or appropriate paper) into the printer, and choose File ➢ Print or press Ctrl+P. If you've filled the entire sheet with labels and want to print several sheets, set the number of Copies to print to the number of sheets you want to print. Choose OK.

10. To exit Word and return to Windows, choose File ➢ Exit from the Word menu bar. If you want to save your work for future use, choose Yes and enter a valid file name (e.g., **mycards**). Then choose OK.

TIPS

- The fancy print in my sample business cards is done in TrueType fonts named Crazed and Logan. As I recall, both are from Swfte International's Typecase collections (see Swfte in Appendix C).
- To type a single label, and perhaps skip over used labels on your sheet, see the section titled *Mailing Label (One)* here in the *Do-It-Now Encyclopedia.*

RELATED SKILLS AND TOPICS

TOPIC	WHERE TO FIND IT
Microsoft Word	*Instant Office*
Select, Then Do	Appendix B

LETTER (BUSINESS OR PERSONAL)

15 min.

When you need to type up a letter, let Word's Letter Wizard do some of the work. You can just have the Wizard format the letter, or even write some sample text to get you started. The Wizard will also give you the option to type up a quick envelope or mailing label to go with the letter.

STEPS

1. Start Microsoft Word.
2. Choose File ➢ New from the Word menu bar.
3. Double-click on Letter Wizard.
4. Choose from among the first three options: *Select a prewritten business* letter (see the list below for letters available if you choose this option), *Write a business letter* (formats a business letter), or *Write a personal letter* (formats a personal letter).
   - Announcement: price increase
   - Apology for delayed delivery
   - Collection letter (30 days past due)
   - Complaint under investigation
   - Credit report request

L

Michael R. Chidlen
P.O. Box 3384
Rancho Santa Fe, CA 92067
June 7, 1993

Mrs. Janda K. Chidlen
1101 Duarte Ave.
Monrovia, CA 92837

Dear Mom,

How are you doing? Everything is fine with me!

I'm sorry that I haven't written for a while, but I've been really busy! As you know, I really like computers, and I'm spending long hours in front of a screen both at work and at home.

In fact, I just bought a great program. It's really neat – a collection of business letters that I can customize any way I want. For example, there's a letter to people who are late paying their bills and another one that complains about a defective product.

I'm sure it'll save me a lot of time and energy — you know how hard it is for me to write letters! Now I'll be able to think about business instead of worrying about what to say in letters.

Too bad they don't have one for writing to you! Ha ha ha. They should also have one for thanking Aunt Patty for the cookies! Nah – form letters could never replace the personal touch!

Gotta run now, Mom! All my love!

- Direct mail offer: Product upgrade
- Landlord: lease expiring: price increase
- Mom: (letter to)
- Order cancellation
- Press Release: new product
- Returned check: (request for payment)
- Thank you: for inquiry
- Thank you: for suggestion

5. Choose Next.
6. Answer questions in each remaining Wizard window until you get to the checkered flag. Choose Finish from that last Wizard window.

Printing the Envelope/Label

If you opted to print an envelope or mailing label, you'll first be taken to the Envelopes and Labels dialog box (see Figure L.1). There you can choose between printing an Envelope or Label using the tabs at the top of the dialog box. If necessary, change the delivery address, return address, or any of the other options in the dialog box. Then choose the Print button in the dialog box. If your printer requires manual feed for labels or envelopes, be sure to insert labels or an envelope into the printer. After printing the envelope or label, Word will redisplay the letter on the screen.

Finishing the Letter

The letter may contain placeholders in square brackets and may be underlined, as in the example below. You may need to scroll around and read the letter to find all those placeholders. If you want, you can have Word find the underlines for you. To do so, choose Edit ➢ Find then press Ctrl+U. (The Find What box stays empty, but "Underline" appears just beneath.) Then choose Find Next (or Find First) to jump to the next underlined text. Choose Cancel to get rid of the dialog box. After

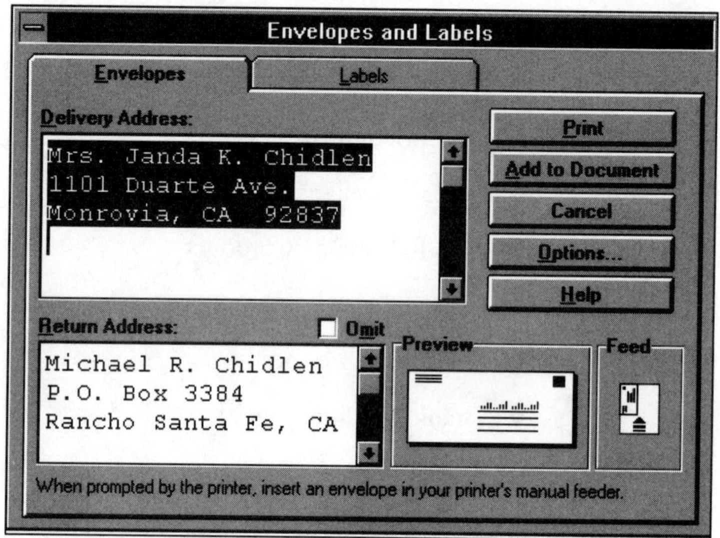

FIGURE L.1

The Envelopes and Labels dialog box lets you print an envelope or mailing label for your letter.

changing the underlined text, you can just press Shift+F4 to repeat the last find, which will move you to the next underlined phrase, if any. You can also use Edit ➢ Find to search for open square brackets (just type the [character into the Find What dialog box, then choose Find First or Find Next).

```
Dear [Name]:

     We are again contacting you about your check number
9999 for $120.69, which was returned to us because of
insufficient funds. We wrote to you once before about this
matter, but you have not responded.
```

To complete the letter, you need to replace the bracketed and underlined text with your own information. To do so, just select the text that you want to replace, then type in the new text. Or press Delete (Del) to delete unwanted text. To remove underlines from any text, select that text and then press Ctrl+U, or click the Underline button (U) in the Formatting toolbar.

NOTE: *If new text you type does not replace selected text, then that feature is probably turned off. You can activate, or deactivate that feature by choosing Tools ➢ Options. Click on the Edit tab, then either select or clear the Typing Replaces Selection option. Then choose OK.*

TIPS

- **To print the letter,** press Ctrl+P or choose File ➢ Print from the Word menu bar. Then choose OK.
- **To exit Word,** choose File ➢ Exit from the Word menu bar, or press Alt+F4. If you wish, you can save this copy of the letter for printing and editing later. You'll be returned to home base, the Windows Program Manager.
- **If you want to send the letter to several people**, refer to *Form Letters* here in the *Do-It-Now Encyclopedia.*
- **For a list of label sizes the Microsoft Word supports,** see Table L.1 under *Labels, Tags, and Cards* here in the *Do-It-Now Encyclopedia.*

RELATED SKILLS AND TOPICS

TOPIC	WHERE TO FIND IT
Microsoft Word	*Instant Office*
Select, Then Do	Appendix B
Type Text and Numbers	Appendix B
Wizards	Appendix B

L

LETTERHEAD

15 min.

There's no need to pay for custom letterhead when you can easily create your own with Microsoft Word. If you want to add a splash of color, order a predesigned paper from Paper Direct, Premier Papers, or Queblo (see Appendix C). In this example, I used the Water Colors paper from Paper Direct. See the front cover of this book for a color illustration.

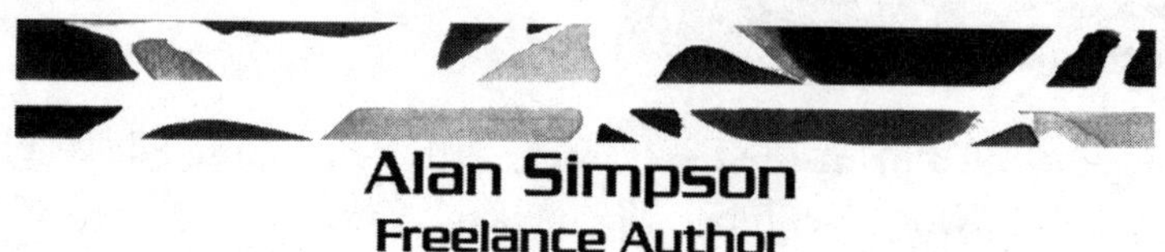

Alan Simpson
Freelance Author

P.O. Box 630
Rancho Santa Fe, CA 92067
Ph: (619)555-1234 Fax: (619)756-0159

NOTE *If you already have preprinted letterhead and just want to set up a template for using that letterhead, skip to the section titled* Steps: Creating a Letterhead Template.

STEPS

Creating a Custom Letterhead

Before you start pounding the keyboard, decide what margins you want to use for the letterhead. If you're using predesigned paper, just take a ruler and measure from the top of the page to where you want the top of your own letterhead to appear, and from the bottom of the page to where you want the bottom of your letterhead to appear, as in the examples presented in Figure L.2. Jot down your own margin measurements in the space provided (you need not get them exact, you can easily adjust them later).

If you're using plain white paper rather than predesigned paper, set your top and bottom measurements each to about .5". After you've

FIGURE L.2

Use a ruler to determine how large you want your margins, as in the example. Then jot down your margins in the space provided.

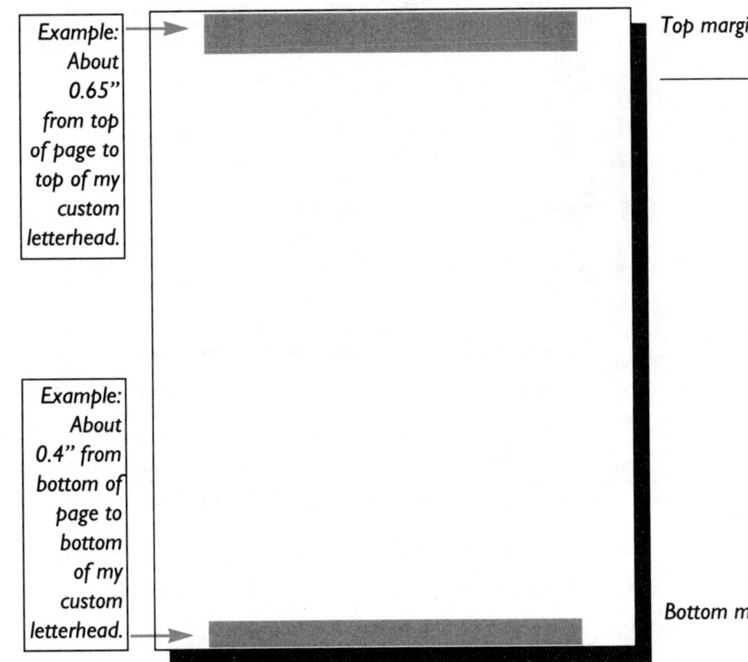

Your measurements:
Top margin:
Example: About 0.65" from top of page to top of my custom letterhead.
Example: About 0.4" from bottom of page to bottom of my custom letterhead.
Bottom margin:

determined your (approximate) margin measurements, you're ready to go online and create your custom letterhead.

1. Start Microsoft Word. If you don't have a blank document window ready on the Word screen, choose File ➢ New ➢ OK.
2. Choose File ➢ Page Setup, click the Margins tab, and set the top and bottom margins to the measurements you jotted down in Figure L.2. For example, here's how I would set up the margins in my example.

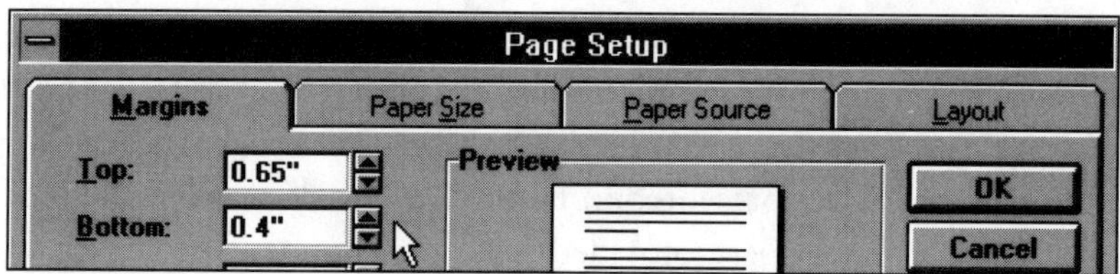

3. Now type the text of your letterhead, pressing ↵ after each line. As an example, here's how my letterhead looked when I first typed it in.

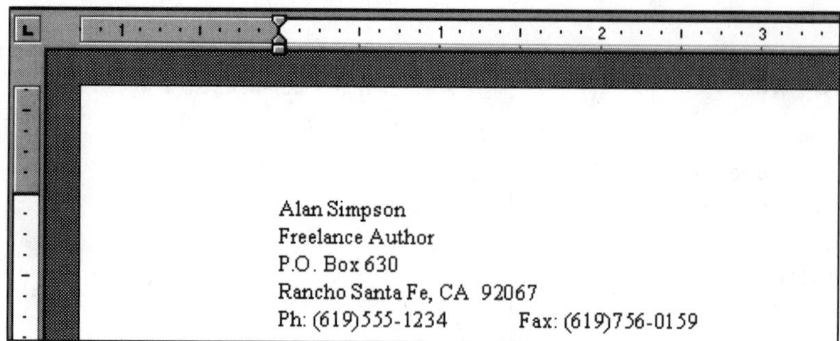

4. To center the text of your letterhead, first choose Edit ➢ Select All, or press Ctrl+A, to select all your text. Then click the Center button in the Formatting toolbar; or choose Format ➢ Paragraph, click the Indents and Spacing tab, and choose Centered under Alignment. Then choose OK. All your text should now be centered.
5. To choose a font for your text, first select whatever text you want to assign a font to. Then use the Font and Font Size boxes on the

toolbar, or choose Format ➢ Font from the menu bar, to choose a font for that selected text.

In the example below, I selected the first line (my name) and set the font to ChainLink Semi-Bold 24pt. Then I selected the second line, and assigned the same font in 18pt. Then I selected the last three lines, and chose the same font at 10 points. (I purchased the Chainlink font from Swtfe. See Appendix C for their address.)

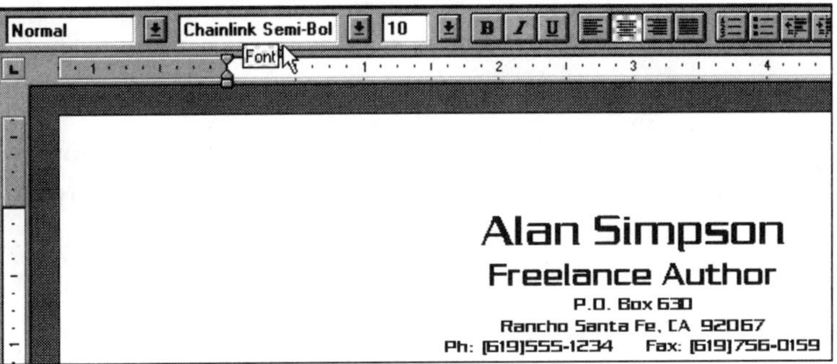

6. If you want *don't* want to move any text to the bottom of the page, then skip to step 12.

7. Select the text that you want to move to the bottom of the page, by dragging the mouse pointer through it.

8. Choose Insert ➢ Frame. You should see a gray frame with little black sizing handles around your selected text.

9. Choose Format ➢ Frame. Then set the Horizontal Position to Center, Relative to Margin, and set the Vertical Position to Bottom, Relative to Margin, as shown below.

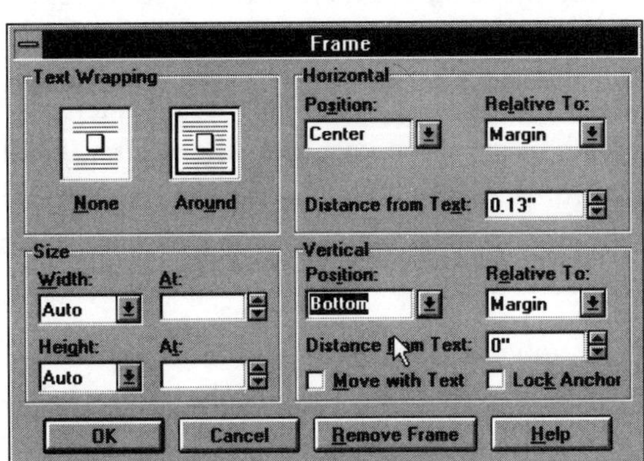

L

10. Choose OK.

11. If you want to remove the dark (printed) border around the text, choose Format ➢ Borders and Shading and then click the Borders tab. Under Presets, choose None. Then choose OK.

12. Print one copy of your letterhead. If you're using predesigned paper, be sure to put a sheet of that paper into the printer first. Then choose File ➢ Print ➢ OK.

13. Review the printed copy. If you need to make refinements, use any of these techniques:

    - **To move your custom text up or down**, choose File ➢ Page Setup ➢ Margins and adjust the margins. For example, to move your text up, decrease the top margin. To move it down, increase the top margin.

    - **To change the font or size**, just select the text you want to adjust and use the font buttons or Format ➢ Font from the menus.

    - **To change the alignment**, select the text you want to realign, then choose one of the alignment options on the Formatting toolbar, or by choosing Format ➢ Paragraph Indents and Spacing ➢ Alignment.

    - **To adjust spacing between lines**, first select all the text in those lines. Then choose Format ➢ Paragraph and click the Indents and Spacing tab. Under Line Spacing, choose Multiple and set the At box to some percentage. For instance, to reduce the spacing by 10%, you'd enter **0.90**. To increase the spacing by 10%, enter **1.1** under At. Choose OK.

14. When you're happy with your custom letterhead, you can print a bunch of copies to keep near the printer. Just load as many sheets of your predesigned paper as necessary, choose File ➢ Print, set the Copies option to however many copies you want to print, then choose OK.

15. Now you can close and save your letterhead. Choose File ➢ Close ➢ Yes, type in a file name, such as **letterhd**, and then choose OK or press ↵.

STEPS

Creating a Letterhead Template

When you type a letter, you'll want to use appropriate margins for your letterhead design. You might also want to center text vertically on the page. Here we'll create a template to make that a simple job. You can follow the steps in this section to create a template for your own custom letterhead or for a preprinted letterhead from a professional printer.

Before you begin, you need to determine what your top and bottom margins will be. Grab a copy of your preprinted letterhead and a ruler, then measure from the edges of the page to where you want your text to begin. Figure L.3 shows an example, where I decided on two inches for both the top and bottom margins. Jot down your own measurements right in that figure, if you like.

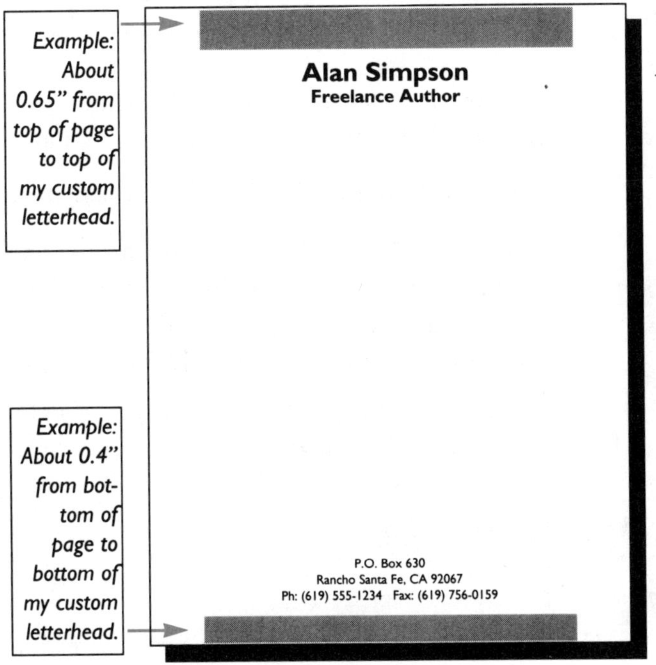

FIGURE L.3

Before printing on your custom letterhead, figure out the top and bottom margins for your letter text, as in my example.

Now you're ready to create the template. Follow these steps:

1. If you're not in Microsoft Word at the moment, start that application.
2. Choose File ➢ New. Under New, choose Template and then choose OK.
3. Choose File ➢ Page Setup, click the Margins tab, then set the Top and Bottom measurements to whatever you decided on back in Figure L.3. You can also adjust the left and right margins to your liking here, if you wish. Here's how I set up the margins for my custom letterhead.

4. If you want to vertically center the text of your letters, click on the Layout tab. Under Vertical Alignment, choose Center.
5. Choose OK to leave the Page Setup dialog box.
6. Choose File ➢ Close ➢ Yes. Type in a file name, such as **Letterhd**, then choose OK. (Because this is a template, it will be saved under the file name LETTERHD.DOT, and so won't conflict with your previously saved LETTERHD.DOC.)

That's it. In the next section, I'll show you exactly how to use your letterhead paper and template.

STEPS

Starting a Letter from Scratch

So now, whenever you want to type up a letter from scratch, and you know you want to use your letterhead, follow the steps at the top of the next page to first select your Letterhd template.

1. If you haven't already done so, start Microsoft Word.
2. Choose File ➢ New, then scroll down to, and double-click on, the name of your letterhead template (Letterhd in my example, as shown below.)

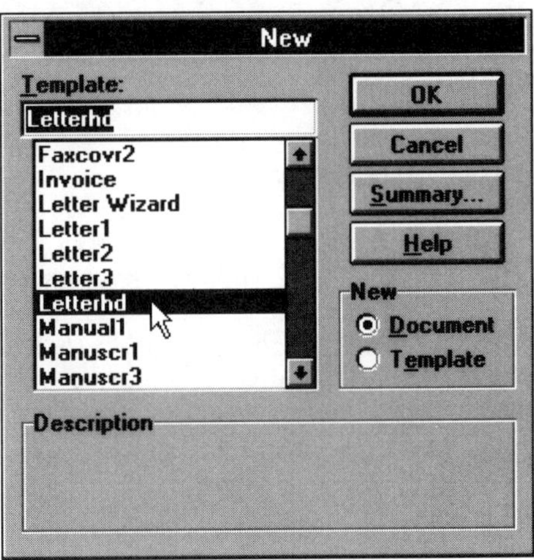

3. You'll be taken to an apparently blank sheet of paper, but its margins will be preset for your letterhead. Type the text of your letter normally.
4. When you're ready to print the letter, put a sheet of your preprinted letterhead into the printer. Then choose File ➢ Print ➢ OK.

That's all there is to it. Beautiful, no? (Don't forget to save your letter, and exit Word, when you're done.)

STEPS

Applying Letterhead to an Existing Letter

Let's suppose you've already typed up a letter without using your letterhead template. Now you want to use that template to print your letter. Here's how you can do that:

1. With the letter you want to print on your Word screen, choose File ➢ Templates from Word's menu bar.

2. Click on Attach, then double-click the name of your letterhead template (LETTERHD.DOT in this example.)
3. Choose OK.
4. Put your preprinted letterhead paper into the printer, the choose File ➢ Print ➢ OK.

Couldn't be easier!

RELATED SKILLS AND TOPICS

TOPIC	WHERE TO FIND IT
Letter	*Do-It-Now Encyclopedia*
Logo	*Do-It-Now Encyclopedia*
Select, Then Do	Appendix B
Signature	*Do-It-Now Encyclopedia*
Type Text and Numbers	Appendix B

LOGO

5 min.

This section isn't about creating a logo. Rather, it's about putting your logo into the documents you create. First, you'll need a digitized copy of your logo stored on disk. Then you'll need to open the document that you want to put the logo into. Here, I'll assume you want to put the logo into a document that you've created using Microsoft Word. I'll discuss other applications under the Tips *heading in this section.*

STEPS

Putting Your Logo in a Word Document

To use your logo, you must know the name and location of the file that the logo is stored in. In this example, I'll assume that your logo is stored in a file named LOGO.TIF on the C:\MSOFFICE\CLIPART directory.

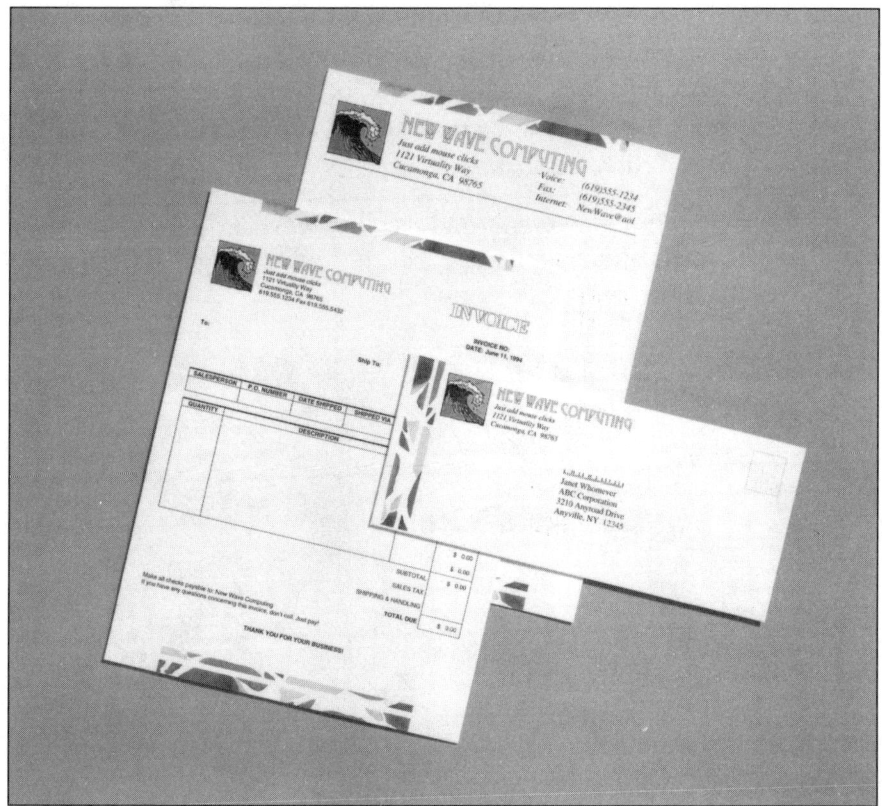

1. Start Microsoft Word, then open or create the document that you want to put the logo in.
2. Move the insertion point to about where you want to put the logo.
3. Choose Insert ➢ Picture from Word's menu bar.
4. Under Drives, choose the drive that your clip-art file is located on (if it's not already the correct drive.) For example, to find C:\MS-OFFICE\CLIPART\LOGO.TIF, you'd want to choose drive C:.
5. Under List Files of Type, choose **All Graphics Files** or the specific type of file you're looking for [e.g., **Tagged Image Format (*.tif)** if you're certain you want to limit your choices to files that have .TIF as the file name extension].

6. Under Directories, work your way to the directory that your logo is stored on. For example, to get to C:\MSOFFICE\CLIPART, scroll to, then double-click on **c:** at the top of the directory tree. Scroll to, and double-click on, the **msoffice** directory name. Then double-click on the **clipart** directory name.

7. Under File Name, scroll down to, and double-click on the name of the file that contains your logo, which would be **logo.tif** in this example (Figure L.4).

FIGURE L.4

Ready to open C:\MSOFFICE\CLIPART\LOGO.TIF. Double-click that file name, or click the file name once and choose OK.

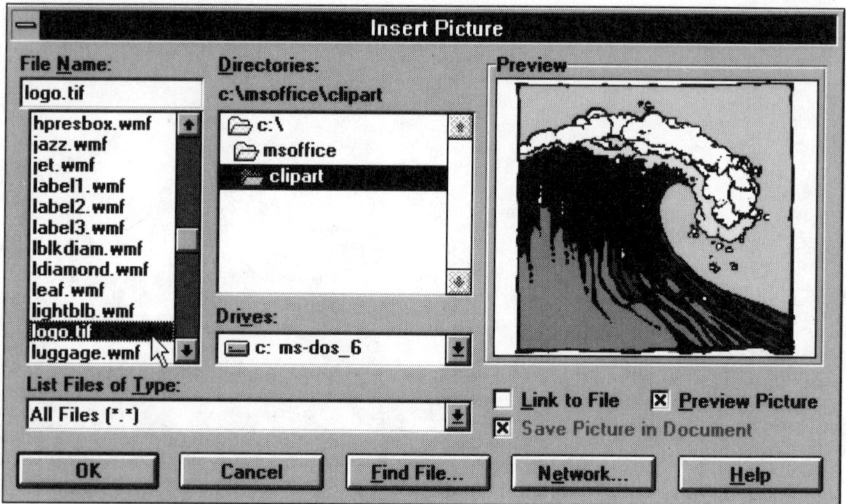

8. To size the image, click it once so it gets sizing handles, as in the example below. Then drag from any corner to enlarge or shrink the image. Don't drag from the side, or you may distort the logo! See *Pictures (Clip Art)* here in the *Do-It-Now Encyclopedia* for more information.

9. To position the image (assuming you're in Microsoft Word), first frame it. To do so, click the image so it has sizing handles, then choose Insert ➢ Frame. Once the logo is framed, you can drag it to any position in the document. You can also choose Format ➢ Frame to control the logo's position, and how text wraps around the logo. See *Pictures (Clip Art)* here in the *Do-It-Now Encyclopedia* for more information.

10. Optionally, to change the border around the logo choose Format ➢ Borders and Shading [also discussed in more detail under *Pictures (Clip Art)*].

11. Don't forget to save your entire document with the logo in place (choose File ➢ Save from Word's menu bar).

TIPS

- If you have a printed logo, but no electronic version on disk, you can just scan the logo into a graphic file. If you don't have a scanner, check with your local print shop or desktop publishing service. Or see the coupon titled *Logos, Photos, and Signatures* near the back of this book.
- A logo is just like any other picture (clip art, photo, signature). Be sure to read the *Pictures (Clip Art)* entry here in the *Do-It-Now Encyclopedia* for more information on moving, sizing, cropping, and framing pictures.
- To insert a logo in an Excel worksheet, click the cell where you want the logo to appear, then choose Insert ➢ Picture from Excel's menu bar. Then follow steps 3–8 above. You can also position the picture, without framing it, simply by dragging it to a new location.
- To insert a logo in a PowerPoint presentation, create or open the presentation, and get to the slide that you want to put the logo on. Move the insertion point to about where you want the logo, choose Insert ➢ Picture, and choose your logo file as in steps 3–8 above. You can move and size the picture by dragging it.
- To add a logo to a Microsoft Access form or report, open that form or report in design view. Move the cursor to about where you want

the logo to appear, then choose Edit ➢ Insert Object. Choose Create from File and ➢ Browse, and locate the logo's file as in steps 3–8 above. For additional help, choose Help ➢ Cue Cards, and explore topics under *Design a Form* or *Design a Report or Mailing Labels.*

RELATED SKILLS AND TOPICS

TOPIC	WHERE TO FIND IT
Drives, Directories, and Files	Appendix B
Microsoft Word	*Instant Office*
Pictures (Clip Art)	*Do-It-Now Encyclopedia*
Signature	*Do-It-Now Encyclopedia*

MAILING LABEL (ONE)

5 min.

Follow the steps in this section to type up a single mailing label. In the example pictured above, I used this method to print the one mailing label on a sheet where the first seven labels had already been used. If you need to type up lots of labels for a mass mailing, please see Labels (Many), *the section that follows this one, so you don't waste a lot of time typing each label individually.*

STEPS

1. Start Microsoft Word.
2. Choose Tools ➢ Envelopes and Labels from the Word menu bar.
3. Click on the Labels tab.
4. Choose the Options button, then either Dot Matrix or Laser, depending on which type of printer you're using.

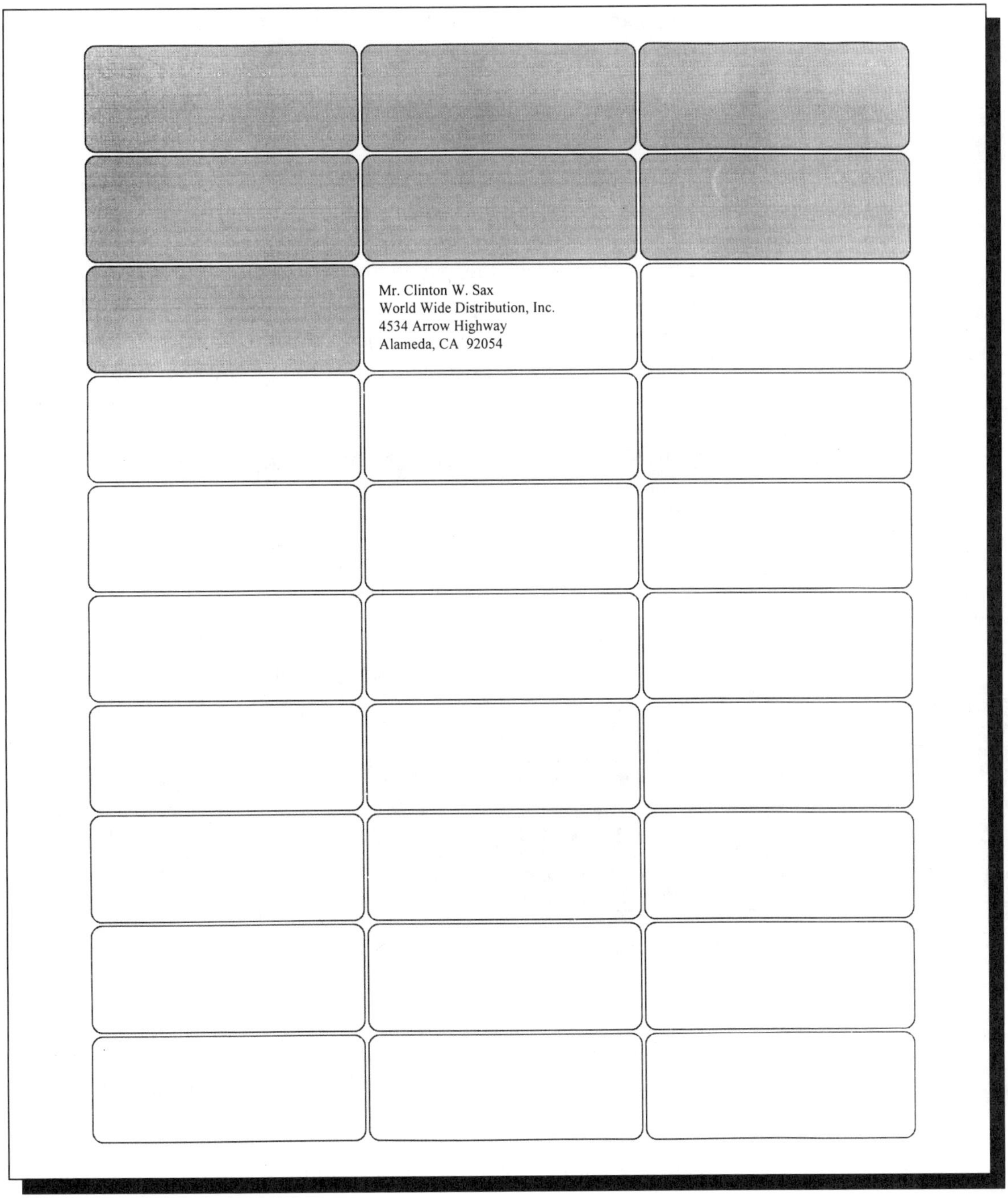

Mr. Clinton W. Sax
World Wide Distribution, Inc.
4534 Arrow Highway
Alameda, CA 92054

5. Choose an option under Label Products. (In this book, I generally assume you're using Avery labels. See *Tips* below.)

6. Under Product Number, choose the type of label you're using. The labels are listed by their product numbers.

7. Choose OK.

8. Type whatever you want to print on the label in the box labeled Address. Most likely, this will be the recipient's name and address. Just type normally and press ↵ after typing one line to move down to the next line. (If you want to put your own name and address on the label instead of the recipient's, just choose the Use Return Address option.)

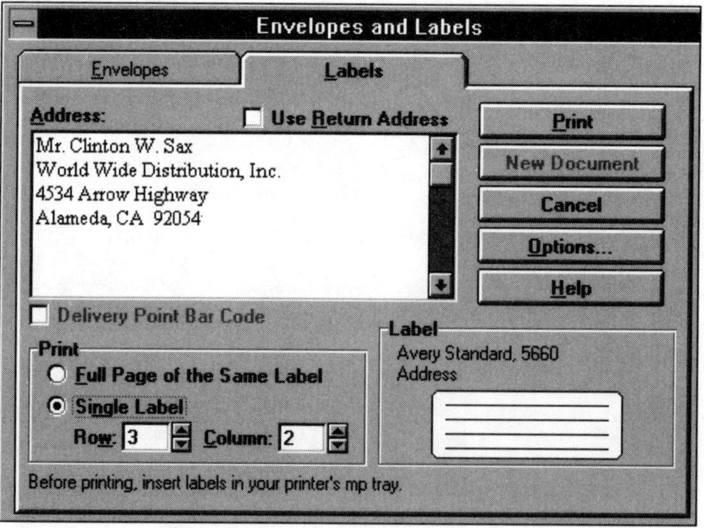

9. Now you have three choices:

- If you want to print a sheet full of the same label, choose Full Page of Same Label.
- If you want to print a single label only, choose Single Label.
- Optionally, if you need to skip over any blank labels on the sheet, indicate which Row and Column you want to start printing. For example, in the figure at the start of this section, the first seven labels have already been used on the sheet. So I

printed my new label at row 3, column 2. (Rows go across. Columns go down, like newspaper columns)

10. Load the labels into the printer, then choose Print.

11. To return to home base, the Windows Program Manager, choose File ➢ Exit ➢ No.

M

TIPS

- If the label isn't printed within a few seconds, make sure you've inserted a sheet of labels snugly into the printer.
- For a summary of commonly used laser printer label sizes, please see Table L.1 under *Labels, Tags, and Cards* here in the *Do-It-Now Encyclopedia.*
- You can buy laser printer labels at most office supply and computer stores. Or purchase by mail from Paper Direct, Premier Papers, or Queblo, all listed in Appendix C. (Get their catalogs!)

RELATED SKILLS AND TOPICS

TOPIC	WHERE TO FIND IT
Dialog Boxes	Appendix B
Microsoft Word	*Instant Office*

MAILING LABELS (MANY)

15 min.

If you need to print mailing labels for lots of people, your best starting point will be to create an Access database to store people's names and addresses. If you have not already done so, create the PEOPLE.MDB database, and add some names and addresses to it, as described under Database (Create) and Database (Use) here in the Do-It-Now Encyclopedia. *Then come back to this section to create your mailing label format, and print your labels.*

Mr. Andy Zeeborp President ABC Corporation 1121 El Verdugo Way Encinitas, CA 92345	Ms. Sally Rambunctuous P.O. Box 4434 Rancho Santa Fe, CA 92067	Mr. Andy Adams President ABC Corporation 123 A St. San Diego, CA 91234
Miss Marie Miller Software Consultant P.O. Box 1234 Encinitas, CA 92024	Dr. Robert Baker Radiology Dep't St. Elsewhere Hospital 1234 Washington Lane New York, NY 12345-1232	Mr. Robert Miller Botanist Evergreen Nursery 11711 Reposo Alto Encinitas, CA 92026
Miss Maria Adams Author 4323 Moonglow Rd. Wyandotte, OK 74370	Mr. John Newell President Newell Construction 212 Riverside Dr. Bernalillo, NM 88004	Dr. Susita Schumack Neurosurgeon Reese Clinic 3313 Park Ave Philadelphia, PA 23456
Mr. Richard Rosiello President Rickdontic Labs P.O. Box 117 Chicago, IL 60606	Mr. Frank Watson Greenskeeper Whispering Palms Golf Club 8771 Concha de Golf Bangor, ME 01876	Miss Anita Smith Accounts Payable Sunshine Gardens 3221 Encinitas Blvd. Encinitas, CA 92024
Ms. Thelma Gillis Author P.O. Box 3384 Rancho Santa Fe, CA 92067	Mr. Henry Smythe Zodiac Gardens 91 Delaware Ave Eugene, OR 98765	Mrs. Helga Königer Königer-Verlag GmbH Von-Erckert Str. 36 München, D-8000 West Germany
Mr. Gören Janulf CITES Uitgeverij B.V. Birkstraat 95 Soest, CJ-3487 The Netherlands	Dr. Sandra Davis, Jr. Botanist Florália P.O. Box 110.123 Niterói, Rio de Janeiro 24.001 Brasil	Ms. Rita Wilson President High Tech Applications 1101 West Squander Dr. San Diego, CA 92067

STEPS

Creating the Mailing Label Format

You can use either Microsoft Access or Microsoft Word to format and print mailing labels. In these steps, we'll use Microsoft Word, since you may already have some experience with Word if you've printed form letters or envelopes. Remember, you need to create the label format only *once*, not every time you want to print labels. Follow these steps to create your mailing label format:

1. Start Microsoft Word.
2. Choose Tools ➤ Mail Merge from the Word menu bar. You'll be taken to the Mail Merge Helper dialog box.
3. Under Main Document, choose Create.
4. Choose Mailing Labels.
5. Choose Active Window.
6. Under Data Source, choose Get Data.
7. Choose Open Data Source.
8. Under List Files of Type, choose **MS Access Databases (*.mdb).**
9. Switch to your Access directory. (Assuming your database is stored on C:\ACCESS, you'll want to double-click on **c:** at the top of the Directories list, then double-click on **access.**)
10. Under File Name, click the name of you Access database (e.g., **PEOPLE.MDB**), then choose OK. Wait about half a minute for Access to load.
11. When the Microsoft Access dialog box appears, click the Tables tab, click the name of the Access table that contains your address list (e.g., **Mailing List**), then choose OK.
12. When the next dialog box appears, choose Set Up Main Document.

13. In the Label Options dialog box, choose your printer type (Laser or Dot Matrix), the label manufacturer under Label Products, and under Product Number, choose the label size you'll be printing on.

NOTE: *You can purchase Avery laser printer labels at most stationery and computer stores. Or contact Paper Direct, Premier Papers, or Queblo, listed in Appendix B, for a catalog.*

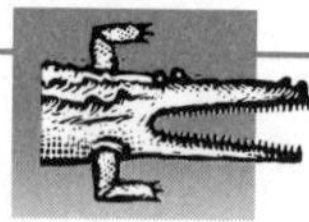

WARNING: *Postal Bar Codes might not fit on small labels. Also, be forewarned that addresses lacking a United States zip code will print a little error message in place of the bar code.*

14. Choose OK. You'll be taken to the Create Labels dialog box.

15. If you want to print postal bar codes on your mailing labels, choose Insert Postal Bar Code. Then use the drop-down list button to choose the name of the field in your Access table that contains zip codes (most likely **PostalCode**), then choose OK. Then press the End key to move past the message. Then press ↵ to move down to the next line.

16. Use the Insert Merge Field button to select fields from your table in exactly the format you want them to appear on the mailing label. For example, click Insert Merge Field, then click Prefix to place the prefix field first. Then:

   - If you want to print a blank space before the next field, press the spacebar.
   - If you want to type a comma or any other text after the field you just entered, type that text. For example, you'll probably want to type a comma and blank space after you place the City field.
   - If you want to print the next field on the next line, press ↵.
   - If you want to indent a tab stop, press Ctrl+Tab.

NOTE: *If you make a mistake while placing fields, and want to correct that mistake later, you can do so through the normal Word document editing window.*

17. Repeat step 16 until all the fields that you want to print are placed in the space provided, in "normal" name and address format.

Figure M.1 shows an example where I've organized the fields named Prefix, FirstName, LastName, and so forth from my Mailing List table into mailing label format.

NOTE: *I've tried to minimize the height of each label by putting Title and OrganizationName on one line, because my labels are only 1" tall in this example.*

FIGURE M.1

A mailing label format designed from fields in 0the table named Mailing List in my PEO-PLE.MDB Access database.

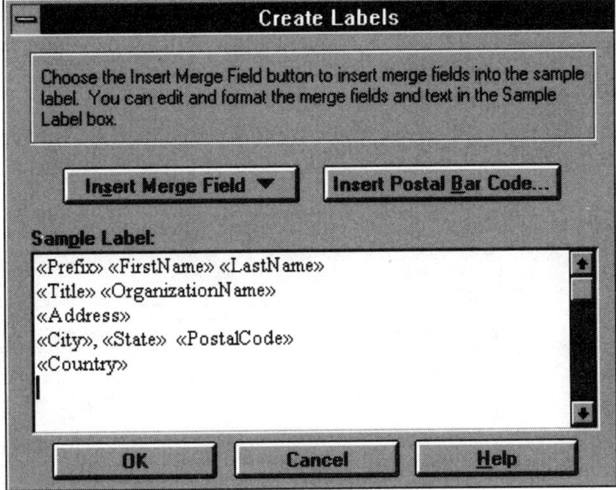

18. Choose OK after you've placed all the fields on the mailing label format.

19. Now, under Main Document, choose Edit, then choose the first option that appears on the drop-down menu. Mailing labels with merge fields in place of actual names and addresses appear on your screen.

20. Let's just save this format now, so you can reuse it as necessary whenever you want to print labels in the future. Choose File ➢

Close ➢ Yes. Type a valid file name, such as **mrglabs** (for Merge Labels), then choose OK.

Your mailing label format is done (finally), and now you have a format you can use, quite easily, whenever you need to print up a bunch of mailing labels in the future. The next section explains how.

STEPS

Printing the Mailing labels

To merge your mailing label format with names and addresses from your Access database, just follow these simple steps:

1. If you haven't done so yet, start Microsoft Word.
2. Choose File ➢ Open, and double-click the name of your mailing label format document (e.g., **mrglabs.doc**)
3. When the labels appear on the screen, click the View Merged Data button in the Mail Merge toolbar (see below). Your labels should now show actual names and addresses from your Access table.

4. Load the mailing label(s) into the printer.
5. Now you have a couple of choices. (If you're not sure which button is which on the Mail Merge toolbar, just touch the mouse pointer to a button, and wait a second for the button name to appear on your screen.)

    - **To print all the mailing labels**, click the Merge to Printer button.

    - **To preview all the mailing labels before printing,** choose the Merge to New Document button. You can then scroll through, and change text using the standard Word navigating and editing techniques. When you're ready to print the mailing labels, choose File ➢ Print ➢ OK.

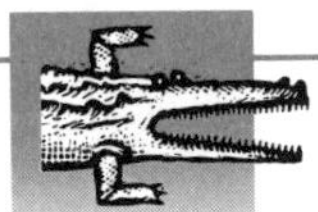

WARNING: *Changes that you make to the mailing labels in Word are not carried back to your Access database. If you need to make a change in the database, do so through Access, as discussed under* Database (Use) *in this book, or by using the Edit Data Source button in the Word Mail Merge toolbar.*

- **To print mailing labels for one person, or some people,** in your database, click the Mail Merge button, and then choose Query Options. Fill out the Filter Records form to define which records you want to print mailing labels for. For example, in Figure M.2 I've opted to print mailing labels only for people who live in the 92*xxx* zip code area (i.e., 92000 through 92999-9999). If you need help defining your query, choose the Help button. If you want, you can choose the Sort Records to define a sort order for printing. When you've finished defining your query, choose OK, then choose Merge. When the labels appear on the screen, choose File ➢ Print ➢ OK to print the mailing labels.

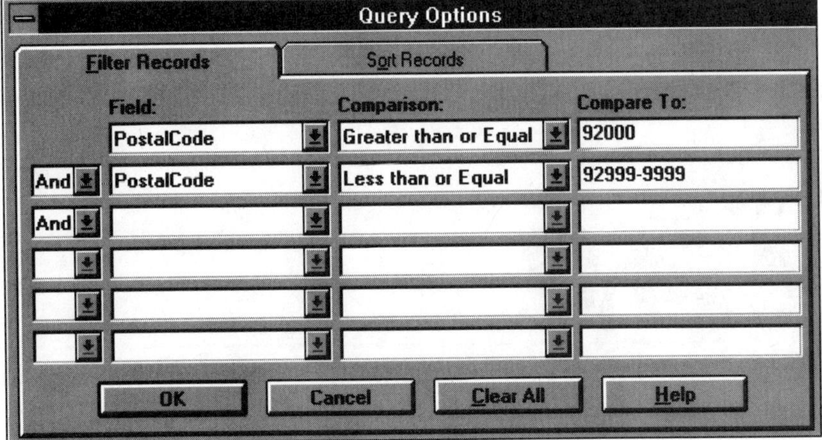

FIGURE M.2

Here I've opted to print mailing labels for addresses in the 92xxx zip code area only (i.e., PostalCodes from 92000 up to 92999-9999). I didn't use this query to print the labels shown at the start of this section.

6. After the mailing labels are printed, you can exit Word without saving anything by choosing File ➢ Exit ➢ No. You'll be returned to your home base, the Windows Program Manager.

TIPS

- The reason you can exit Word without saving anything in step 6 above is because your names and addresses and mailing label format are still stored on disk, and neither has been changed. The two have just been merged into one.
- See the entries titled *Envelopes (Many)*, *Form Letters*, and *Directory (Names and Addresses)* here in the *Do-It-Now Encyclopedia* for other things you can do with your Access database and Word.

RELATED SKILLS AND TOPICS

TOPIC	WHERE TO FIND IT
Drives, Directories, and Files	Appendix B
Help	Appendix B
Microsoft Access	*Instant Office*
Microsoft Word	*Instant Office*

MEMO

5 min.

Need to whip up a quick memo? Use Word's Memo Wizard to get the job done in a flash. You can choose from among three styles—Classic, Contemporary (shown here), or Typewriter.

STEPS

1. Start Microsoft Word.
2. Choose File ➢ New from the Word menu bar.
3. Scroll down to and double-click on Memo Wizard.

M

INTEROFFICE MEMO

Date: 03/01/95

To: Janet, Rocco, Moe, Curly Joe

CC: Everyone in DP

From: Alfonso Bell

Subject: Computer competence at last!

I think everyone should buy a copy of Alan Simpson's book, *Instant Office for Microsoft Office*. It tells you how to do all sorts of useful things on a PC, even if you don't know diddley-squat about computers.

For example, I was able to type up this memo in just a couple of minutes, by looking up Memo in Alan's book, and following the simple step-by-step instructions. (And you all know what a computer klutz *I* am!)

What's even cooler is that, after you've created the memo, you can use the full power of Microsoft Word to make changes and corrections. For example, I chose Tools ➡ Speller before I printed this memo. So you don't see my usual typos.

I must confess that I never even knew you could do so *much* with a computer. And I didn't realize how *easy* it all can be. So trash those big boring tech manuals and get the book that gives you instant gratification—in spite of your technological timidity!

AB/AS

03/01/95

4. When the first Wizard window appears, answer the question(s) that appear, then choose Next. (Ignore the Header/Footer toolbar that appears, it will go away in a few moments.)

5. Repeat step 5 until you get to the last Wizard window (which shows the checkered flag). Choose a help option, then choose Finish.

When the memo is finished, you'll see the sample text *[Type your memo text here]* already selected on the screen. Just type the text of your memo normally remembering to press ↵ only at the end of complete paragraphs (not at the end of each line).

NOTE: *If new text you type does not replace selected text, then that feature is probably turned off. You can activate, or deactivate that feature by choosing Tools ➢ Options. Click on the Edit tab, then either select or clear the Typing Replaces Selection option. Then choose OK.*

You can scroll up and down through other sample text, and replace it as appropriate. For example, you might see a line like this:

```
To:    [Names]
```

To change that, select the bracketed text by dragging the mouse pointer through it, or by holding down the Shift key while moving the cursor with the arrow keys (see Appendix B if necessary). Then type the new replacement text. Or press Delete (Del) to just delete the selected text.

TIPS

- **To print the memo**, press Ctrl+P or choose File ➢ Print from the Word menu bar. Choose however many copies you want to print, then choose OK.
- **To exit Word** and return to home base, choose File ➢ Exit from the Word menu bar. If you want to keep a copy of this particular memo on disk, for future reference, choose Yes and type in a valid file name (e.g., **memo1**), then choose OK. If you don't need to save a copy of the memo, just choose No.

RELATED SKILLS AND TOPICS

TOPIC	WHERE TO FIND IT
Help	Appendix B
Microsoft Word	*Instant Office*
Select, Then Do	Appendix B
Wizards	Appendix B

MORTGAGE PAYMENT

15 min.

Suppose you need to borrow $100,000 for 30 years to buy a house. Interest rates are at about 6.5%. What would your monthly payment be? Here's an easy-to-create Excel worksheet that will give you the answer instantly. (If this is your first attempt at using Excel, please see the Instant Office section for Excel basic skills before you try this example. Mainly, you just need to know what a cell is.)

MORTGAGE.XLS

	A	B	C
1	Loan Payment Worksheet		
2			
3	Loan Amount	$ 100,000.00	
4	Annual Interest Rate	6.50%	
5	Term (Years)	30	
6			
7	Payment will be	$632.07	
8	Payback will be	$ 227,544.49	
9			
10			
11			
12			
13			
14			
15			
16			
17			
18			
19			
20			

Sheet1 / Sheet2 / Sheet3

STEPS

1. Start Microsoft Excel.
2. Widen the first two columns of the worksheet. To do so, drag the mouse pointer through the column headings A and B, so that both columns are selected as shown below. Then choose Format ➢ Column ➢ Width, type **20** and choose OK.

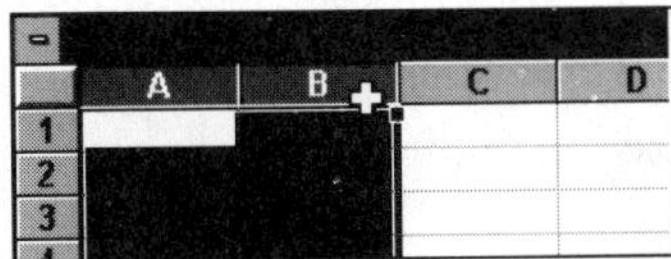

3. Use Table M.1 as a guide to creating the worksheet. Click the cell listed in the first column, then type exactly (and literally) what's shown in the second column. For example, to get started, move to cell A1 (Column A, Row 1) and type the words **Loan Payment Worksheet**. Then click in cell A3 and type the words **Loan Amount.** Do so until you get to the end of Table M.1.

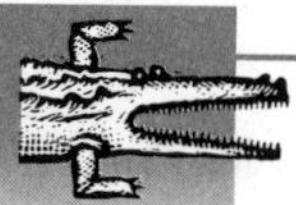

WARNING: *When typing in formulas (the things that begin with an = sign), you must type every character correctly, or the formula won't display its proper result.*

TABLE M.1

The exact contents of cells in the Loan Payment Worksheet Excel example

CELL	EXACT CONTENTS
A1	Loan Payment Worksheet
A3	Loan Amount
A4	Annual Interest Rate
A5	Term (UYears)
A7	Payment will be
A8	Payback will be
B3	100000
B4	6.5%
B7	=PMT(B4/12,B5*12,-B3)
B8	=(B5*12)*B7

4. To spruce up the worksheet, first open the Formatting toolbar if it isn't already open (choose View ➢ Toolbars, click on Formatting so that it's marked with an X, then choose OK).

5. Click on cell A1, and use the Font Size drop down list to set that cell's size to about 18 points (see below). You can also click the Bold button just to the right, to make the title a little darker.

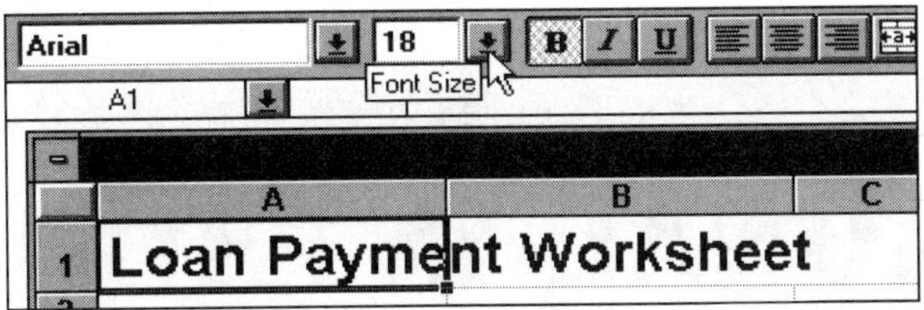

6. Click on cell B3, then click on the Currency Style button (indicated by a $) in the Formatting toolbar.
7. Click on cell B8, and again click on the Currency Style button in the Formatting toolbar.
8. Now to try out different loan scenarios, click on and change the contents of cell B3, B4, or B5. Cells B7 and B8 will be recalculated instantly to show you the monthly payment and pay back.
9. To print the worksheet, choose File ➢ Print ➢ OK.
10. When you're done, close and save the worksheet. That is, choose File ➢ Exit ➢ Yes. Type in a valid file name such as **mortgage** and then press ↵. You'll be returned to your home base, the Windows Program Manager.

TIPS

- If you want to reuse the worksheet in the future, don't bother with steps 1–10 above. Just start Excel, choose File ➢ Open, and double-click on the file name you entered in step 10 (e.g., **MORTGAGE.XLS** in this example).
- For more examples of financial calculations that Excel can do, search Excel's help **financial functions.**

RELATED SKILLS AND TOPICS

TOPIC	WHERE TO FIND IT
Microsoft Excel	*Instant Office*
Select, Then Do	Appendix B
Type Text and Numbers	Appendix B

M

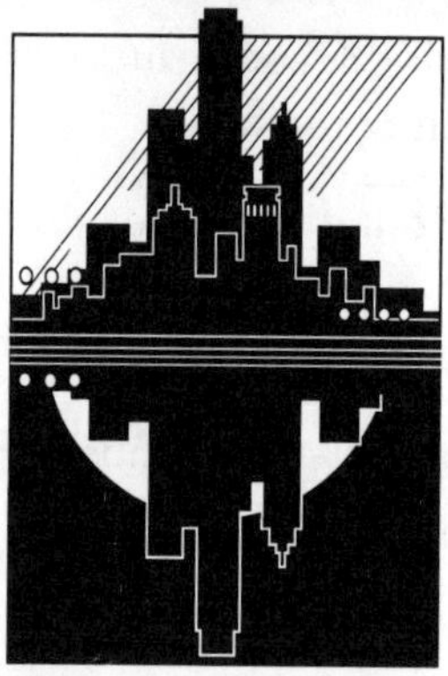

March '95 — Volume 1.1

NATIONAL INTRUDER

LV BLUES

A salesman driving across country checked into a Las Vegas hotel to get a good night's sleep. Not being a gambler, he went straight to his room, undressed, and went to bed.

During the night, thieves broke into his room and stole everything but the underwear he was sleeping in.

When the salesman discovered the robbery, he ran out of his room, through the crowded casino, and out into the street, in hopes of catching the perpetrators.

A drunk passerby saw the man standing there in his underwear. Feeling pity, the drunk put his arm across the salesman's shoulder. In slurred words, the drunk said "Aw geez, pal, that's a darn shame. But ya never know when yer luck will change. Ya shoulda' bet yer underwear."

R-E-S-P-E-C-T

Pop Quiz: What do the following phrases have in common: 1) The candyman can, 2) Chestnuts roasting on an open fire, 3) R-E-S-P-E-C-T, 4) Come and listen to my story 'bout a man named Jed.

Answer: If you're over the age of 30, most will automatically launch your brain into an entire song. Even if you hate the song, your mind will insist on playing it over and over until it (your mind) gets sick of it. You have no control over this.

KID PSYCH

Yesterday my six-year-old daughter pointed to her eyes, and (seriously) asked me this profound question: "Daddy, why do we have to call these things 'eyes'?"

I explained how we just have different words for different things, and "eyes" is what we happen to call those little round things you see with. I explained that if everyone had decided to call them "shmorps" instead, we'd all be gazing into each others' shmorps. She nodded approval, like she understood.

She thought for a while, and asked "Then why do we have to call these things 'noses'?", pointing to her nose.

I took a different tack this time: I told her, "Because if we called everything a

INSIDE

1. UFO Lands in Washington
2. Miracle Diet Cures Amnesia
3. Liz Stubs Toe
4. Erica Weeps at Awards
5. Amazing Gnat-Boy Flies!

NEWSLETTER

50 min.

A newsletter is a very ambitious project. Word's Newsletter Wizard can help simplify things a little, and here I'll show you the easiest way to get the job done. But even so, I wouldn't recommend trying this until you've had some experience creating a few easier Word documents.

STEPS

Create and Save the Text

Take it from a guy who's been around the block a few times. A highly formatted document, like a newsletter, is *much* easier if you divide it into two separate jobs—writing, and formatting. Start by writing your articles in a "regular" Word document. Then later, you can create your newsletter format and "pour" your text into that format. Here's how I recommend you get started:

1. Start Microsoft Word.
2. Choose File ➢ New➢OK to get to a blank sheet of paper.
3. Type up the text of your newsletter, without regard to formatting. Just start each article with a headline followed by a press on the ↵ key. Figure N.1 shows an example.
4. When you've written all the articles for the newsletter, choose File ➢ Close ➢ Yes. Enter a valid file name such as **newstext** then choose OK.

The text of your newsletter is now safely stored on disk. Now you can use Microsoft Word's Newsletter Wizard to quickly set up a newsletter format, as described next.

N

FIGURE N.1

Before you start formatting your text into a newsletter format, just type up that text in a regular (unformatted) document. Add a headline to each article.

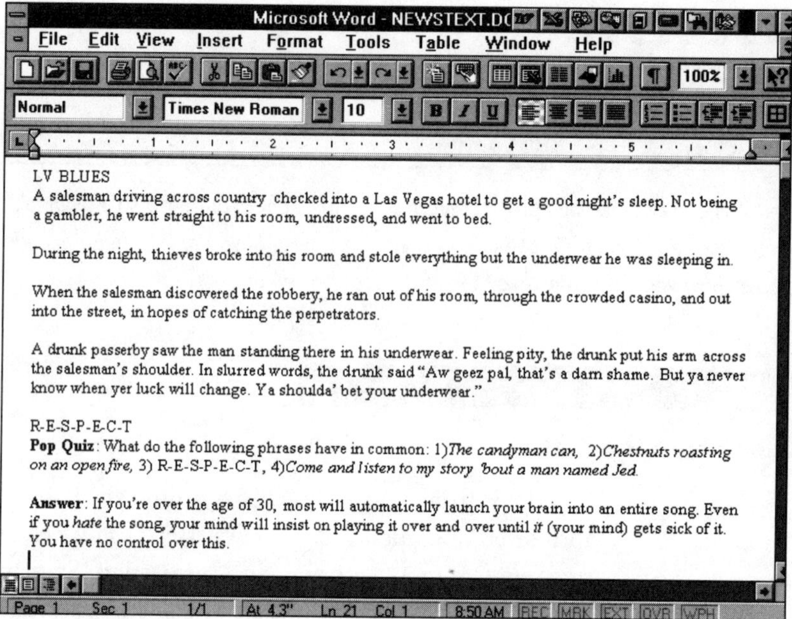

STEPS

Create the Newsletter Format

To create the newsletter format, follow these steps:

1. If you exited Microsoft Word after typing your newsletter text, restart Word.
2. Choose File ➢ New from the Word menu bar.
3. Scroll down to **Newslttr Wizard** and double-click on it.
4. Answer the question(s) in the Wizard Window to your liking, keeping an eye on the little preview document to monitor your choices. Choose Next when you're ready to move onto the next Wizard window.
5. Repeat Step 4 until you get to the last Wizard screen (which shows you the checkered flag). Then choose Finish.
6. When the Wizard is done, the sheet of paper on your screen looks like the start of a newsletter, as in Figure N.2.

- To change the magnification of the newsletter, use the Zoom Control button on the Standard toolbar, or choose View ➢ Zoom, and setting, and OK.

FIGURE N.2

The Newsletter Wizard displays an empty sheet of paper, preformatted into a newsletter.

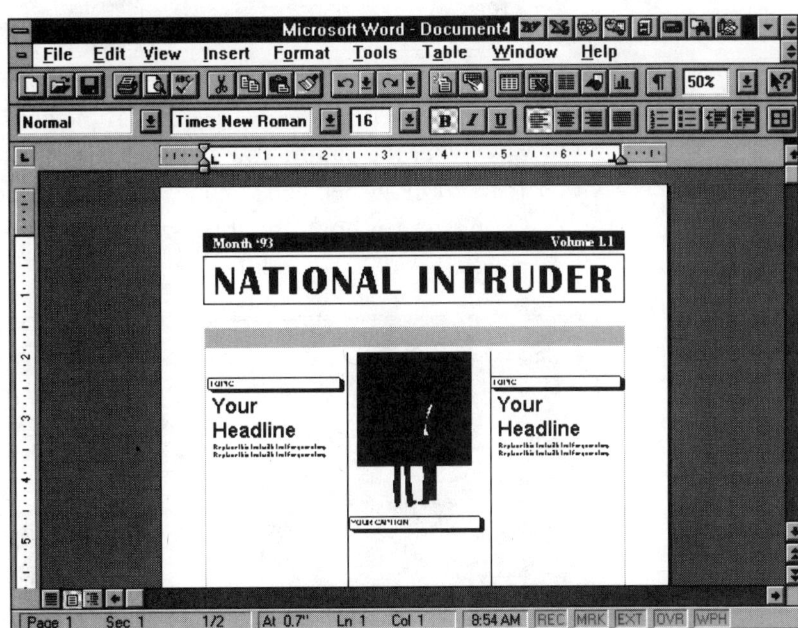

7. Make sure the Standard and Formatting toolbars are visible (choose View ➢ Toolbars, click on Standard and Formatting so that each is marked with an X, then choose OK).

8. Move the cursor down to the first article headline, just to the left of the large letter *Y* in *Your Headline*, as shown here:

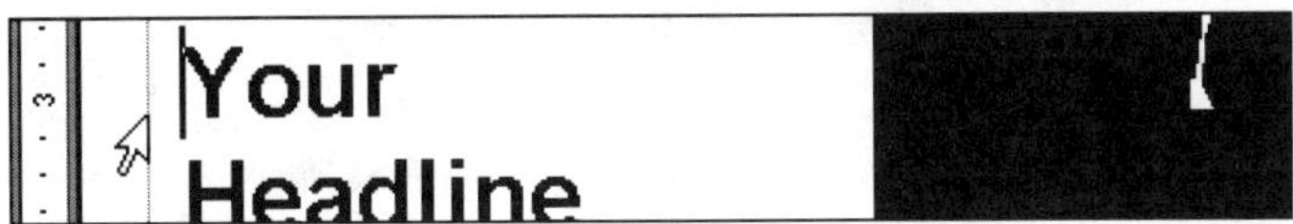

9. Press Ctrl+Shift+End to select everything from the cursor on down, and then press Delete (Del) to delete the sample headlines and text. (You'll be pouring in your own text shortly.)

10. Notice the little topic headings in rounded boxes. Those can be a pain, so I recommend you delete those as well. To delete them,

click the border of one until it has sizing handles as shown here, then press Delete (Del).

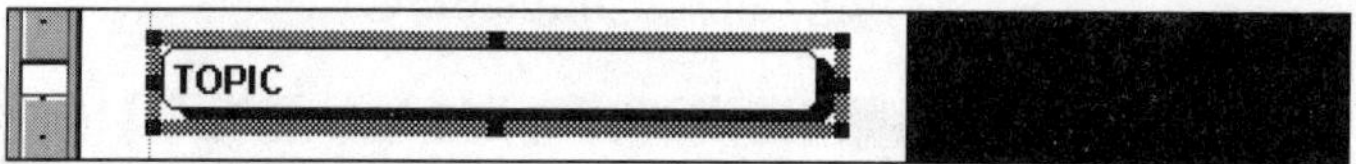

11. Repeat Step 10 to delete the other Topic box, as well as the box under the picture (the box that contains the text *YOUR CAPTION*. When you're done, your newsletter won't have any sample text or boxes. So if you zoom to Whole Page view, the newsletter looks something like this:

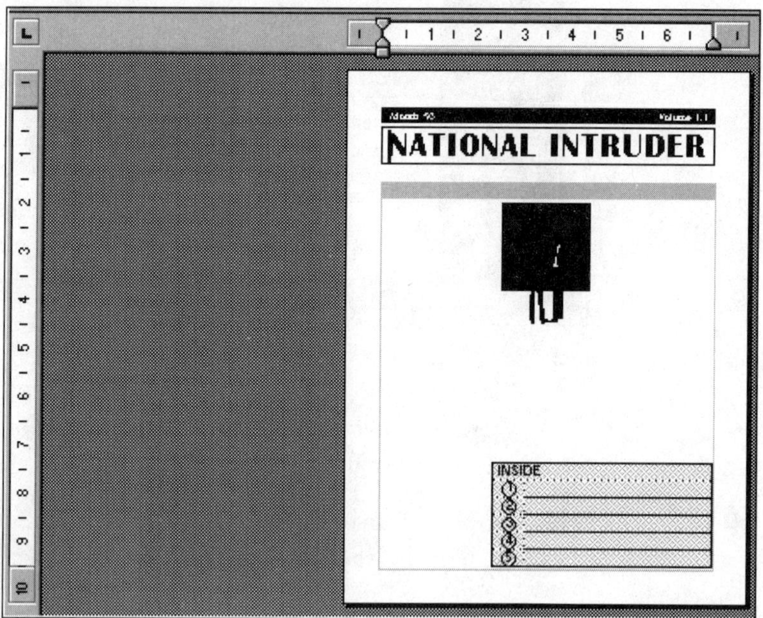

12. I suggest you save this clean version of your newsletter in its own file (but don't close it yet). Choose File ➢ Save, enter a file name like **newsfrmt** and then choose OK.

STEPS

Pour Your Text into the Newsletter

Now you're ready to pour your text into the newsletter. You have to position the incoming text precisely, so follow these steps carefully:

1. Zoom to about 100% (View ➢ Zoom ➢ 100% ➢ OK) to get a closer view.
2. Turn on the paragraph marks (click the ¶ button on the Standard toolbar.) The marks will appear on the screen.
3. Move the blinking insertion point close to the top of the first column, but *below* the paragraph mark that shows *End Of Section,* as shown below.

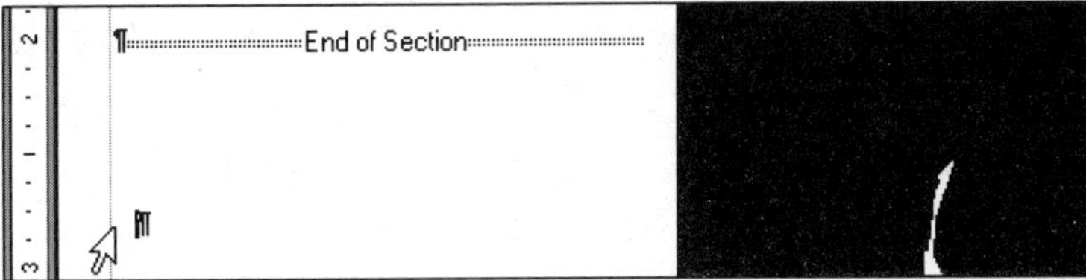

4. Choose Insert ➢ File and then double-click on the file that contains your text (e.g., **newstext.doc** in my example—*not newsfrmt*). Your text should come into the newsletter, neatly formatted into three columns. (If you want to insert other documents into this format, press Ctrl+End to move to the end of the existing text. then use choose Insert ➢ File again to insert the next document.)
5. Now, apply the Headline style to a headline. That is, select any one headline by dragging the mouse pointer through it, as in the example below:

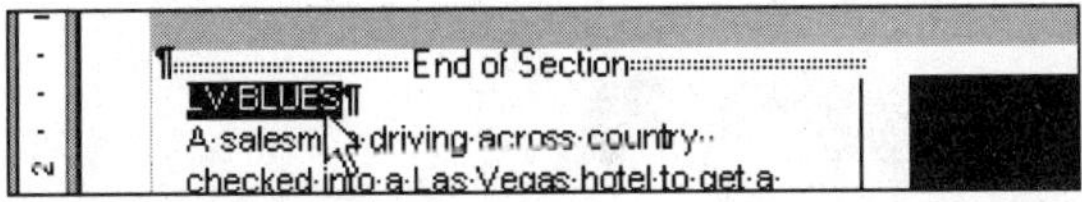

6. Then click the Style drop-down list in the Formatting toolbar and choose **Headline,** as shown here.

N

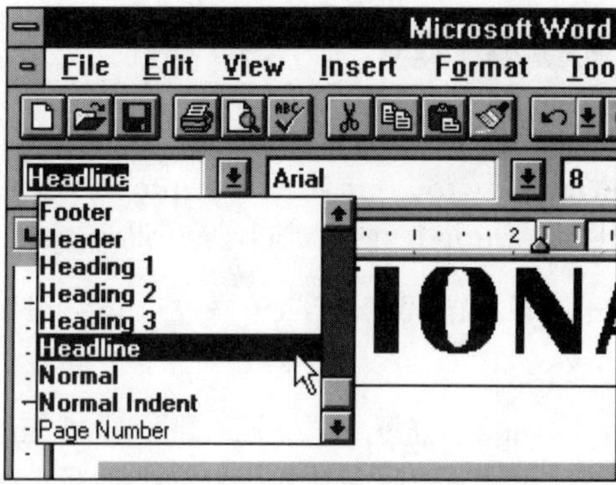

7. Next, select all the text under the headline (up to but *excluding* the next headline), and choose Body Text from the Style drop-down list.

8. Repeat Steps 5 through 7 for each article in your newsletter.

9. When you've finished applying the Headline and Body Text styles, you can turn off those paragraph marks by clicking the ¶ button in the Standard toolbar again. Also, you might want to zoom to Whole Page so you can see how things are shaping up. Figure N.3 shows how the main body of my sample newsletter looked on the screen at this stage.

10. Now is a good time to save your work (without closing it). Choose File ➢ Save As, enter a file name such as **newslttr** and then choose OK.

The rest of the job is largely a matter of tweaking and refining. I can't give you step-by-step instructions on that—it's something you need to experiment with on your own. But I will point out some tips to get you headed in the right direction.

TIPS

- **To change the magnification** of the newsletter, use the Zoom Control button or View ➢ Zoom from the menu bar. You might find it easiest to do large formatting in Whole Page view. Use 100% or higher magnification for smaller detail work.

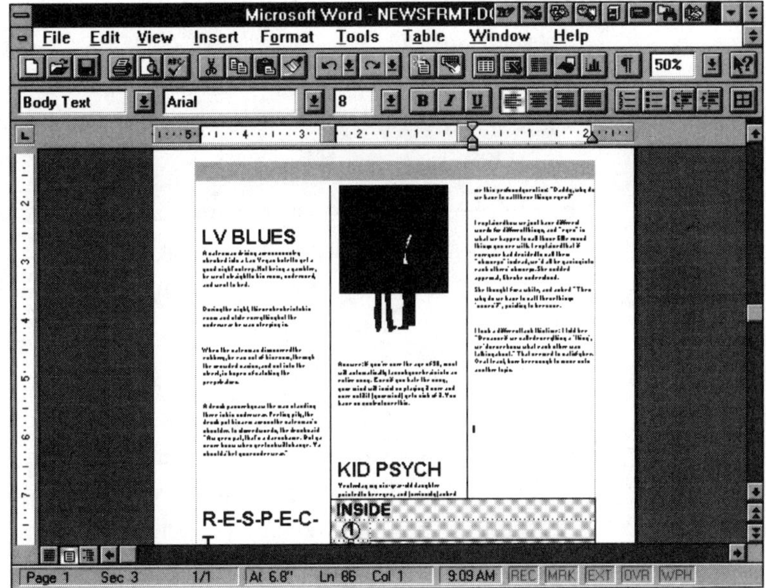

FIGURE N.3

The Newsletter format after adding the text I'd written earlier and applying Headline and Body Text styles

- **To reduce the amount of white space** above headlines, first click on any one article headline. Then choose Format ➢ Style, make sure Headline is the selected style under Styles, then choose Modify. In the Modify Style dialog box, choose Format ➢ Paragraph and under Spacing reduce the Before setting. (I reduced it to 0 pt). Then choose OK and Close until you get back to the document window. This will change all the headlines with that style, so you need only do it once.
- **To delete blank lines between paragraphs** within each article, just move the cursor to the start of the blank line and press Delete (Del).
- **To modify the style or size of the text,** choose Format ➢ Style and then either Body Text or Headline, depending on which you want to change. Then choose Modify ➢ Format ➢ Font, and choose your font and point size. (I switched to Arial, Regular, 10 pt.) Choose OK and Close until you get back to the document. Once again, changing the style will affect all the text to which you've applied that style. (If you did want to change the font of a particular body of text, you *wouldn't* go through Format ➢ Style. Instead, just select whatever you want to change, then choose Format ➢ Font, or Format ➢ Paragraph, or whatever commands you need.)

N

- **To change the picture**, first click near the center of the picture, then press Delete (Del). Next, click on the edge of the remaining picture frame, so that frame has sizing handles. Choose Insert ➢ Picture, then double-click the name of the picture that you want to insert.
- **To change the size of the picture's frame**, click the frame so it has sizing handles, then drag the frame to whatever seems the appropriate size for the picture. (For information on cropping the picture, search Word's help for *cropping graphics.*)
- **To add text to the table of contents box** (titled *INSIDE*), click at the start of any blank line and type your text. If you told the Wizard to include the date, volume number, and so forth, scroll around and find the placeholders for that information, and replace them with your own text. (The Date and Volume number are usually at the top of the page.)
- **Remember that patience is a virtue.** I almost omitted this example because it's complicated and goes beyond what most of us would consider just "taking care of business." If you really hate this sort of thing, you can always hire someone to do a newsletter for you!
- **To print the newsletter,** press Ctrl+P or choose File ➢ Print from the Word menu bar. Then choose OK.
- **To exit Word** and return to home base (Windows), choose File ➢ Exit from the Word menu bar. When asked about saving the newsletter, choose Yes if you want to be able to do more work on the newsletter later, then choose OK.

RELATED SKILLS AND TOPICS

TOPIC	WHERE TO FIND IT
Microsoft Word	*Instant Office*
Select, Then Do	Appendix B
Wizards	Appendix B

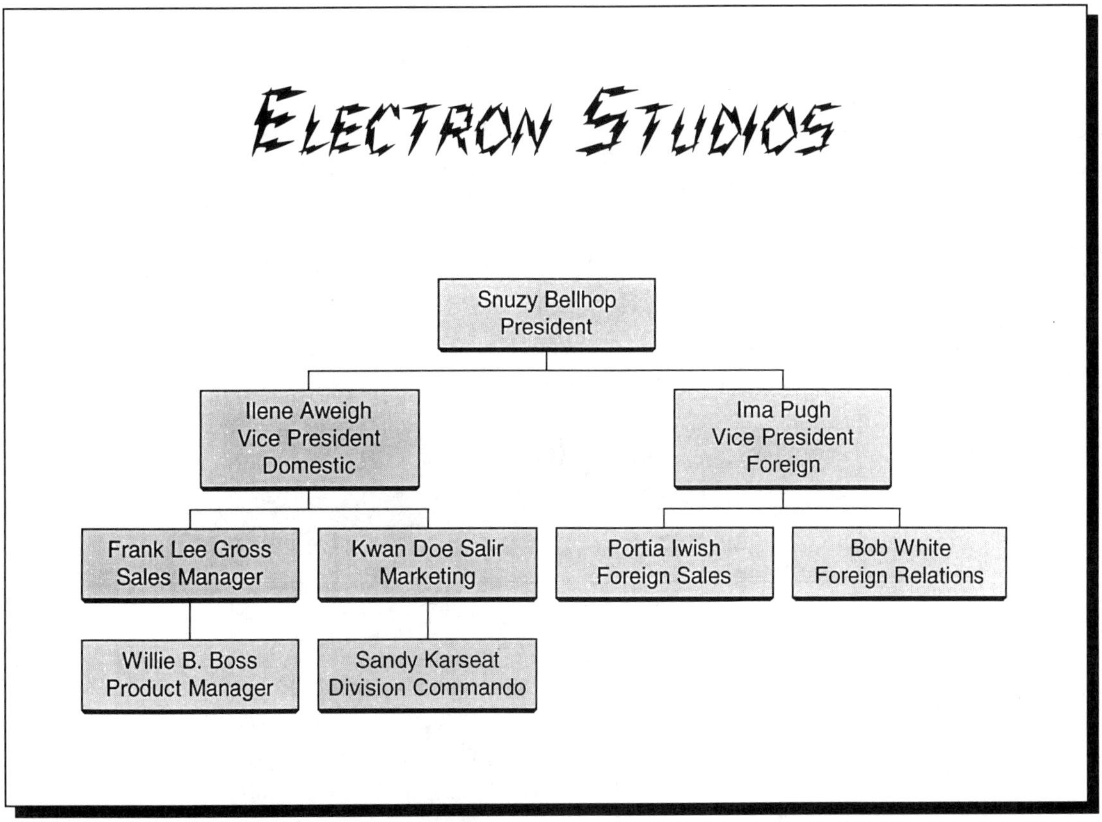

ELECTRON STUDIOS

Snuzy Bellhop
President

Ilene Aweigh
Vice President
Domestic

Ima Pugh
Vice President
Foreign

Frank Lee Gross
Sales Manager

Kwan Doe Salir
Marketing

Portia Iwish
Foreign Sales

Bob White
Foreign Relations

Willie B. Boss
Product Manager

Sandy Karseat
Division Commando

ORGANIZATION CHART (ORG CHART)

5 min.

Typing up an Organization Chart, with or without the aid of a computer, has never been easy. But now, thanks to Microsoft's Org Chart tool, it's not only easy, it's actually kind of fun. Try it for yourself.

O

STEPS

1. Start the application you need:

   - If you want to make a full-page Org Chart, start Microsoft PowerPoint. (If the Tip of the Day dialog box appears, choose OK to remove it.)

- If you want to make the Org Chart part of a Word document, start Microsoft Word and open (or create) the document that you want to put the chart into. Move the insertion point to where you want to display the chart, and choose Insert ➢ Object ➢ Microsoft Organization Chart 1.0 ➢ OK. Then skip to step 6 below.

2. From the first dialog box to appear, choose Blank Presentation, then choose OK.

3. In the New Slide dialog box, click on the Org Chart slide (shown below) then choose OK. Wait a few seconds.

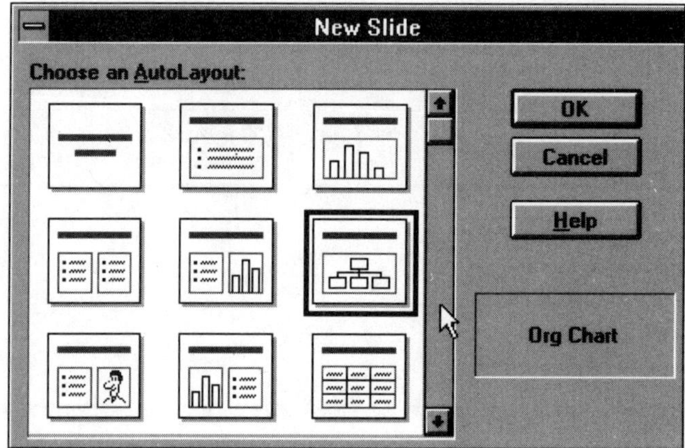

4. Click where it says *Click to add title*, and type in a title. (Optionally, you can select whatever you typed and then choose a font and size from the Formatting toolbar.)

5. Double-click where indicated to add the Org Chart.

6. Wait for the Microsoft Organization Chart dialog box to appear. If you wish, you can maximize that dialog box to see more of your chart. (Click the Maximize button in the upper-right corner of the window.)

7. Now you can construct your Org Chart by doing any of the following, in any order you wish:

   - **To fill a box**, select the text that says *Type name here* or *Type title here* (by dragging the mouse pointer through that text) and then type in your own text. When you're done typing, just click some other box.

- **To add a box**, first choose whichever toolbar button best describes where you want to place the new box (e.g.,Subordinate, Co-worker, Manager, etc.). Then click whichever box you want to attach this new box to. (If you make a mistake, choose Edit ➢ Undo Insert.)
- **To fill a new box**, just click that box and replace its placeholders with your own text.
- **To delete a box**, click the box and press Delete (Del). (If you change your mind, choose Edit Undo Delete to undo that one deletion.)
- **To delete several boxes**, select the boxes to delete by dragging a frame around them. Then press Delete (Del). If you change your mind, choose Edit ➢ Undo Delete.
- **To move a box**, drag it to its new location. If you make a mistake, just choose Edit ➢ Undo Move (watch the screen for helpful tips).
- **To add styles to the chart**, select the box or boxes you want to change (either by dragging the mouse through them or by choosing an option under Edit ➢ Select). Then choose options from the Boxes pull-down menu.

8. When you've finished your chart, exit by pressing Alt+F4 or by choosing File ➢ Exit from the Microsoft Organization Chart menu bar. Unless you've really made a mess of things and want to start over, choose Yes when asked about saving your work.

You'll be returned to PowerPoint, or to your Word document, whichever you started from.

TIPS

- **To size or change the shape of the completed chart**, click it once. Then drag its sizing handles.

- **To work on the chart some more**, double-click it. Wait for the Microsoft Organization Chart dialog box to appear. Then make your changes using the same techniques you used to create the chart, then press Alt+F4 or choose File ➢ Exit from the Microsoft Organization Chart menu bar.
- **To print the org chart**, choose File ➢ Print ➢ OK.
- **To close your chart and return to home base** (the Windows Program Manager), choose File ➢ Exit from the current application's menu bar. If you want to be able to work with the chart in the future, when asked about saving your work, be sure to choose Yes and enter a valid file name.

RELATED SKILLS AND TOPICS

TOPIC	WHERE TO FIND IT
Microsoft PowerPoint	*Instant Office*

PHOTO

5 min.

If you want to put a copy of a photograph in a document, you'll first need to scan the photo, to store a copy of it on disk. If you don't have a scanner, see the Tips section below for some tips on getting your photo scanned.

Here, I'll assume you want to put the photo into a document that you've created using Microsoft Word. Then I'll discuss other applications under the Tips heading in this section.

STEPS

To put your photo in a document, you need to know the name of the file that it's stored in and that file's location on your hard disk. In this example, I'll assume that your photo is stored in a file named PHOTO.-TIF in the C:\MSOFFICE\CLIPART directory.

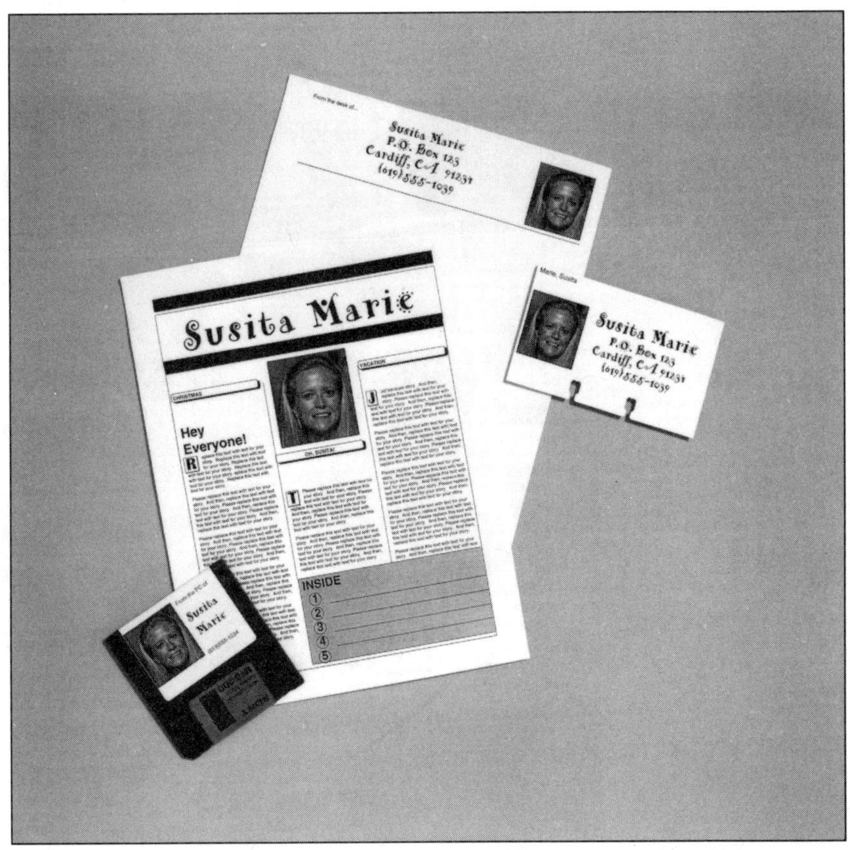

1. Start Microsoft Word and open or create the document that you want to put the photo in.

2. Move the insertion point to about where you want the photo.

3. Choose Insert ➢ Picture from Word's menu bar.

4. Under Drives, choose the drive that your clip-art file is located on (if it's not already the correct drive.) For example, to find C:\MS-OFFICE\CLIPART\PHOTO.TIF, you'd want to choose drive C:.

5. Under List Files of Type, choose **All Graphics Files** or the specific type of file you're looking for [e.g., **Tagged Image Format (*.tif)** if you're certain you want to limit your choices to files that have .TIF as the file name extension].

6. Under Directories, work your way to the directory that your photo is stored on. For example, to get to C:\MSOFFICE\CLIPART, scroll to, then double-click on **c:** at the top of the directory tree. Scroll to, and double-click on, the **msoffice** directory name. Then double-click on the **clipart** directory name.

7. Under File Name, scroll down to, and double-click on the name of the file that contains your photo, which would be PHOTO.TIF in this example (Figure P.1).

FIGURE P. 1

Ready to open C:\MSOFFICE\CLIPART\PHOTO.TIF. Double-click that file name, or click the file name once and choose OK.

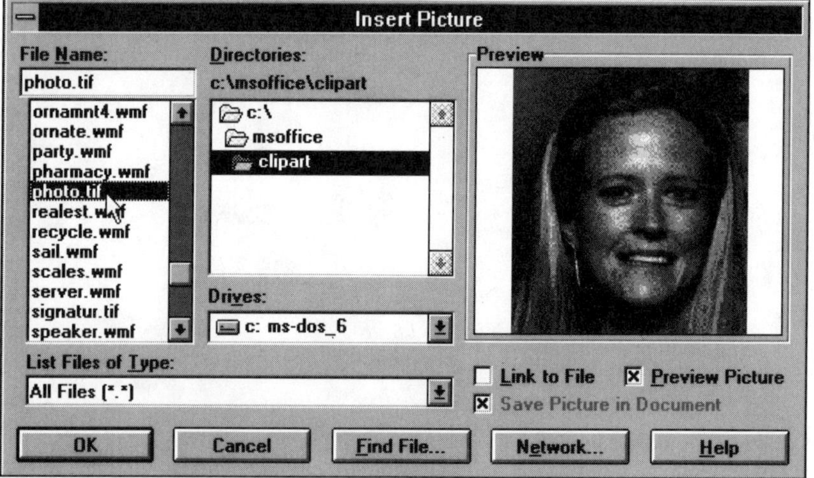

8. To size the photo, click it once so it gets sizing handles, as in the example below. Then drag from any corner to enlarge or shrink the image. Don't drag from the side, or you might distort the photo! See *Pictures (Clip Art)* here in the *Do-It-Now Encyclopedia* for more information.

9. To position the photo, first frame it. To do so, click the image so it has sizing handles, then choose Insert ➢ Frame. Once the photo is framed, you can drag it to any position in the document. You can also choose Format ➢ Frame to control the photo's position and how text wraps around the photo. See *Pictures (Clip Art)* here in the *Do-It-Now Encyclopedia* for more information.

10. Optionally, to change the border around the picture choose Format ➢ Borders and Shading [this is also discussed in more detail under *Pictures (Clip Art)*].

11. Don't forget to save your entire document with the photo in place (choose File ➢ Save from Word's menu bar).

TIPS

- If you have a printed photo, but no electronic version on disk, you can just scan the photo into a graphic file. If you don't have a scanner, check with your local print shop or desktop publishing service. Or see the coupon titled *Logos, Photos, and Signatures* near the back of this book.
- A photo is just like any other picture (clip art, logo, signature). Be sure to read the *Pictures (Clip Art)* entry here in the *Do-It-Now Encyclopedia* for more information on moving, sizing, cropping, and framing pictures.
- To insert a photo in an Excel worksheet, click the cell where you want the photo to appear, then choose Insert ➢ Picture from Excel's menu bar. Then follow steps 3–8 above. You can also position the picture without framing it, simply by dragging it to a new location.
- To insert a photo in a PowerPoint presentation, create or open the presentation and get to wherever you want to put the photo. Movc the insertion point to about where you want the photo, choose Insert ➢ Picture, and choose your photo file as in steps 3–8 above. You can move and size the picture by dragging it.
- To add a photo to a Microsoft Access form or report, open that form or report in design view. Move the cursor to about where you

want the photo to appear, then choose Edit ➢ Insert Object. Choose Create from File ➢ Browse and locate the photo's file as in steps 3–8 above. For additional help, choose Help ➢ Cue Cards and explore topics under *Design a Form* or *Design a Report or Mailing Labels.*

RELATED SKILLS AND TOPICS

TOPIC	WHERE TO FIND IT
Drives, Directories, and Files	Appendix B
Logo	*Do-It-Now Encyclopedia*
Microsoft Word	*Instant Office*
Pictures (Clip Art)	*Do-It-Now Encyclopedia*
Signature	*Do-It-Now Encyclopedia*

PICTURES (CLIP ART)

1 min.

Art, cartoons, photos, logos, even your signature, are all examples of pictures (also called graphics). In this section I'll show you how to put a picture in any Word, Excel, PowerPoint, or Access document.

To complete the steps in this section, you should have already completed (or at least gotten started on) the document that you want to add a picture to. That document can be anything: A letter you created with Word's Letter Wizards, a spreadsheet, or a form or a report in an Access database. Furthermore, that document should be visible on your screen, in whatever application you used to create that document.

STEPS

Insert a Picture from the Clip Art Gallery

The easiest way to insert a picture into a document is via the Microsoft Clip Art Gallery. The gallery comes with version 4.0 of PowerPoint, and is automatically installed along with that application. But once the Clip

Art Gallery is installed, you can use it to put a picture in just about any document you create.

1. If you have not already done so, start the application you want to use (Word, Excel, PowerPoint, or Access), and create or open the document that you want to add a picture to.

2. Follow *one* of the instructions below, depending on which application you're using at the moment:

   - **If you're using Word:** Move the insertion point to about where you want to place the picture. Then choose Insert ➢ Object from Word's menu bar. Double-click on **Microsoft ClipArt Gallery**, then skip to step 3.

- **If you're using Excel**: Click on a cell where you want to place the upper-left corner of the picture, then choose Insert ➢ Object from Excel's menu bar. Double-click on **Microsoft ClipArt Gallery**, then skip to step 3.
- **If you're using PowerPoint:** Open your presentation, and get to, or create, the slide to which you want to add a picture. To do so, choose View ➢ Slides, then choose Insert ➢ New Slide. Then click the *Text and Clip Art* or *Clip Art and Text* template (both show a tiny picture of a person's face). Then choose OK. Double-click where indicated on the slide to add clip art, then skip to step 3.
- **If you're using Access:** Open your database (choose File ➢ Open Database). Then create, or open in design view, the form or report you want to add a picture to. Click near where you want to display the picture in the form or report, then choose Edit ➢ Insert Object ➢ Create New. Then double-click on **Microsoft ClipArt Gallery** and continue with the next step.

3. If Office detects some pictures that aren't already in the Clip Art Gallery, you'll be asked if you want to add those pictures. Choose Yes and wait for the Gallery (shown in Figure P.2) to appear.

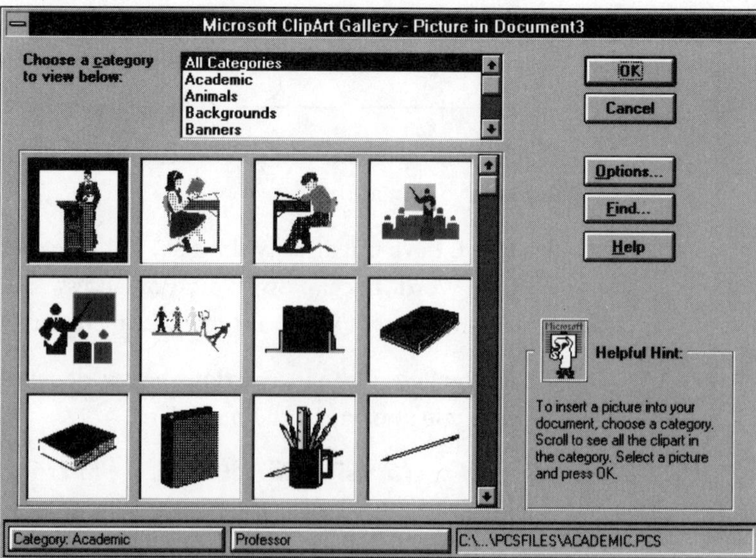

FIGURE P.2

The Microsoft Clip Art Gallery lets you add pictures to any Microsoft Office document.

4. In the drop-down list near the top of the dialog box, choose a category (or All Categories, if you prefer).

5. In the set of pictures, click whichever picture you want to put into your document. Note that in some categories, you can use the scroll bar to scroll to additional pictures. After clicking on the picture that you want to put into your document, choose the OK button.

The picture comes into your document, and you're done! If you need to change the picture a little, skip to *Move, Size, or Crop a Picture* a little later in this section.

P

STEPS

Insert a Picture from a File

If you want to add a picture that's not in the ClipArt gallery to a document, you must know the name and location of the file that the picture is stored in. Then you can follow the steps below to locate the picture, and bring it into your document. To illustrate an example as we go through the text, I'll assume that you're trying to add a picture named **0694111B.TIF** from the directory named **D:\0694CLIP\TIFF** on a compact disc in CD-ROM drive **D:**. But you'll need to choose the appropriate drive, directory, and file name of the picture that you want to add to *your* document as you follow the steps.

NOTE: *Strange names like 0694111B.TIF are often used to identify pictures that come from a clip-art subscription service. The name indicates the date (e.g.* ***0694*** *for June 94), picture ID number (e.g.,* ***111****), and whether it's in black-and-white or color. For more information on clip art subscriptions, contact Art Parts, Electronic Clipper, or Software of the Month Club, all listed in Appendix C.*

1. If you're in **Word**, **Excel**, or **PowerPoint,** move the insertion point to about where you want to insert the picture. If you're in **Access**, create or open in design view the form or report to which you want to add a picture, then click at about where you want to place the picture.

2. If you're in **Word**, **Excel**, or **PowerPoint**, choose Insert ➢ Picture. If you're in Access, choose Edit ➢ Insert Object ➢ Create from File ➢ Browse.

3. Under List Files of Type, choose **All Files (*.*)** or the specific type of file you're looking for (e.g. **Tagged Image Format (*.tif)** if you're certain you want to limit your choices to files that have .tif as the file name extension.

4. Under Drives, choose the drive that your clip art file is located on (if it's not already the correct drive). For example, to find D:\0694-CLIP\TIFF\0694111B.TIF**,** you'd want to choose drive **d:**.

5. Under Directories, work your way to the directory that your picture is stored on. For example, to get to D:\0694CLIP\TIFF**,** double-click on **d:** at the top of the directory tree. Scroll to, and double-click on, the **0694clip** directory name. Then double-click on the **tiff** directory name.

6. Under File Name, scroll down to, and double-click on the name of the file that contains your picture, which would be **0694111B.TIF** in this example (Figure P.3).

FIGURE P.3

Ready to open D:\0694CLIP\TIFF\0694111B.TIF. To preview the picture, check the Preview Picture box. To put the picture in your document, choose OK, or double-click the picture's file name.

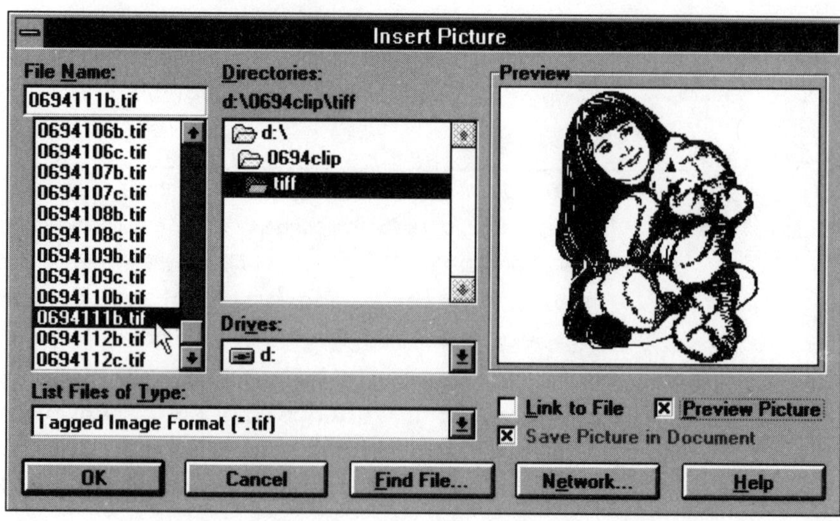

That should do it—the picture will be in your document. If you need to size, move, or crop the picture, see the next section.

STEPS

Move, Size, or Crop a Picture

Once you have a picture in your document, you can generally select it, and then drag any sizing handle to size the picture. Or drag the entire picture from one place to another. For example, in Microsoft Word, do any of the following to move, size, or crop the image to your liking:

1. Select the picture (click it once, so it has sizing handles). Then:
   - To size the picture without distorting, drag from any corner (in Excel/PowerPoint, hold down the Shift key while you drag).
   - To size the picture and scale it to its frame, drag from any side. The picture will be distorted to fit in the new frame shape, which is OK with some types of pictures.

NOTE: *In Access, you determine how the picture fits within its frame by setting the Size Mode property. Choose View ➢ Properties from the Access menu bar to get to the properties sheet.*

   - In Word, you can easily crop the picture. Just hold down the Shift key while dragging any sizing handle. (This is a very handy technique, and I hope Microsoft will add it to future versions of other Office applications.)
2. If you're using Microsoft Word and want to move the picture, first select the picture, then choose Insert ➢ Frame from Word's menu bar to frame the picture. If you're not using Word, skip this step.
3. Drag the picture to any location.

Figure P.4 illustrates the Microsoft Word techniques for sizing and cropping a picture. For other applications, click on any sizing handle and take a look at the status bar for instructions. Or press F1 while the mouse pointer is on a sizing handle. Or search that application's help for Picture, Graphics, and similar topics.

FIGURE P.4

An original picture, and the same picture after sizing and cropping using the techniques that Microsoft Word provides.

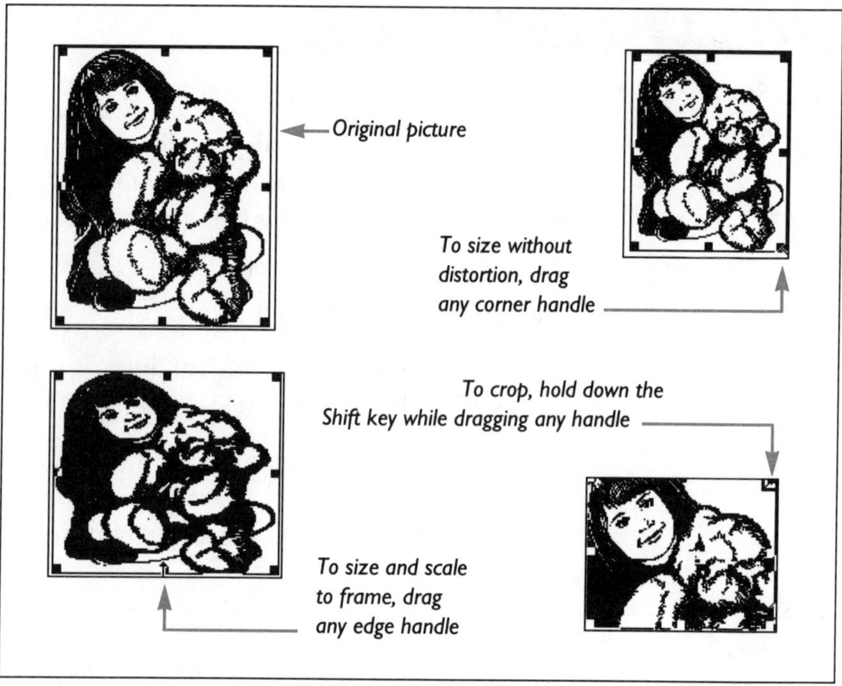
Original picture
To size without distortion, drag any corner handle
To crop, hold down the Shift key while dragging any handle
To size and scale to frame, drag any edge handle

STEPS

Add Your Own Pictures to the Clip Art Gallery

The easiest way to insert a picture into a document is via the Microsoft Clip Art Gallery. But, when initially installed, the Gallery only shows you pictures from Microsoft Corporation. If you want to make it easier to find a particular picture, follow the steps below to add that picture to the Clip Art Gallery:

1. First, if the picture that you want to add to the Gallery isn't on your hard disk, copy it to your hard disk. You can use the Windows File Manager to copy files (please see your Windows documentation).
2. Start the Microsoft Clip Art Gallery. To do so, you can start Word, get to a blank document, choose Insert ➢ Object, then double-click on **Microsoft ClipArt Gallery**.
3. Click on the Options button, then choose Add.

4. Use the List Type of File, Drives, and Directories options to work your way to the drive and directory that contains the pictures that you want to add to the Clip Art Gallery.

5. Under Picture Name, do any of the following:

   - If you want to add just one picture, click its name.
   - If you want to add several pictures, hold down the Ctrl key while you click each picture's name.
   - If you want to add all the pictures shown in the list, choose Select All.

6. Choose OK. If you selected more than one picture to add, you'll be asked if you want to categorize the pictures. Choose Yes, then choose OK.

7. You'll then be taken to the Add Clipart dialog box shown below.

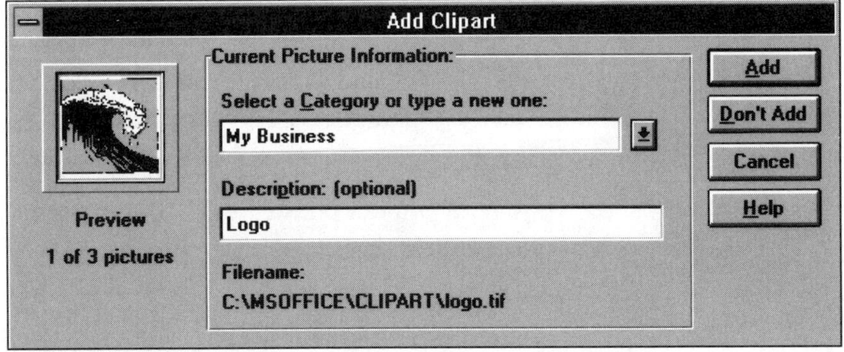

8. The Preview box shows the name of one picture. To categorize that picture, choose a category from the Select a Category drop down list. Or type in a new category name of your own choosing (I typed in *My Business* in the example shown above).

9. Optionally, type in a brief description under the Description option (I typed *Logo* in my example).

10. Choose Add to add the picture to the Gallery.

11. Repeat Steps 8–10 to categorize and describe each picture. If you come across a picture that you decide not to add to the Gallery, just choose Don't Add.

12. When you've finished categorizing and describing, you'll be returned to the Gallery dialog box. Choose Close to close the Gallery and return to Word.

From now on, you can follow the steps under *Insert a Picture from the ClipArt Gallery* rather than the steps under *Insert a Picture from a File* whenever you want to add one of those pictures to an Office document.

TIPS

- To add more pictures to your clip art collection, contact any of the publishers listed under *Clip Art* in Appendix C. Or just take a stroll through a nearby computer store. Some art supplies store also carry electronic clip art these days.
- When purchasing clip art, stick with modern graphics formats like TIF, CMG, and WMF. If you have a PostScript printer, you can also use high-quality EPS-formatted files.
- Whenever you're viewing the Microsoft Clip Art Gallery on your screen, you can press F1 or choose an option from the Help menu to get help that's relevant to the Clip Art Gallery.
- If you don't have an electronic version of the picture you want to put into a document, you just need to have that picture digitized (scanned). Check with your local print shop or desktop-publishing bureau. Or see the coupon titled *Logos, Photos, Signatures* near the back of this book.
- If you need to convert a picture from one format to another (e.g., from bitmap [.BMP] to Tiff), use an application like Hijaak Pro, available from Inset Systems in Brookfield CT, Phone 800-374-6738.

RELATED SKILLS AND TOPICS

TOPIC	WHERE TO FIND IT
Create a Document	Appendix B
Drives, Directories, and Files	Appendix B
Graph	*Do-It-Now Encyclopedia*
Open (Retrieve) Saved Work	Appendix B
Organization Chart	*Do-It-Now Encyclopedia*

P

PLEADING

5 min.

If you need to type up a pleading for a court of law, Microsoft Word's Pleading Wizard might be a good way to get started. Though it can't type up the entire pleading, the Wizard will format the first page and print line numbers in the margin.

STEPS

1. Start Microsoft Word.
2. Choose File ➢ New from Word's menu bar.
3. Scroll down to Pleading Wizard and double-click on it. Wait a few seconds for the Legal Pleading Wizard window to appear.
4. Choose options from the Wizard window. The preview shows you the effect of your choices. Choose Next when you're ready to move onto the next Wizard window.
5. Repeat Step 4 until you get to the checkered flag. Then choose a Help option, and then choose Finish.

The formatted first page of the pleading appears on the screen, with the insertion point where you want to start typing your text. You can type and edit text normally.

Malcolm Weepdip, Esq.
Sheepdip, Weepdip, and Kern
11021 West Valley Parkway
Escondido, CA 92039
Telephone: (619)555-9485
Fax:(619)555-9486

Attorney For: Gertie Gooose

UNITED STATES DISTRICT COURT

CENTRAL DISTRICT OF CALIFORNIA

Page 1

TIPS

- **To check your spelling** before printing the pleading, click the Spelling button on the Standard toolbar, or choose Tools ➢ Spelling from the menus, or press F7.
- **To print the pleading,** click the Print button on the Standard tool bar, or choose File ➢ Print from the menus, or press Ctrl+P. Then choose OK.

- **To close Word and return to Windows,** choose File ➢ Exit from the Word menu bar. You can save this copy of the pleading for printing and editing later, if you like, by choosing Yes when asked about saving, and entering a valid file name.

RELATED SKILLS AND TOPICS

TOPIC	WHERE TO FIND IT
Microsoft Word	*Instant Office*
Wizards	Appendix B

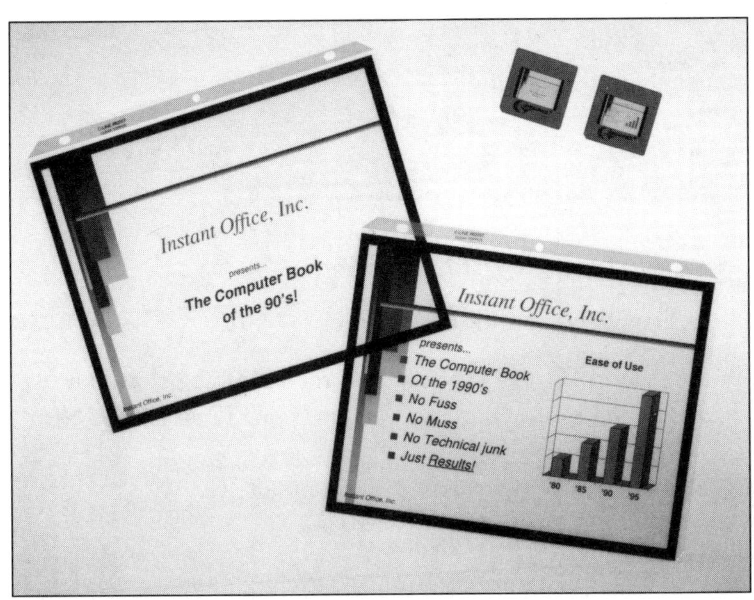

PRESENTATION

60 min

Do you need to whip up a quick presentation for a sales pitch, recommendation, or progress report? Need handouts, slides, or overheads to go with it?

Let PowerPoint's AutoContent Wizard get you started and help you along.

STEPS

1. Start Microsoft PowerPoint.
2. If the Tip of the Day appears, you can just choose OK to move on. You should then come to this dialog box. (If you don't get to that dialog box, choose File ➢ New from Presentation's menu bar.)

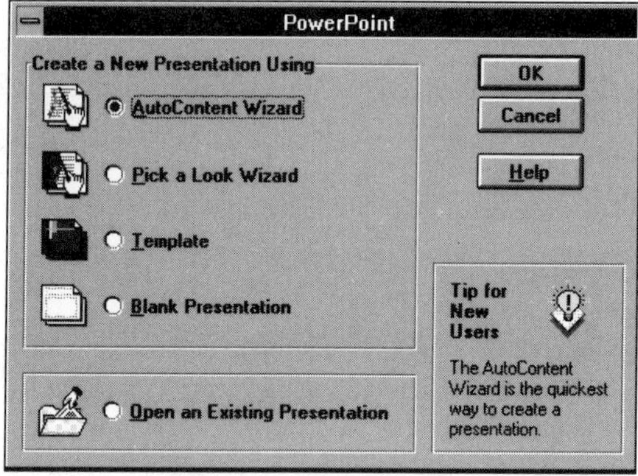

3. Choose AutoContent Wizard, then choose OK.
4. Read the first Wizard window, then choose Next.
5. Fill in the second Wizard window as in the example below, but use information relevant to your own presentation. Then choose Next.

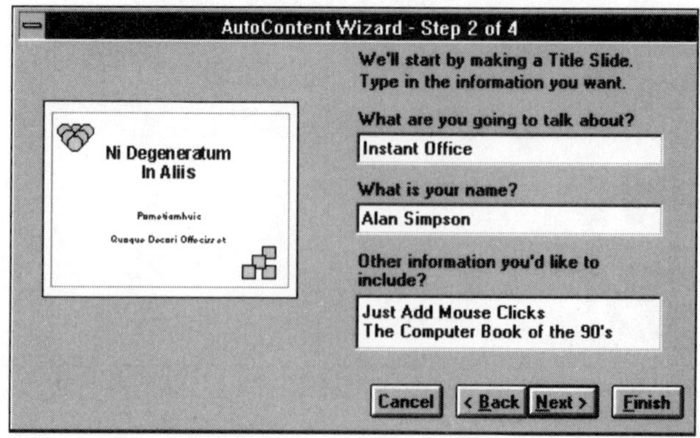

6. In the third Wizard window, choose the type of presentation you plan to give, as in the example below. Then choose Next.

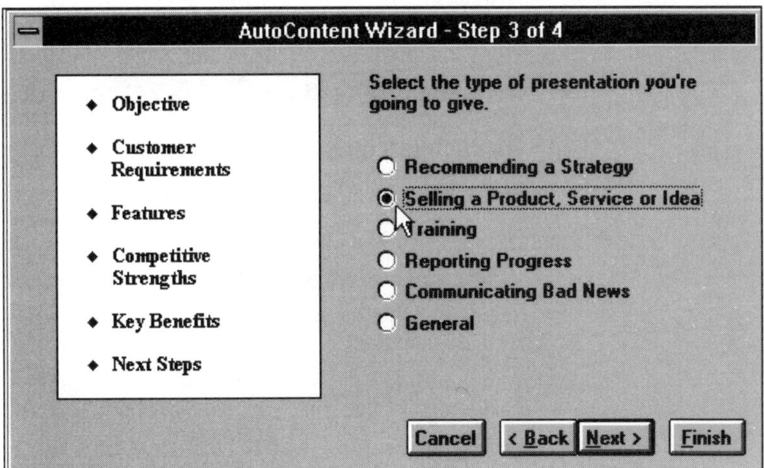

7. Read the fourth Wizard window, then choose Finish. A suggested outline for your presentation, and helpful Cue Card, appear on your screen, as in the example shown in Figure P.5.

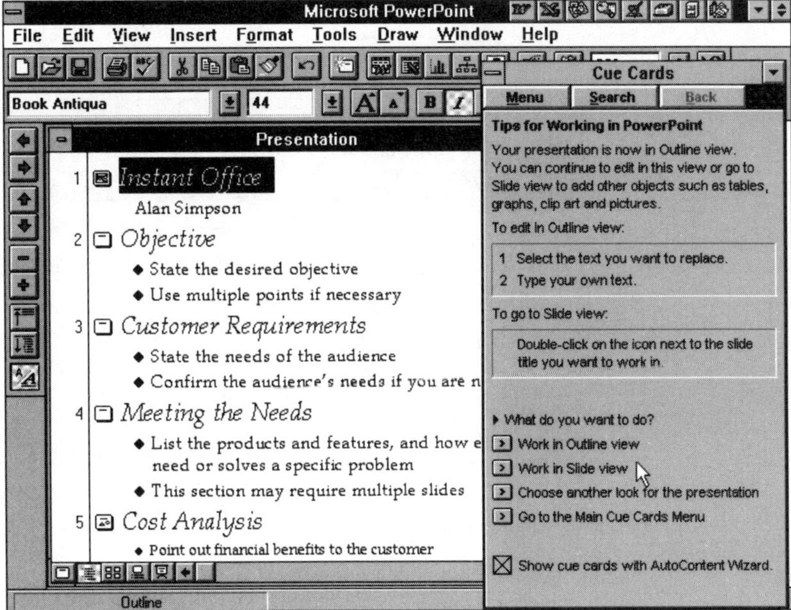

FIGURE P.5

A sample outline for a presentation, created by PowerPoint's AutoContent Wizard.

8. From here on out, you should be able to create your presentation using the techniques below, in any order you wish. Use the Cue Cards on the screen for additional direction and help. As always, you can just press F1 when you need more help.

Remember, if the Cue Card covers something you're trying to see on the screen, just drag the Cue Card out of the way.

- To change a line of text in the outline, select that text by dragging the mouse through it. Then type in your own text.
- To delete a line, select the line and press Delete. If you also want to delete the bullet, press Backspace Not necessary if whole line is selected—bullet will go anyway. You won't see it highlighted, but it will go.
- To insert a new line, put the insertion point one line above where you want the new line to go. Press End to move to the end of that line, then press ↵. A bullet matching the one above appears at the start of the new line.
- To promote (outdent) the current line, press Shift+Tab.
- To demote (indent) the current line, press Tab.
- To undo your most recent change, choose Edit undo or press Ctrl+Z.

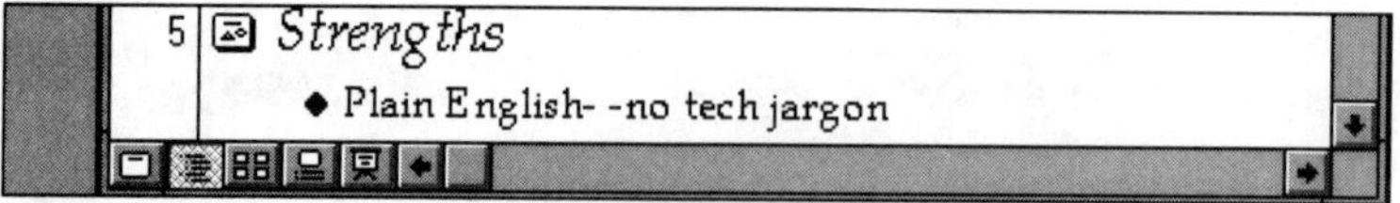

- To view the slide for a topic in your outline, click the Slide View button near the bottom of the screen, or double-click the little slide icon next to any topic.
- To view multiple slides, click the Slide Sorter button
- To change the general look and feel of the slides, choose Format ➢ Pick A Look Wizard, and follow the instructions presented in each Wizard window until you get to the checkered flag.

- To change the color scheme or background of the slides, choose Format ➢ Slide Background, or Format ➢ Slide Color Scheme. Make your selections from the dialog box that appears, then choose OK.
- To switch back to outline view, click the Outline View button near the bottom of the screen.

Figure P.6 shows how I rearranged the initial outline that PowerPoint gave me, using just the techniques above. Figure P.7 shows that same presentation in Slide Sorter view.

FIGURE P.6

My presentation after modifying the outline that PowerPoint originally suggested back in Figure P.5.

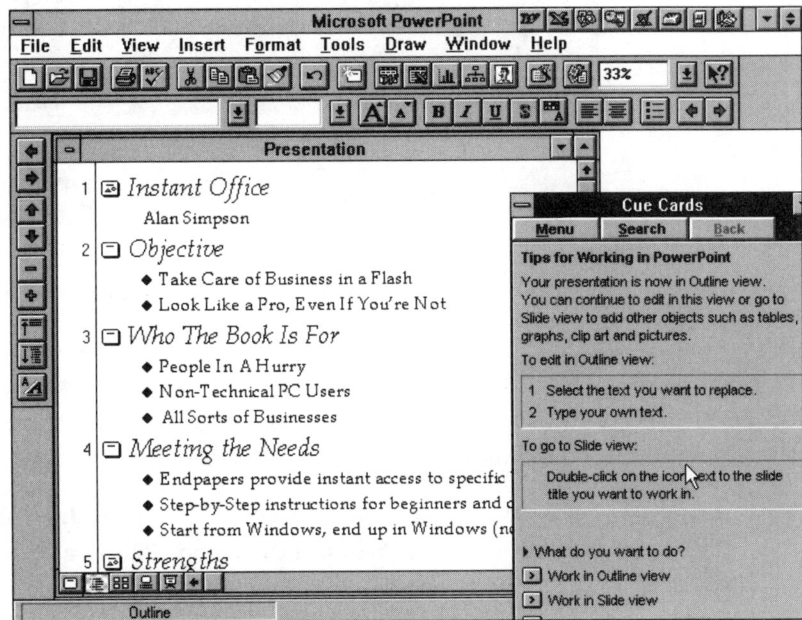

STEPS

Print/Save/Exit the Presentation

When you're happy with your presentation, or when you're ready to save or print a draft, just follow these steps:

1. Choose File ➢ Save from PowerPoint's menu bar. Type in a valid file name (such as **myprsnt**), then choose OK. If the Summary Info

FIGURE P.7

The same presentation shown in Figure P.6, but shown here in Slide Sorter view.

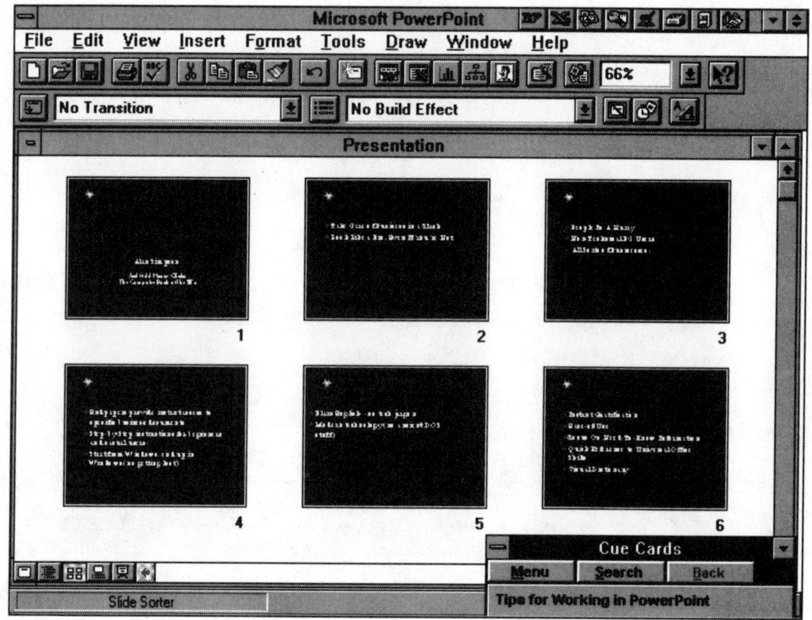

dialog box appears, you can fill it in however you wish (or not fill it in), then choose OK.

2. To print your outline, choose File ➢ Print. Then, in the Print dialog box that appears, choose Outline View from the Print What drop-down list. Then choose OK.

3. To print your transparencies or 35mm slides, choose File ➢ Print to return to the Print dialog box. Choose Slides from the Print What drop-down list. Then:

   - If you want to print transparencies yourself, load your blank laser transparencies into the printer and choose OK.

NOTE: *The Avery label company makes overhead transparency sheets specifically designed for laser printers. You can usually find them at a computer or office supply store. Or order them from Paper Direct, Premier Papers, or Queblo, all listed in Appendix C.*

- If you want professionally printed color 35mm slides, overhead transparencies, or glossies, choose Slides from the Print What drop-down list. Then choose Printer, double-click on **Genigraphics® Driver on GENI**, then choose OK. You'll be taken to the Genigraphics Job Description form, shown below. Fill out the form, choose Help if you need additional information. For prices, and the name and phone number of the Genigraphics Service Center nearest you, see your GeniGraphics manual. Or call their central offices at (800) 638-7348. (It *is* a tad expensive, so make sure you understand how the pricing works!)

Genigraphics Job Instructions

Copies
1 sets, 35mm Slides (plastic mounts)
0 sets, 35mm Slides (glass mounts)
0 sets, 8"x 10" Overheads
0 sets, 8"x 10" Prints
v4.0
OK
Cancel
Help
Send Via
Modem Diskette
Return Via
Courier Mail
Hold for Pickup
Save As MYPRSNT
Custom >>

4. To save your work and exit PowerPoint, choose File Exit. If prompted on the screen, choose Yes to save your changes. You'll be returned to your home base, the Windows Program Manager.

If you want to work on the presentation some more in the future, start PowerPoint. Then choose Open an Existing Presentation OK from the first dialog box. Or choose File Open from PowerPoint's menu bar. Click on the name of your presentation, then choose OK.

TIPS

- The steps described here help you whip up a presentation in a jiffy. But PowerPoint can do much, much more. See your PowerPoint documentation, or the Cue Cards and help screens, for more information.

- If you want to create individual slides, transparencies, or overheads without a complete presentation, see Slides/Transparencies here in the *Do-It-Now Encyclopedia.*

RELATED SKILLS AND TOPICS

TOPIC	WHERE TO FIND IT
Cue Cards	Appendix B
Dialog Boxes	Appendix B
Select, Then Do	Appendix B
Slides/Transparencies	*Do-It-Now Encyclopedia*
Wizards	Appendix B

PRESS RELEASE

30 min.

Microsoft Word comes with templates to help you format a press release. Though not quite as easy as using a Wizard, the templates can help you maintain a consistent format. Choose from among three styles: Classic, Contemporary, or Typewriter.

STEPS

1. Start Microsoft Word.
2. Choose File ➢ New from the Word menu bar.
3. Scroll down to one of these press-release templates and double-click on it, depending on which style you want to give your press release:

PressRel1	Classic
PresRel2	Contemporary
PresRel3	Typewriter

ELECTRON PRODUCTIONS

11021 Marcy Vista Way
Wilmington, DE 54321

EP Releases Mondo Man

Virtual Reality Comes Home

For Immediate Release

Tuesday, June 07, 1994

Contact: Meg Acidopholous

Wilmington—[*Type information here*]

4. A press release page appears with placeholders (text inside square brackets) to indicate where you'll want to type your own information.

5. To replace a placeholder with your own text, select the placeholder by dragging the mouse pointer through it. Then type your own replacement text.

6. Replace the *[Type information here]* placeholder with the text of your press release.

7. If you want to change the style of any text in your press release, select that text, and then choose a style from the Style list in the Formatting toolbar, or by choosing Format ➢ Style, selecting the name of the style you want to apply to the selected text, and then choosing Apply.

TIPS

- **To view the handy Formatting toolbar**, choose View ➢ Toolbars, click on Formatting, then choose OK.
- **To see which style is currently applied** to text in the press release, click that text and look at the style name displayed in the Style box at the left side of the Formatting toolbar.
- **To check your spelling**, click the Spelling button in the Standard toolbar. Or choose Tools ➢ Spelling from the Word menu bar.
- **To print the press release,** click the Print button in the Standard toolbar. Or choose File ➢ Print from the Word menu bar. Choose OK when you're ready to start printing.
- **To save and close the press release**, choose File ➢ Exit ➢ Yes from the Word menu bar. Type in a valid file name for this press release (e.g., **pressrel**) and then choose OK. You'll be returned to home base, the Windows Program Manager.

RELATED SKILLS AND TOPICS

TOPIC	WHERE TO FIND IT
Microsoft Word	*Instant Office*
Select, Then Do	Appendix B

PROMOTIONAL KIT

60 min.

If you want to create an entire business promotional kit complete with letterhead, envelopes, business cards, and so forth, you first need to purchase appropriate papers for the job. If you want to make life really easy, you can also purchase templates for use with Microsoft Word, to make formatting your custom documents even easier.

STEPS

Here's the quickest, easiest way to create a complete promotional kit for a new business, or for an old business in need of a makeover:

1. Contact Paper Direct, Premier Papers, and Queblo (all listed in Appendix C) for their catalogs.
2. When the catalogs arrive, find the paper style that best projects the image you want to create.
3. If the paper company also offers templates for using their papers, get them. Be sure to specify templates for Microsoft Word version 6.0.

4. When the papers and templates arrive, follow the instructions that come with the templates to install and use those templates.

It doesn't get any easier than that. Honest! Granted, you might be spending $150.00 or more to get started. But that's cheap compared to what professional printers charge. And you get the satisfaction of having complete control over the results, and the convenience of using your own laser printer.

RELATED SKILLS AND TOPICS

TOPIC	WHERE TO FIND IT
Letterhead	*Do-It-Now Encyclopedia*

PURCHASE ORDER

5 min.

Microsoft Word comes with a handy Purchase Order template (PURCHORD.DOT) that you can tailor to your own business. When you later need to type up a purchase order, just call up the template and fill in the blanks.

STEPS

Personalizing the Purchase Order

You need only follow the steps presented here once, to personalize the purchase order template:

1. Start Microsoft Word.
2. Choose File ➢ Open from the Word menu bar.
3. Under List Files of Type, choose **Document Templates (*.dot)** (see Figure P.8).

P

ABC Corporation

No Hay Problema
1234 Porkerville Way
Cucamonga, CA 91234
213.555.1234 Fax 213.555-1235

The following number must appear on all related correspondence, shipping papers, and invoices:
P.O. NUMBER:

To: **Ship To:**

P.O. DATE	REQUISITIONER	SHIP VIA	F.O.B. POINT	TERMS

QTY	UNIT	DESCRIPTION	UNIT PRICE	TOTAL
				$ 0.00
				$ 0.00
				$ 0.00
				$ 0.00
				$ 0.00
				$ 0.00
				$ 0.00
			SUBTOTAL	$ 0.00
			SALES TAX	
			SHIPPING & HANDLING	
			OTHER	
			TOTAL	$ 0.00

1. Please send two copies of your invoice.
2. Enter this order in accordance with the prices, terms, delivery method, and specifications listed above.
3. Please notify us immediately if you are unable to ship as specified.
4. Send all correspondence to:
   Janet Kerrington
   ABC Corporation
   1234 Porkerville Way
   Cucamonga, CA 91234
   714.555.1234 Fax 714.555-1235

Authorized by Date

4. Under Directories, choose the **template** directory by double-clicking. (If you have trouble finding a directory, see *Drives, Directories, and Files* in Appendix B.)

5. Under File Name, scroll down to **PURCHORD.DOT** and double-click on it.

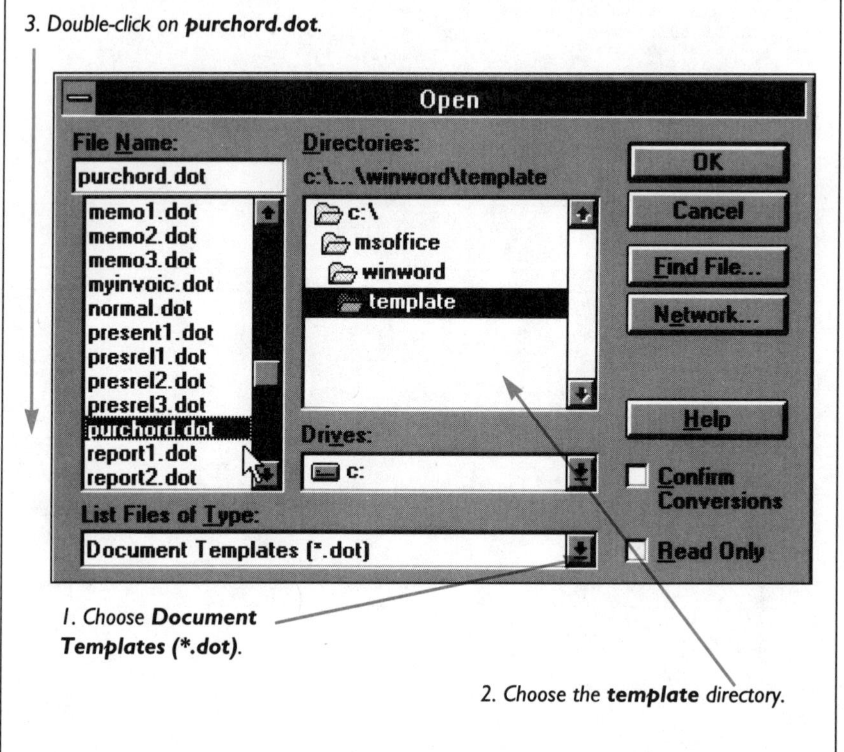

FIGURE P.8

To personalize the Purchase Order template, first open the document template named PURCHORD.DOT in the templates directory.

6. Choose Tools ➢ Unprotect Document from the Word menu bar.

7. Select the placeholder **Your Company Name** (by dragging the mouse pointer through it) and then type in your own company name.

8. Repeat Step 7 to replace the placeholders for your company slogan, address, and phone numbers, as in the example shown below. There are also some placeholders under *Send all correspondence to...* near the bottom of the document. Change those as well.

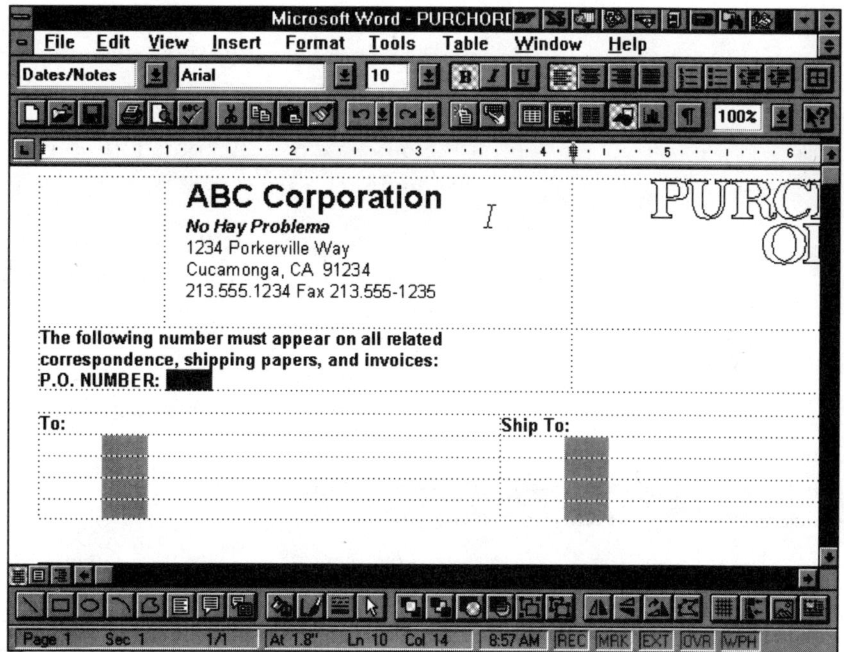

9. Choose Tools ➢ Protect Document ➢ Forms ➢ OK.
10. Choose File ➢ Close ➢ Yes.

At this point, your personalized version of PURCHORD.DOT replaces the original version of that template.

STEPS

Typing Up a Purchase Order

Once you've personalized your purchase order template, you need only open it up and fill in the blanks. Here's how:

1. Start Microsoft Word (if it isn't already started).
2. Choose File ➢ New from the Word menu bar.
3. Scroll down to, and double-click on **Purchord**.
4. Move the cursor to any blank field (gray area), using the mouse or Tab and Shift+Tab keys. Then type your entry into that field (the status bar near the lower-left corner of the screen shows a brief description of what's expected in each blank).

5. As you fill in quantities, prices, sales tax, shipping and handling, subtotals, and totals will be recalculated instantly.

6. After you've filled in all the blanks and are happy with your work, print the purchase order (choose File ➢ Print, the number of to print, and then OK).

7. When you're done, choose File ➢ Close. You can then decide whether to keep a copy of that particular purchase order on disk.

You can type up another purchase order immediately by repeating steps 2–8. Or, if you've exited Word and then want to type up a new purchase order later, repeat the seven steps listed in this section.

TIPS

- As an alternative to using up disk space to save a copy of each purchase order, you can just print two copies of each one. Send one to the supplier and keep the other copy on file for your own records.

RELATED SKILLS AND TOPICS

TOPIC	WHERE TO FIND IT
Microsoft Word	*Instant Office*
Select, Then Do	Appendix B
Type Text and Numbers	Appendix B

REPORT/THESIS

Depends on length

It would be great if you could just tell a Wizard the topic of a report, and then have it write up the report for you. But unfortunately, life at the PC isn't quite that easy. (Yet.) But you can use some predefined Word templates to give your report a consistent look and feel.

Chapter 1

Welcome to Word

Typing Reports with Templates

This is the first page of a report typed with Microsoft Word's report2.dot template. I just typed my text, then applied styles to whatever text I wanted to reformat. Quick and easy, once you get the hang of it.

HOW TO APPLY A STYLE

To apply a style to text you've already typed, first select that text. Or just put the insertion point (not the mouse pointer) anywhere within the text to which you want to apply the style. Then, use either of these methods to assign a style:

- If the Formatting toolbar is open, just choose a Style from the Style drop-down list.
- Or, if that toolbar isn't open, choose Format ➤ Style, click the name of the style you want, then click the Apply button in the Style dialog box.

The heading that follows is formatted with the Heading 2 Style.

Why Use Styles?

Styles let you easily maintain a consistent format throughout a lengthy document. Furthermore, you can change the appearance of stylized text throughout your entire document, just by changing a style. To change a style:

1. Move the insertion point anywhere within text to which you've already applied the style.
2. Choose Format ➤ Style. Make sure the name of the style you want to modify is highlighted in the list of style names.
3. Click the Modify button.
4. Use the Format button to change the font, spacing, or other characteristics of the style.
5. Choose OK and Close, as necessary, to work your way back to your document.

Document templates that are especially good for stylizing lengthy documents include those named Manual, Manuscr, Report, and Thesis. You can choose one right after choosing File ➤ New from Word's menu bar.

R

STEPS

1. Start Microsoft Word.
2. If the Tip of the Day appears, you can just choose OK to move on.
3. Choose File ➢ New. Then click whichever template name listed below best matches the general look and feel you want to give to your report. Choose OK.

TEMPLATE	LOOK AND FEEL	EXAMPLE
Manual1	Typeset book	Figure R.1
Manuscr1	Classic manuscript	Figure R.2
Manuscr2	Typewritten manuscript	Figure R.3
Report1	Classic business report	Figure R.4
Report2	Contemporary business report	Figure R.5
Report3	Typewritten business report	Figure R.6
Thesis1	Classic thesis	Figure R.7

FIGURE R.1

The Manual1 template gives your document the look of a typeset book or manual.

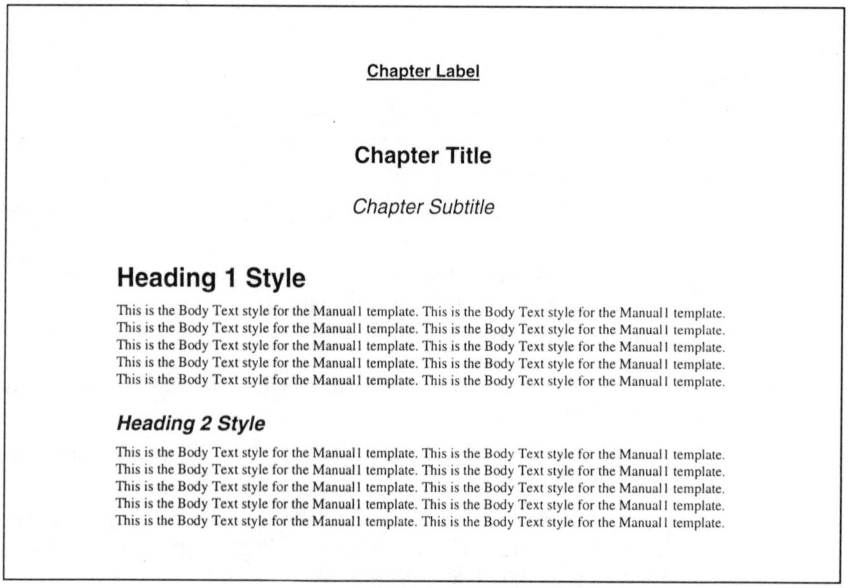

FIGURE R.2

The Manuscr1 template gives your document the look of a classic manuscript for a book or play.

Chapter Label

Chapter Title

Chapter Subtitle

Heading 1 Style

This is the Body Text style for the Manuscr1 template. This is the Body Text style for the Manuscr1 template. This is the Body Text style for the Manuscr1 template. This is the Body Text style for the Manuscr1 template. This is the Body Text style for the Manuscr1 template. This is the Body Text style for the Manuscr1 template. This is the Body Text style for the Manuscr1 template. This is the Body Text style for the Manuscr1 template. This is the Body Text style for the Manuscr1 template. This is the Body Text style for the Manuscr1 template.

Heading 2 Style

This is the Body Text style for the Manuscr1 template. This is the Body Text style for the Manuscr1 template. This is the Body Text style for the Manuscr1 template. This is the Body Text style for the Manuscr1 template.

FIGURE R.3

The Manuscr2 gives your document the look of a typewritten manuscript.

Chapter Label

Chapter Title

Chapter Subtitle

HEADING 1 STYLE

This is the Body Text style for the Manuscr3 template. This is the Body Text style for the Manuscr3 template. This is the Body Text style for the Manuscr3 template. This is the Body Text style for the Manuscr3 template. This is the Body Text style for the Manuscr3 template. This is the Body Text style for the Manuscr3 template. This is the Body Text style for the Manuscr3 template. This is the Body Text style for the Manuscr3 template. This is the Body Text style for the Manuscr3 template.

Heading 2 Style

This is the Body Text style for the Manuscr3 template. This is the Body Text style for the Manuscr3 template. This is the

FIGURE R.4

The Report1 gives your document the look of a classic business report.

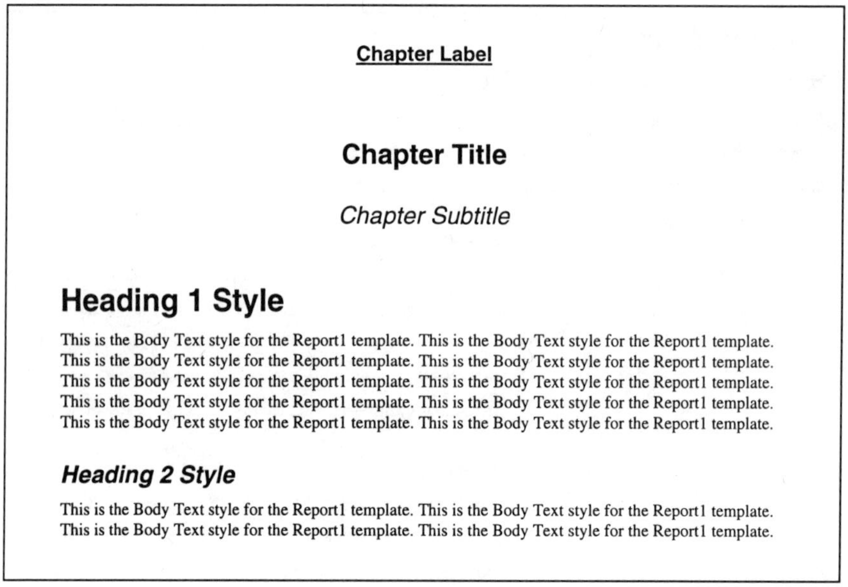

Chapter Label

Chapter Title

Chapter Subtitle

Heading 1 Style

This is the Body Text style for the Report1 template. This is the Body Text style for the Report1 template. This is the Body Text style for the Report1 template. This is the Body Text style for the Report1 template. This is the Body Text style for the Report1 template. This is the Body Text style for the Report1 template. This is the Body Text style for the Report1 template. This is the Body Text style for the Report1 template. This is the Body Text style for the Report1 template. This is the Body Text style for the Report1 template.

Heading 2 Style

This is the Body Text style for the Report1 template. This is the Body Text style for the Report1 template. This is the Body Text style for the Report1 template. This is the Body Text style for the Report1 template.

FIGURE R.5

The Report2 template gives your document the look of a contemporary business report.

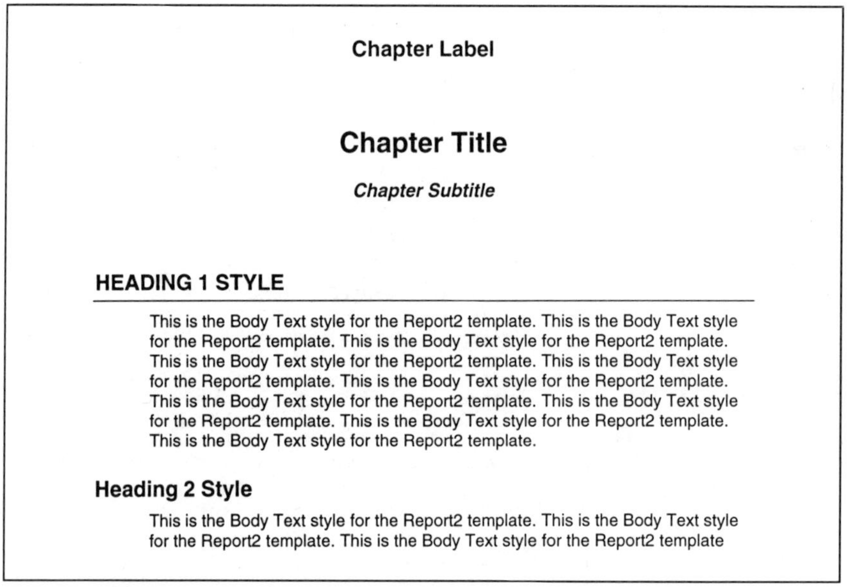

Chapter Label

Chapter Title

Chapter Subtitle

HEADING 1 STYLE

This is the Body Text style for the Report2 template. This is the Body Text style for the Report2 template. This is the Body Text style for the Report2 template. This is the Body Text style for the Report2 template. This is the Body Text style for the Report2 template. This is the Body Text style for the Report2 template. This is the Body Text style for the Report2 template. This is the Body Text style for the Report2 template. This is the Body Text style for the Report2 template.

Heading 2 Style

This is the Body Text style for the Report2 template. This is the Body Text style for the Report2 template. This is the Body Text style for the Report2 template. This is the Body Text style for the Report2 template

FIGURE R.6

The Report3 template gives your document the look of a typewritten business report.

Chapter Label

Chapter Title

Chapter Subtitle

HEADING 1 STYLE

This is the Body Text style for the Report3 template. This is the Body Text style for the Report3 template. This is the Body Text style for the Report3 template. This is the Body Text style for the Report3 template. This is the Body Text style for the Report3 template. This is the Body Text style for the Report3 template. This is the Body Text style for the Report3 template. This is the Body Text style for the Report3 template. This is the Body Text style for the Report3 template. This is the Body Text style for the Report3 template.

Heading 2 Style

This is the Body Text style for the Report3 template. This is the Body Text style for the Report3 template. This

FIGURE R.7

The Thesis1 template gives your document the look of a classic thesis or dissertation.

Chapter Label

Chapter Title

Chapter Subtitle

Heading 1 Style

This is the Body Text style for the Thesis1 template. This is the Body Text style for the Thesis1 template.

This is the Body Text style for the Thesis1 template. This is the Body Text style for the Thesis1 template.

This is the Body Text style for the Thesis1 template. This is the Body Text style for the Thesis1 template.

This is the Body Text style for the Thesis1 template. This is the Body Text style for the Thesis1 template.

This is the Body Text style for the Thesis1 template. This is the Body Text style for the Thesis1 template.

Heading 2 Style

This is the Body Text style for the Thesis1 template. This is the Body Text style for the Thesis1 template.

This is the Body Text style for the Thesis1 template. This is the Body Text style for the Thesis1 template.

4. If it isn't already visible, display the Formatting toolbar (choose View ➢ Toolbars, select Formatting so it's marked with an X, then choose OK.)

5. Now it's time to start typing your report. Sorry, we can't help you with the content, that's up to you. But here's how you can apply the styles from whatever template you chose back in Step 3 as you go along:

   - After you type a chapter or section title, keep the insertion point on that line. Or, if you already pressed ↵, just click the line, or use the ← key, to move the insertion point back into the line.
   - Choose a style from the Style drop-down list in the Formatting toolbar, as in the example below.

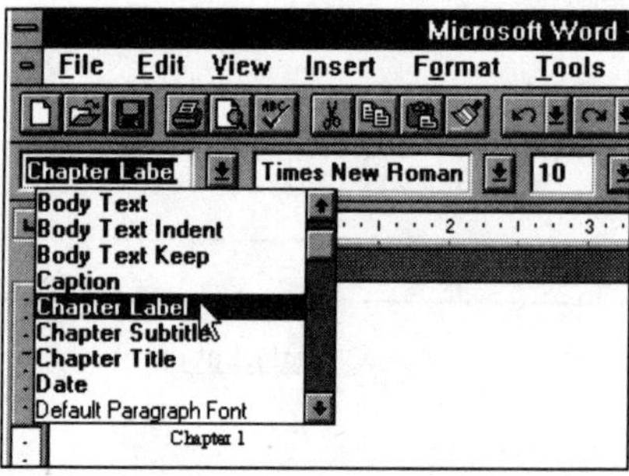

   - After you make your selection, the paragraph or line takes on the format you chose, as below. Press the End key to move to the end of that line, then press ↵ to move down to the next line.

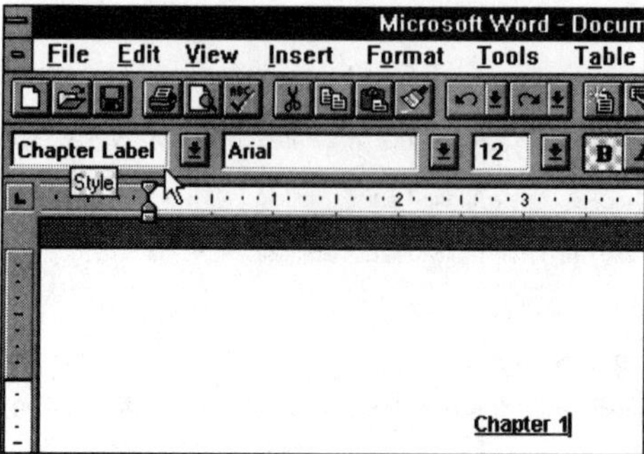

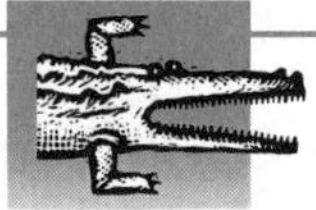

WARNING: *Use the Heading 1 style for all main-level headings within the report. Use Heading 2 for all first-level subheads (a sub-topic under a main head). Use Heading 3 for all second-level subheads, and so forth.*

- The Body Text style is automatically applied to any text you type after marking a line with a Heading style, as in Figure R.8.

FIGURE R.8

When you apply a Heading style (Heading 1, Heading2, and so forth), the text in the next line automatically takes on the Body Text style.

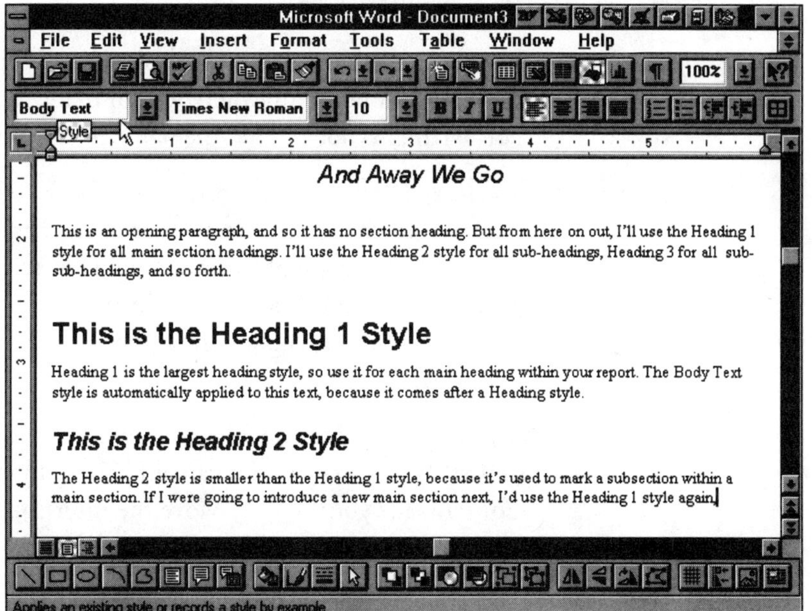

6. Save your work frequently! Choose File ➢ Save to give your document a name, such as MyReport. Then choose File ➢ Save or press Ctrl+S every five minutes or so just to protect yourself from lost work in the event of a power failure or some other mishap.
7. To check and correct your spelling, click the Spelling button in the Standard toolbar, or choose Tools ➢ Spelling from Word's menu bar. Follow the instructions in the Spelling dialog box until the spell check is complete.
8. When you're ready to print your report, just choose File ➢ Print ➢ OK. When you're ready to save your work and exit Word, choose File ➢ Exit ➢ Yes.

You'll be returned to the Windows Program Manager. To resume work on your report later, start Microsoft Word, choose File, and then click your report name at the bottom of the File menu. (Or, if you don't see your report name there, choose File ➢ Open and double-click your report name in the File Name list in the Open dialog box.)

TIPS

- To see what style is currently applied to a section of text, just move the insertion point anywhere within that text. The Style box on the Formatting toolbar shows the name of the currently applied style.
- To change a style consistently throughout your document (for example, to change the Body Text style), choose Format ➢ Style, then click the name of the style you want to change. Then choose Modify. Use the Format button in the Modify Style dialog box to change the font, spacing (Paragraph) or other characteristics of that style.
- If you used the built-in Heading styles (Heading 1, Heading 2, and so forth) consistently, you can automatically create a Table of Contents for your report. Move the insertion point to the bottom of the document (press Ctrl+End), and insert a page break (press Ctrl+↵). Type **Table of Contents** and press ↵ a couple of times to insert blank lines. Then choose Insert ➢ Index and Tables and click on the Table of Contents tab. Choose a format and any other options, then choose OK. When you print the report, the Table of Contents will be printed last. But you can just shuffle it up to the start of the document before you bind the pages.
- For more information and examples of styles within each template, see the *Quick Results* manual for Microsoft Word that came with your Microsoft Office package.

RELATED SKILLS AND TOPICS

TOPIC	WHERE TO FIND IT
Microsoft Word	*Instant Office*
Open (Retrieve) Saved Work	Appendix B
Save Your Work	Appendix B
Select, Then Do	Appendix B
Type Text and Numbers	Appendix B

RÉSUMÉ (CURRICULUM VITAE)

15 min.

Let the Résumé Wizard help you create a professional-looking résumé or Curriculum Vitae. Of course, the Wizard doesn't "know" your work experience, but it can help you insert choose headings and format the résumé. Pick from a variety of styles and formats, and optionally print a separate cover letter and/or envelope.

R

STEPS

1. Start Microsoft Word.
2. Choose File ➢ New from the Word menu bar.
3. Scroll down to, and double-click on, Resume Wizard (or CV Wizard, or Curriculum Vitae Wizard, whichever option is available in your list).
4. Answer questions in the Wizard window. As usual, the little preview changes to reflect your current changes. Choose Next when you're ready to move on to the next Wizard window.
5. Repeat step 4 until you get to the last Wizard window (the one with the checkered flag). Then choose one of the three options there, and then choose Finish.

Wilma Wangdoodle
P.O. Box 4811
Cardiff-By-The Sea, CA 920624
(619)555-0159 (W) (619)555-9320 (H)

Objective

To earn a living

Education

1993 - 1995 **Acme Beauty School**
San Diego, CA
Received full training in haircuts, manicures, pedicures, and cosmetic tattooing. Graduated with honors, third in my class.

Awards received
Best Power Bob, Woman's short-do championships
Nicest Toe Work, Vanity Fair

Interests and activities
When I'm not working to help people look their best, I like to snow ski, walk on the beach, ride horses, watch tabloid news shows on TV.

Languages
English, Spanish

Work experience

1994 - 1995 **Quick Cuts**
Encinitas, CA 92019
Worked as a trainee in hair, nails, and tattooing during their Summer trainee programs.

References
Available on request.

6. If you opted to print a separate cover letter in step 5, you'll be taken to the Letter Wizard dialog box with Resume cover letter already highlighted. Choose Next and complete the Wizard windows for the cover letter wizard in the usual manner.

7. If you opt to create an envelope or label at the last Wizard in step 6 above, you can choose Print to print the envelope immediately, or choose Labels, then Print, to print a label. Your printer may wait

for a "manual feed," meaning that it won't print anything until you manually insert an envelope or mailing label into the printer.

If you opted to create both the résumé and the cover letter, you can choose Window ➢ 1 or 2 (or whatever) from the bottom of the pull-down menu to switch from one document to the other.

To complete the résumé, select any placeholder text by dragging the mouse pointer through it, as in the example here:

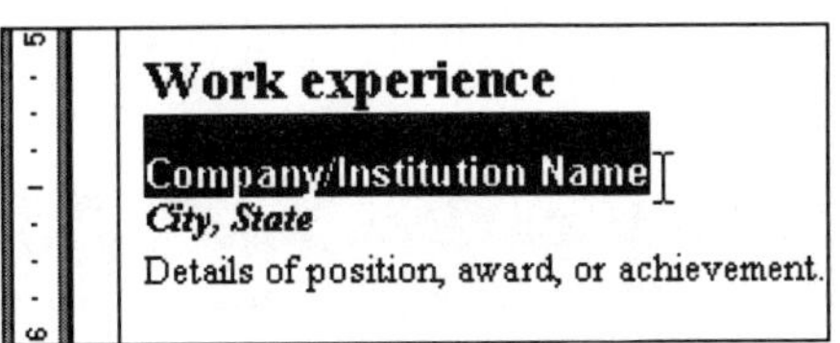

Type in your new text, or press Delete (Del) to just delete the currently selected text. Scroll through the entire résumé to make sure you find all the placeholders. Optionally, you can use Edit ➢ Find to search for placeholders. See *Finishing the Letter* under *Letter (Business or Personal)* here in the *Do-It-Now Encyclopedia* for some tips on using Find.

R

TIPS

- **To check your spelling**, choose Tools ➢ Spelling from the Word menu bar, or press F7, or click the Spelling button on Word's Standard toolbar.
- **To print**, choose File ➢ Print from the Word menu bar or press Ctrl+P. Then choose OK.
- **To exit Word,** choose File ➢ Exit from the Word menu bar. You'll be given the usual options for saving your work. To save this copy, choose Yes and enter a file name you're likely to remember (e.g., **myresume**). Then choose OK to return to the Windows Program Manager.
- **Whenever you need to print and/or update your résumé,** just start Microsoft Word and choose File ➢ Open to open the saved résumé, which would be named MYRESUME.DOC in this example.

RELATED SKILLS AND TOPICS

TOPIC	WHERE TO FIND IT
Microsoft Word	*Instant Office*
Select, Then Do	Appendix B
Wizards	Appendix B

FUTURVAL.XLS

	A	B	C	D	E	F
1	Future Value of Deposits					
2						
3	Annual Interest Rate	6%				
4	Years	10				
5	Monthly Deposit	$ 100.00				
6	Starting Balance	$ 1,000.00				
7						
8	**You will have:**	$ 18,289.27				
9						
10						
11						
12						
13						
14						
15						

Sheet1 / Sheet2 / Sheet3 / Sheet4 / Sheet5 / Sh

SAVINGS/RETIREMENT GOAL

5 min.

Here's a worksheet that lets you pick a savings goal, the amount of time you have to reach that goal, and an interest rate. From those assumptions, the worksheet tells you how much you'll need to invest each month to achieve that goal.

STEPS

1. Start Microsoft Excel.

2. Type the text and numbers shown in Table S.1 into the cells indicated. Be sure to type the text and formulas literally, *exactly* as shown. For example, to get started, you should click on cell A1, then type the words **Future Value of Deposits.** Then click on cell A3, type the words **Annual Interest Rate**, and so forth.

TABLE S.1:

Contents of the Saving Goal worksheet.

CELL	LITERAL (EXACT) CONTENTS
A1	Future Value of Deposits
A3	Annual Interest Rate
A4	Years
A5	Monthly Deposit
A6	Starting Balance
A8	You will have:
B3	6%
B4	10
B5	100
B6	1000
B8	=FV(B3/12,B4*12,-B5,-B6,1)

3. To format the worksheet, first open the Formatting toolbar (View ➢ Toolbars, choose Formatting, then OK). Then select the cell(s) you want to format, and choose formatting options. For example, in my worksheet, I selected cell A1 and chose the Arial 18-pt font, to make the title larger. Then I selected the dollar amounts in cells B5, B6, and B8, and clicked the Currency Style ($) button in the toolbar. (If the numbers change to ###### symbols, the column is

S

too narrow. Widen the column by dragging the right border of the columns heading.)

4. To try out different scenarios, change the value in cells B3 through B6. The required monthly deposit will change instantly to show you what's needed to reach that goal.

TIPS

- **To print the worksheet,** choose File ➢ Print.
- **To save the worksheet** for future use and close it, choose File ➢ Close ➢ Yes. Enter a valid file name such as **savings** and then choose OK. When you want to reopen this same worksheet in the future, start Excel, choose File ➢ Open, and double-click on whatever file name you saved the worksheet under (e.g., **SAVINGS.XLS**).
- **For more examples of financial calculations,** search Excel's help for **PMT** or **financial functions.**

RELATED SKILLS AND TOPICS

TOPIC	WHERE TO FIND IT
Microsoft Excel	*Instant Office*
Select, Then Do	Appendix B
Type Text and Numbers	Appendix B

WET
PAINT

SIGN

5 min.

You can easily create a sign using a landscape paper orientation and a large font in Microsoft Word.

STEPS

1. Start Microsoft Word.
2. Choose File ➢ New ➢ OK from the Word menu bar.

S

3. Choose File ➢ Page Setup from the Word menu bar.
4. If you want to print the sign in landscape orientation (sideways on the page), choose the Paper Size tab, then choose Landscape under Orientation.
5. If you want to center text on the sign vertically, choose the Layout tab. Then choose Center under Vertical Alignment.
6. Choose OK.
7. Type the text of the sign, pressing ↵ wherever you want to end a line (don't worry about fonts or centering just yet).
8. If it's not already visible, open the Formatting toolbar (choose View ➢ Toolbars ➢ Formatting ➢ OK, or right-click any visible toolbar and choose Formatting).
9. To center the text horizontally, select it (press Ctrl+A to select it all), then click the Center button in the Formatting toolbar or press Ctrl+E.
10. To change the size and appearance of text, select whatever text you want to change (or press Ctrl+A to select all the text). Then choose a font and size from the Formatting toolbar, or choose Format ➢ Font and the Font tab. Then choose a Font, Font Style, and Size, and then choose OK. I used Arial, Bold Italic, 200 pt in the Wet Paint example. But you can use any font that's available to you. (If you want to specify a font size that isn't in the Size list box, just type the appropriate size right into the text box under the Size option.)
11. To print the sign, choose File ➢ Print or press Ctrl+P. Indicate the number of copies you want to print, then choose OK.

TIPS

- To add some pizzazz to your sign, try WordArt. That is, complete *only* steps 1–4 above. Then choose Insert ➢ Object ➢ Microsoft WordArt 2.0 ➢ OK). Type the text of your sign in the box marked Enter Your Text, and experiment with some of the pull-down menus and buttons that now appear in the toolbar. When you've finished, click anywhere outside the framed box. Then size the text by dragging a corner of its box. To edit the WordArt text, double-click it to bring back the WordArt toolbar buttons. You can also align your WordArt by clicking on one of the alignment buttons in the Formatting toolbar.

- To add some color graphics to your sign, contact Paper Direct, Premier Papers, or Queblo (all listed in Appendix C).

RELATED SKILLS AND TOPICS

TOPIC	WHERE TO FIND IT
Microsoft Word	*Instant Office*
Select, Then Do	Appendix B
Type Text and Numbers	Appendix B

SIGNATURE

5 min.

You can scan your signature and put it on disk just like a photo, logo, or any other picture. Then you can put your signature into any document you create with MS Office. This is especially good for form letters, because you need only put your signature on the main document, once. Each printed letter will then be signed automatically as printed.

While you're scanning your signature, you might also want to scan your first name and initials separately for signing more casual correspondence. If you don't have a scanner, see the Tips section below for some tips on getting your signature scanned.

Here, I'll assume you want to put your signature into a document that you've created using Microsoft Word. Then I'll discuss other applications under the Tips heading in this section.

S

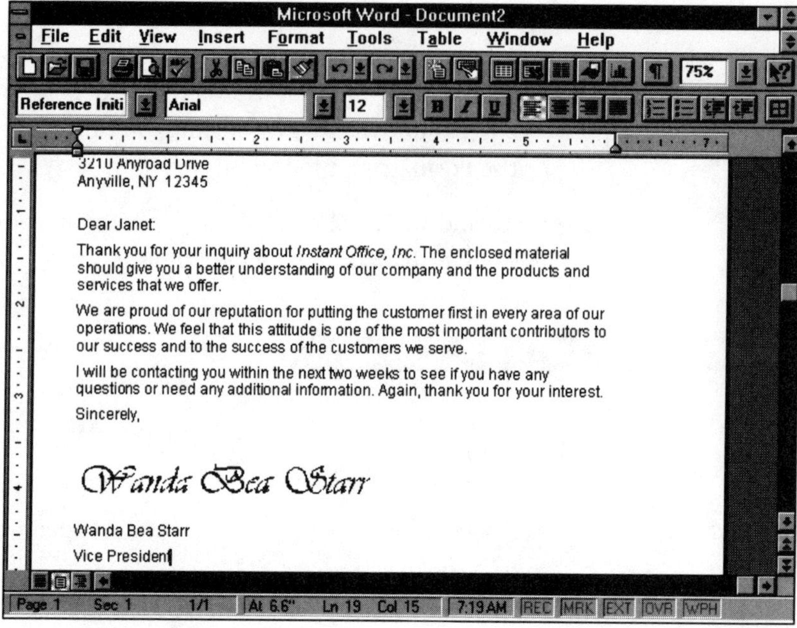

STEPS

Putting Your Signature in a Word Document

To put your signature in a document, you need to know the name of the file that it's stored in, and that file's location on your hard disk. In this example, I'll assume that your signature is stored in a file named SIGNATUR.TIF in the C:\MSOFFICE\CLIPART directory.

1. Start Microsoft Word and open or create the document that you want to put your signature into.
2. Move the insertion point to about where you want your signature placed in the printed document.
3. Choose Insert ➢ Picture from Word's menu bar.
4. Under Drives, choose the drive that your clip-art file is located on (if it's not already the correct drive). For example, to find C:\MSOFFICE\CLIPART\SIGNATUR.TIF, you'd want to choose drive C:.

5. Under List Files of Type, choose **All Graphics Files** or the specific type of file you're looking for [e.g., **Tagged Image Format (*.tif)** if you're certain you want to limit your choices to files that have .TIF as the file name extension].

6. Under Directories, work your way to the directory that your signature is stored in. For example, to get to C:\MSOFFICE\CLIPART, scroll to, then double-click on **c:** at the top of the directory tree. Scroll to, and double-click on, the **msoffice** directory name. Then double-click on the **clipart** directory name.

7. Under File Name, scroll down to, and double-click on the name of the file that contains your signature, which would be SIGNATUR.-TIF in this example (Figure S.1).

FIGURE S.1

Ready to open C:\MSOFFICE\CLIPART\SIGNATUR.TIF. Double-click that file name, or click the file name once and choose OK.

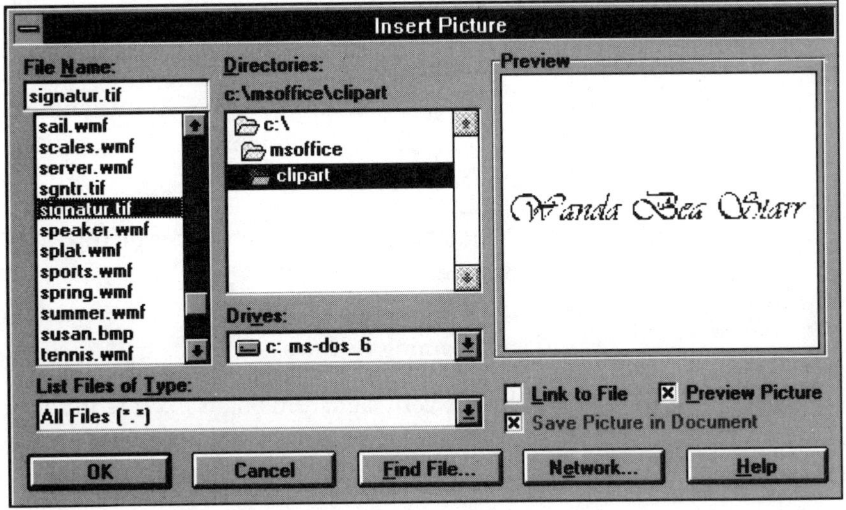

8. To size your signature, click it once so it gets sizing handles, as in the example below. Then drag from any corner to enlarge, or shrink the image. Don't drag from the side, or you'll distort your signature! See *Pictures (Clip Art)* here in the *Do-It-Now Encyclopedia* for more information.

S

9. To position your signature, first frame it. To do so, click the image so it has sizing handles, then choose Insert ➢ Frame. Once it's framed, you can drag it to any position in the document. You can also choose Format ➢ Frame to control its position, and how text wraps around it. See *Pictures (Clip Art)* here in the *Do-It-Now Encyclopedia* for more information.

10. Optionally, to change the border around the picture choose Format ➢ Borders and Shading [this is also discussed in more detail under *Pictures (Clip Art)*].

11. Save your entire document with the signature in place (choose File ➢ Save from Word's menu bar).

TIPS

- If you need to have your signature scanned, and but don't have a scanner, check with your local print shop or desktop publishing service. Or see the coupon titled *Logos, Photos, and Signatures* near the back of this book.
- A signature is just like any other picture (clip art, logo, signature). Be sure to read the *Pictures (Clip Art)* entry here in the *Do-It-Now Encyclopedia* for more information on moving, sizing, cropping, and framing pictures.
- To put your signature on an Excel worksheet, click the cell where you want your signature to appear, then choose Insert ➢ Picture from Excel's menu bar. Then follow steps 3–8 above. You can also position the picture without framing it, simply by dragging it to a new location.
- To put your signature in a PowerPoint presentation, create or open the presentation, and get to the slide that you want to sign. Move the insertion point to about where you want your signature, choose Insert ➢ Picture, and choose your signature file as in steps 3–8 above. You can move and size the picture by dragging it.
- To add your signature to a Microsoft Access form or report, open that form or report in design view. Move the cursor to about where

you want your signature to appear, then choose Edit ➢ Insert Object. Choose Create from File ➢ Browse and locate your signature's file as in steps 3–8 above. For additional help, choose Help ➢ Cue Cards, and explore topics under *Design a Form* or *Design a Report or Mailing Labels.*

RELATED SKILLS AND TOPICS

TOPIC	WHERE TO FIND IT
Drives, Directories, and Files	Appendix B
Logo	*Do-It-Now Encyclopedia*
Microsoft Word	*Instant Office*
Photo	*Do-It-Now Encyclopedia*
Pictures (Clip Art)	*Do-It-Now Encyclopedia*

SLIDES/TRANSPARENCIES

10 min.

Here I'll show you how to whip up some slides or overhead transparencies. If you're looking to create a total presentation with an outline as well as slides or overheads, you might want to use PowerPoint's AutoContent Wizard. That's discussed under Presentations *here in the* Do-It-Now-Encyclopedia.

S

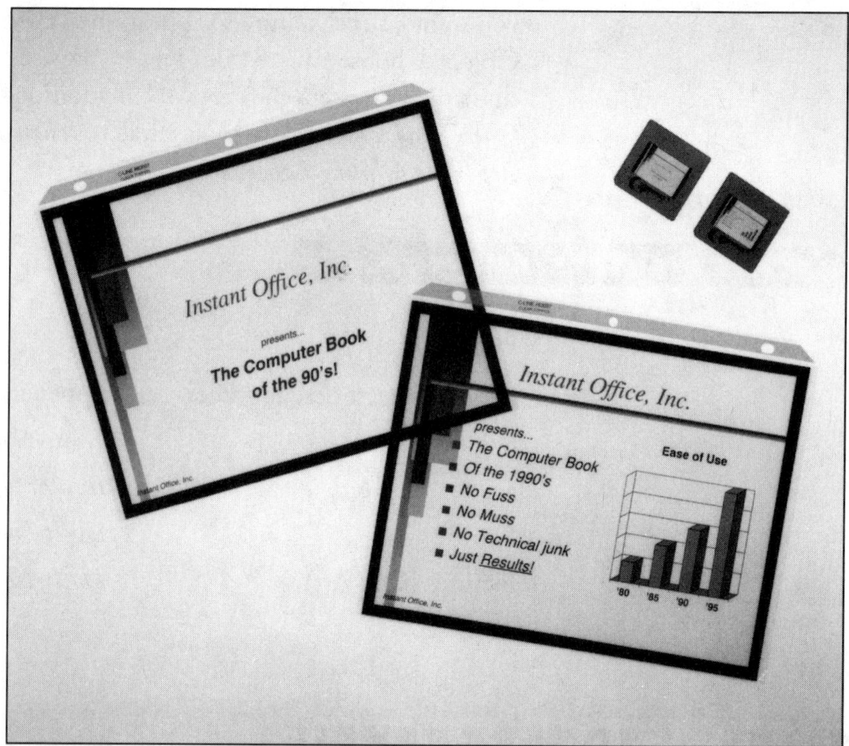

STEPS

Before you begin:

- If you want to print transparencies on your own printer, be sure to use sheets that are suitable for a laser printer. Avery Label Company makes some, and you can find them at many computer stores. Or order from Paper Direct, Premier Papers, or Queblo (see Appendix C for the addresses).

- If you want Genigraphics to professionally print color slides, transparencies, or glossies, have your Genigraphics booklet handy (it should be in your Microsoft Office, or Microsoft PowerPoint box.) If you can't find it, or need more information, contact Genigraphics at (800) 638-7348.

1. Start Microsoft PowerPoint.
2. If the Tip of the Day appears, you can just choose OK to move on.
3. If the dialog box shown below does *not* appear, choose File ➢ New from PowerPoint's menu bar.

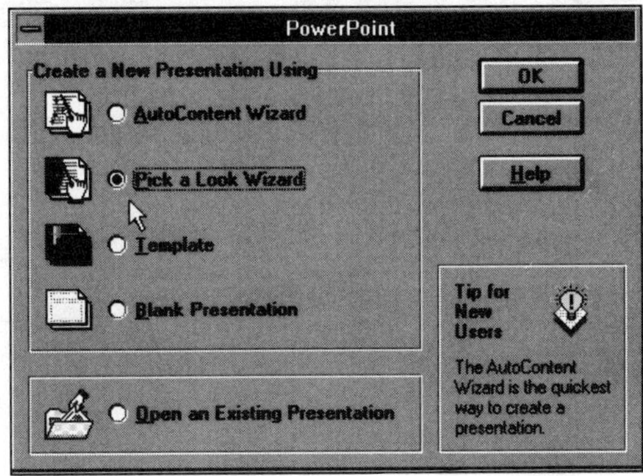

4. Choose Pick a Look Wizard, then choose OK.
5. Read the first Wizard window, then choose Next. You'll then come to this window.

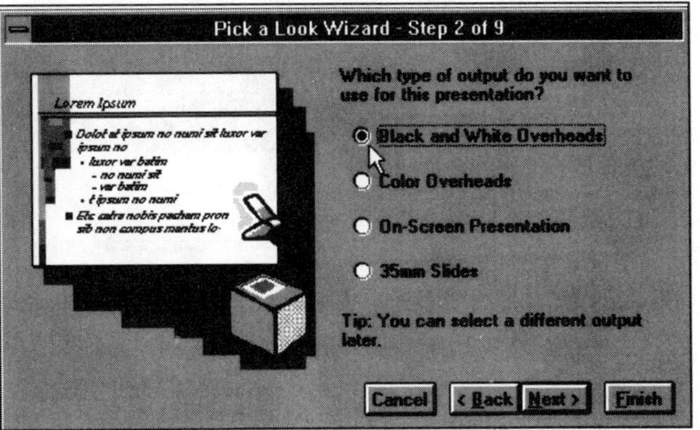

6. Choose whichever type of output you want to create, Black and White Overheads, Color Overheads, 35mm Slides, etc.) Then choose Next.

S

7. Complete each Wizard window that appears, choosing Next after making your selection.

8. When you get to Step 4 of 9, you'll probably want to select only Full Screen Slides, and clear the other options as below.

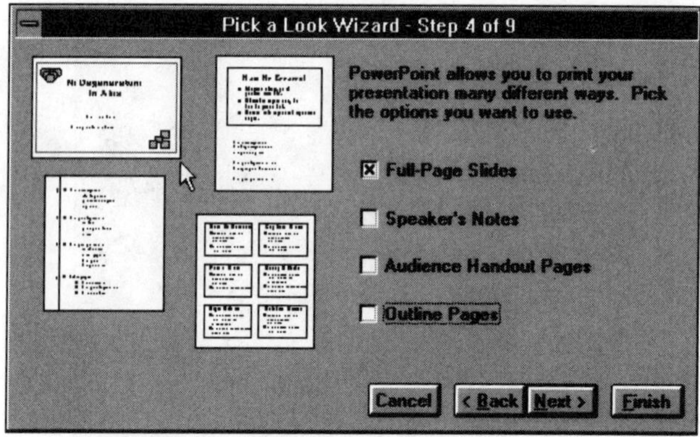

9. When you get to the checkered flag, choose Finish. You'll see a sample slide like the example shown in Figure S.2.

FIGURE S.2

A sample slide on the PowerPoint screen. Instructions appear right on the slide!

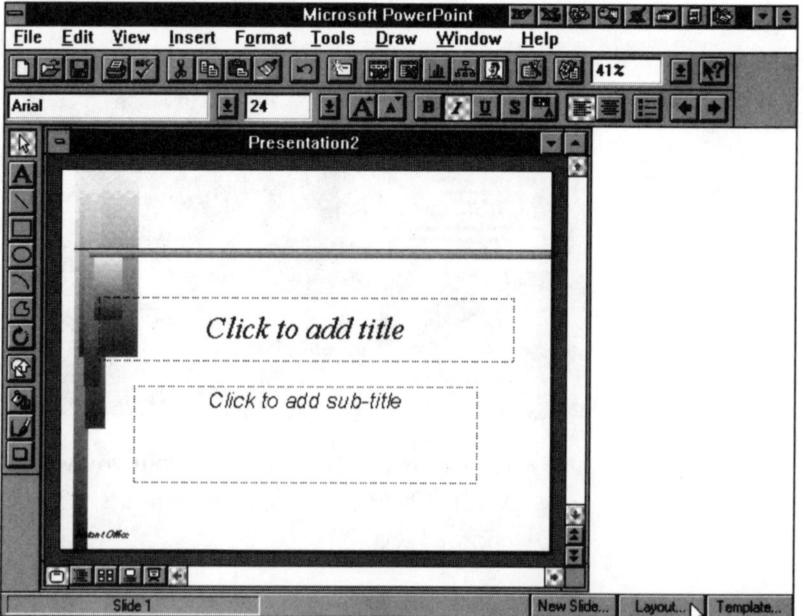

10. To choose a layout for the slide or overhead, click the Layout button near the lower right corner of the screen. You'll see a dialog box of layout options, as shown below.

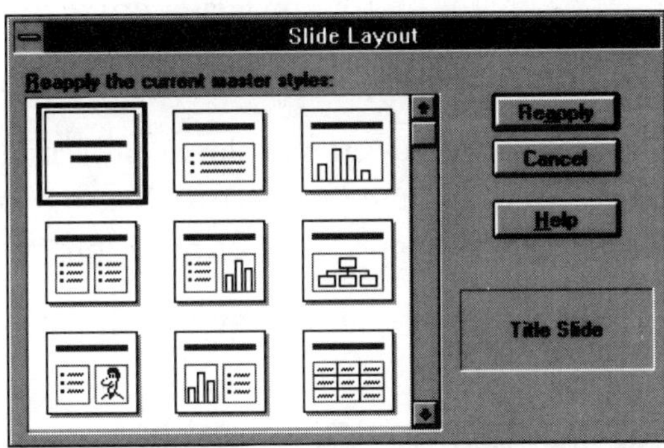

11. Choose a layout option, then click on Apply. The slide on your screen takes on the new layout, and instructions on the slide that tell you how to use that layout. Just follow those instructions. (You can also refer to the sections titled *Display Ad*, *Org Chart*, and *Picture* here in the *Do-It-Now-Encyclopedia* for additional help and suggestions.)

12. After completing your slide/transparency, choose File ➢ Save to save your work. If this is the first time you've saved your work, enter a file name, such as **MySlides**, then choose OK.

13. To create another slide, click the New Slide button near the lower right corner of the screen. Then repeat Steps 11–13 until you've created as many slide or overheads as you need.

TIP: *To view all of your slides, click the Slide Sorter View button near the lower left corner of the window, or choose View ➢ Slide Sorter. To return to single-slide view, click the Slide View button, or choose View ➢ Slides.*

14. When you've finished creating your slides, and are ready to print them, refer to one of the *Steps* sections that follow, depending on whether you want to use your own printer, or have the slides professionally printed.

S

STEPS

Print Overheads Yourself

To print overheads on your own laser printer:

1. Load the laser transparencies into your printer.
2. If you've exited PowerPoint since completing your slides, start PowerPoint, and use the Open an Existing Presentation option, or File ➢ Open, to open your presentation.
3. Choose File ➢ Print from PowerPoint's menu bar. You'll be taken to this dialog box.

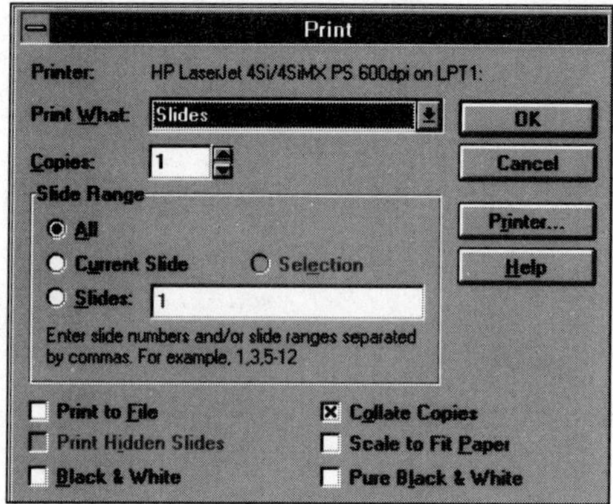

4. If the printer name next to **Printer:** is *not* the printer you want to use, choose Printer, click the name of the printer you want to use, then choose OK.
5. Choose Slides from the Print What drop-down list.
6. Choose OK.

The printed slides should start coming out of your printer in just a few minutes.

STEPS

Have Slides/Transparencies Professionally Printed

If you want Genigraphics Corporation to print full-color 35mm slides, overhead transparencies, or glossies, follow these steps:

1. If you've exited PowerPoint since completing your slides, start PowerPoint, and use the Open an Existing Presentation option, or File ➢ Open commands, to open your presentation.
2. Choose File ➢ Print from PowerPoint's menu bar. You'll be taken to the Print dialog box.

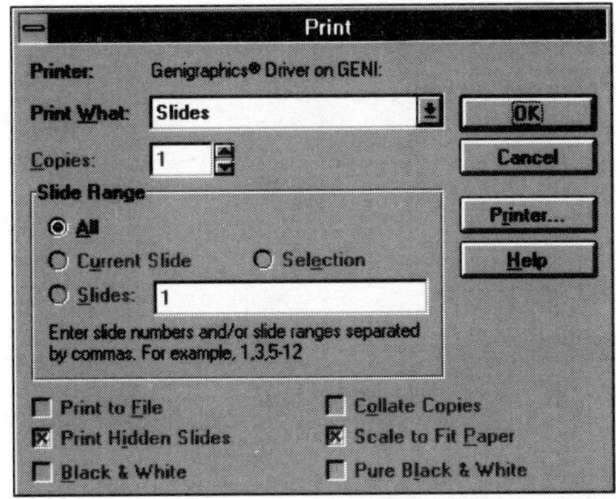

3. If the printer name next to **Printer:** is *not* **Genigraphics® Driver on GENI:**, choose Printer, click on **Genigraphics® Driver on GENI:,** then choose OK.
4. Choose Slides from the Print What drop-down list.
5. Choose OK. You'll be taken to a dialog box like the one on the top of the following page.

S

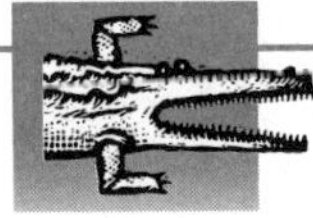

WARNING: *Professional color printing is not cheap. Be sure you understand Genigraphics pricing policies before you place an order! Ballpark estimate: Anywhere from $9.00 to $20.00 per slide, depending on how fast you want them.*

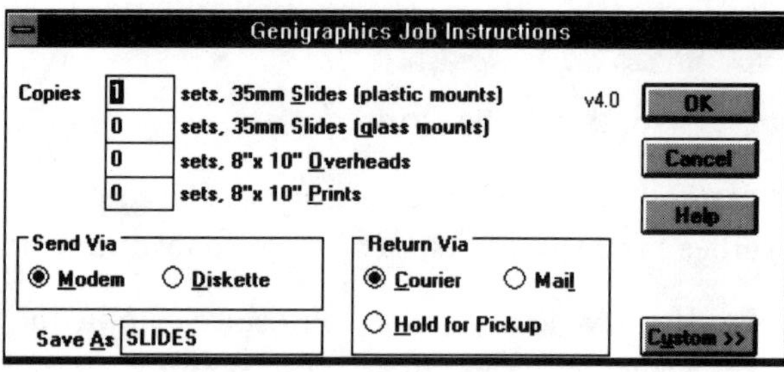

6. Fill in the form as per instructions in your Genigraphics booklet to create file to send to Genigraphics, or to send them your work by telephone (if you have a modem).

RELATED SKILLS AND TOPICS

TOPIC	WHERE TO FIND IT
Microsoft PowerPoint	*Instant Office*
Display Ad	*Do-It-Now-Encyclopedia*
Organization Chart	*Do-It-Now-Encyclopedia*
Pictures	*Do-It-Now-Encyclopedia*
Presentation	*Do-It-Now-Encyclopedia*

SPEED UP YOUR SYSTEM

15 min.

To make programs easy and intuitive to use, the people who create those programs need to put more and more of the workload on the computer hardware. Which means that everything takes longer. A system that seemed like a screaming demon in DOS might feel more like a half-frozen snail under Windows. In this section, I'll describe some general techniques you can use to keep your system running at its fullest potential.

from Presentation Task Force

STEPS

General Tune Up

When a power outage or other mishap turns off your computer without first exiting Windows, you might end up with several files on your hard disk that Windows can no longer connect to a real file name. Even though you can't use those "lost" files, they continue to take up space on your hard disk. They can also slow down the performance of your hard disk.

Even without an abnormal termination, DOS might also *fragment* some of the files you save. Normally, DOS will try to save your file in contiguous chunks on your hard disk. But if there is no single chunk of space large enough to store your file, DOS will fragment the file into whatever smaller noncontiguous chunks are available. This doesn't harm the file. But, when you later read that file, the drive head has to hop all over the place to pull the file into memory. That, in turn, leads to slower disk performance (not to mention more clicking and clacking noises coming from the drive).

To keep your hard disk running at top speed, use SCANDISK (or CHKDSK /F in earlier versions of DOS) to get rid of the lost files. Then use DEFRAG to rearrange all the little fragments of files into contiguous sections on the disk, for faster, smoother reading. I'd recommend that you do so about once a month, or whenever your hard disk seems noticeably noisy or sluggish. Here are the steps to follow:

1. Exit *all* open applications by choosing File ➢ Exit from their menu bars. Exit Windows as well, by choosing File ➢ Exit Windows from Program Manager's menu bar and choosing OK when asked for confirmation. You should end up at the DOS command prompt, which will look something like C:\> or C:\WINDOWS\>.
2. Find out what version of DOS you're using. Type **ver** and press ↵. You should see a message (something) like this:

   ```
   MS-DOS Version 6.20
   ```

3. If you're *not* using version 6.0, 6.2, or 6.21 (or higher), stop here. You won't be able to complete the remaining steps until you upgrade to the latest DOS. Check with your computer dealer or Microsoft Corporation (Appendix C) for upgrade information.
4. Now, clean up your hard disk. Type **scandisk** and then press ↵. Follow the instructions on the screen. If all you get is *Bad command or file name,* rather than instructions, type **chkdsk /f** and press ↵. If either command asks whether you want to get rid of lost files or directories, choose Yes to get rid of them. (There's really no reasonable way to recover them anyway.)
5. Follow any additional instructions on the screen, until SCANDISK or CHKDSK finishes its job. At that point, you'll be returned to the DOS command prompt.
6. Type **defrag** and press ↵. When you come to the screen that asks which drive you want to defragment, choose your hard disk (typically C:).
7. Choose OK or press ↵.
8. When you get to the dialog box titled *Recommendation,* choose Configure (even if it only recommends Optimize).
9. From the menu that appears, choose Optimization Method. Then choose Full Optimization, then choose OK.
10. Choose Begin Optimization from the menu.
11. Wait a few minutes while DEFRAG does its job.

NOTE: *If you happen to notice a big chunk of your hard disk marked as Unmovable (X) in DEFRAG, it's probably just your Windows permanent swap file, which reserves disk space to use as virtual memory. In English that means, "don't worry about it."*

12. When DEFRAG is done defragmenting your disk, you'll see a dialog box that says *Finished condensing.* Choose OK or press ↵.
13. Choose Exit Defrag. You'll be returned to the DOS command prompt.

That's it. Now you can run Windows now and resume your work. For more information on performance tuning, see your DOS manual for information on CHKDSK, SCANDISK, DEFRAG, and MEMMAKER.

Windows Tune Up

You can also improve your computer's performance by setting up a permanent swap file, and using 32-bit disk and file access. But exactly how you go about doing that depends on what version of Windows you're using, and also somewhat on what kind of hardware you're using. Therefore, I don't feel confident enough to give you step-by-step instructions here—they might not work.

So, as an alternative, I suggest you consult your Windows documentation. Look up topics like *32-bit disk access, Performance, SMARTDrive,* and *Swap File.*

TIPS

- The best way to speed up your system *dramatically* is to get a faster processor, though this isn't cheap. Call your computer's manufacturer, or a PC professional,and ask them what sort of performance upgrades are available for your system.
- You might also want to check the manual that came with your computer system for performance-tuning tips.
- A graphics accelerator card can also improve windows performance, particularly if you work with a lot of pictures and photos. Ask your computer dealer for details.

RELATED SKILLS AND TOPICS

TOPIC	WHERE TO FIND IT
Version	Appendix B

Special Characters

© ® ™ … — – “ ”

Symbols (Times Roman font)

‰ ¢ £ ¥ ½ é ø ÷

Wingdings (Microsoft)

✂ ☎ ☺ & ☒ ⊞ ☑ ✓

Animations (Swfte)

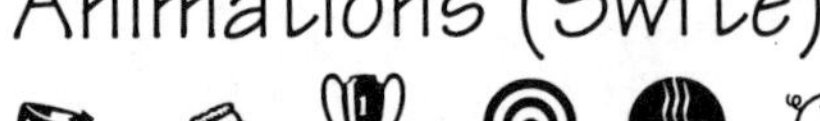

SYMBOLS AND SPECIAL CHARACTERS

1 min.

You're not limited to typing the letters, numbers, and punctuation marks that are on your keyboard. All your Office applications provide easy access to a wide range of other special and foreign characters. You can also purchase optional "dingbat" fonts, which contain only pictures and symbols See Figure S.3 for some examples. (Wingdings comes with Microsoft Windows.)

FIGURE S.3

A few examples of "dingbat" fonts. See Appendix C for names and addresses of these font vendors.

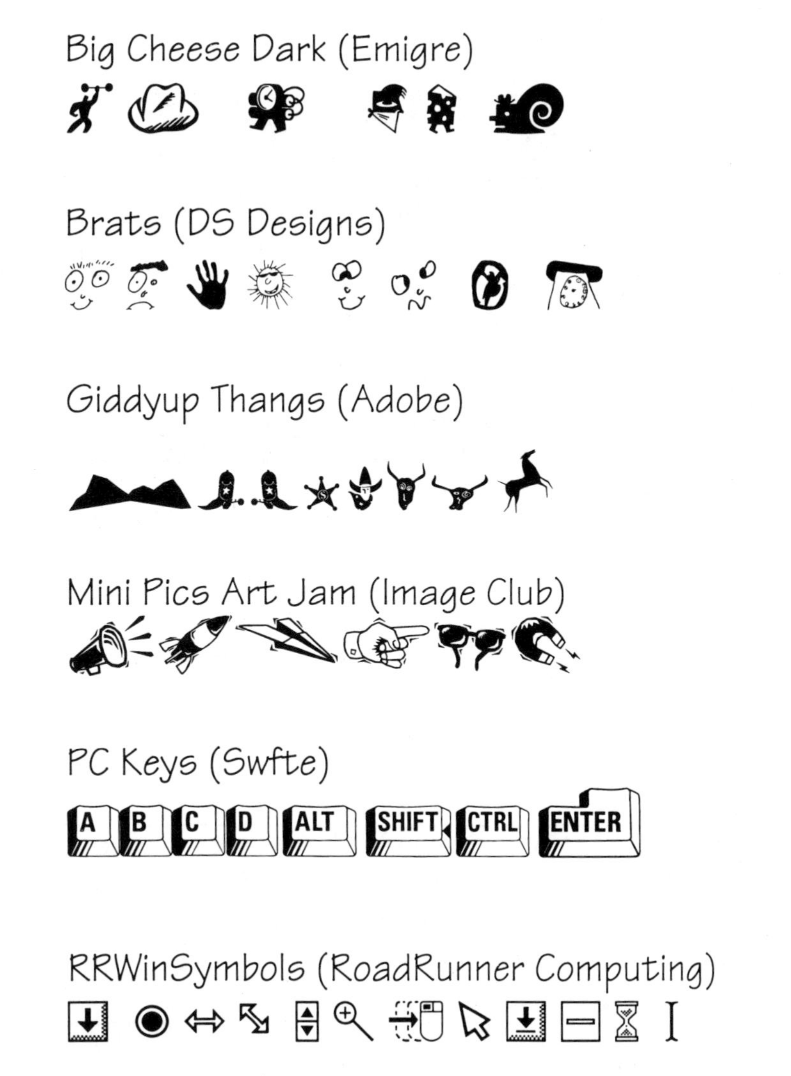

S

STEPS

To insert a special character in your Word document (or spreadsheet, or whatever), follow these steps:

1. In your Microsoft Word document, move the insertion point to where you want to place the special character or symbol.

2. Choose Insert ➢ Symbol from the menu bar. You'll be taken to the Symbol dialog box.

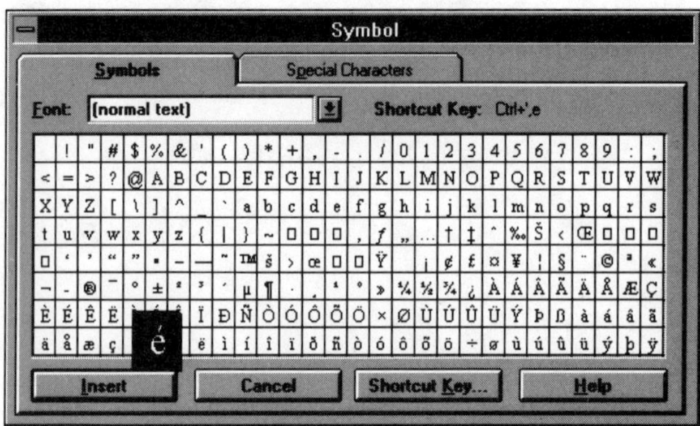

3. Now you can do any of the following, in any order you wish:

- To view commonly used special characters, such as em dashes (—) or copyright symbols (©), click the Special Characters tab.
- To view all the symbols for the current font, click the Symbols tab.
- To view special dingbat characters choose the appropriate font from the Font drop-down list.

NOTE: *The Font option in the Symbol dialog box provides access to all the fonts on your system. But fonts that are based on the standard ANSI or ASCII character set are all listed under the font name* (normal text)*. Dingbat fonts, which don't contain normal alphabetical characters, are listed under the font name.*

- To get a closer look at a symbol, click it once.
- To insert the currently selected (magnified) symbol into your document, click the Insert button.
- When you've finished inserting symbols and special characters, click the Close (or Cancel) button in the Symbol dialog box.
- To change the size of the symbol or special character in your document, first select that character either by dragging the mouse pointer through it, or by holding down the Shift key while pressing the ← or → key. Then choose a font size from

the Formatting toolbar, or choose Format ➢ Font, make your size selection, and choose OK.

STEPS

An Alternative Method

You can use the steps listed above to choose a symbol from any font. Or, as an alternative to going through Insert ➢ Symbol, you can type the appropriate characters and then apply the appropriate font to those characters. Here's how:

1. Type the character or characters that represent the special symbol you want to use. If necessary, you can refer to the character map that comes with most dingbat fonts to determine which character you need to type.
2. Select that text by dragging the mouse pointer through it, or by holding down the Shift key while pressing an arrow key.
3. Select the appropriate font and size from the Font and Size options on the Formatting toolbar, or from the Font dialog box (choose Format ➢ Font in most applications).

Using Special Characters as Bullets

To use a special character as a bullet in a Word document:

1. Choose Format ➢ Bullets and Numbering from Word's menu bar.
2. Click on the Bulleted tab.
3. Click any one of the six bullet designs shown, then choose Modify.
4. Click on the Bullet button in the Modify Bulleted List dialog box that appears.
5. Choose a font from the Symbols From drop-down list.
6. Click on the character that you want to use as the bullet, then choose OK.
7. Choose OK to return to your document.

Creating a Bulleted List

To create a bulleted list in your Word document:

1. If you have not already done so, display the Formatting toolbar (choose View ➢ Toolbars, choose Formatting so it's marked with an X, then choose OK).

2. Type each item in your list, and remember to press ↵ after typing each item.

3. Select the text to be bulleted (or numbered) by dragging the mouse pointer through it, as below.

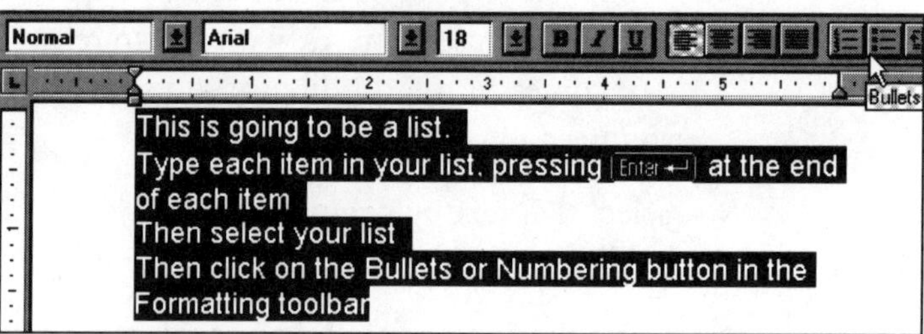

4. Click the Bullets button in the Formatting toolbar (or the Numbering button, if you decide to use a numbered list instead). The list will look something like this:

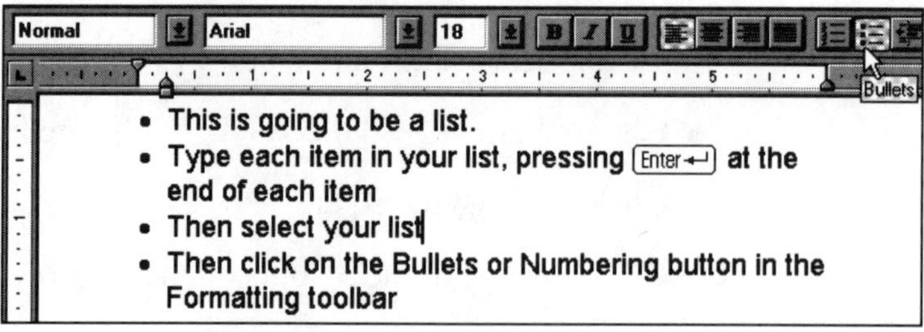

If you end up with too many bullets, just put the insertion point next to any bullet (or number) that has no text next to it, and then click the Bullets (or Numbering) button in the Formatting toolbar again.

To indent or outdent the entire list, first select all the text in the list. Then click the Increase Indent or Decrease Indent button to change the level of indentation.

To modify the format of the bulleted list or change the bullet character, first select all the items in the list. Then right-click the selected text and choose Bullets and Numbering from the menu that appears. Choose Modify, make your selections from the dialog box that appears, then choose OK.

TIPS

- To use a dingbat as a piece of clip art, just display it at a large type size. (72 points equals about 1 inch of height.) If you need to better position the dingbat, select it, then choose Insert ➢ Frame from Word's menu bar. Once the character is framed, you can drag it to any location on the page.
- To rotate a special character or dingbat, use Word Art (see the *Word Art* entry in the *Do-It-Now Encyclopedia*). Choose the font of the symbol from Word Art's toolbar. Then use the Insert Symbol button in the Enter Your Text Here box to insert a character. Then use the Rotate button to rotate.
- For an on-screen demonstration of numbered and bulleted lists, choose Help ➢ Examples and Demos from Word's menu bar. Choose Getting Started, and then click on Adding or removing bullets and numbers in a list. Click on Demo, then follow the instructions on the screen.

RELATED SKILLS AND TOPICS

TOPIC	WHERE TO FIND IT
Help	Appendix B
Microsoft Word	*Instant Office*
Select, Then Do	Appendix B
Typing Text and Numbers	Appendix B
Pictures	*Do-It-Now Encyclopedia*
Word Art	*Do-It-Now Encyclopedia*

METRIC CONVERSION CHART—APPROXIMATIONS

	When You Know	Multiply By	To Find
Length			
	millimeters	0.04	inches
	centimeters	0.39	inches
	meters	3.28	feet
	meters	1.09	yards
	kilometers	0.62	miles
	inches	25.40	millimeters
	inches	2.54	centimeters
	feet	30.48	centimeters
	yards	0.91	meters
	miles	1.61	kilometers
Area			
	square centimeters	0.16	square inches
	square meters	1.20	square yards
	square kilometers	0.39	square miles
	square inches	6.45	square centimeters
	square feet	0.09	square meters
	square yards	0.84	square meters
	square miles	2.60	square kilometers
	acres	0.40	hectares
Mass/Weight			
	grams	0.035	ounce
	kilograms	2.21	pounds
	ounces	28.35	grams
	pounds	0.45	kilograms
Volume			
	milliliters	0.20	teaspoons
	milliliters	0.06	tablespoons
	milliliters	0.03	fluid ounces
	liters	4.23	cups
	liters	2.12	pints
	liters	1.06	quarts
	liters	0.26	gallons
	cubic meters	35.32	cubic feet
	cubic meters	1.35	cubic yards
	teaspoons	4.93	milliliters
	tablespoons	14.78	milliliters
	fluid ounces	29.57	milliliters
	cups	0.24	liters
	pints	0.47	liters
	quarts	0.95	liters
	gallons	3.79	liters

TABLE

   5 min.

Need to organize some text into columns and rows? If it's a fairly small amount of text, use the Microsoft Word Table Wizard to get a head start. If you need to store a lot of information in rows and columns, consider creating an Access database table instead. For instructions, see Database (Create) *here in the* Do-It-Now Encyclopedia.

T

STEPS

1. Start Microsoft Word.
2. Choose File ➢ New from the Word menu bar.
3. Scroll down to Table Wizard and double-click on it.
4. Answer the questions in the Wizard window, then choose Next.
5. Repeat Step 4 until you get to the checkered flag. Answer the questions on that last Wizard window, then choose Finish.
6. You'll be taken to the Table AutoFormat dialog box, where you can further refine the format of your table. Click each option in the Formats list until you see one you like. Figure T.1 on the next two pages shows some examples. Then choose OK.
7. Now you can fill in the table by clicking in any cell and typing into it.

TIPS

- **To print the table in landscape orientation** (sideways on the page), move the cursor to the top of the document (press Ctrl+Home). Choose File ➢ Page Setup, click the Paper Size tab, choose Landscape, and then choose OK.

Grid 1

Train No. ▶	569	571	767	773	575	579	587
San Diego		5:05 A	6:00 A	7:00 A	8:05A	9:00 A	10:05 A
Del Mar		5:40 A	6:35 A	7:35 A	8:40 A	9:40 A	10:45 A
Oceanside		5:58 A	6:53 A	7:53 A	8:55 A	9:55 A	11:05 A
San Clemente		6:31 A	7:23 A	8:20 A	9:22 A	10: 20 A	11:30 A
Capistrano	6:00 A	6:45 A	7:36 A	8:40 A	9:40 A	10:40 A	11:40 A
Irvine	6:13 A	6:57 A	7:48 A	8:48 A	9:48 A	10:50 A	11:50 A
Santa Ana	6:26 A	7:06 A	7:58 A	8:58 A	9:58 A	10:55 A	12:00 P
Orange	6:30 A	7:23 A	8:08 A	9:10 A	10:10 A	11:15 A	12:15 P
Anaheim	6:35 A	8:08 A	8:55 A	9:57 A	10:55 A	11:45 A	12:45 P
Fullerton	6:44 A		9:15 A	10:20 A	11:00 A	12:00 P	1:00 P
Los Angeles	7:02 A		11:00 A	12:00 P	1:00 P	2:00 P	3:00 P

Colorful 3

Train No. ▶	569	571	767	773	575	579	587
San Diego		**5:05 A**	**6:00 A**	**7:00 A**	**8:05A**	**9:00 A**	**10:05 A**
Del Mar		**5:40 A**	**6:35 A**	**7:35 A**	**8:40 A**	**9:40 A**	**10:45 A**
Oceanside		**5:58 A**	**6:53 A**	**7:53 A**	**8:55 A**	**9:55 A**	**11:05 A**
San Clemente		**6:31 A**	**7:23 A**	**8:20 A**	**9:22 A**	**10: 20 A**	**11:30 A**
Capistrano	**6:00 A**	**6:45 A**	**7:36 A**	**8:40 A**	**9:40 A**	**10:40 A**	**11:40 A**
Irvine	**6:13 A**	**6:57 A**	**7:48 A**	**8:48 A**	**9:48 A**	**10:50 A**	**11:50 A**
Santa Ana	**6:26 A**	**7:06 A**	**7:58 A**	**8:58 A**	**9:58 A**	**10:55 A**	**12:00 P**
Orange	**6:30 A**	**7:23 A**	**8:08 A**	**9:10 A**	**10:10 A**	**11:15 A**	**12:15 P**
Anaheim	**6:35 A**	**8:08 A**	**8:55 A**	**9:57 A**	**10:55 A**	**11:45 A**	**12:45 P**
Fullerton	**6:44 A**		**9:15 A**	**10:20 A**	**11:00 A**	**12:00 P**	**1:00 P**
Los Angeles	**7:02 A**		**11:00 A**	**12:00 P**	**1:00 P**	**2:00 P**	**3:00 P**

FIGURE T.1

A few examples of predefined table autoformats (continued on the next page)

3D Effects 3

Train No.	569	571	767	773	575	579	587
San Diego		5:05 A	6:00 A	7:00 A	8:05A	9:00 A	10:05 A
Del Mar		5:40 A	6:35 A	7:35 A	8:40 A	9:40 A	10:45 A
Oceanside		5:58 A	6:53 A	7:53 A	8:55 A	9:55 A	11:05 A
San Clemente		6:31 A	7:23 A	8:20 A	9:22 A	10: 20 A	11:30 A
Capistrano	6:00 A	6:45 A	7:36 A	8:40 A	9:40 A	10:40 A	11:40 A
Irvine	6:13 A	6:57 A	7:48 A	8:48 A	9:48 A	10:50 A	11:50 A
Santa Ana	6:26 A	7:06 A	7:58 A	8:58 A	9:58 A	10:55 A	12:00 P
Orange	6:30 A	7:23 A	8:08 A	9:10 A	10:10 A	11:15 A	12:15 P
Anaheim	6:35 A	8:08 A	8:55 A	9:57 A	10:55 A	11:45 A	12:45 P
Fullerton	6:44 A		9:15 A	10:20 A	11:00 A	12:00 P	1:00 P
Los Angeles	7:02 A		11:00 A	12:00 P	1:00 P	2:00 P	3:00 P

- **To change the width of columns**, drag the column boundary in the horizontal ruler to the left or right, as illustrated below. Or choose Table ➢ Select Table, then choose Table ➢ Cell Height and Width ➢ the Column tab ➢ AutoFit. Or, select the column you want to resize by clicking just above the top of the column. Then choose Table ➢ Cell Height and Width ➢ the Column tab, enter measurements for the Width of Column and Space Between Columns options, then choose OK. (Each method has the same result, they're just different ways of doing the same thing.)

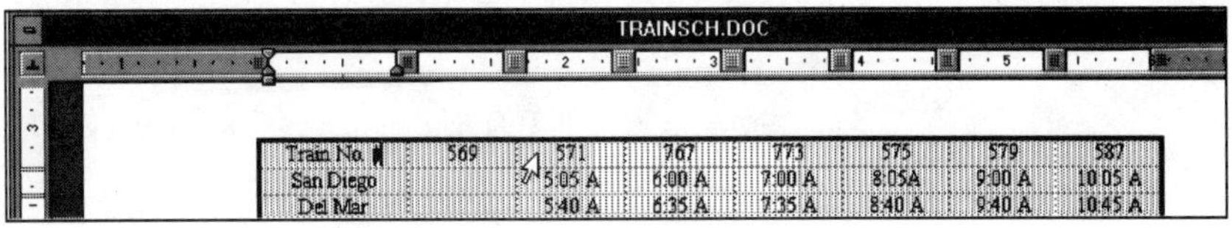

TRAINSCH.DOC

Train No.	569	571	767	773	575	579	587
San Diego		5:05 A	6:00 A	7:00 A	8:05A	9:00 A	10:05 A
Del Mar		5:40 A	6:35 A	7:35 A	8:40 A	9:40 A	10:45 A

- **To change the font, size, weight, or alignment of text or numbers** in a column, select the column by clicking its top edge or by choosing Table ➢ Select Column. Then use the various buttons on the Formatting toolbar to format and align the selected text. If the Formatting toolbar (shown below) isn't visible, choose View ➢ Toolbars ➢ Formatting ➢ OK.

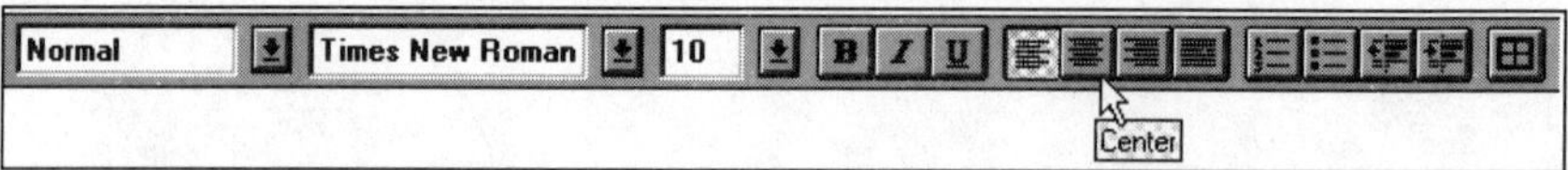

- **To border or shade a column or row,** first select the column(s) or row(s) by clicking at the top edge of the column or the left edge of the row. Then, choose Format ➢ Borders and Shading, then choose appropriate options from the Borders and Shading Tabs. Choose OK.

- **To change the print style in a row or column,** select the row or column that you want to change. Then make your selections from the Formatting toolbar. (If that toolbar is hidden, choose View ➢ Toolbars ➢ Formatting ➢ OK.)

- **To move or copy the table** to another document, put the insertion point anywhere within the table, then choose Table ➢ Select Table. Then, if you want to *move* the table, choose Edit ➢ Cut or press Ctrl+X. If you want to *copy* the table, choose Edit ➢ Copy or press Ctrl+C. Open or switch to the document that you want to put the table in, and position the cursor where you want the table to go. Then choose Edit ➢ Paste or press Ctrl+V.

- **To print the table,** choose File ➢ Print from the Word menu bar or press Ctrl+P. Then choose OK or press ↵.

- **To exit Word,** choose File ➢ Exit from the Word menu. If you want to save the table for future use, or to put into another document, choose Yes, type in a valid file name, then choose OK.

RELATED SKILLS AND TOPICS

TOPIC	WHERE TO FIND IT
Microsoft Word	*Instant Office*
Select, Then Do	Appendix B
Type Text and Numbers	Appendix B
Wizards	Appendix B

T

TEMPLATES (GET MORE)

5 min.

If you like the Invoice, Purchase Order, and Weekly Time sheet templates, illustrated under those headings here in the Do-It-Now Encyclopedia, *I know where you can get a whole bunch more. If you're using pre-designed papers from Paper Direct, you can also get some templates that'll make it much easier to format text on those papers.*

Please don't interpret this section as an inducement to spend money. Neither I, nor the publisher of this book, is affiliated with Paper Direct. We didn't get one red cent for adding this section, nor do we get any money if you place an order with Paper Direct. I've added this section to the Do-It-Now Encyclopedia *only because my goal in this book is to show you the quickest, easiest way to "take care of business" using Microsoft Office, and I would be remiss in that duty if I didn't tell you about these optional time-saving Word templates!*

TEMPLATES FOR ANY PAPER

If you want to make quick work of any business document that's not described in this book, consider purchasing *Smart LaserForms for Word Processing* from Paper Direct (Appendix C). Be sure to get the latest version for Microsoft Word 6.0 for Windows. At about $40.00, it'll probably save about 40 hours of your time even if you just use a few of the

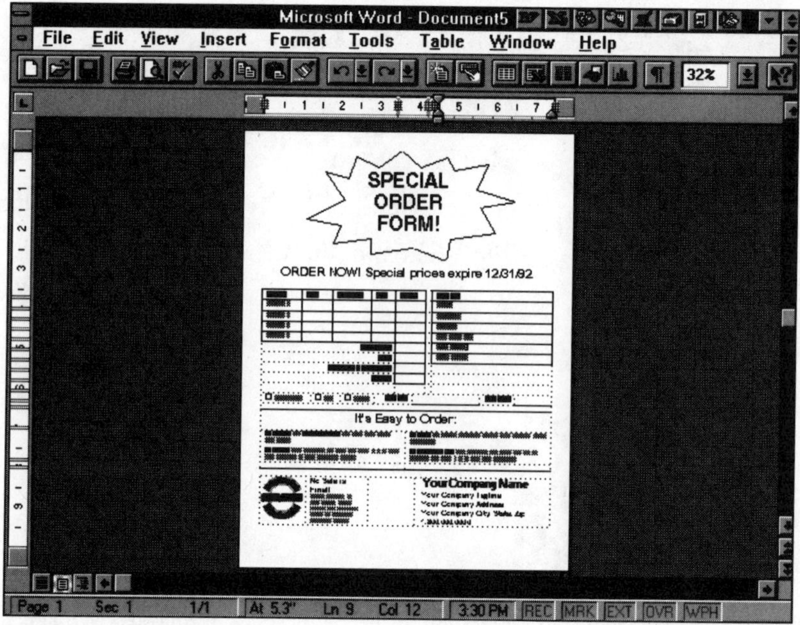

templates. Comes with complete instructions for use with Word, and all of these templates:

Automobile Expense Form
Bill of Lading
Cash Receipt
Commercial Credit Application
Company Phone List
Company Property Receipt
Conference Room Scheduler
Credit Reminder
Daily Calendar
Employee Index
Employee Performance Review
Employee Self-Evaluation Form
Employee Time Off Record
Expense Report

Job Estimate
Monthly Calendar
Order Form Flyer
Packing List
Past Due Notice
Phonebook Advertisement
Price List
Product Data Sheet
Purchase Order
Purchases Log
Quarterly Travel Itinerary
Seminar Evaluation
Service Invoice
Statement of Account

- Fax Cover Sheet
- Fax Log
- Final Credit Notice
- Flyer
- Graph Paper
- Hourly Invoice
- Interview Summary Form
- Invoice
- Job Application Form
- Statement of Services
- Stub Invoice
- Telephone Message Slips
- Telephone Sales Order
- Vacation Checklist
- Weekly Calendar
- Weekly Expense Form
- Weekly Time Sheet
- Yearly Calendar

T

TEMPLATES FOR PREDESIGNED PAPERS

If you use any of Paper Direct's predesigned papers, you'll probably want to get a hold of their Paper Templates Software as well. It contains forms that look just like the predesigned paper, so you can lay out your text correctly on the first try. Costs about $39.95 for the whole set, and comes with complete instructions. Be sure to get the version for Microsoft Word 6.0 for Windows.

RELATED SKILLS AND TOPICS

TOPIC	WHERE TO FIND IT
Invoice	*Do-It-Now Encyclopedia*
Purchase Order	*Do-It-Now Encyclopedia*
Weekly Time Sheet	*Do-It-Now Encyclopedia*

TIMEARIT.XLS

	A	B	C	D
1	TIME ARITHMETIC (Fill shaded cells only)			
2				
3	Known Duration	Duration	Total Duration	Running Time
4	(Min.Sec)	(Seconds)	(Seconds)	(Min.Sec)
5	3.5	230	230	3.50
6	4.25	265	495	8.15
7	2.05	125	620	10.20
8	3.11	191	811	13.31
9	6.5	410	1221	20.21
10	4.55	295	1516	25.16
11	6.1	370	1886	31.26
12	3.46	226	2112	35.12
13	4.11	251	2363	39.23
14	5.55	355	2718	45.18
15	7.5	470	3188	53.08
16	3.12	192	3380	56.20
17	2.58	178	3558	59.18
18	4.5	290	3848	64.08
19	3.33	213	4061	67.41
20	4.53	293	4354	72.34
21	6.15	375	4729	78.49
22	3.55	235	4964	82.44
23	4.32	272	5236	87.16
24	5.05	305	5541	92.21
25	3.15	195	5736	95.36
26	4.01	241	5977	99.37
27	6.05	365	6342	105.42
28	5.05	305	6647	110.47
29	3.55	235	6882	114.42
30	4.5	290	7172	119.32
31				

Sheet1 / Sheet2 / Sheet3 / Sheet4 / Sheet5 / Sheet6

TIME ARITHMETIC

15 min.

If you add 3 minutes 50 seconds (3.50), 4 minutes 25 seconds (4.25) and 2 minutes 5 seconds (2.05), how much time is that all combined? Not easy to work this out in your head, but here is a worksheet that can do this kind of math in a jiffy. Just type your time durations into column A, and Column D will keep a running total of those times. Might come in handy when you need to estimate how long a large job will take, based upon smaller tasks. Or when you're making a cassette or video tape, and need to make sure all the songs or clips will fit onto the tape.

STEPS

Creating the Worksheet

1. Start Microsoft Excel.
2. Select columns A through D by dragging the mouse pointer through the column headings, as shown below.

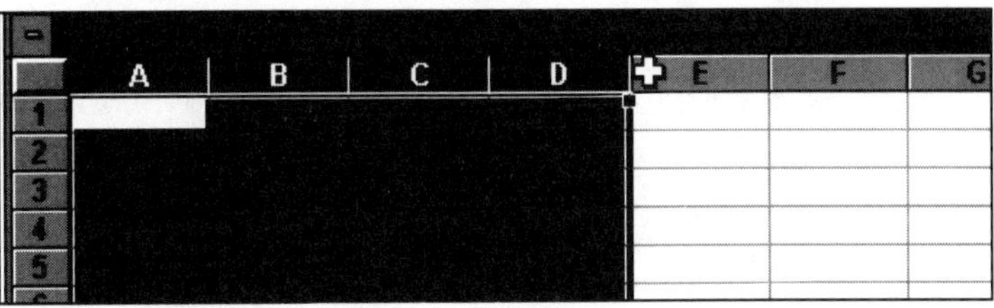

3. With those columns still selected, choose Format ➢ Column ➢ Width,type in **20,** and then choose OK.
4. Using Table T.1 as guide, click on the cell listed in the first column, and then type (literally and exactly) what's shown in the second column. For example, click on cell A1 and type the text **TIME ARITHMETIC (Fill Shaded Cells Only)**. Then click on cell A3 and type the words **Known Duration**. Continue to do so until cells A1 through D5 have been filled.
5. If the Formatting toolbar is not visible, choose View ➢ Toolbars, click on Formatting so it's marked with an X, then choose OK.
6. Click on cell A1, then increase its point size to about 18 using the Size button as shown here.

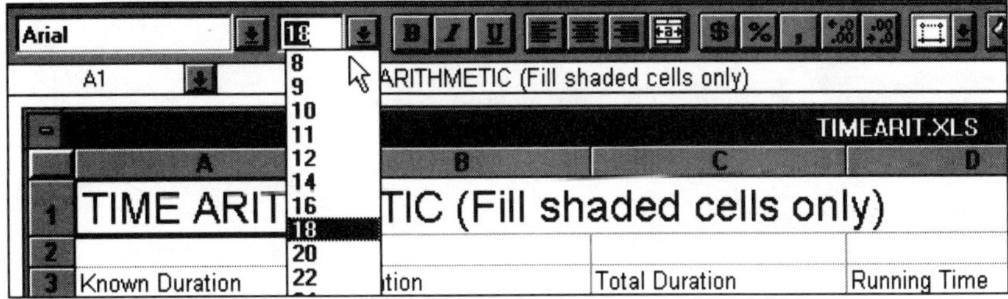

7. Select cells A3 through D4 as shown here. Then click the Bold and Center buttons in the Formatting toolbar.

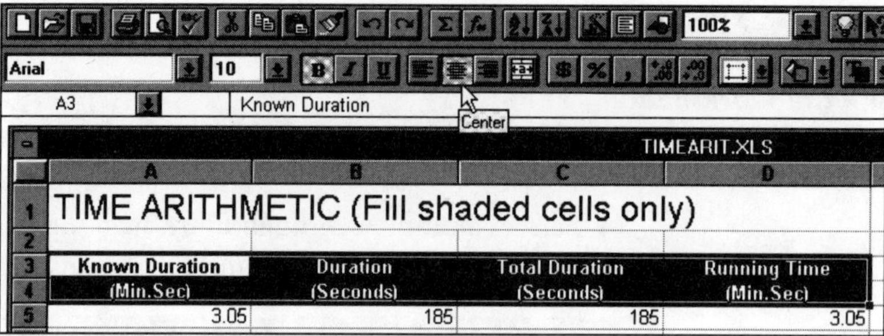

8. Right-click on cell A5, then choose Format Cells from the pop-up menu.

9. Click on the Border tab, then choose Outline. Then click on the Patterns tab and click on a light gray color. Choose OK. Cell A5 is now bordered and shaded.

TABLE T.1

Contents of cells A1 through D5 in the Time Arithmetic worksheet

CELL	EXACT CONTENTS
A1	TIME ARITHMETIC (Fill shaded cells only)
A3	Known Duration
A4	(Min.Sec)
A5	3.05
B3	Duration
B4	(Seconds)
B5	=IF($A5>0,INT($A5)*60+($A5-INT($A5)*100),NA())
C3	Total Duration
C4	(Seconds)
C5	=SUM($B$5:B5)
D3	Running Time
D4	(Min.Sec)
D5	=INT($C5/60)+MOD($C5,60)/100

10. Click cell A5 again, and choose Edit ➢ Clear ➢ Contents. Cell A5 is now empty but still shaded. The formulas to the right show *#N/A* now, which stands for "number not available." That's OK for right now.

11. Right-click on cell D5 and choose Format Cells from the pop-up menu. Click on the Number tab and choose **0.00** under Format Codes. Choose OK. The cell still shows *#N/A*, but will show numbers with two decimal places later when you start using the worksheet.

12. Select cells A5 through D5 by dragging the mouse pointer through them. Notice the fill handle in the lower-right corner of the selected group of cells.

	A	B	C	D
1	TIME ARITHMETIC (Fill shaded cells only)			
2				
3	Known Duration	Duration	Total Duration	Running Time
4	(Min.Sec)	(Seconds)	(Seconds)	(Min.Sec)
5	3.05	185	185	3.05
6				
7				
8				
9				

13. Now put the mouse pointer right on that little fill handle. You'll know the pointer is properly positioned when the mouse pointer changes to a solid black plus sign (+).

14. Drag the fill handle down to about row 30. Press Ctrl+Home to move back to the top of the worksheet. Your screen should now look something like Figure T.2.

15. To protect formulas and headings, first clear the locks from the cells you'll be changing. That is, select cells A5 to A30 (the shaded cells) by dragging the mouse pointer through them. Then choose Format ➢ Cells, click the Protection tab, clear the Locked checkbox, then choose OK.

16. To protect those cells which remain locked, choose Tools ➢ Protection ➢ Protect Sheet ➢ OK.

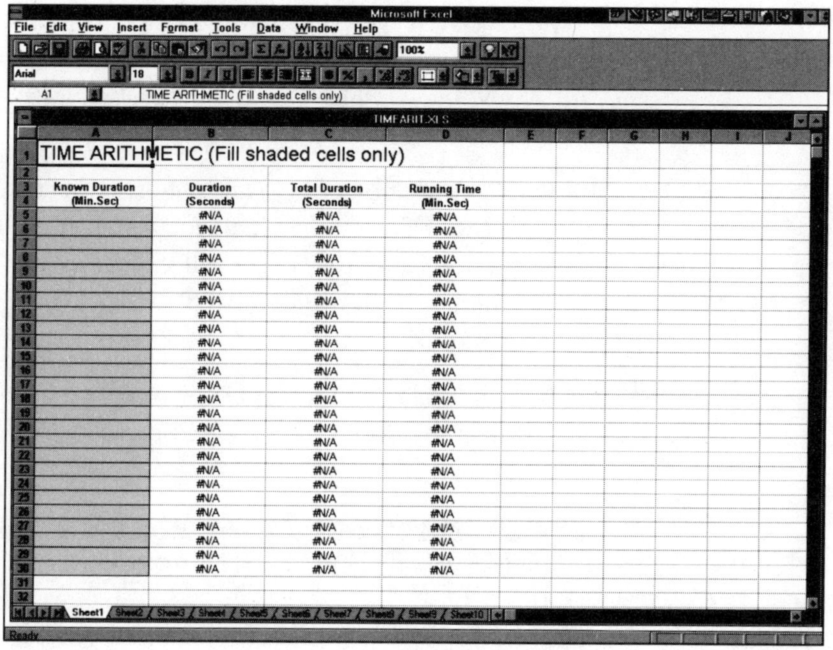

FIGURE T.2

After you copy cells A5 through D5, and copy them down to about row 30, your worksheet will look something like this. So far, so good.

17. Now close and save the completed worksheet. To do so, choose File ➢ Close ➢ Yes, type in a valid file name such as **timearit**, and then choose OK.

That's it—the worksheet is created and saved. Now you can follow the steps below at any time you wish to use that worksheet.

STEPS

Using the Time Arithmetic Worksheet

1. If Excel isn't on your screen right now, start Microsoft Excel.
2. Choose File ➢ Open and double-click the name of the time arithmetic worksheet (e.g., **TIMEARIT.XLS**).
3. Move to cell A5 and type in a time in *mm.ss* format. For example, to type in 3 minutes and 5 seconds, you would type **3.05**. To type in 4 minutes and 55 seconds, type in **4.55**.
4. Move down to the next shaded cell, and type in the next number in the same *mm.ss* format. Keep doing so until you've typed in all the time durations that you need to sum.

Notice how columns B, C, and D convert and sum the times that you enter, as follows:

COLUMN	SHOWS
A	Time you entered in *mm.ss* format, or nothing if blank.
B	Your time, from column A, converted to seconds. Or #N/A if no data in column A of this row
C	Running total of seconds, or #N/A if no data available in this row
D	Running total of times, in *mm.ss* format, or #N/A if no data available in column A of this row

Any row that you don't put a duration into just shows #N/A where the calculations would normally appear, to inform you that there is no data on that row to add to the existing totals.

TIPS

- When you're ready to print the completed worksheet, use the standard technique (click the Print button, or choose File ➢ Print ➢ OK).
- For more information on ways you can manage dates and times with Excel, search Excel's help for time functions.
- The INT (integer) and MOD (modulo) functions used in the Time Arithmetic worksheet are general math functions. Search Excel's help for *math functions.*
- To close the worksheet when you're done with it, choose File ➢ Exit ➢ No. You'll be returned to home base, the Windows Program Manager.

RELATED SKILLS AND TOPICS

TOPIC	WHERE TO FIND IT
Microsoft Excel	*Instant Office*
Select, Then Do	Appendix B
Type Text and Numbers	Appendix B

Electron Studios
Where Electrons Dance
11021 Montgomery Highway
San Diego, CA 92056
619.555.3920 Fax 619.555.3921

Employee Name: Mindy Monkhouse — Title: Editorial Assistant
Employee Number: A-123 — Status: Full-time
Department: Editorial — Supervisor: DEK

Date	Start Time	End Time	Regular Hrs.	Overtime Hrs.	Total Hrs.
9/5/94	8:00 AM	4:30 PM	8.5		8.5
9/6/94	9:00 AM	5:00 PM	8		8
9/6/94	5:00 PM	7:00 PM		2	2
9/7/94	8:00 AM	5:00 PM	8		8
9/8/94	8:00 AM	5:00 PM	8		8
9/9/94	8:00 AM	5:00 PM	8		8
9/10/94	8:00 AM	12:00 PM		4	4
		WEEKLY TOTALS	40.5	6	46.5

Employee Signature: — Date:
Supervisor Signature: — Date:

WEEKLY TIME SHEET

15 min.

Microsoft Word includes a template for typing up a weekly time sheet. To use the template, first personalize it to your own needs. You only have to do that once. In the future, whenever you need to type up a time sheet, just fill in the blanks on the screen.

STEPS

Personalizing the Time Sheet

Before you actually use the weekly time sheet for the first time, you'll want to personalize it a bit. To do so, follow the steps on the next page.

1. Start Microsoft Word.
2. Choose File ➢ Open from the Word menu bar.
3. Under List Files of Type, choose **Document Templates (*.dot)** (see Figure W.1).
4. Under Directories, choose the **TEMPLATE** directory by double-clicking that name. (If you have trouble finding a directory, see *Drives, Directories, and Files* in Appendix B.)
5. Under File Name, scroll down to, and double-click on **WEEK-TIME.DOT.**

FIGURE W.1

To personalize the Weekly Time Sheet template, first open the document template named WEEKTIME.DOT on the templates directory.

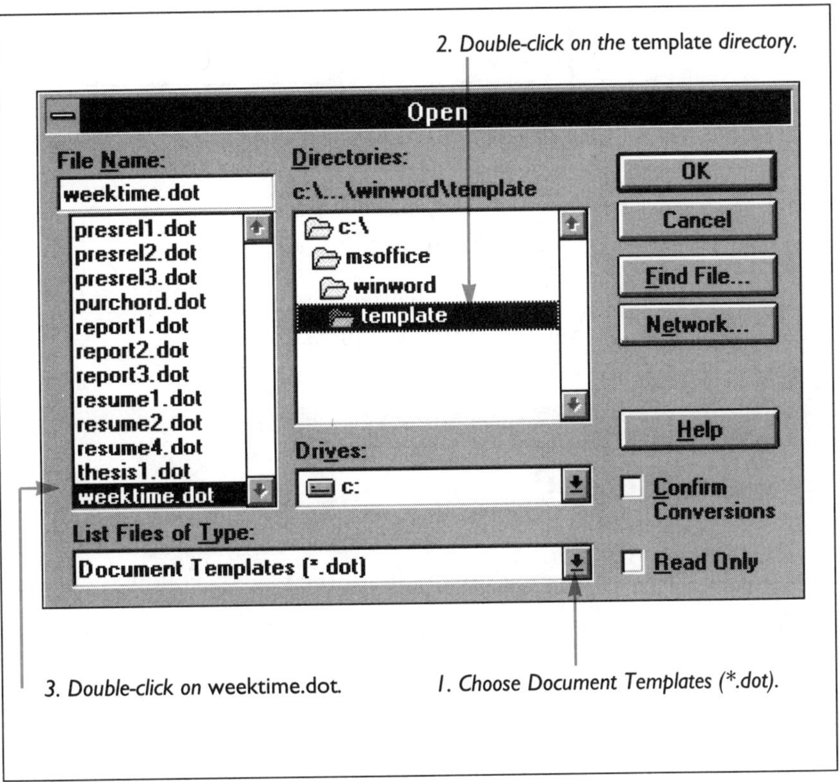

6. Choose Tools ➢ Unprotect Document from the Word menu bar.
7. Select the placeholder **Your Company Name** by dragging the

mouse pointer through it. Then type in your own company name.

8. Repeat Step 7 to replace the placeholders for your company slogan, address, and phone numbers, as in the example shown below.

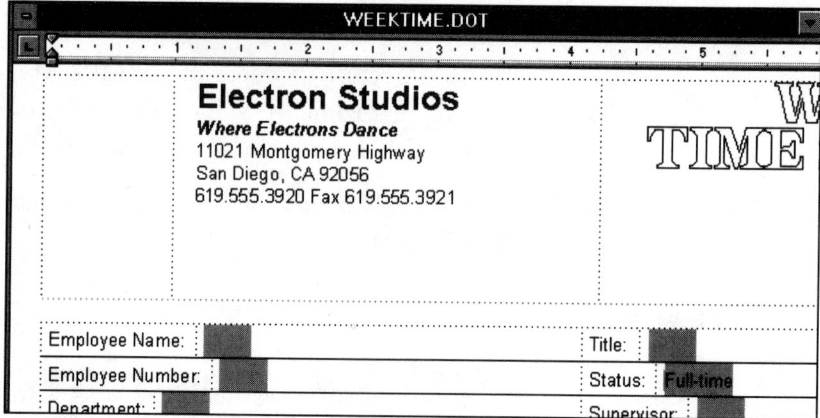

9. Choose Tools ➢ Protect Document ➢ Forms ➢ OK.

10. Choose File ➢ Close ➢ Yes.

Your personalized version of WEEKTIME.DOT replaces the original version of that template.

STEPS

Typing Up a Time Sheet

Once you've personalized your time sheet template, you need only open it up and fill in the blanks. Follow these steps:

1. Start Microsoft Word (if it isn't already started).
2. Choose File ➢ New from the Word menu bar.
3. Scroll down to, and double-click on **Weektime**.
4. Move the cursor to any blank field (gray area), using the mouse or Tab and Shift+Tab keys. Then type your entry into that field. The status bar near the lower-left corner of the screen shows a brief description of what's expected, and the format to use when typing

in information (e.g., **8:00 AM** for eight o'clock in the morning).

5. Be sure to type in the number of Regular Hours and/or Overtime Hours worked in each row. Those times are *not* calculated automatically from the Start Time and End Time. However, Total Hours and Weekly Totals *are* computed automatically from the Regular Hours and Overtime Hours you type in.

6. After you've filled in all the blanks required to complete your time sheet, choose File ➢ Print ➢ OK to print it.

7. When you're done, choose File ➢ Exit to start working your way back to the Windows Program Manager. You can then decide whether to keep a copy of that particular time sheet on disk when asked about saving it.

TIPS

- As an alternative to using up disk space to save a copy of every time sheet, you can just print two copies of each one; one to submit, the other to keep in your own files.

RELATED SKILLS AND TOPICS

TOPIC	WHERE TO FIND IT
Microsoft Word	*Instant Office*
Select,Then Do	Appendix B
Type Text and Numbers	Appendix B

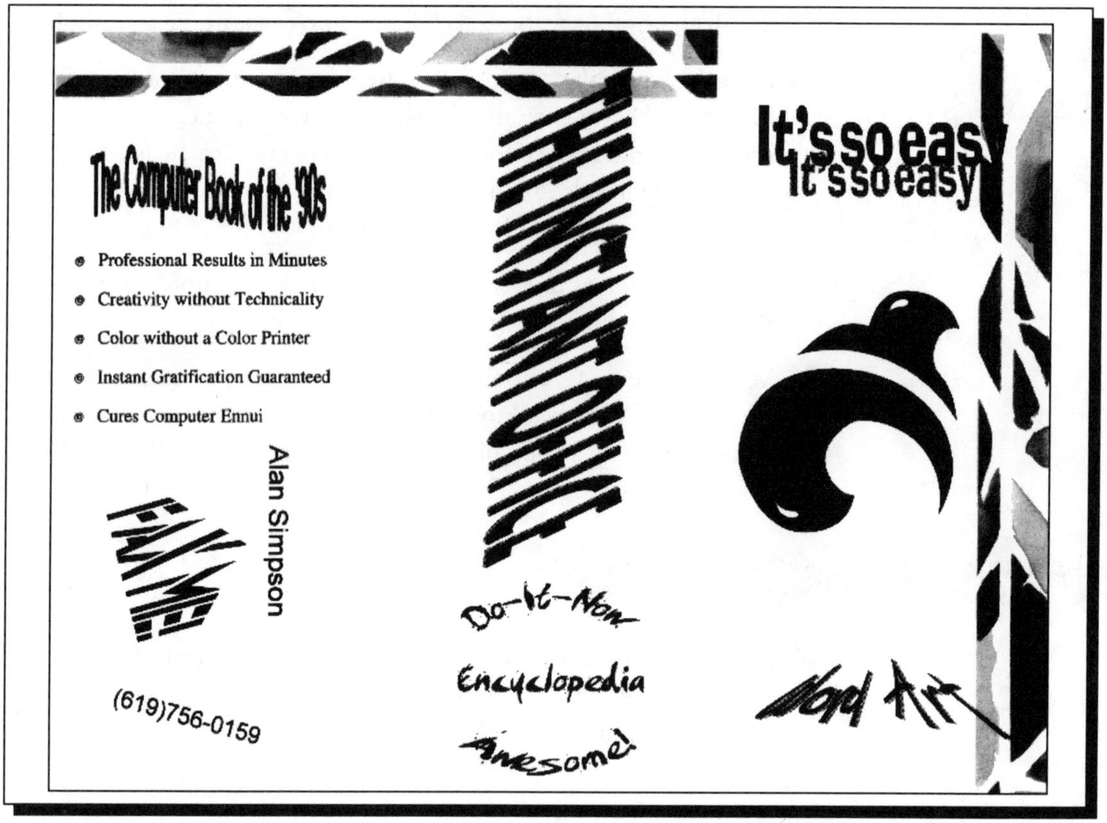

The Computer Book of the '90s

- Professional Results in Minutes
- Creativity without Technicality
- Color without a Color Printer
- Instant Gratification Guaranteed
- Cures Computer Ennui

Alan Simpson

FAX ME!

(619)756-0159

THE INSTANT OFFICE

Do-It-Now

Encyclopedia

Awesome!

It's so easy

It's so easy

Word Art

WORD ART

Depends how hooked you get.

When you really want to add a little pizzazz to a document, try a little Word Art. It'll let you stretch, bend, slant, rotate, shape, and add all kinds of special effects to your text. It's fun. It's easy. But be careful, because it's also habit-forming!

STEPS

You can get to Word Art from any Microsoft Office application by following the steps below. But since you're most likely going to want to use it in your Word documents, I'll assume you're starting from Word.

1. Start Microsoft Word and either create or open the document that you want to put some Word Art into.
2. Move the cursor to about where you want to place your Word Art, then choose Insert ➢ Object from Word's menu bar.
3. Click on Microsoft Word Art 2.0, then choose OK. The menu bar and toolbar both change to Word Art commands. A small Enter Your Text Here dialog box for typing your Word Art also appears on the screen, as in Figure W.2. (You can still see your regular document behind the Word Art window as well.)

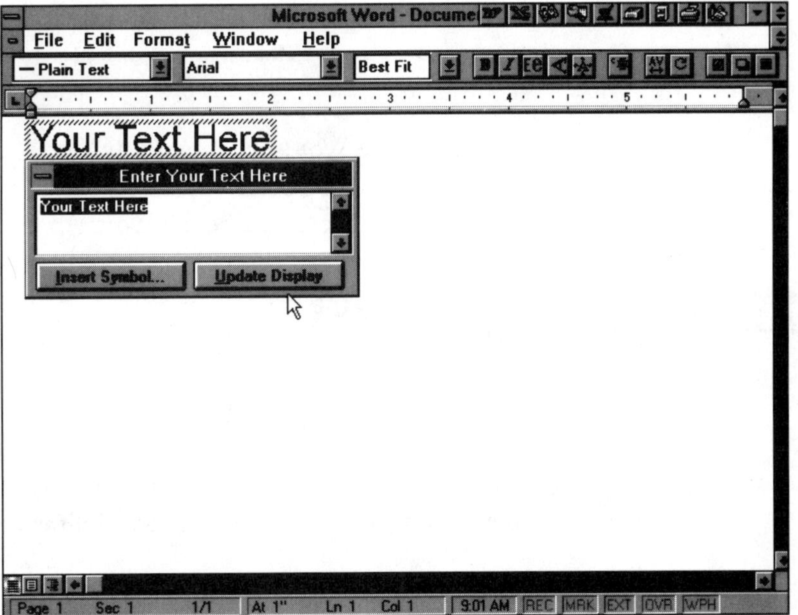

FIGURE W.2

When Word Art is in control, the menu bar and Toolbar display Word Art commands, and a small Enter Your Text Here dialog box appears.

4. Type the text you want to apply Word Art to. To type several lines, just press ↵ after each line (but keep it to a maximum of three or four lines, for simplicity's sake). Then click the Update Display button.
5. If you can't see your newly typed text behind the Word Art box, just drag that box to a new location.
6. Now have some fun. Try out the various tools on the toolbar, as shown in Figure W.3, just to see what you get. Go on, be brave, have some fun. Experiment! You can't hurt anything.

W

FIGURE W.3

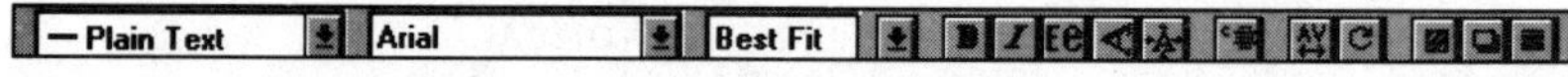

Use options in the Word Art toolbar to stylize your text.

7. When you're done stylizing your text, just click anywhere in your document *except* on the actual Word Art and its dialog box. The normal Word menu bar and toolbar(s) reappear. The Word Art is in a box, with sizing handles.
8. If you need to resize the Word Art box, drag any sizing handle.
9. To better position the box, first make sure it's selected (so it has sizing handles). Then choose Insert ➢ Frame from Word's menu bar. Then you can drag the Word Art to any location in your document. To size/position the framed Word Art more precisely, choose Format ➢ Frame. Make your choices in the Frame dialog box, then choose OK.
10. To change the Word Art, double-click it. The Word Art menu bar, toolbar, and dialog box reappear. As before, when you're done editing, click anywhere outside the Word Art and its dialog box.

TIPS

- Word Art has its own help system. When the Word Art Enter Your Text dialog box is visible, pressing F1 brings up help for Word Art.
- The best way to learn about Word Art is to just relax and experiment with all the options. The possibilities are endless!

RELATED SKILLS AND TOPICS

TOPIC	WHERE TO FIND IT
Pictures	*Do-It-Now Encyclopedia*
Promotional Kit	*Do-It-Now Encyclopedia*
Symbols and Special Characters	*Do-It-Now Encyclopedia*

APPENDIX A

Absolute "How To" Basics

THIS APPENDIX COVERS the absolute basics—the very things that most computer books assume you already know, and don't bother to explain. Those basic skills include:

- How to start your PC and Windows
- How to use a mouse (click, double-click, right-click, etc.)
- How to work a keyboard (press *key+key* combination keystrokes and such)
- How to work Microsoft Windows (open, close, size, move, and uncover windows on your screen)

If you already know how to do all that, skip this appendix. No need to relearn all those basic skills just to learn about Office.

But those of you who are new to PCs and don't know a mouse click from a monitor should definitely start here. A word of advice: You'll probably find it all to be much, much easier than you thought it would be. But just in case you have problems, I've added a *First Aid* section to the end of this appendix, to help you resolve those common problems quickly.

Get Fired Up

First things first, let's start with how to turn on your computer. Refer to Figure AA.1 for some buzzwords. Then follow these steps.

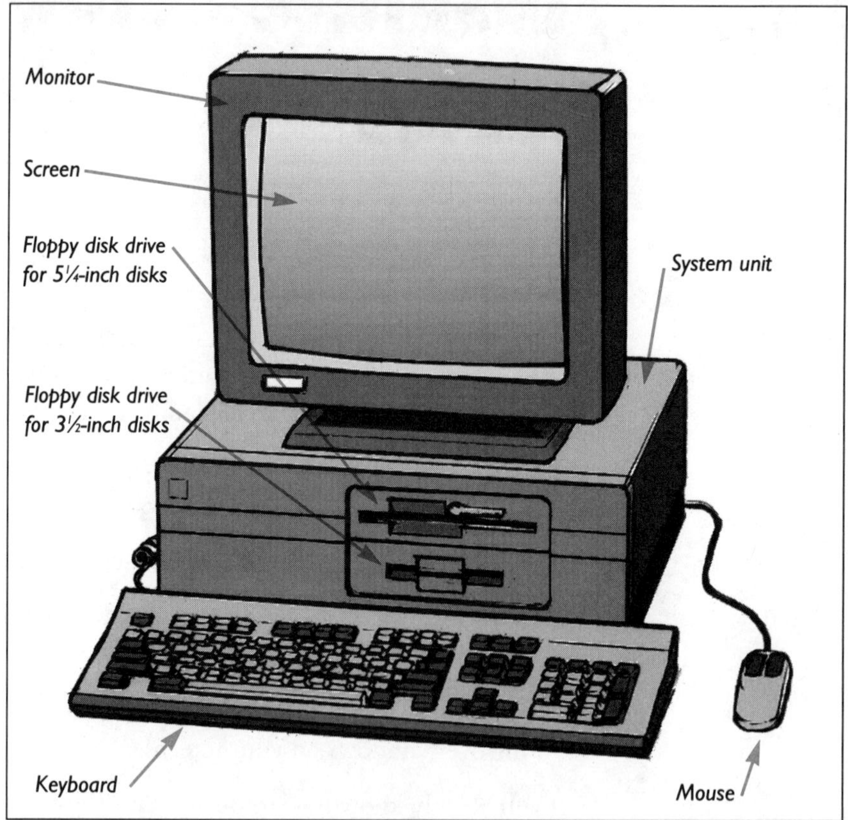

FIGURE AA.1

A typical desktop computer system.

1. Make sure the floppy disk drive is empty, or at least open. To do that, press the little Eject button on the front of the drive. Or, if the drive has a latch in front, swing that latch to the right and up, so the slot into the drive is no longer blocked, as in Figure AA.1 (the 5.25" drive). If you have two floppy drives, open or empty both of them.

TIP: *In case you're wondering, the floppy drives need to be open or empty at startup to force your computer to "boot up" from the hard disk that's inside the computer. That's where DOS and Windows, the programs you want to start with, are located. If your hard disk ever "crashes," you can always start your computer by putting a "bootable floppy" disk in drive A. If you ever have that problem, see your DOS documentation for more information.*

2. Turn on the printer and any other gadgets that are connected to the computer (such as a CD-ROM drive). Look around for the appropriate On/Off switches, which may be labeled 0 for Off and 1 for On.
3. Turn on the monitor (if it has its own on/off switch).
4. Turn on the main power switch, which is most likely on the system unit, and wait a few seconds.

You may hear some beeping and buzzing, and see indecipherable little messages whiz by on the screen as the computer goes through its warm-up (called, officially, the Power On Self Test or POST). You can ignore any messages that you don't understand.

When the computer is "booted up" (finished with its little warm-up ritual), the screen stops changing and awaits your commands. Your computer might start up in DOS, or Windows (see Figure AA.2), or something else. What you do next depends on where your screen ends up:

- **If your computer starts in Windows**, you've learned your first basic skill. Go straight to the next section, titled *How to Work a Mouse.*
- **If your computer starts in DOS**, go to the section titled *Get into Windows* below.
- **If your computer starts in neither DOS nor Windows**, refer to *First Aid: Startup Troubles* near the end of this appendix.

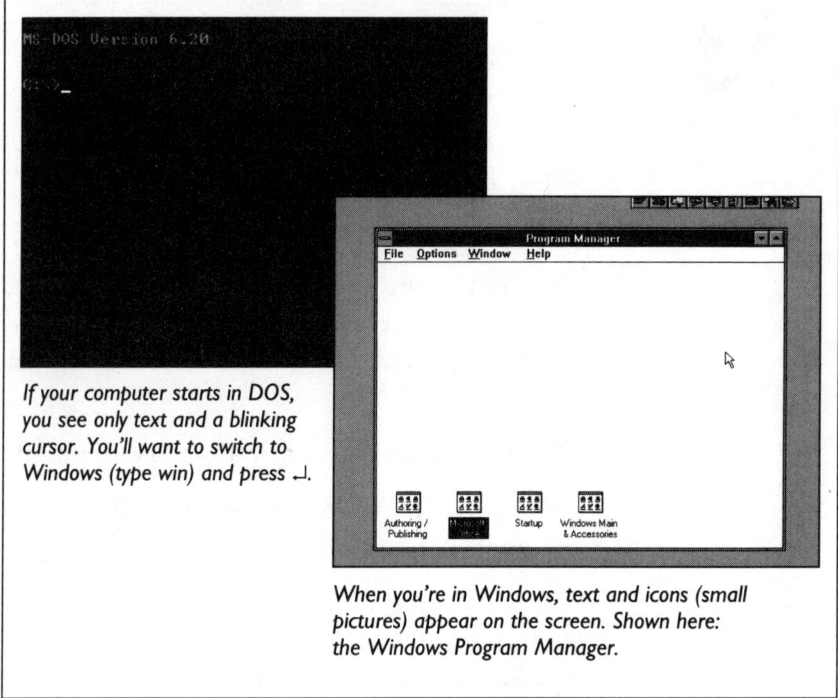

If your computer starts in DOS, you see only text and a blinking cursor. You'll want to switch to Windows (type win) and press ↵.

When you're in Windows, text and icons (small pictures) appear on the screen. Shown here: the Windows Program Manager.

FIGURE AA.2

If your computer starts in DOS, you see only text and a DOS prompt (typically C:\> followed by a blinking cursor). If your computer starts in Windows, you see text and icons (little pictures).

Get into Windows

Windows (not DOS) will be your "home base" whenever you're using Microsoft Office. If your computer starts in DOS, follow this one step to switch to Windows:

- Using your keyboard, type **win** and then press ↵.

Windows should appear on your screen within a few seconds.

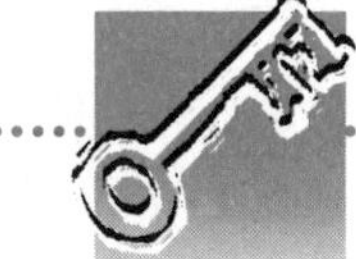

How to Work a Mouse

The easiest way to bark orders at the computer when you're using Windows is with your mouse. As you'll see, the basic idea is simple. You roll the mouse around until the mouse pointer on the screen is touching the thing you want. Then you just click (or double-click) the little mouse button to say "I want *that* thing."

Taming the Mouse

To use a mouse, just lay your hand on it comfortably, so that your right index finger rests gently on the left mouse button, as below. Or, if you're left-handed, use your left hand, and rest your index finger on the mouse button that's on the right side of the mouse.

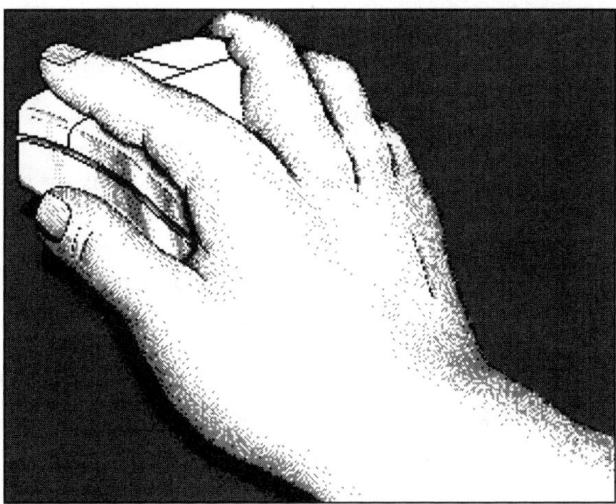

As you roll the mouse around on your desktop or rubber mouse pad, you should see a small *mouse pointer* moving around on the screen, in the same general direction that you move the mouse. (If your "pointing device" is a trackball or j-mouse, see the manual that came with that pointing device for instructions on using it.)

Mouse Clicks

To use the mouse productively, you first need to understand a few terms:

Mouse pointer: The thing on the screen that moves when you move the mouse. Most of the time it just looks like a little arrow.

Icon: A little picture on your screen. Here are a couple of icons that may (or may not) be visible on your screen at the moment.

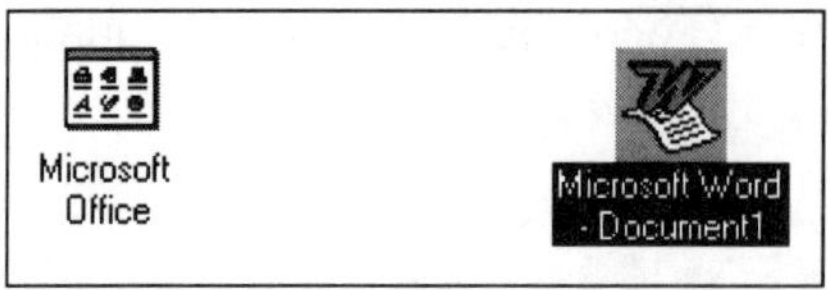

Point to: This means to move the mouse pointer so that it's touching the icon you want. For example, below I'm *pointing to* the Microsoft Office icon.

Mouse button: The mouse button that naturally rests under your index finger—the button on the left when you're using a "normal" (right-handed) mouse.

Click: Point to an object on the screen, then press and quickly release the mouse button (once). The mouse makes a little clicking sound and (usually) something happens on the screen.

Double-click: Point to an object on the screen, then press and release the mouse button twice in rapid succession. Click-click, as fast as you can.

Right-click: Point to an object on the screen, then press and release the "other" mouse button (usually the one on the right-hand side, or the button that rests under your middle or ring finger).

Drag: Point to an object on the screen, then press and hold down the mouse button, while moving the mouse. The pointer "drags" the object across the screen as you move the mouse. Don't release the mouse pointer until you've finished dragging.

Hands-On Mouse Workout

If you want to get a little hands-on practice using a mouse, try the Windows tutorial. Follow these steps:

1. Assuming you can see the Windows Program Manager on your screen, first click the Window titled Program Manager to bring that window to the forefront. If Program Manager is a just a little icon,

as below, first double-click that icon to open the Program Manager window. Or, if you can't get the double-click right, just click the icon once. Then click on Restore in the little menu that appears.

2. Now, look to the menu bar just under the Program Manager title, and click on Help. A menu appears. Click on Windows Tutorial, as illustrated below.

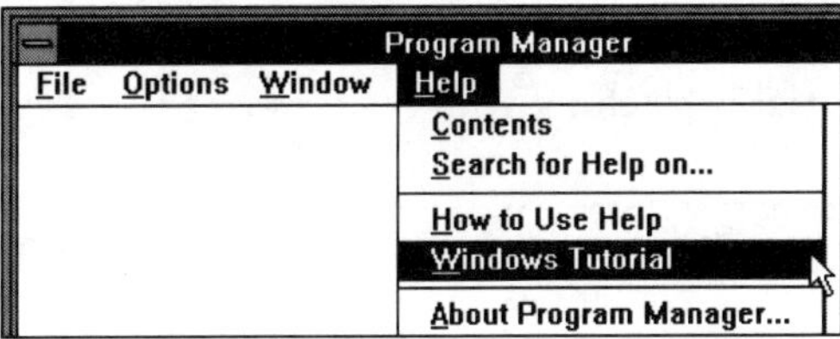

3. Type the letter **m** to try the mouse lessons.

4. Follow all the instructions that appear on the screen.

TIP: *The ENTER key that the tutorial refers to from time to time may be labeled Enter, Return, or just ↵, on your keyboard.*

5. When you've finished with the tutorial, press the Escape key (sometimes labeled Esc), and follow the instructions on the screen.

You'll be returned to your home base, the Windows Program Manager.

Mouse Tips

It takes a little time to get your hand-eye coordination just right when you're first learning to use a mouse. Here are some tips that might help if you have problems:

- Keep your eye on the screen, and make sure the mouse pointer is touching *exactly* the thing you want before you click or double-click.

- Be careful not to move the mouse as you click, otherwise you might inadvertently click the wrong thing (which can be confusing).
- You can switch between a right- and left-handed mouse using the Mouse icon in the Windows Control Panel (please see your Windows documentation)
- You can also control the double-click rate using the Mouse icon in the Windows Control Panel.
- If your mouse has three buttons, you can just ignore the middle button.
- If you still feel klutzy with a mouse, try repeating the Windows Tutorial until you feel comfortable. And pay attention to what that tutorial is teaching you!

How to Work the Keyboard

Most of the keys on the computer keyboard are laid out like a standard typewriter's keys. That's good news for those of you who can type, because you'll be able to type just as well on a computer. If you can't type worth beans, well, that may not be too much of a problem. Use the mouse whenever possible, and limit your typing to things you must type. More on this under *First Aid: Keyboard Troubles* near the end of this appendix.

Good Keys to Know

There are a few special keys on the keyboard that you'll need to use from time to time. Most of these keys do *nothing* when you're in the Windows Program Manager. So don't bother to try them right now. But for future reference, those special keys are pointed out in Figure AA.3 and summarized below:

Esc (escape): Generally used to "escape" from unknown territory and hence likely to be your best friend for a while. Pressing Esc won't back you out of *every* conceivable jam. But it's a good thing to try first when there's something weird on your screen. You can live by this motto:

> **If in doubt,**
>
> **Escape key out**

FIGURE AA.3

A few special keys you'll need to use from time to time.

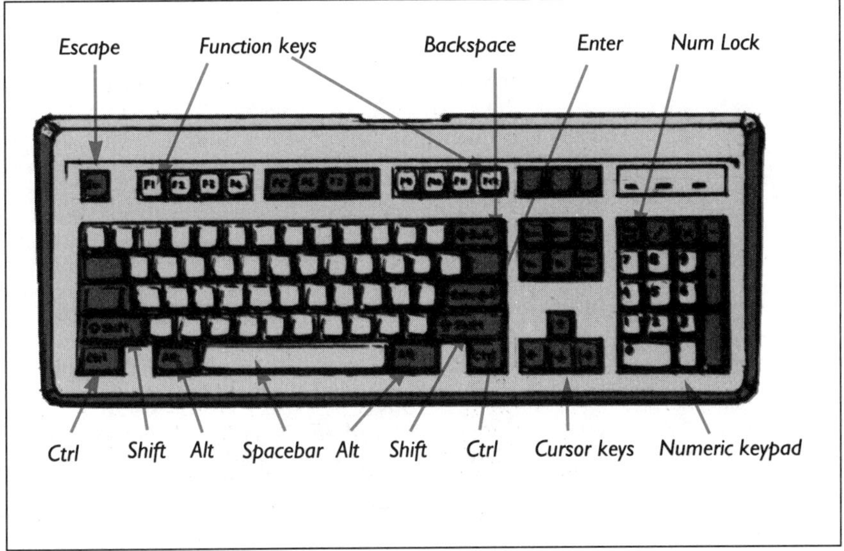

Function Keys: Keys labeled F1, F2, and so forth are called *function keys.* When you see an instruction like "press F2," press the function key labeled F2 (don't type the letter F, then the number 2).

Backspace: Erases the character to the left of the cursor on the screen. Use this to correct simple mistakes when you're actually typing on the screen.

Numeric Keypad: The numeric keypad keys are laid out like an adding machine's keys. However, these keys type numbers *only* when the Num Lock is turned on. When the Num Lock key is turned off, the cursor keys take effect.

Cursor Keys: (Also called the cursor-positioning keys). The →,←, ↑, ↓, Home, End, PgUp, and PgDn keys will all help you move around on the screen. But they only work in certain situations, which I'll describe a little later (when you can actually use those keys). For now, just know that some keyboards have their cursor keys on the numeric keypad. However, those cursor keys only take effect when the Num Lock key is turned off.

Num Lock: Determines whether the keys on the numeric keypad type numbers or move the cursor. Turning Num Lock "On" activates the number. Turning Num Lock "Off" activates the cursor-positioning keys.

Enter (↵): This key (sometimes called the *return* key, or *carriage return*) plays a couple of roles on the computer. In general, you'll use it to select a highlighted item on the screen, or to start a new line when you're typing.

Tab: Depending on what you're doing at the moment, pressing Tab either indents your text, as on a regular typewriter, or, when you're making a decision about what option to go to, moves you from one option to another.

Spacebar: As on a regular typewriter, inserts a blank space between words.

Shift, Alt, and Ctrl: The Shift, Ctrl (control), and Alt (alternate) keys don't do anything by themselves. Instead, they're always used in combination keystrokes (described next). On most keyboards there are two sets, so you can use either hand to hold down one of these keys while tapping another key.

Combination Keystrokes (Key+Key)

When using your computer, you may occasionally be given instructions like "press Shift+F1" or "press Ctrl+A" or "press Alt+X." Whenever you see a plus sign (+) between two keys, that means "hold down the first key, tap the second key, then release the first key." Don't even *try* to press the keys simultaneously.

For example, when you see an instruction that says "press Ctrl+Esc," that means *(1)* Hold down the Ctrl key, *(2)* Press, and release the Esc key, and *then (3)* release the Ctrl key.

Incidentally, if you just pressed Ctrl+Esc, you may now be looking at a dialog box named Task List on your screen. Just press Esc to escape out of it.

O is not Zero, L is not 1

If you took typing eons ago, they may have told you to use the letter *O* for the number zero, and use the letter *l* for the number one. *Don't* do that on a computer keyboard. When you need to type a one or zero, use the appropriate number keys near the top of the keyboard, or on the numeric keypad when Num Lock key is on.

"Any" Key

Occasionally, you might see a message on your screen that says something like:

```
Press any key to continue...
```

Actually, the message should say "Press a letter, number, ↵, or the space bar," because pressing any other key might not work. If in doubt, just press the spacebar or ↵ (the two largest keys on most keyboards).

Take Control of Windows

When you first start your computer and Windows, you're automatically taken to the Windows Program Manager. You can easily recognize the Program Manager window by its title bar (see Figure AA.4).

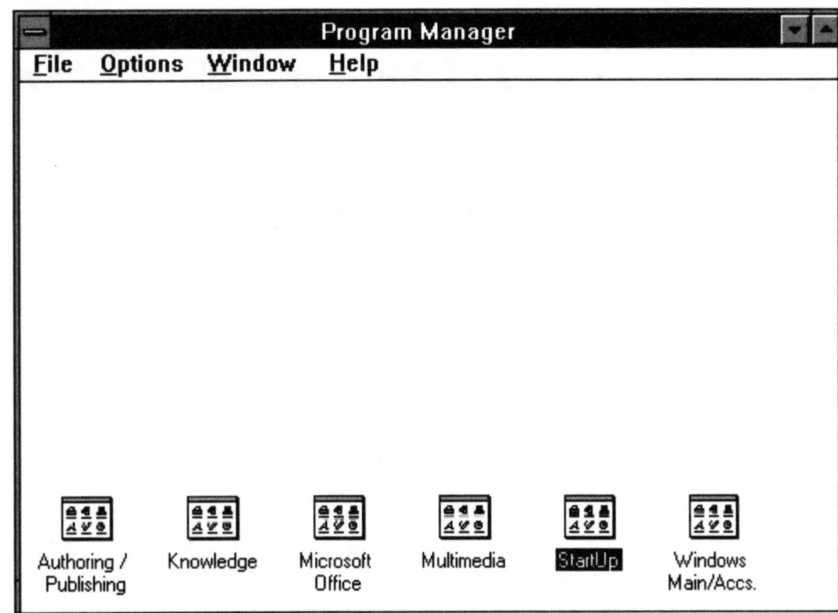

FIGURE AA.4

The Windows Program Manager with application groups appearing as icons within the Program Manager window. Yours probably won't look exactly like this one. But it will have the words "Program Manager" in the title bar up top.

Life would be simple if everyone's screen looked just like my Figure AA.4 at startup. But not everyone's figured out how to keep their screen quite so tidy and uncluttered. In fact, when I fire up someone else's computer, their screen often comes up looking more like Figure AA.5.

FIGURE AA.5

Program Manager is also on this person's screen. But there's so much clutter, it's hard to tell.

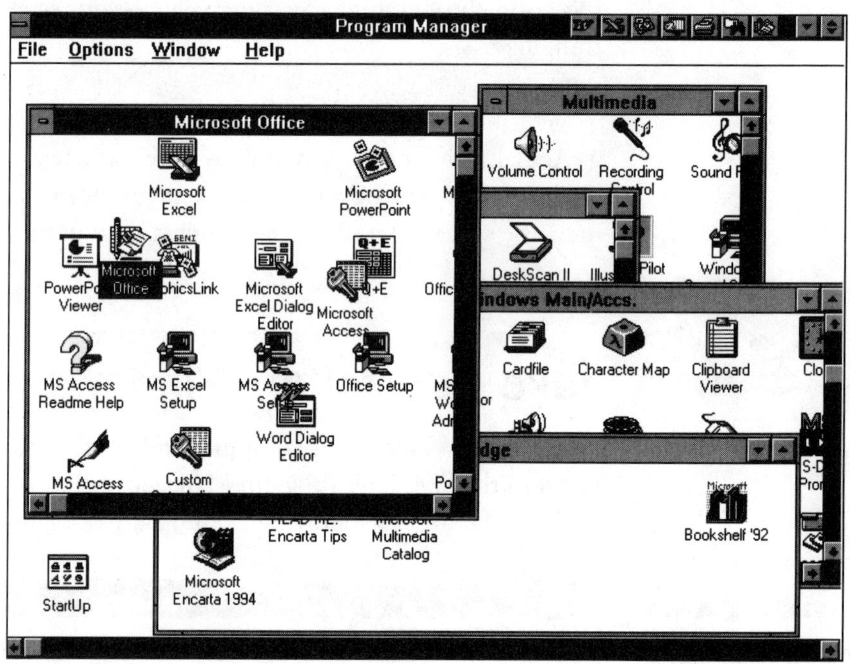

It's important to realize, however, that even though Figures AA.4 and AA.5 look dramatically different, both are showing the same two kinds of things: *windows* and *icons.* And those windows and icons can be tidied up with just a few mouse-clicks.

Windows and Icons

An *icon* is a window that's currently minimized, meaning it's at its smallest possible size. All you see when you look at an icon is a tiny picture and a brief description, like these examples:

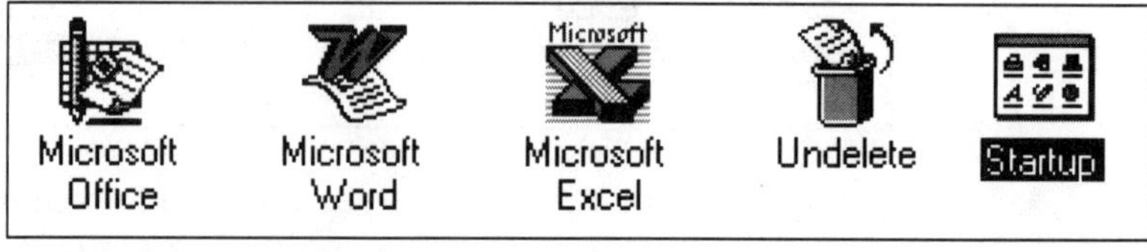

Though it might be hard to tell at first glance, all the icons on your screen are grouped into windows. Each window has a frame that looks something like this (but with different words in the title bar up top):

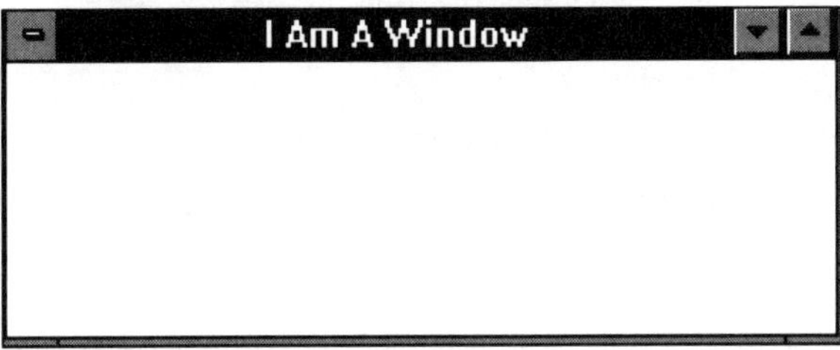

If your screen is a mess, you should really clean it up by reading the next section. If your screen is already uncluttered, like Figure AA.4, then you can skip this part and move on down to the section titled *It's All in the Frame.*

Clean Up Your Act

If you need to get your screen whipped into shape, I suggest you follow these steps. You'll learn a few Windows tricks along the way:

1. First, *maximize* Program Manager to full-screen size by double-clicking on its title bar. Put the mouse pointer right on the words *Program Manager* and double-click. If the window shrinks, it was already maximized. Double-click on Program Manager again to re-maximize its window.

2. If there are any open windows visible on your screen (as there are back in Figure AA.5), first arrange the icons in that window. To do so, click anywhere on the window that contains poorly arranged icons. That window jumps into the forefront, and its title bar will probably change color, indicating that it's currently the *active window.*

3. Look for the Program Manager title bar and click on the Window menu command that's just under that title bar. A menu will drop down, as in the example below.

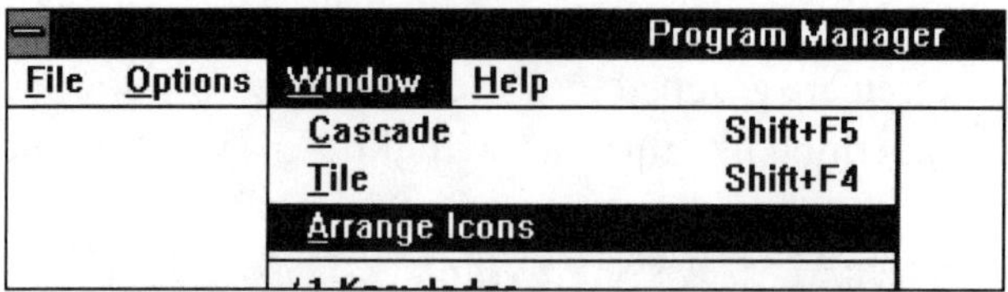

4. Choose (click on) Arrange Icons. The icons in the active window arrange themselves into a neat grid, as illustrated in the example below.

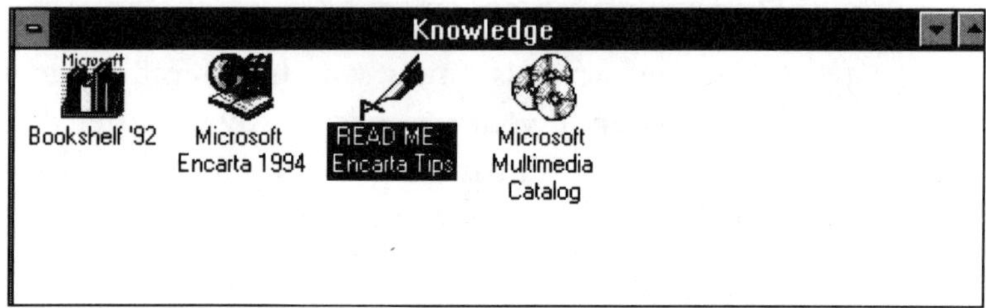

TIP: *If your icons overlap one another after choosing Arrange Icons, you can increase the space allotted to each icon. Get to the Windows Control Panel, choose Desktop, and increase the Spacing setting. For more information, please see your Windows documentation.*

5. After tidying up the icons in the window, you can resize the window for a better fit. Just move the mouse pointer to the lower-right corner of the window that you want to resize so that the pointer changes to a double-headed arrow, and then drag that corner in whatever direction you want to go. For example, below, I dragged the lower-right corner of a window up and to the left to get rid of wasted white space. You can repeat steps 4 and 5 until you get a nice fit.

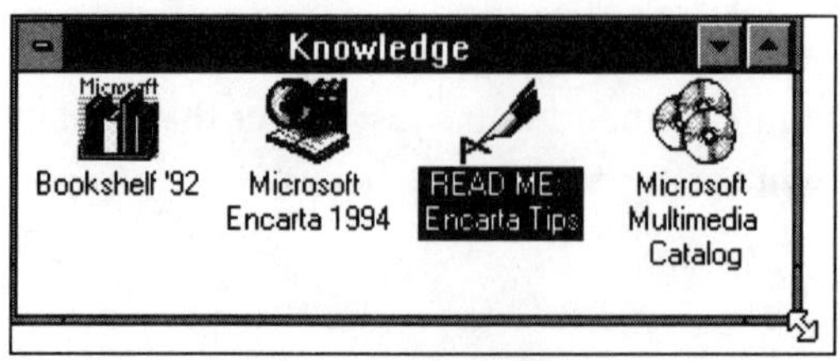

6. Now you can *close* the active window by double-clicking the control-menu bar in the upper-left corner of the window. *But don't close Program Manager's window, or you'll end up in DOS.* (If you close Program Manager by accident, type **win** ↵ at the DOS command prompt to get back to Windows.)

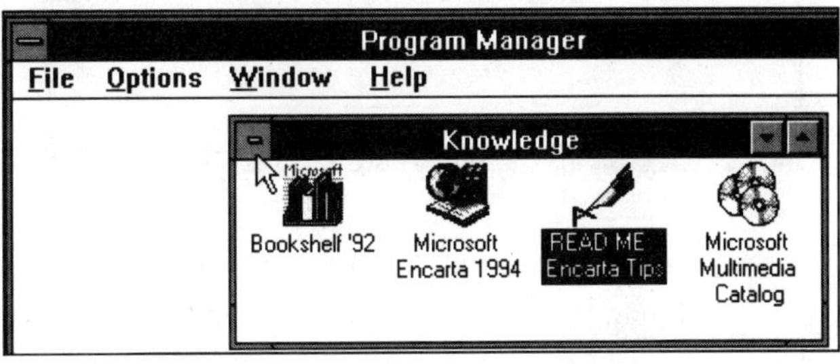

7. Now you can repeat steps 2 through 6 for every open window, *except* Program Manager, until your group windows are all closed. At which point, your screen should look something like Figure AA.6.

FIGURE AA.6

Program Manager with all its group windows shrunk down to icons.

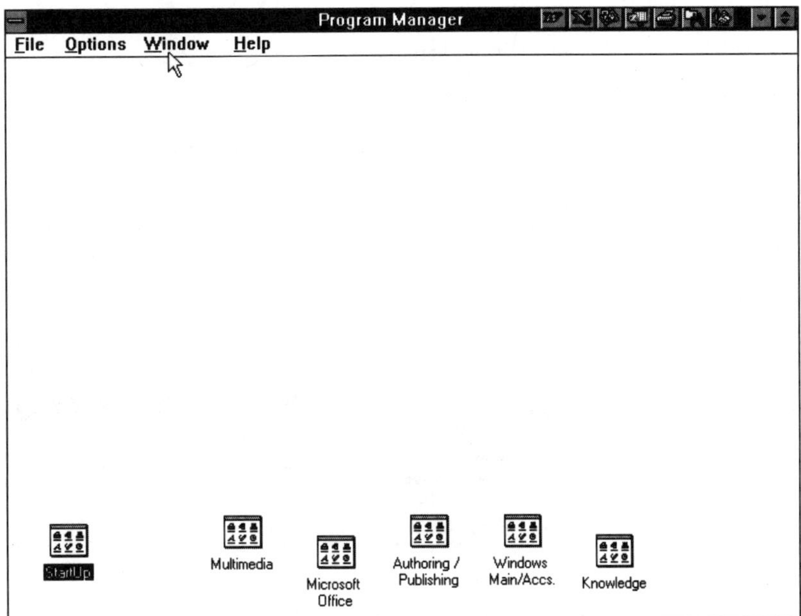

8. Now, there's no need to keep Program Manager sized to full screen. So once again, double-click its title bar. It may shrink down so

small that you can't even see its group icons, as below. Don't worry, we'll fix that in a moment.

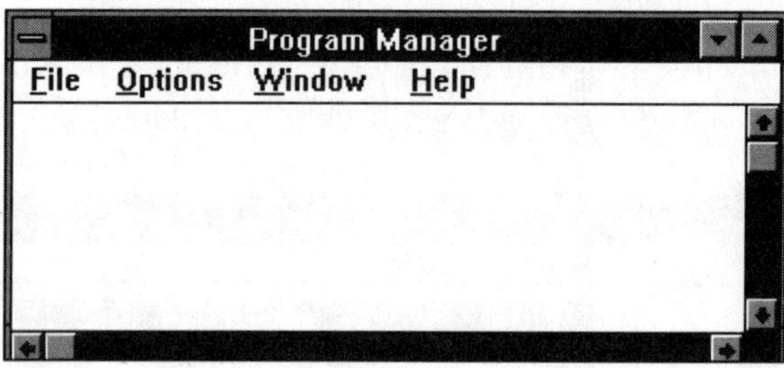

9. Now once again, click on the Window option under Program Manager, and choose Arrange Icons. Program Manager's icons should be arranged neatly now.

10. If you like, you can now size the Program Manager window, by dragging its borders, until the icons fit nicely into the window. You can also drag the Program Manager to a new location, by dragging its title bar.

11. Repeat steps 9 and 10, as necessary, until you're happy with the way things look.

Save the Neat Screen

If you're happy with the general appearance of your screen, save those settings for future Windows sessions. Here's how:

1. Click on the Options menu command under Program Manager, to reveal the menu shown below.

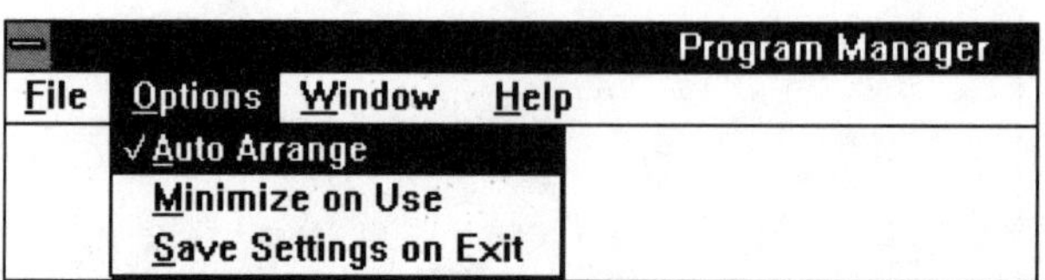

2. If (and *only if*) you *don't* see a check mark next to Auto Arrange, click that option. If Auto Arrange already does have a check mark next to it, press the Escape (Esc) key to leave that setting unchanged. The menu disappears.

3. Now once again, click on Options under Program Manager to open that menu. If you pressed Esc in the previous step, you'll need to click twice to get the menu again.

4. If (and *only* if) you do see a check mark next to Save Settings on Exit, click that option. If you *don't* see a check mark next to Save Setting on Exit, leave it unchecked (press Esc). The menu disappears.

5. Now save this screen arrangement. First hold down the Shift key, and don't let go until I tell you to.

6. In Program Manager's window, click on the File command, then choose (click on) Exit Windows from the bottom of the menu that appears.

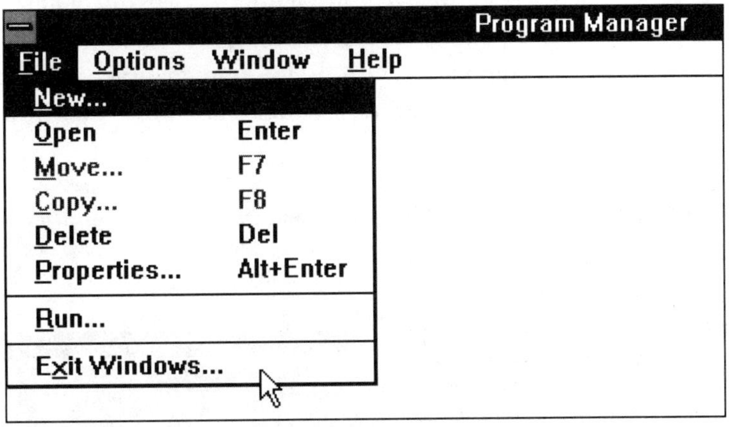

Program Manager	
File Options Window Help	
New...	
Open	Enter
Move...	F7
Copy...	F8
Delete	Del
Properties...	Alt+Enter
Run...	
Exit Windows...	

7. Now you can let go of the Shift key.

Let me tell you what you've just done:

- By turning on Auto Arrange, you've told Program Manager to auto matically rearrange icons inside windows from time-to-time, so you won't have to do it manually as often.
- By turning off Save Settings On Exit, you've essentially told Windows "I might exit Windows with the screen in a complete mess. Please *do not* save that mess for me. I want to come back to the settings I'm about to save right now."

- By holding down the Shift key while choosing File ➢ Exit, you defined your current screen arrangement as the settings that you want to save, and what you want to see when you first start Windows in the future.

If you've been following along, it may seem as though you just went through a pretty strange ritual just to groom your screen. But in fact, you've just had some exposure to basic tools and techniques for taking control of your screen at all times. If your screen gets messy in the future, try these same steps again to tidy it up. You'll get the hang of it pretty soon.

It's All in the Frame

Virtually everything you need to know about managing windows and icons is summarized in Figure AA.7. If you're new to Windows, you might want to make a photocopy of that figure and tape it right near your computer screen. Refer to it whenever you feel your screen is a total mess, for tips and techniques that'll help you get things back in order.

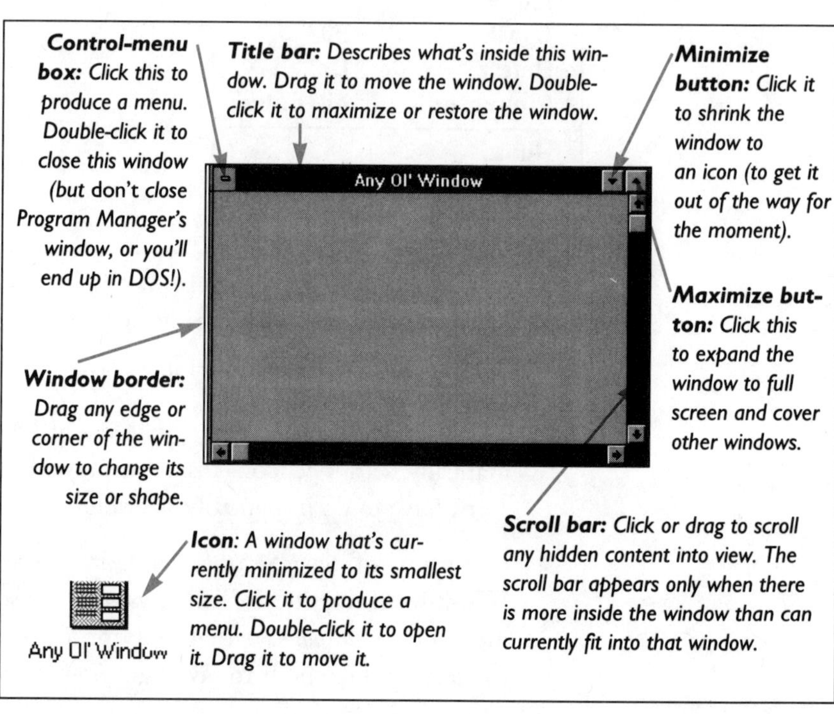

Control-menu box: Click this to produce a menu. Double-click it to close this window (but don't close Program Manager's window, or you'll end up in DOS!).
Title bar: Describes what's inside this window. Drag it to move the window. Double-click it to maximize or restore the window.
Minimize button: Click it to shrink the window to an icon (to get it out of the way for the moment).
Any Ol' Window
Maximize button: Click this to expand the window to full screen and cover other windows.
Window border: Drag any edge or corner of the window to change its size or shape.
Scroll bar: Click or drag to scroll any hidden content into view. The scroll bar appears only when there is more inside the window than can currently fit into that window.
Any Ol' Window
Icon: A window that's currently minimized to its smallest size. Click it to produce a menu. Double-click it to open it. Drag it to move it.

FIGURE AA.7

All you really need to know to manage windows and icons is summarized right here.

Home Base: Program Manager

If you don't have a "home base" to work from when you use a computer, you'll spend a lot of time wondering things like "Where am I?", "How did I get here?" and "How do I get to...?" Program Manager is the perfect window to use as your home base. For several reasons:

- Program Manager is the first Window to appear when you first start Windows.
- You can start any Windows application (program) that's on your system from Program Manager.
- Program Manager is *always* available when you're in Windows. If you don't see it on your screen, just hold down the Alt key, and press the Tab key (Alt+Tab), until you see the little box below. Then release the Alt key. Program Manager will pop to the forefront of any other open windows on your screen.

- When you exit Program Manager or close its window, you're actually exiting *all* of Windows. You don't really want to do that unless you plan on shutting down the computer or need to use some non-Windows program.

Of course, you'll probably close Program Manager by accident from time to time. But before you're booted out of Windows completely, you'll see this message and options:

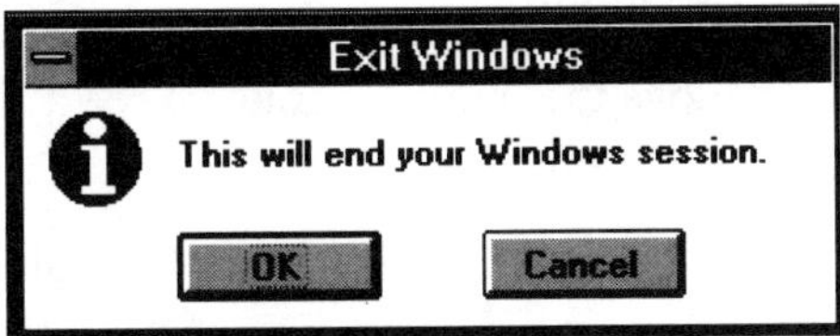

When you see that, think before you act:

- If you don't really want to exit Windows, choose Cancel or press Esc.
- If you're sure you do want to leave Windows, choose OK or press ↵.

If you choose OK, you'll be taken to DOS (that **C:\>** thing). That is an excellent time to turn off your computer because you can rest assured that any work you've done has been saved.

Where Does DOS Fit In?

Given that you have Windows and Microsoft Office, there's probably no need for you to learn a whole lot about DOS.

If you feel you *must* learn something about DOS, I would recommend that, if you're using DOS 6.2, you look into the commands MEMMAKER, SCANDISK, and DEFRAG. You can use them to give your computer an occasional tune-up. But other than those three commands, anything you can do in DOS is easier to do in Windows.

In any event, if you find yourself at the DOS command prompt (C:\>) and want to get back to Windows, just type **win** ↵.

First Aid: Startup Troubles

If you cannot get into DOS or Windows, try some of these troubleshooting tips.

Problem: The screen is blank or hard to read, even though the computer sounds like it's turned on.

Solution: Try these options:

- Press ↵ or move the mouse around to see if the screen is just temporarily blanked out.
- Look around for, then fiddle with, the Brightness and Contrast knobs on the monitor until you can see the screen.

- If the monitor has its own On/Off (or 1/0) switch, make sure the monitor is turned on.
- If you're not using a small laptop computer, make sure the monitor is plugged into the wall, and plugged into the system unit as well.
- If the screen is off-center, fiddle with the alignment buttons, which may be on the front, side, or back of the monitor.

Problem: The screen shows a message saying that this is "...not a system disk..." or "not a bootable disk..."

Solution: Most likely, you forgot to open or empty the floppy disk drives before you turned on the computer. Remove any floppy disks from the floppy disk drives, and then press the ↵ key to try again.

Problem: Nothing happened after you typed **win** ↵.

Solution: If absolutely *nothing* happens on your screen, maybe you forget to press ↵, in which case the screen just sits there waiting for you to type more. Remember you must type **win** *and* press ↵ to switch from DOS to Windows.

If that's not the problem, then try these solutions:

- If you see a little message on the screen that says *Bad command or file name*, make sure you typed correctly. You must type **win** exactly, not **windows** or **wim.** Try again, and don't forget to press ↵.
- If typing **win** ↵ correctly always displays the *Bad command or file name* message, then perhaps Windows isn't even installed on this computer. You'll need to ask your dealer or some local computer guru for advice on purchasing and installing Microsoft Windows. (Windows is optional, so you might not even have it!).

Problem: Your computer doesn't start in DOS, or Windows.

Solution: Some computers are set up to start in a custom menu system or some alternative interface. If your computer is like that, try some of these techniques to switch to Windows:

- If you see an option on the screen that says "Windows," pick that option.

- Look around the screen for clues on how to "Exit" whatever is on the screen. For example, if you see *Esc=Exit*, then press the Escape key. If you see *Ctrl+X=Exit*, press Ctrl+X (hold down the Ctrl key, tap the letter X, then release the Ctrl key). If you can get to DOS in that manner, you can then type **win** ↵ to switch over to Windows. (You might want to make a note of that in the Basic Skills list.)
- If you're really stuck and can't get to either DOS or Windows, you'll need to ask your local computer guru how to get into Windows. Unfortunately, I can't see your screen at the moment, so I can't even venture a guess for you. Sorry.

First Aid: Mouse Troubles

Problem: Your mouse is dead.

Solution: If there is no mouse pointer on the screen, or the mouse pointer does not move when you roll the mouse, one of the following may be to blame:

- Perhaps you're in some program that doesn't support a mouse (such as DOS). Get to Windows as described near the start of this appendix.
- Perhaps your mouse has never been properly installed on your computer. Refer to the manual that came with your mouse, or your local computer guru.

Problem: Nothing happened when you clicked or double-clicked.

Solution: There are several reasons why clicking something on your screen may have no effect:

- The most common problem is moving the mouse slightly just before you click or double-click. Once the mouse pointer is pointing to the thing you want, then *gently* click or double-click, without jerking the mouse.

- Perhaps the thing you clicked isn't a "clickable" object on the screen. Try the Windows Tutorial mentioned earlier.

First Aid: Keyboard Troubles

Problem: Your keyboard is dead as a doornail.

Solution: You're probably in a situation where the computer doesn't accept much keyboard input, such as the Windows Program Manager. Try using the mouse instead.

Or maybe your keyboard isn't plugged into the computer. Check all connections and, if you find that the keyboard is loose, *turn off everything, then plug in the keyboard, then turn everything back on.*

Problem: Your keyboard or computer is beeping wildly.

Solution: There are three possible solutions to the problem of the chronically beeping computer:

- You're typing too fast. Stop typing, wait for the beeps to stop, then pick up where you left off.
- Something is leaning against the keyboard holding a key down. Make sure nothing heavy (like a book) is pressing against the keyboard, and wait for the beeping to stop.
- You're pressing a key that does not make sense in the current situation. "If in doubt, Escape key out." If pressing Esc doesn't help, look around the screen for other clues on how you might back out, using the mouse.

Problem: You can't type worth beans.

Solution: Chances are, you'll use the mouse most of the time, so atrocious typing skills may not be too much of a handicap. However, if you plan on using the computer to do a lot of typing or writing, then you better also plan on polishing up those typing skills. Consider taking a typing course. Or go to your local computer store and ask for a "typing tutor" program.

First Aid: Windows Troubles

Problem: I made one little mouse click, and my whole window/icon just disappeared.

Solution: Maybe you just covered it up by accident. Try some of these solutions:

- Hold down the Alt key and press Tab repeatedly until you find the thing you lost. Then release the Alt key.
- Press Ctrl+Esc to bring up the Task List. Then click on Cascade. Look for the missing window's title bar.
- Click on Window in Program Manager's title bar, then, if you can find the thing you're looking for listed near the bottom of the window, click that thing.
- Press Ctrl+F4 until all the document windows are closed. Maybe you'll then be able to see the missing window or icon.
- Minimize every open window by clicking the Minimize button near its upper-right corner. If you can't see the Minimize button, drag the window by its title bar until you can see the Minimize button.

Problem: You're stuck because there's some message on the screen that you can't get rid of.

Solution: Press Esc (Escape) to back up until you get to more familiar territory. If that doesn't help:

- Look for a button that says Cancel, and click that button.
- If there is no Cancel button, click the OK button.
- Close the pesky window by double-clicking its control-menu box. Or try one of the other general techniques summarized back in Figure AA.7 to close, size, or move the window.

Problem: The screen is practically blank, except for the **C:\>** prompt. How do I get back to Program Manager?

Solution: You're probably in DOS. Type **ver** and press ↵. If you see a little message on the screen saying something like *MS-DOS Version...*, then you are definitely in DOS. Type **exit** ↵ to see if that takes you back to Windows. If that doesn't take you back to Windows, type **win** to get back to Windows.

APPENDIX B

Universal Office Skills Quick Reference

THIS APPENDIX PROVIDES a quick reference to basic Windows and Microsoft Office skills. Unlike Appendix A, which should be read from start to finish by anyone who is just getting started with PCs, you can use this appendix as a reference, to look up things as needed.

For example, if you see an instruction in this book, such as "Choose..." or "Select...." or "Start...", and don't know how to do that, you can flip to this appendix for a quick lesson or reminder. Here are the tools and skills covered in this appendix.

Arrange Windows and Icons

It's nearly impossible to get along with your PC when your screen is a confusing pile of overlapping windows and icons. If you get in the habit of closing any windows that you're not using at the moment, you won't end up with a confusing mess on your screen.

Arranging Program Manager

Program Manager is your home base when using Windows. Figure AB.1 shows an example of how Program Manager might look when poorly arranged, shows the names of some things on the screen, and also provides tips on how to get it neatly arranged.

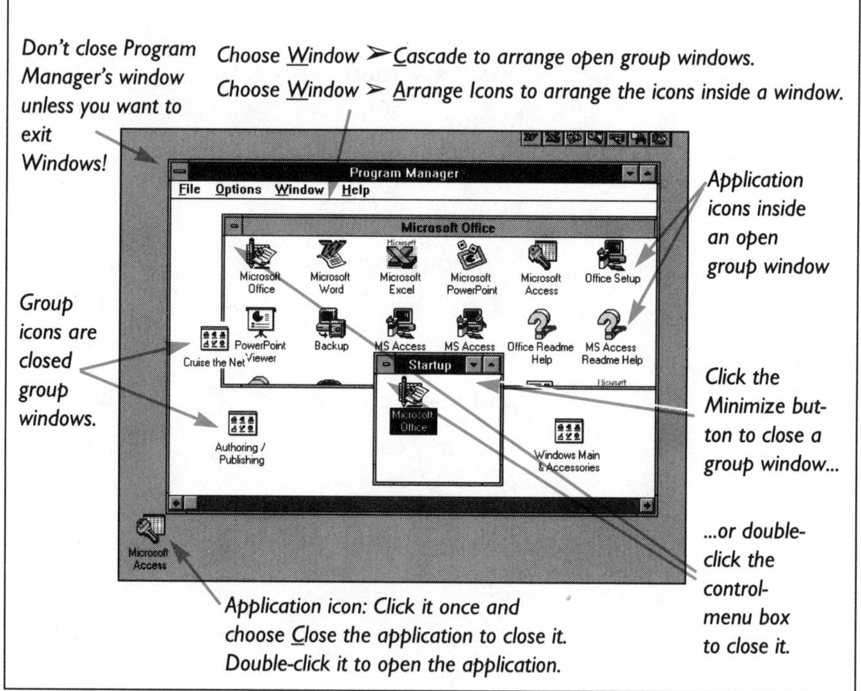

FIGURE AB.1

Before: A messy Windows Program Manager screen and tips on how to tidy up

Figure AB.2 shows how Program Manager would look after closing all open group windows and application icons.

Arranging Application Windows

When too many open applications are cluttering your screen, press Ctrl+Esc to pop up the Task List (shown in Figure AB.3). Use the Cascade and Arrange Icons in the Task List to tidy up.

FIGURE AB.2

After: A much tidier and more manageable Program Manager

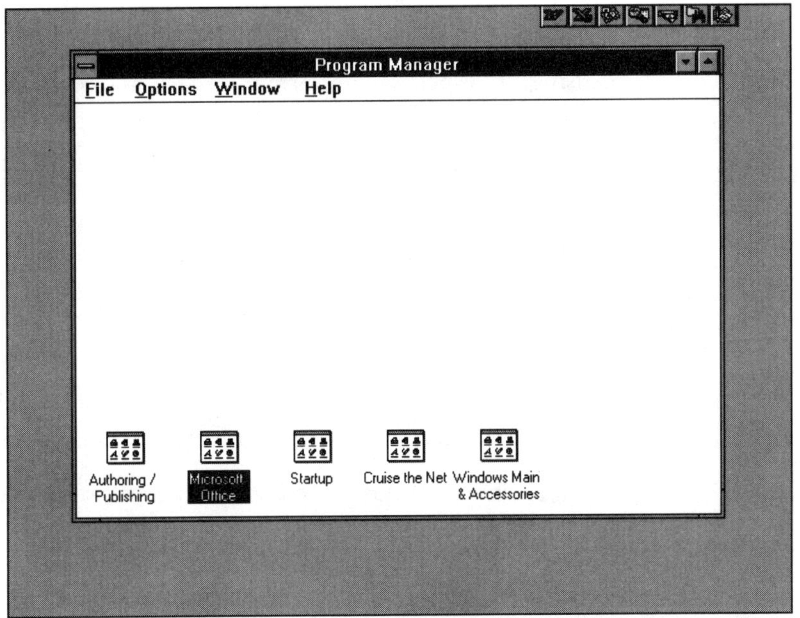

FIGURE AB.3

Use the Cascade and Arrange Icons buttons in the Task List (press Ctrl+Esc) to tidy up the desktop. Close any applications that you're no longer using.

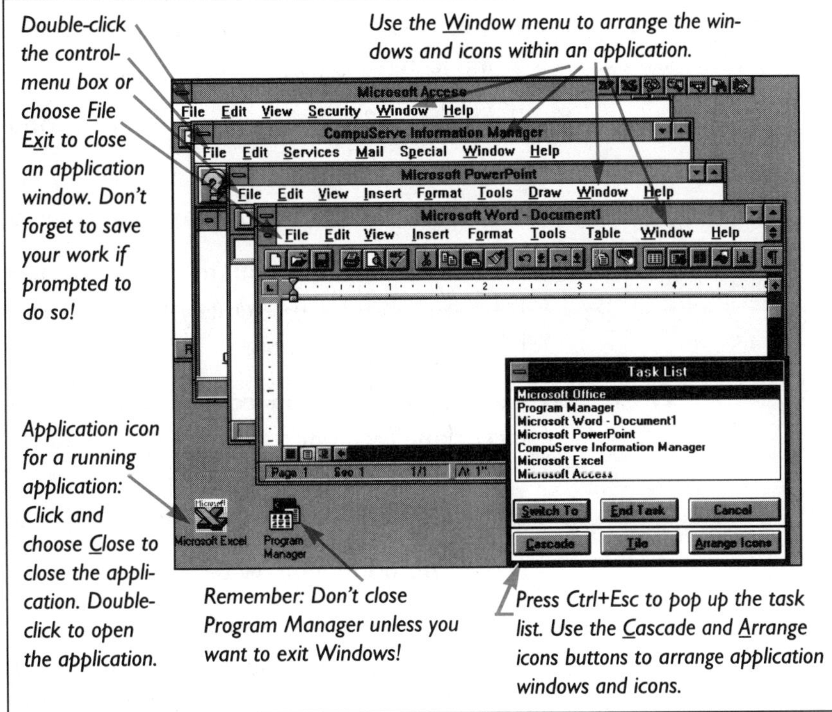

Use the Window menu inside any application window to tidy up the contents of that window. Be sure to close any applications that you're not using. It's especially important to close all applications and save the work you've done before you exit Windows or turn off the computer. Otherwise, you'll probably lose any work you've accomplished.

The Clean-Up Ritual

So here's how you can use the tools you've just learned about to tidy up your Program Manager screen:

1. Close or minimize any open application windows (*except* Program Manager), as described in Figure AB.3.
2. Choose Window ➢ Cascade from Program Manager's menu bar to arrange all the open group windows.
3. Choose Window ➢ Arrange Icons to arrange all the icons in the current group window.
4. Close the group window by clicking its Minimize button or by double-clicking its Control-menu box to shrink it down to a group icon.
5. Repeat steps 3 and 4 until all the group windows are closed.
6. Then choose Window ➢ Arrange Icons from Program Manager's menu again, to arrange the group icons inside Program Manager.
7. Press Ctrl+Esc to bring up the Task List, then click the Arrange Icons button there to arrange open application icons in the lower-left corner of the screen.
8. Close each application icon in the lower-left corner of the screen by clicking each once, and choosing Close from the little menu that appears.
9. To save your tidy screen, hold down the Shift key and choose File ➢ Exit from Program Manager's menu bar.
10. Then, click on Options in Program Manager's menu bar. *If* (and *only* if) the Save Settings on Exit command has a check mark next to it, choose that option to turn it off. If Save Settings on Exit *does*

have a check mark next to it, just click outside the menu or press Escape to leave that setting unchanged.

Related Topics

- *Start an Application* here in Appendix B
- *Exit an Application* here in Appendix B
- *Take Control of Windows* in Appendix A

Choose

To *choose* something, you usually just click it with the mouse. In this book, an instruction such as

```
Choose Help ➢ About Program Manager
```

means "Choose Help from the menu bar, then choose About Program Manager from the drop-down menu that appears," as illustrated below.

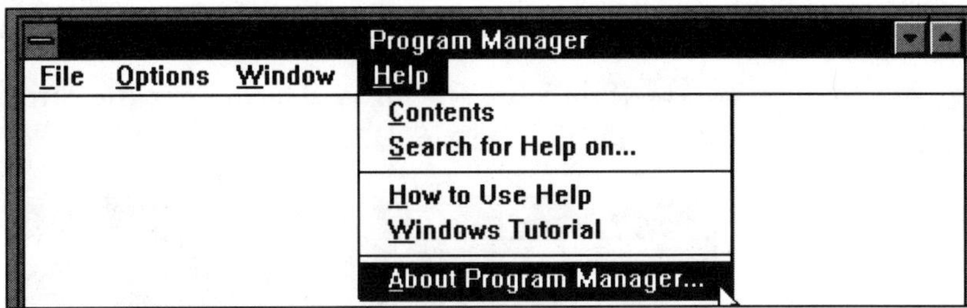

In some cases, the instruction might refer to a control in a dialog box. For example:

```
Choose OK.
```

means "Click the command button labeled OK," like the one shown at the top of the following page.

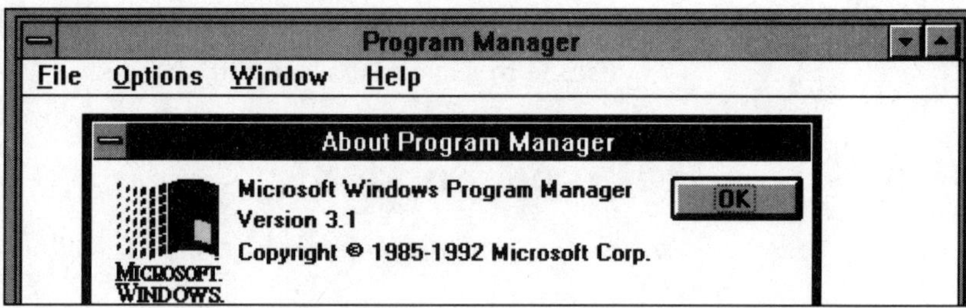

Related Topics

- *Menus* here in Appendix B
- *Dialog Boxes* here in Appendix B

Close a Document

To close the document that's on your screen without exiting the application you used to create that document:

1. Choose File ➢ Close from the application's menu bar.
2. If there are any unsaved changes in the current document, you'll see a dialog box similar to this one:

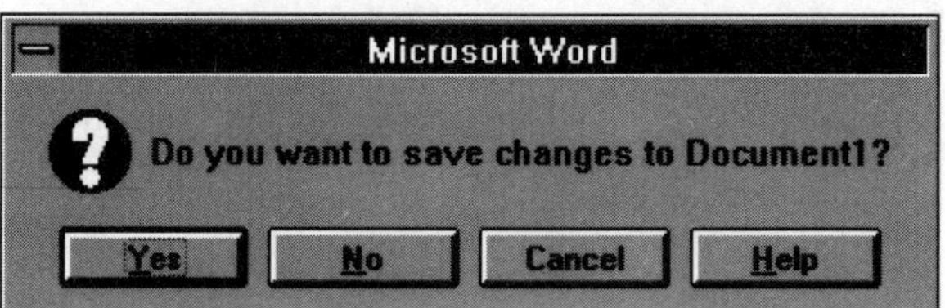

3. Choose one of the following options:
    - Yes: If you want to save this document so you can work on it more later, choose Yes then proceed to Step 4.
    - No: To trash the current document, choose No. Be aware that once you choose this option, there will be no way to retrieve the document in the future.

NOTE: *Actually, when you choose No, only the changes you've made since the last time you saved the file will be trashed. Everything that was in the document up to the last time you saved it will remain on the disk, under the same file name.*

- Cancel: If you got to this dialog box by accident, choose Cancel. The document remains on your screen.
- Help: Provides help with saving the document.

4. If you chose Yes in Step 3, and have never saved this document, you'll see a Save As dialog box similar to the one below:

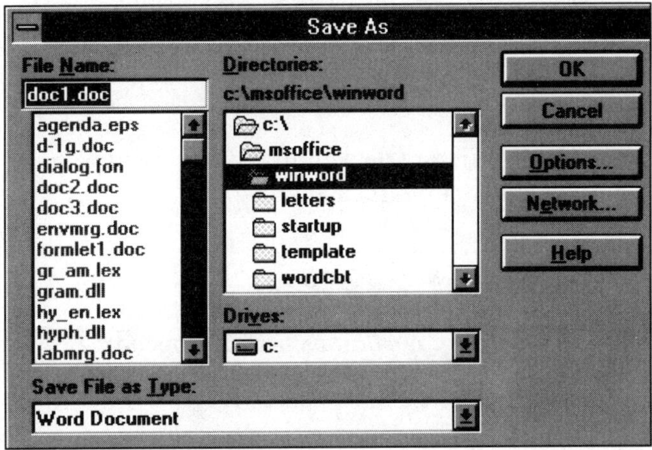

5. Type in a valid DOS file name (eight characters maximum length, no spaces or punctuation marks), then choose OK.

The application window remains on the screen, but its document window is empty. Now you can choose File ➢ New to start a new document, or File ➢ Open to open a previously saved document.

Related Topics

- *Exit an Application* here in Appendix B
- *Save Your Work* here in Appendix B

Create a Document

To create a new document, starting from the Windows Program Manager:

1. Start whichever application will best help you create that particular type of document. (See Table IO.1 in the *Instant Office* section for a summary.)
2. If no document window (or database window) appears for you to work in, choose File ➢ New from the application's menu bar.
3. If you're using Word at the moment, you can choose OK from the New dialog box to get to a "plain sheet of paper."

Now you can type within the document window or respond to the Wizard that appears (if any).

Related Topics

- *Start An Application* here in Appendix B
- *Menus* here in Appendix B
- *Type Text and Numbers* here in Appendix B

Cue Cards

Cue Cards give you on-screen coaching so that you can learn as you go. Access, Excel, Office Manager, and PowerPoint all offer Cue Cards. Here's how to get into those Cue Cards from within each application:

WHEN YOU'RE IN...	...DO THIS TO GET TO CUE CARDS
Access	Choose Help ➢ Cue Cards from Access's menu bar

Office Manager	Right-click the Office Manager toolbar, then choose Cue Cards from the menu that appears.
PowerPoint	Choose Help ➢ Cue Cards from PowerPoint's menu bar

Once a Cue Card is on the screen, it covers anything that's beneath it. You might need to move the Cue Card, or reduce it to an icon, to see what's behind the Cue Card. See Figure AB.4.

FIGURE AB.4

Cue Cards float above all other windows. To see what's behind the Cue Card, move, minimize, or close the Cue Card's window.

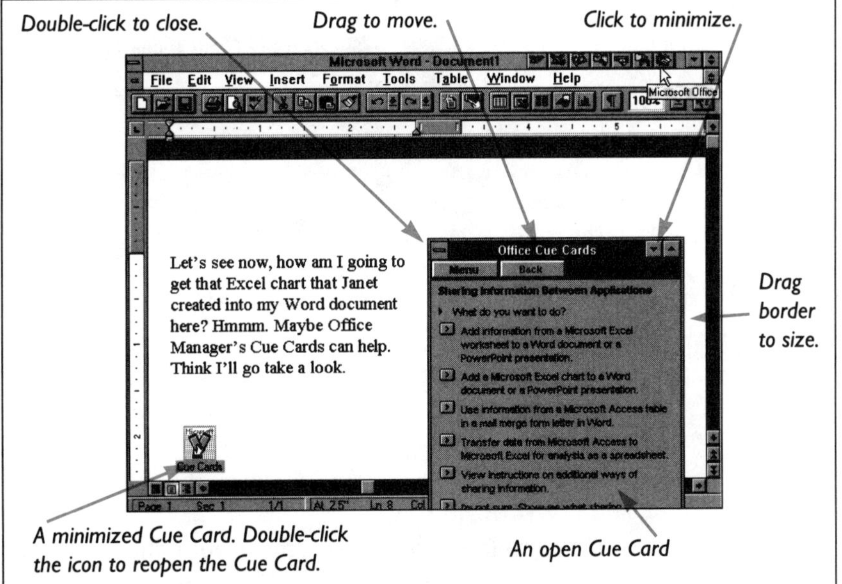

To Close Cue Cards

Double-click the control-menu box in the upper-left corner of the Cue Card's window (Figure AB.4) to close a Cue Card.

Related Topics

- *Help* here in Appendix B
- *Menus* here in Appendix B
- *Wizards* here in Appendix B

Dialog Boxes

A dialog box appears whenever the computer needs more information from you before starting a task. A sample dialog box might contain any of the controls shown in Figure AB.5.

FIGURE AB.5

A dialog box asks for more information before starting a particular task.

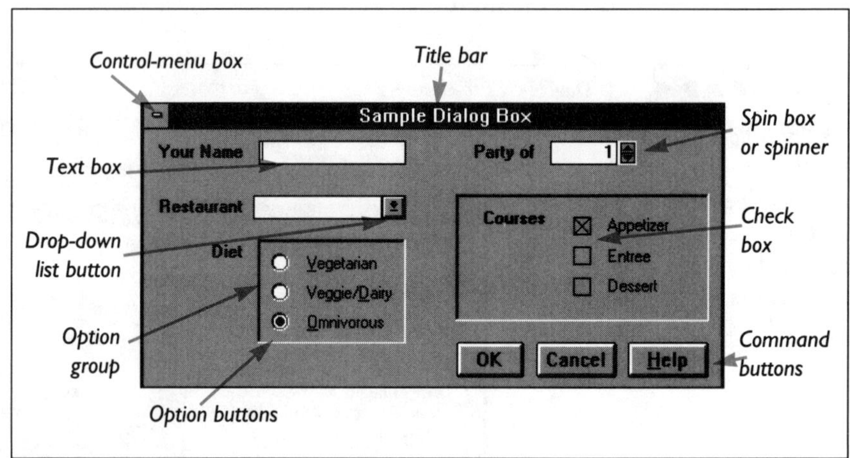

To Complete a Dialog

To complete a dialog, you make your choices from the options provided, typically by clicking on the option you want, or by typing into a text box. Then choose the OK button to proceed.

To Move a Dialog Box

If you need to see something that's covered by the dialog box, just drag it out of the way by its title bar.

To Cancel a Dialog Box

If you don't want to proceed with the dialog, or get to a dialog box by accident, click the Cancel button or press Escape.

To Get Help with a Dialog

If you're not sure what an option in a dialog box means, click its Help button. You'll be taken to the help screen for that particular dialog box.

Related Topics

- *Menus* here in Appendix B
- *Help* here in Appendix B

Drives, Directories, and Files

Understanding how and where the "stuff that's inside your computer" is stored is an important part of using a PC effectively. It's not terribly complicated if you think of it in terms of a regular file cabinet. A file cabinet contains drawers, and each drawer contains its own set of files.

On a PC, each *drive* acts as sort of a file cabinet for storing applications and the documents you create. The disk in that drive might be divided up into two or more *directories,* kind of like the way a file cabinet is divided into drawers. Each directory on a disk contains its own set of files, just like each drawer in a file cabinet holds its own set of files, as illustrated in Figure AB.6.

Let's take each concept one a time, starting with *drives.*

Understanding Drives

A *drive* (also called a *disk drive*) is a mechanical device that can read from, and in most cases write to, a disk. A bare-bones PC might have two drives: a floppy drive, for reading from, and writing to, floppy disks, and an internal hard drive for storing all your applications and documents. The floppy drive is named A:, the hard drive is named C:.

But a system can easily have more than two drives. You might have two floppy drives (A: and B:), an internal hard drive (C:), perhaps a CD-ROM drive (typically named D: or E:), and perhaps a network drive that you share with other users in your workgroup. The network drive might be named F: or N:, or some other letter, as in Figure AB.7.

NOTE: *Your hard disk might be divided into several logical drives, named C:, D:, E:, and so forth. Just because you have a drive named D: (or higher) doesn't necessarily mean you have a CD-ROM drive in your computer!*

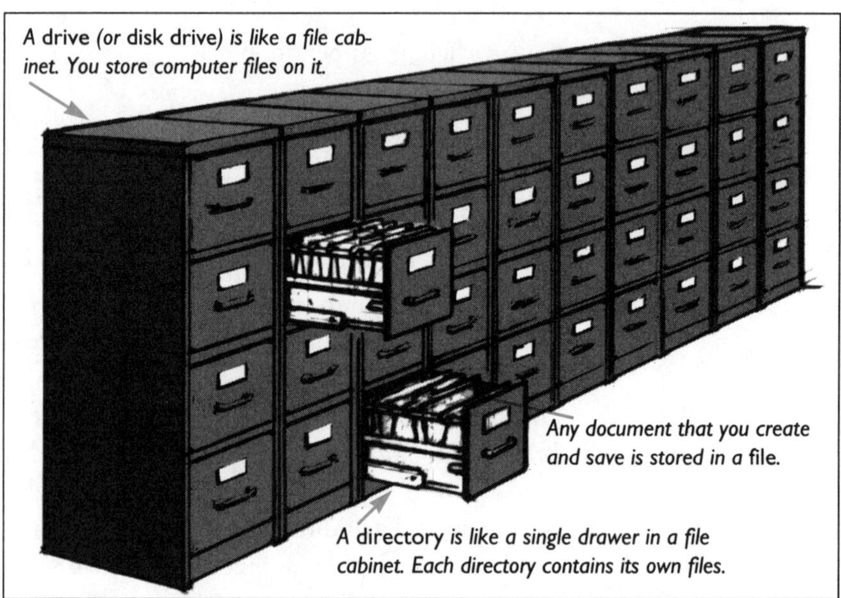
A drive (or disk drive) is like a file cabinet. You store computer files on it.
Any document that you create and save is stored in a file.
A directory is like a single drawer in a file cabinet. Each directory contains its own files.

FIGURE AB.6

On a computer, a drive plays a role similar to that of a file cabinet. The disk in a drive might be divided into several directories. Each directory contains its own files.

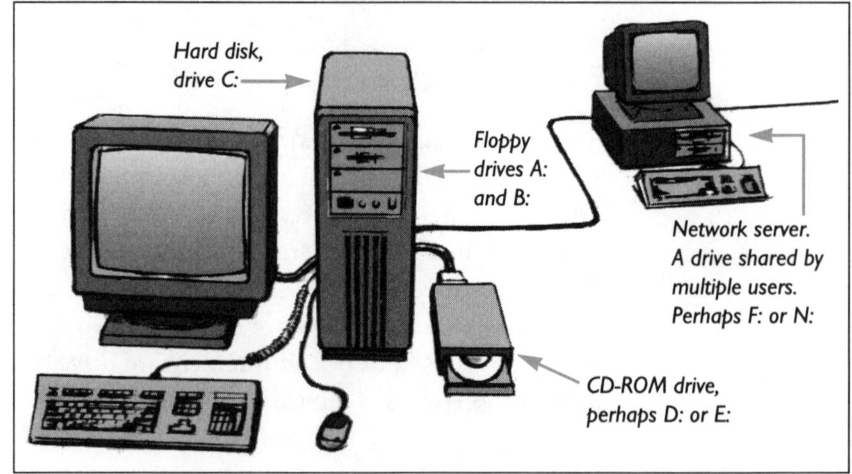
Hard disk, drive C:
Floppy drives A: and B:
Network server. A drive shared by multiple users. Perhaps F: or N:
CD-ROM drive, perhaps D: or E:

FIGURE AB.7

A computer might have several drives connected to it, including floppy drives, a hard disk, a CD-ROM drive, and a network drive.

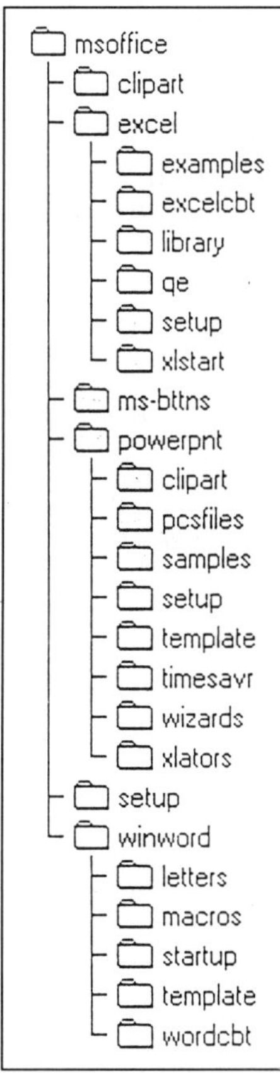

Understanding Directories

As mentioned, any given disk drive might be organized into several directories. Each directory has its own unique set of files—just as a drawer in a file cabinet contains its own files.

But one big difference between a disk drive and a file cabinet is that a disk drive can have *subdirectories.* A subdirectory would be sort of a drawer-within-a-drawer. Like, you open a file-cabinet drawer and, lo and behold, there are *more* drawers inside there. This, of course, never happens in real life. But you'll eventually need to start thinking like that if you're going to fully understand how files are organized on your disks.

Anyway, directories don't just happen on your computer. They're created in two ways:

- When you install a new application, chances are it will create its own directory, and perhaps some subdirectories, automatically. For example, when you installed Microsoft Office (the whole kit and caboodle), it created a directory named MSOFFICE, and several subdirectories beneath it, something like the arrangement illustrated here.
- You can also create your own directories, using the File ➢ Create Directory commands in the Windows File Manager. For more information, please refer to your Windows documentation.

Understanding Files

The smallest unit of storage on a computer disk is a file. A file might contain a document (something that *you* created, and saved), or it might contain an application, or even just part of an application. Any PC might have thousands of files in it. In fact, a single directory on a drive could contain thousands of files.

Every file has a name that's anywhere from one to eight characters in length, including letters and numbers, but no spaces. The file name can be followed by an *extension,* which is up to three-letters in length, and preceded by a period (dot). Table AB.1 shows examples of valid and invalid file names.

The Not-So-Beaten Path

In order to specify the exact drive, directory, and name of any given file, you construct a *path* to that file. The path starts with the drive letter, names the directories and subdirectories, and finally the file. Here's an example:

```
c:\msoffice\winword\mydoc.doc
```

That thing is called a path because it describes to the computer not only the name of the file (MYDOC.DOC), but also the file's location. Translating the various parts of the path down into English gives us:

c:\	Start at the root (highest level) directory of drive C:.

TABLE AB.1:

Valid and invalid file names

FILE NAME	OK/NOT OK
X	OK (but not very informative!)
MyLetter	OK
Qtr1Tax	OK
Tax_1994	OK (the underscore character is OK)
Alan-Let	OK (hyphens are OK too)
01-01Fig	OK (numbers are OK)
01-01Fig.Doc	OK, but I recommend that you don't add your own three-letter extension to file names. It's easier, in the long run, if you let each application automatically add its own three-letter extension.
My Letter	Not OK—spaces are not allowed
MyLetterToMom	Not OK—eight characters is the maximum length
Saved?	Not OK—because of the question mark

msoffice\	Go down to the directory named MSOFFICE.
winword\	From MSOFFICE, go down to the subdirectory named WINWORD.
mydoc.doc	And there you'll find a file named MYDOC.DOC.

You might want to think of it as taking a path from the top of a hierarchy to a final location, as in Figure AB.8.

How You Follow A Path

Whenever you attempt to open a document, by choosing File ➢ Open from some application's menu bar, you're presented with a dialog box that looks something like the one in Figure AB.9. You can use the Drives and Directories options to specify the directory to look at. The List Files of Type option limits the display of file names to certain file name extensions (.DOC in this example).

If you don't try to do anything fancy with directories, you'll rarely need to go looking around for your files. But here's how you can search for a missing file, should the need arise. First, choose File ➢ Open from your application's menu bar to get to that dialog box shown in Figure AB.9. Then:

1. Choose the drive that the file is on using the Drives drop-down list.

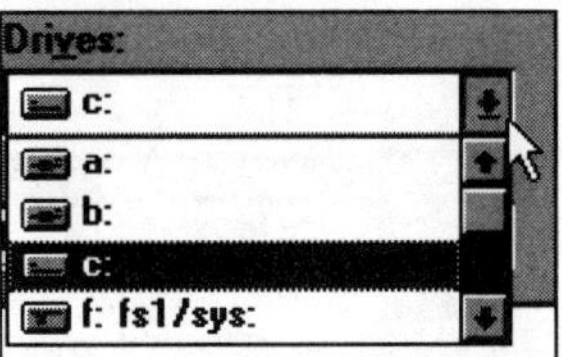

2. Choose the directory that you need from the Directories list. If you don't see that directory name, double-click the little folder next to the root directory name (**C:**) to view only the first-level directories. Then scroll down through directory names until you find the directory you want. Double-click the little folder of the directory you need to explore, and its subdirectories (if any) will appear.

FIGURE AB.8

A path tells the computer the name of a file and how to get to that file.

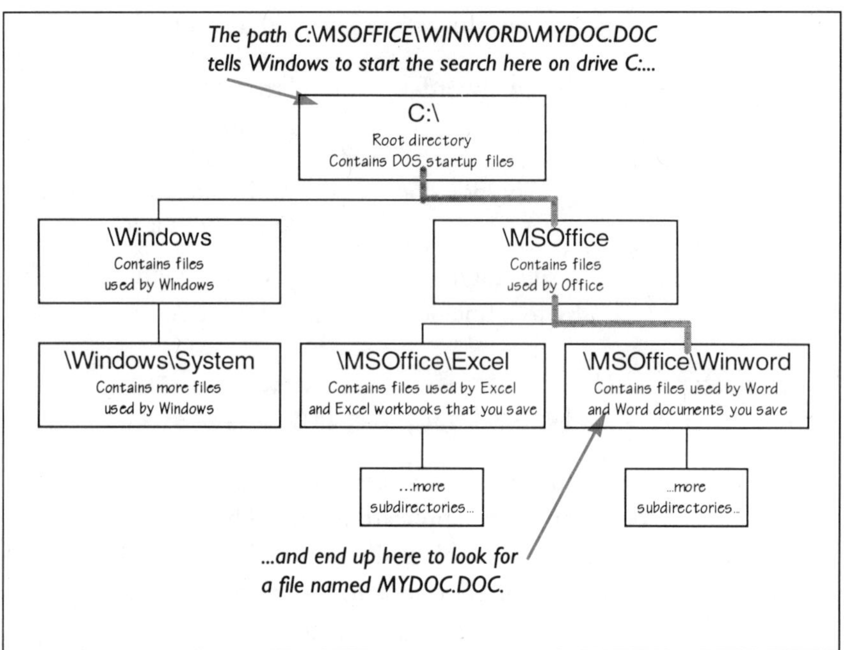

FIGURE AB.9

The Open File dialog box lets you choose a drive and directory to search through, as well as specific types of files to display.

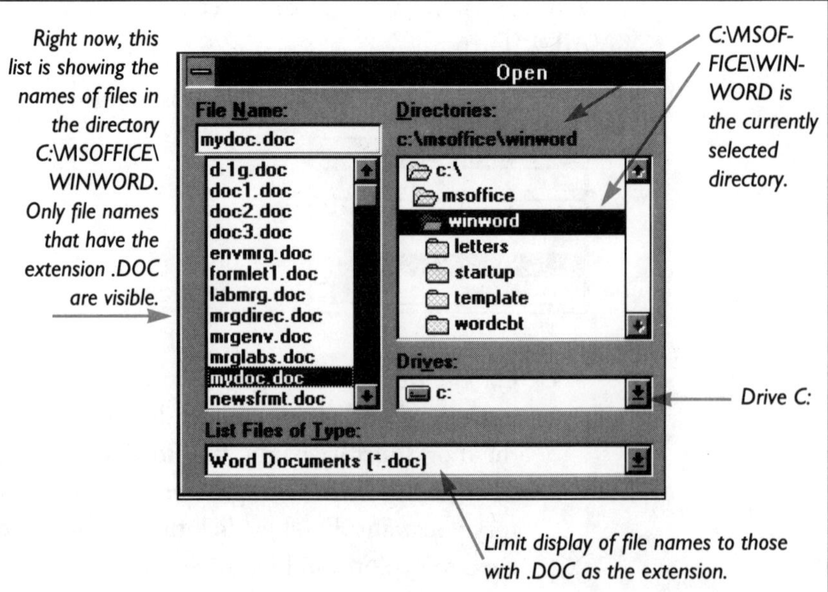

3. If you want to see the names of all the files on that particular directory, you can choose All Files (*.*) from the List Files of Type drop-down list.

4. When the path that's just above the Directories list displays the correct location of your file, and the List Files of Type box contains All Files (*.*), then the list of File Names displays, in alphabetical order, all the files on that particular directory.

5. To open a file, scroll down to its file name, then double-click that file name. (Or click the file name once, then choose OK.)

NOTE: *If you're faced with a long list of file names, type the first few letters of the name of the file you want. The highlighter will jump to that section of the list.*

And that is how it all works. Of course, this method assumes that you know the exact location and name of the file you're looking for. If you don't know all of that, you can base a search on whatever information you do know about the file. See *Find a Lost File* here in Appendix B.

Related Topics

- *Open (Retrieve) Saved Work* here in Appendix B
- *Start an Application* here in Appendix B

Exit an Application

You should get into the habit of exiting all applications, and saving your work, before you turn off the computer. For that matter, it's a good idea to exit an application as soon as you've finished using it, just to reduce screen clutter. Exiting an application is easy:

1. If you have several applications visible on the screen, as in Figure AB.10, double-click the title bar of the application you want to exit. Doing so will expand that application's window to full screen, so you're not distracted by a lot of other menu bars.

2. Choose File ➢ Exit from the application's menu bar. (Or, if you prefer, you can just double-click the control-menu box in the upper-left corner of the application's window.)

3. If you've left any unsaved work on the screen, you'll see a message similar to the one below:

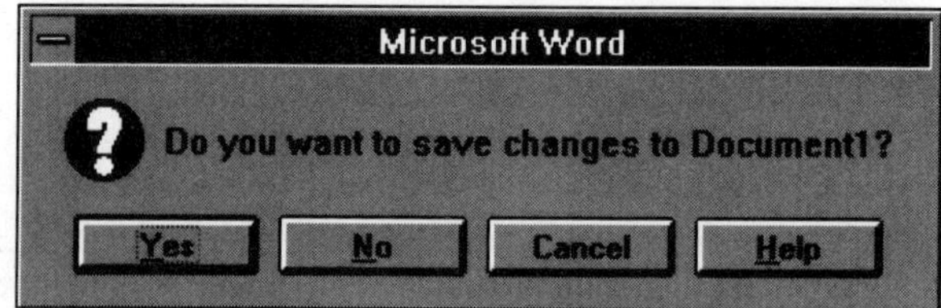

4. Choose one of the following:

- If you want to save the document, choose Yes, and enter a valid file name (eight characters maximum length, no spaces or punctuation marks). Then choose OK.

FIGURE AB.10

Menu bars look alike. Before choosing anything from an application's menu bar, first make sure you're looking at the correct menu bar.

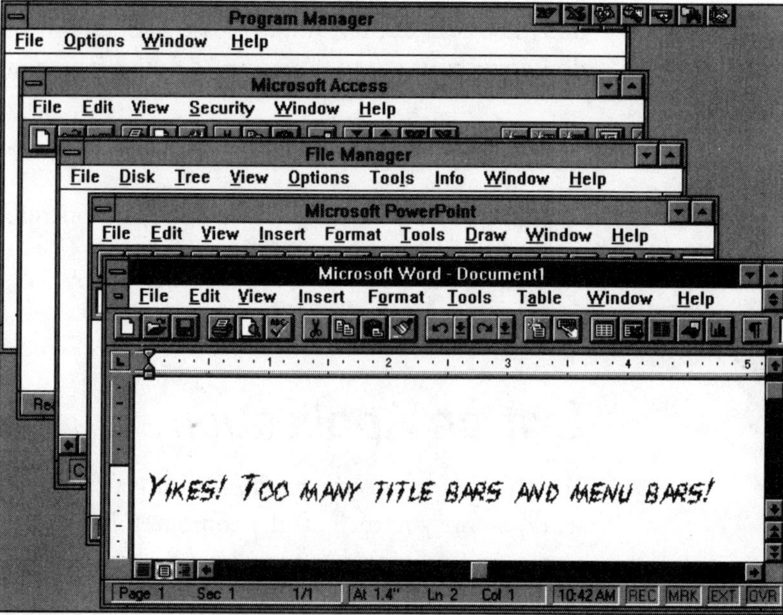

- If you want to trash the current version of the document you've been working on, choose No. If you've never saved this document before, you'll lose the entire document. If you *have* saved this document before, you'll only lose the changes you made since the last time you saved the document.

- If you want to go back and take another look at the document on the screen, before you decide, choose Cancel.

5. If more than one document is open, you'll be prompted to save or discard each one. Repeat steps 3 and 4 until the application stops asking if you want to save.

After all the open documents have been either saved or discarded, the application closes. You'll be back to the Windows Program Manager, or wherever you were before you started this application.

Exiting Windows

Keep in mind that if you exit the Windows Program Manager, you exit Windows entirely and are taken back to DOS. That's actually the safest time to shut down the computer. But if you exit Windows by accident, you can restart it right on the spot by typing **win**, then pressing ↵, at the DOS command prompt.

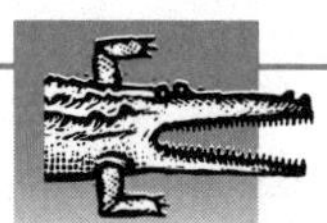

WARNING: *Beside losing your work, turning off your computer while Windows is still running leads to lots of temporary (.TMP) files on your hard disk. Those files just waste disk space. So always remember to exit Windows before you turn off your PC!*

Related Topics

- *Drives, Directories, and Files* here in Appendix B.
- *Save Your Work* here in Appendix B.

Find a Lost File

Computers don't just "devour" files. Files don't just disappear all by them selves. If you choose File ➢ Open from an application, but don't see the name of the file that you want to open, the problem could be any of the following:

- You're looking at files on the wrong drive/directory.
- You don't remember the name of the file, or exactly how you spelled that name.
- You have deleted the file from the disk (or somebody else has).

Before you assume the worst case (someone deleted the entire file), try using Microsoft Office's Find Files applet to look around for the missing file. Here's how:

1. Click on the Find File button in the Office Manager toolbar (shown below).

TIP: *You can also choose File ➢ Find File from some applications' menu bars.*

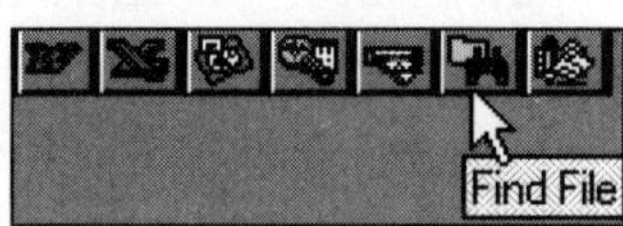

2. You'll be taken to the Search dialog box shown in Figure AB.11. (If you get to the dialog box shown in Figure AB.12 instead, click the Search button in that dialog box to get to the Search dialog box.)
3. Use the drop-down list button next to Location to choose the drive you want to search. (Your hard disk is drive C:, which will appear as **c:** after you make your selection.)
4. If you want to search *all* the directories on the drive, select the Include Subdirectories check box, so that it's marked with an x.
5. What you do next depends on what you know about the file you're looking for:
   - If you know the first few letters of the missing file's name, type those letters followed by *.*. For example, to search for files that begin with the letters *aug*, you type **aug*.*** into the File Name box.

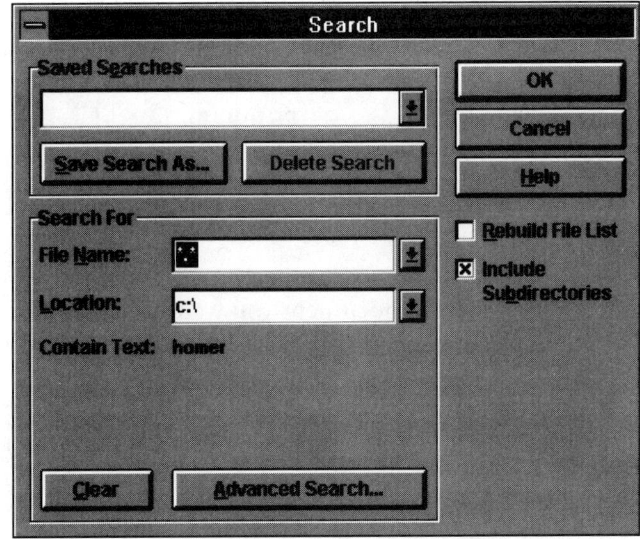

FIGURE AB.11

The Search dialog box lets you search an entire drive for a particular file, based on the file's name, extension, date, contents, or summary information.

- Or, if all you know is a bit of the information in the file's Summary Info, choose Advanced Search, click on the Summary tab, then type in whatever summary information you want to search for.
- Or, if all you know is a little content that might be unique to that particular document, choose Advanced Search, and type that little bit of known text into the text box beneath Containing Text. For example, if you're looking for a letter to Homer Frizbomb that you wrote umpteen weeks ago, you could type **Homer** or **Frizbomb** into the Containing Text box.

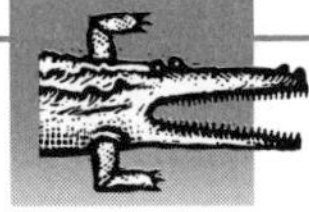

WARNING: *Searching through files for specific content can take a lo-o-o-o-ng time. Use that method only if you have no other recourse.*

- Or, if you know the approximate date that you created, or last saved, the file, choose Advanced Search. Then click the TimeStamp tab, and enter a range of dates under Last Saved, or Created (depending on which date you know).

6. Choose OK until you see the dialog box indicating that Find Files is searching for the file and building a file list.

When Find File has completed its search (which might take a while) the names of any files that match your search criterion will be listed under Listed Files in the Find File dialog box, as in the example shown in Figure AB.12. There LETTER99.DOC is the only file that matched the search in this example.

To get an idea of what's inside a file, move the highlighter to its name. Then, under View, choose Preview, File Info, or Summary to pick which kind of information you want to view about the file.

If you find the document you want to open, just double-click its name, or click its name once and choose Open.

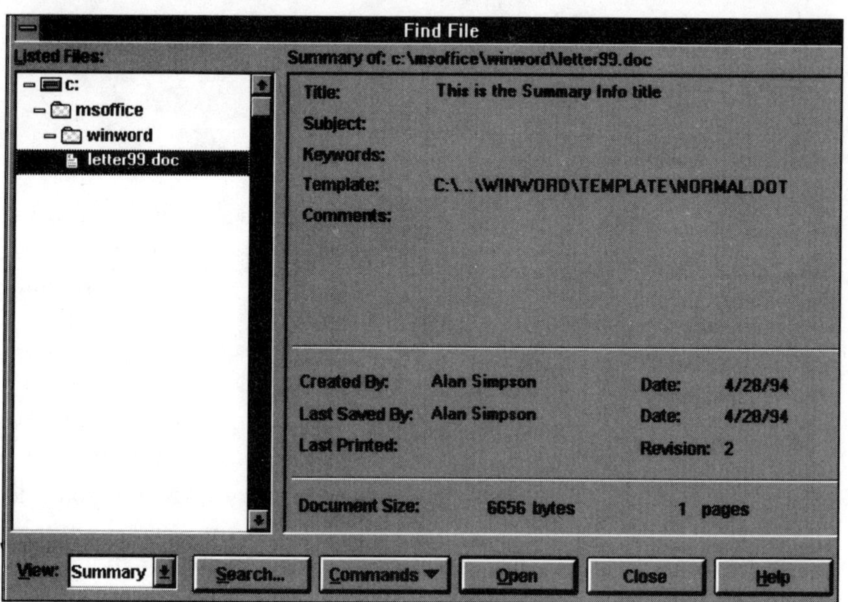

FIGURE AB.12

When Find File has completed its search, this dialog box appears. Any files that match your search criterion will be listed under Listed Files. To open a file, double-click its name.

Related Topics

- *Summary Info* here in Appendix B.
- *Open (Retrieve) Saved Work* here in Appendix B.
- Find File's help screens (press F1 or click the Help button while you're in Find File).

Fonts

A font (typeface) is a particular style, weight, and size of print. Typically you measure the height of a font in *points*, where 1 point equals roughly 1/72 of a inch. Windows, Microsoft Office, and your printer each come with fonts you can use in any document. Plus, you can purchase and install additional fonts.

There are thousands of fonts available for the PC. Figure AB.13 shows just a few examples—some of which you already own because they come with Windows or Office.

FIGURE AB.13

Sample fonts. The name in parentheses, where shown, indicates the publisher of that font. Appendix C lists their addresses and phone numbers.

Arial Bold Italic
Courier
Times Roman
Script
Certificate
COMIC STRIP (Swfte)
Lucida Calligraphy (Microsoft)
MYTHOS (Adobe)
Remedy (Emigre)

Neither your computer, nor printer, can *create* fonts. You can only use fonts that you've purchased and installed on your computer.

To Use a Font

To use a font:

1. In Word, Excel, or PowerPoint, type the text to which you want to apply the font.

NOTE: *In Access, you can apply fonts to text on forms and reports by opening that form or report in design view. For more information, search Access's help for Fonts.*

2. Select the text to which you want to apply the font by dragging the mouse pointer through that text or by using any of the other techniques described under *Select, Then Do* here in Appendix B.
3. Now you can do either of the following to apply a font to that selected text:
   - If the Formatting toolbar is open, choose a font, size, and a weight (such as Bold, Italic, Underline) from the Formatting toolbar.
   - If the Formatting toolbar isn't handy, or if you want to control the color and other special effects, choose Format ➢ Font from the application's menu bar. You'll be taken to the Font dialog box which looks something like Figure AB.14. Make your selections then choose OK.

That's all there is to it!

Related Topics

- *Select, Then Do* here in Appendix B
- *Toolbars* here in Appendix B

FIGURE AB.14

The Font dialog box for Microsoft Word. Your list of fonts might be different.

Help

Learning to use the Windows help system is the most important skill of all. There is no quicker, easier way to get "How To" instructions, and answers to your questions.

Getting into Help

Each application has its own built-in help system. Even Program Manager has its own help. So the first thing you want to do, always, is make sure you're starting help from the application that you want help with.

For instance, if you want help with Microsoft Word, you should be using Word at the moment. And when you go for help, make sure you choose the Help command from Word's menu bar.

In any given Windows application, there are generally three ways to get into help:

- Press the F1 key for context-sensitive help (meaning, the help that appears will usually be relevant to whatever menu or dialog box is on your screen at the moment).

- Or, choose Help ➢ Contents (or some other command) from the application's menu bar.
- Or, if you see a command button labeled Help, click that button for help with the current dialog box.

A help window appears, most likely covering some portion of your work.

The Case of the Disappearing Help

It's important to understand that the Help information is in a window. So if you click any window *outside* the help window, that clicked window jumps to the forefront, most likely covering your help window. If that happens, you can return to help by holding down the Alt key and pressing Tab repeatedly until you see a small box with the Help icon (question mark) in it, as in the example below.

Release the Alt key to bring the help window back to the forefront.

Stopping Help from Disappearing

If you want to be able to see the help window while working in the associated application, you need to tell help to keep its window "on top." To do so, choose Help ➢ Always on Top from the help window's menu bar, as illustrated in Figure AB.15.

In some cases, you might also see a command button labeled "On Top" in the help widow. In that case, you can just click that button to keep the window on top of other windows.

Moving, Sizing, and Scrolling through Help

You can also size and position the help window like you would any other. For example, you can drag its title bar to move the window or drag its borders to size it. To scroll through help, use the scroll bar or cursor keys (PgUp, PgDn, ↓, ↑).

FIGURE AB.15

Normally when you click outside a help window, the help window gets covered and disappears from view. To prevent that, choose Help ➢ Always On Top from the Help window's menu bar (not the application's menu bar).

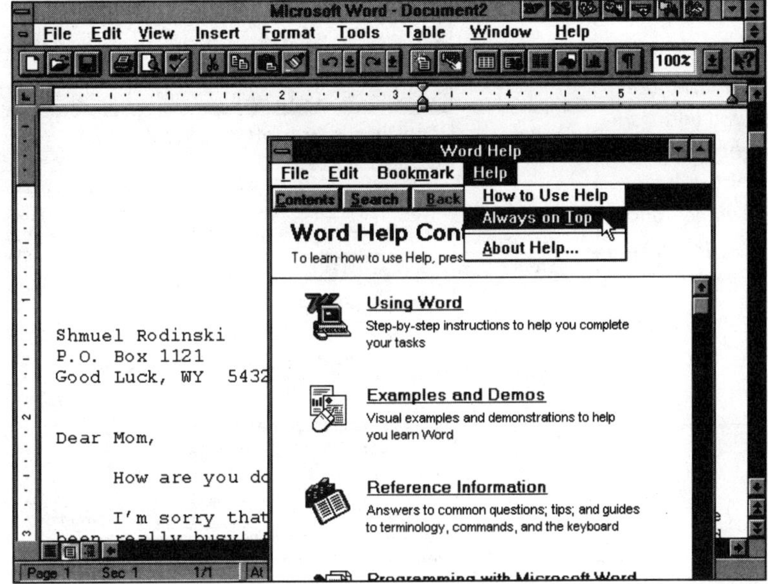

To Use Help

Once you're in Help, you can use all the tools presented in the help window to find information. Though the exact tools in a help window varies, most offer some combination of a menu bar, some command buttons, jump topics, glossary terms, and perhaps some cross-reference, like the example shown in Figure AB.16. Just click whichever item you want to use.

To Print a Help Topic

To print the help information that's currently on your screen, choose File ➢ Print Topic from the help window's menu bar. Or, in a "How To" help Window, just click the Print command button.

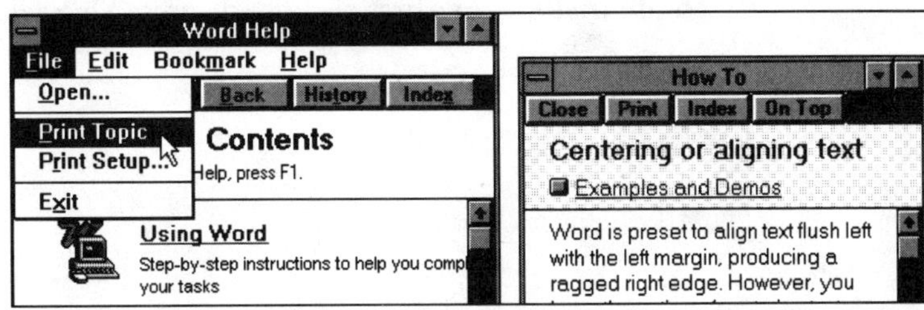

FIGURE AB.16

Help windows have their own menu bar and command buttons, and might also have jump topics, glossary entries, and cross-references.

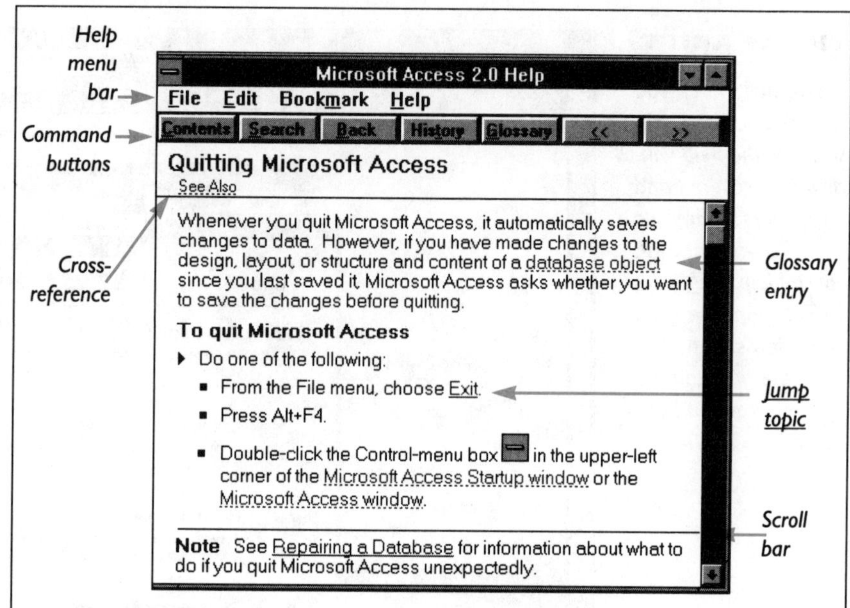

Asking "What Does That Command Do?"

Some applications offer a help button that you can use to answer a question like "What is *that* thing?" or "What does *that* command do?" The button looks like this on the Standard toolbar (when the mouse pointer is on the button, of course):

To use that button, first click it (or press Shift+F1). The mouse pointer changes to this:

Next, to get help with a command, just go through the menus as though you were actually going to select that command. Or, to get help with a toolbar button, click that toolbar button. A help screen will appear describing the feature that that command or button gives you access to.

TIP: *Many objects on the screen are "right-clickable." So another way to get some clues about how to use or change something on your screen is to right-click it and see if you get a menu of commands to choose from.*

How to Search Help

If you want to know how to do a particular task, or just want information about a particular topic, you can search help for that topic. Here's how:

1. To get started, complete one of the steps below to get to the help Search dialog box (Figure AB.17):
    - If you're already in a help window, click the Search command button.
    - If you're not already in a help window, choose Help ➢ Search from the application's menu bar.

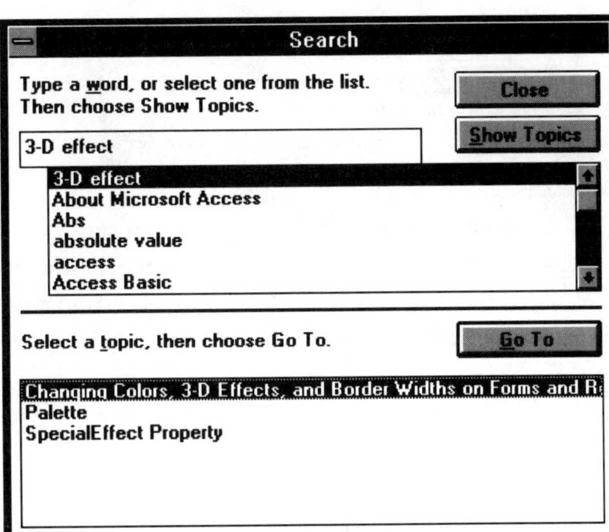

FIGURE AB.17

The Search dialog box lets you search help for any topic.

2. Type a word, or scroll through the list of topics shown. Then click on the Show Topics button or press ↵.

3. In the lower half of the Search window, click on a specific topic. Then click the Go To button or press ↵. (Optionally, you can just double-click a topic and skip the Go To button.)

You'll be taken to the help topic you specified. If you need to return to Search to try a different topic, just click the Search command button near the top if the help window.

To Close Help

When you've finished with help, close it as you would any other window:

- Double-click the control-menu box in the upper-left corner of the Help window (*not* the application's window).
- Or choose File ➢ Exit from the Help window's menu bar (*not* the applications' menu bar!)

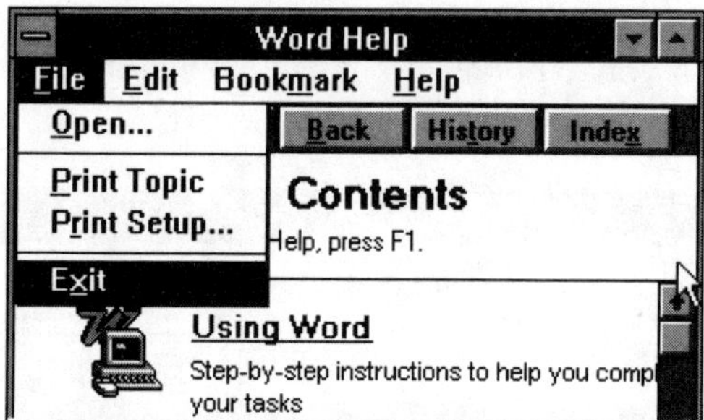

When you close Help in this way, you can't get back to it by pressing Alt+Tab. Pressing Alt+Tab only uncovers open windows that are currently covered by some other window. But you can just press F1 or choose a Help command from the application's menu bar again when you need help.

Hands-On Help

I highly recommend that you let Windows teach you a bit about the help system. Starting from Program Manager, press F1, wait for the Help window to appear, then press F1 a second time. Read the contents of the help window, then go exploring.

Related Topics

- *Cue Cards* here in Appendix B.
- *Wizards* here in Appendix B.

Install a Windows Application

When you buy new software for your PC—be it an application, fonts, clip art, whatever—it will come with installation instructions. All you really need to do to install the software is read and follow those instructions.

Of course, if you're like me and 99% of the other human beings here on Earth, you probably prefer to read the instructions only as a last resort, when all else fails. In that case, you can try using the technique I always use to install a new product on my PC. But be forewarned. I'm not guaranteeing that this will work in *every* case. This is just the way I try to install Windows software before digging around the manual for installation instructions:

1. Get to the Windows Program Manager.
2. Insert into floppy drive A: or B: the floppy disk (or Disk #1 of the series of floppies that contains the software you want to install).
3. Choose File ➢ Run from Program Manager's menu bar.
4. Click the Browse button.
5. Under Drives choose whichever drive you put the floppy into back in step 2 (A: or B:)
6. Click on whichever file name looks like it might be the installation program (e.g.., SETUP.EXE or INSTALL.EXE), then choose OK.
7. When you get back to the Run dialog box, choose OK again.

At this point, the installation program should take over, and you can just follow the instructions on the screen. If it *doesn't* work, you'll need to read the instructions. (Bummer.)

Menus

The most basic of basic skills in using computers is learning to use the menus. It's also a very easy skill to learn, once you know how to work a mouse (which is discussed in Appendix A of this book).

Virtually every Windows application has its own menu bar. That bar is always just beneath the application's title bar (Figure AB.18). To get an application to do something, you choose commands from its menu bar.

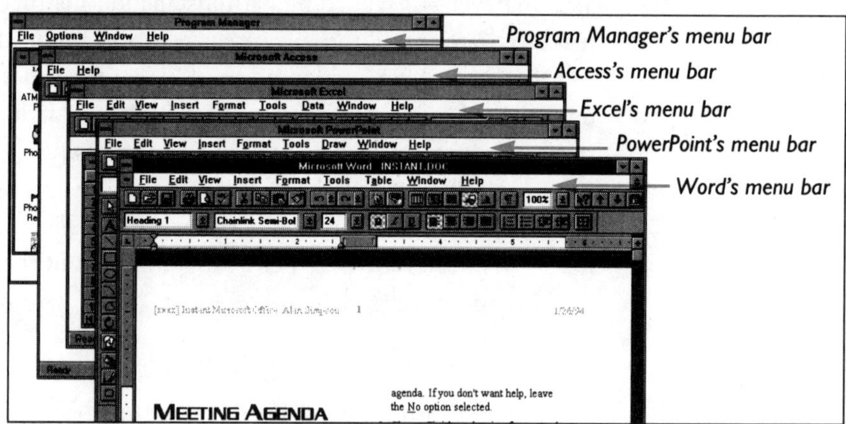

FIGURE AB.18

Every Windows application has its own menu bar, just beneath that application's title bar. The menu commands affect only the document(s) inside that particular application's window.

Each menu bar affects only the document or documents inside that application's window. For example, to get Excel to do something, you must choose something from Excel's menu bar. For this reason, it's always a good idea to glance up at the title bar just before you choose a menu command, especially when you have two or more open applications on your screen, just to make sure you're indeed using the correct menu bar.

NOTE: *Remember, if you maximize the window of the application you're using, you'll avoid the common mistake of making your selections from the wrong menu bar. You can maximize/restore an application's window by double-clicking its title bar or by clicking the Maximize/Restore button at the far right end of the title bar.*

How to Work the Menus with a Mouse

To work the menus using a mouse:

1. Click whatever command you want in the menu bar. A drop-down menu appears.

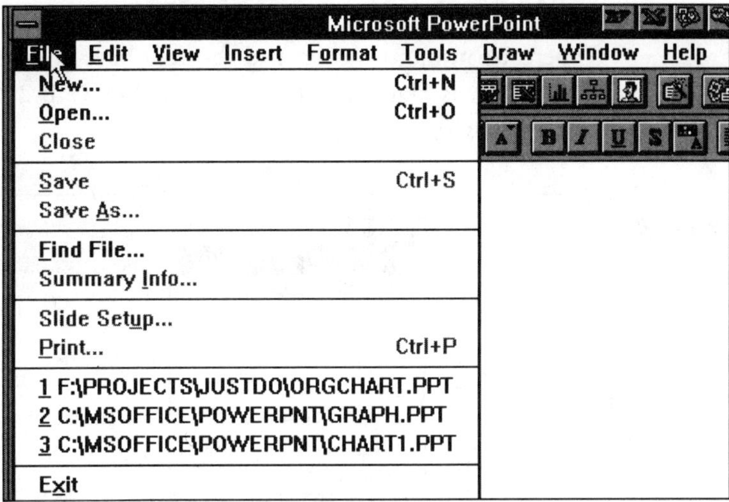

2. In the drop-down menu, click whatever command you want.

That's all there is to it. You might get to a third menu, or to a dialog box eventually. But wherever you end up, the same basic principal holds true: You just click on whatever you want.

How to Work the Menus with a Keyboard

If you prefer to use the keyboard, you can work the menus like this:

1. Hold down the Alt key and type the underlined letter in the command you want. For instance, to choose File from the menu bar, press Alt+F.

2. To choose a command from the drop-down menu, just type the letter that's underlined in the command. (You don't need to hold

down the Alt key once the drop-down menu appears, though you can keep holding it down. If you press Alt a second time, however, the menu will vanish.)

That's all there is to that.

What's on the Menu?

There are numerous clues and shortcut keys on the menu bars to help you along, as Figure AB.19 illustrates. Table AB.2 summarizes what each clue means.

FIGURE AB.19

Clues on menu bars

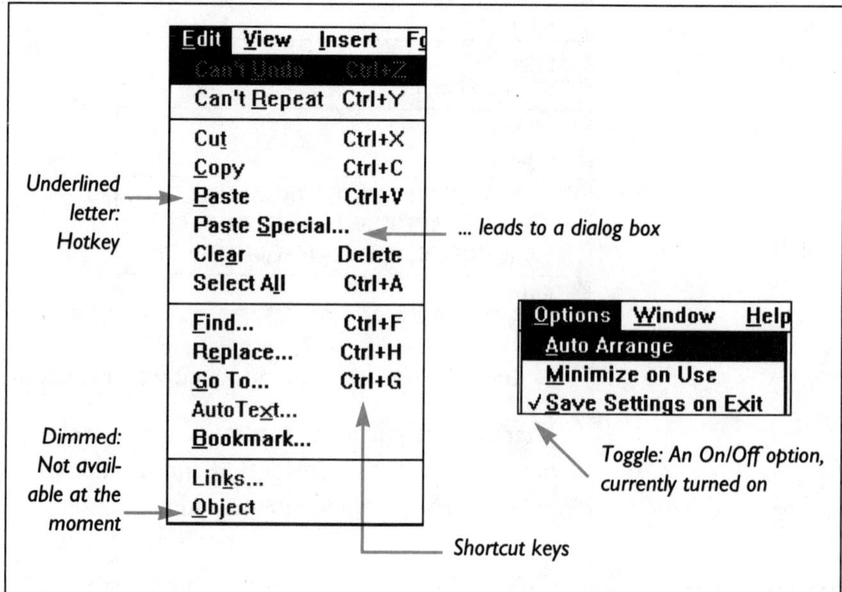

Dimmed Commands

If a menu command is dimmed, it just means that that particular command isn't relevant at the moment, so you can't select it. If you're not sure why a particular command is dimmed, try searching Help for that command to see what might be wrong.

TABLE AB.2

Symbols on menus

MENU SYMBOL	MEANING
x	Underlined letter is the hotkey. On the menu bar, hold down Alt and tap the underlined letter to open that menu. On the drop-down menu, just tap the hotkey letter.
...	Command leads to a dialog box.
√	Indicates that a toggle (a command that can be "on or "off") is currently "on." Choosing a toggle switches to the opposite setting.
Dimmed (gray)	This command is not relevant at the moment, so cannot be selected. Maybe you need to select text first, or open a document.
Shortcut key	The key or combination keystroke to the right of a menu command is the shortcut key, which you can press instead of going through the menu.

(Almost) Universal Menu Commands

Even though every application has its own unique set of menu commands, there are certain commands that are available in *almost* every Windows application you'll ever come across. They're listed in Table AB.3.

Related Topics

- *Start an Application* here in Appendix B
- *How to Work a Mouse* in Appendix A
- *How to Work the Keyboard* in Appendix A
- *Shortcuts* here in Appendix B

TABLE AB.3

(Almost) Universal menu commands.

ACTION	COMMON MENU SEQUENCE	COMMON SHORTCUT
Copy to Clipboard	Edit ➢ Copy	Ctrl+C
Exit	File ➢ Exit	Alt+F4
Font	Format ➢ Font	—
Help	Help ➢ Contents	F1
Move to Clipboard	Edit ➢ Cut	Ctrl+X
New document	File ➢ New	Ctrl+N
Open a document	File ➢ Open	Ctrl+O
Paste from Clipboard	Edit ➢ Paste	Ctrl+V
Print	File ➢ Print	Ctrl+P
Save document	File ➢ Save	Ctrl+S
Select All	Edit ➢ Select All	Ctrl+A
Toolbars (view)	View ➢ Toolbars	—
Undo	Edit ➢ Undo	Ctrl+Z

Open (Retrieve) Saved Work

Any document that you create and save is stored on the disk in a file. To resume work on that document, you need to open that file. Here's how:

1. Start the application that you (or whomever) originally used to create the document.

TIP: *If you've recently edited the document you're trying to open, choose File from the menu bar. Then, if you see the name of the file you want to open down near the bottom of the menu, just click that name.*

2. Choose File ➢ Open from that application's menu bar. You'll get to the Open dialog box, which will look something like this.

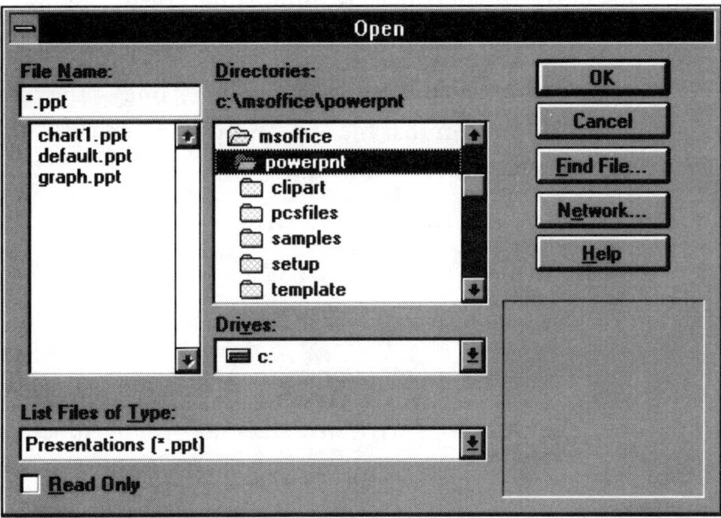

3. Double-click the name of the file that contains the document you want to open.

If you don't see the name of the file you want to open in Step 3, then try these steps:

- The file names are in alphabetical order. So if you don't see a particular file name, perhaps it's just scrolled out of view. Scroll down the list using the scroll bar. Or press Tab until the highlighter is in the list of file names, then press the PgDn or ↵ keys to scroll.

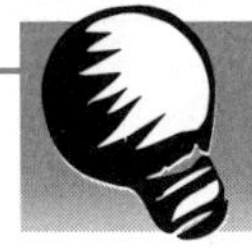

TIP: *Here's yet another way to quickly locate a file. Leave the insertion point in the File Name text box, press Home, then type the first few letters of the file name. For example, if you're looking for a Word document that begins with the letters app, change the File Name entry from* ****.doc*** *(or whatever it is) to* ***app*.doc****. Then press ↵.*

- If you still don't see the file you're trying to open, perhaps it's stored on a different drive or directory. Choose the appropriate Drive, Directory, and List File of Type options to zero in on the file you're looking for. (See *Drives, Directories, and Files* here in Appendix B if you don't understand what that means.)

- If you still can't find the file you're looking for, use Find File to search entire disk drives. See *Find a Lost File* here in Appendix B.

After you've double-clicked the name of the file you want to open, the document in that file appears on your screen. You can edit, print, or do whatever you want with that file using all the features of the application.

Related Topics

- *Start an Application* here in Appendix B
- *Find a Lost File* here in Appendix B
- *Drives, Directories, and Files* here in Appendix B

Print

Printing is easy in any Office application. In general, you just follow these steps:

1. If you want to print the document, worksheet, or presentation that's currently on your screen, skip to step 4 right now.
2. To print a document that's *not* on your screen, first start the application you used to create that document.
3. Then choose File ➢ Open from the application's menu bar, and open the document that you want to print.
4. Choose File ➢ Print from the application's menu bar. You'll be taken to a Print dialog box that looks something like the one at the top of the next page (which is from Word).

TIP: *Do you like shortcuts? Here's a couple for printing: Click the Print button in the toolbar, or press Ctrl+P!*

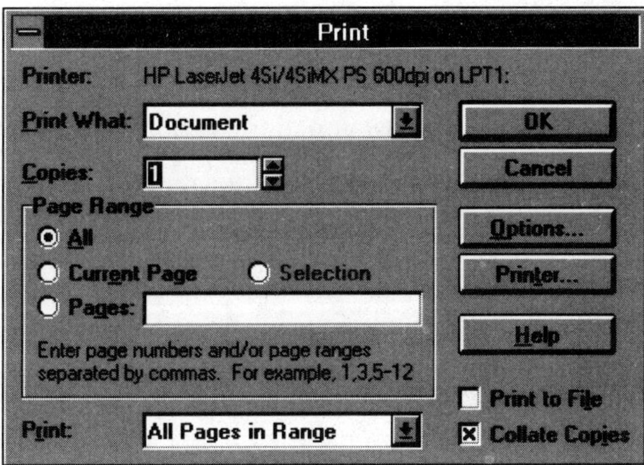

- If you want to print the whole thing, choose OK.
- If you have several printers connected to your computer and want to print on a specific printer, choose the Printer button, double-click the name of the printer you want to use, then choose Close.
- If you want to print only certain pages or if you want to print multiple copies, select the appropriate options in the dialog box (click the Help button if you need help with those options).

5. Choose OK from the Print dialog box.

It might take a while for the printer to actually start printing. However, you need not wait for the entire print job to be done before you resume work. As soon as the print message box disappears and the hourglass changes back to a normal mouse pointer, you can go back to using your computer. Basically, you can do anything you want *except* exit Windows or turn off the computer. Don't do either of those things until the print job is complete.

To Print in Access

Printing in Access is a little different from most other applications:

1. If you want to print an object in the current database, skip to step 4 now.

2. Start Microsoft Access.

3. Choose File ➢ Open Database from Access's menu bar, then open the database that contains the object you want to print.

4. Complete the three steps illustrated in Figure AB.20 (starting with Step 1, of course).

FIGURE AB.20

To print in Access, click the name of the object you want to print. Then choose File ➢ Print from Access's menu bar or click the Print button on the toolbar.

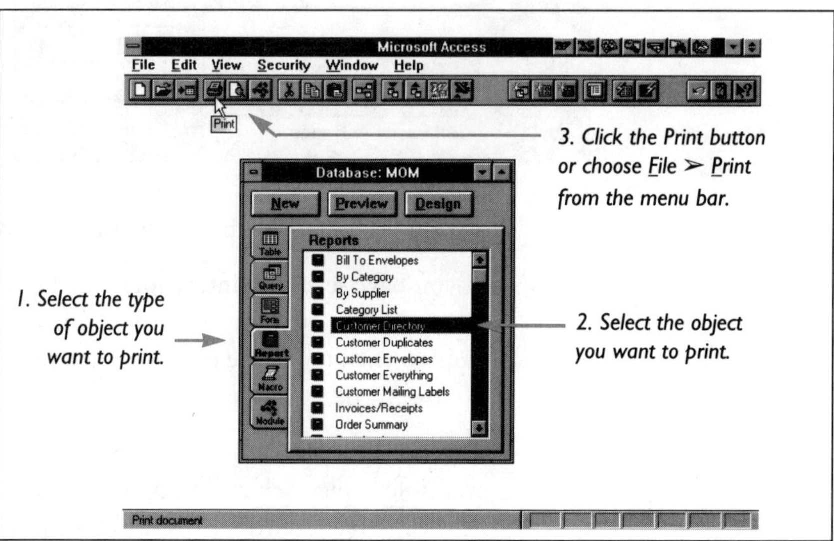

Related Topics

- *Start an Application* here in Appendix B.
- *Open (Retrieve) a Document* here in Appendix B
- *Menus* here in Appendix B.

Save Your Work

It's crucial to understand that any new document you create, or any change you make to a document, is initially stored only in the computer's RAM (Random Access Memory). And when you turn off the computer, or even when you just exit Windows, everything in RAM is erased.

If you want to be able to resume work, or reprint, that document in the future, you must *save* the document. Saving a document puts a copy of the document on the hard disk, which doesn't get erased when you turn off the computer.

When to Save Your Work

Certainly it makes sense to save your work as soon as you've finished with it for the day. In fact, if you get into the habit of always exiting an application before you turn off the computer, you'll be notified on the screen if you're leaving behind any unsaved work. You'll also be given an opportunity to save that work, before the application closes.

It's also a good idea to get into the habit of saving your work every few minutes, just in case a power outage or some other mishap erases everything in RAM for you.

Another good habit to get into is to save your work just before you try some daring new procedure. That way, if the experiment makes a complete mess of your document, you can just close the messed up version (choose File ➢ Close ➢ No), then open up the "clean" version you just saved (choose File, then click the name of the file near the bottom of the File drop-down menu).

If the new procedure proves fruitful, rather than disastrous, then perhaps you'll want to save this new accomplishment right away (choose File ➢ Save).

To Save a Document

To save the document that's currently on your screen:

1. Choose File. ➢ Save from the application's menu bar (or just press Ctrl+S in most applications).
2. If you've previously saved this document and given it a filc name, you're done. The current version of your document just instantly replaces the older version on the disk, and you can skip the remaining steps.
3. If you've never given the document a file name, you'll see a dialog box that looks something like the one at the top of the next page.

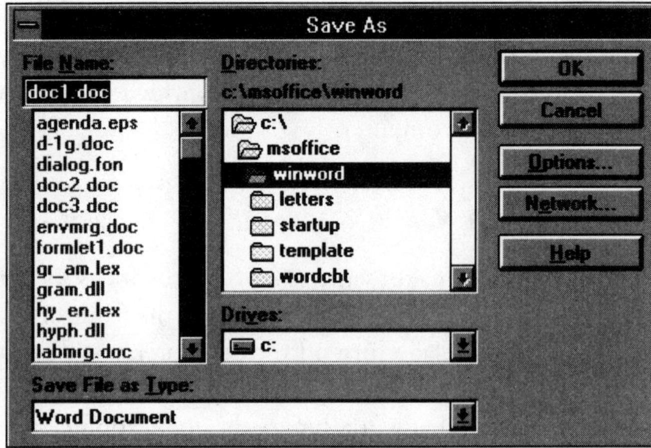

4. Type in a valid DOS file name, eight letters maximum length, no blank spaces. No punctuation. (See Table AB.1 under *Drives, Directories, and Files* here in Appendix B for some examples of valid and invalid file names.)

5. Optionally, you can add a period followed by a three-letter extension to the file name you type. However, you'll surely find it easiest to omit that extension and let the application add its own automatically. Table AB.4 shows the extensions each Office application automatically adds to the file name you provide.

6. Choose OK.

7. If you see a message asking if you want to replace the existing copy of that file, that means the file name you chose already exists. You need to think carefully before you choose Yes or No:

   - If you know for certain what's in the file you're about to replace, and know you can safely trash that work, choose Yes to replace that document with your new one.
   - If you *don't* know what's in the file you're about to replace, choose No. Then type in a different file name and choose OK.
   - If you're not quite sure what you want to do right now, or if you got to this dialog box by accident, choose Cancel. You're work, however, is *not* saved.

TABLE AB.4:

The three-letter extension that each Office application adds to the file name you make up.

APPLICATION	EXTENSION	STANDS FOR
Access	.MDB	Microsoft Database
Excel	.XLS	Excel Spreadsheet
PowerPoint	.PPT	PowerPoint
Word	.DOC	Document

- If you want help with the dialog box, choose Help.

The only thing you're likely to see on your screen is a little odometer racing along the status bar near the lower-left corner of the application's window. You won't see any other change on the screen. But you can rest assured that any work you've achieved up to this point is safely stored on disk.

Related Topics

- *Start an Application* here in Appendix B
- *Open (Retrieve) Saved Work* here in Appendix B
- *Summary Info* here in Appendix B

Select, Then Do

Any time you want to do something to a "chunk of stuff" in your document, you must first *select* that chunk. After you've made the selection, you can use menu commands or toolbar buttons to do whatever it is you want to do.

Here's an example, using a Microsoft Word document, and Word's Formatting toolbar. Suppose I type a title and some text into a Word document, like the one at the top of the next page.

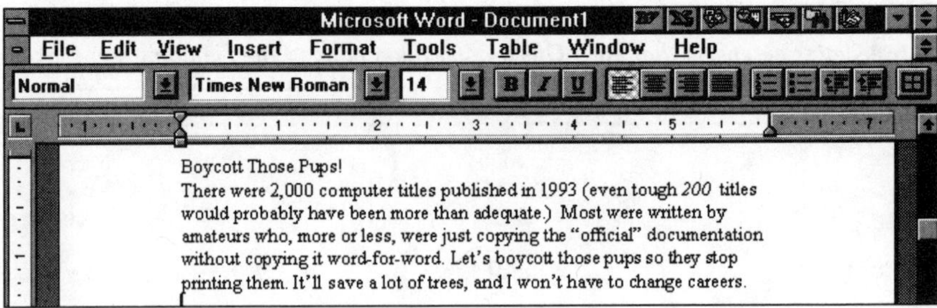

Now suppose I want to center the title, and change its font to something more attention-grabbing. First I'd select that text by dragging the mouse pointer through it, so it's selected (highlighted) like this:

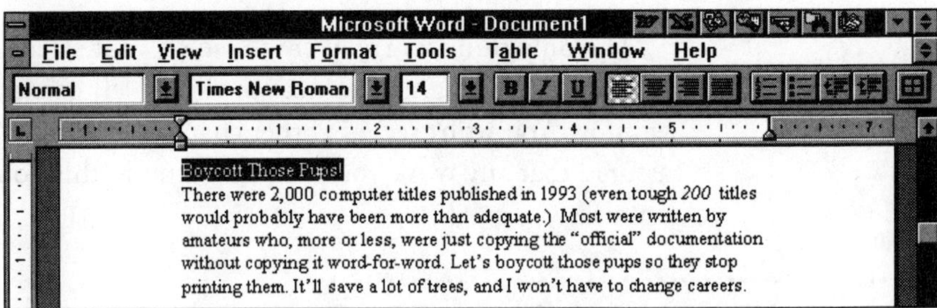

Next, I could choose a font, size, and the Center button on the Formatting toolbar to format that selected text, as below.

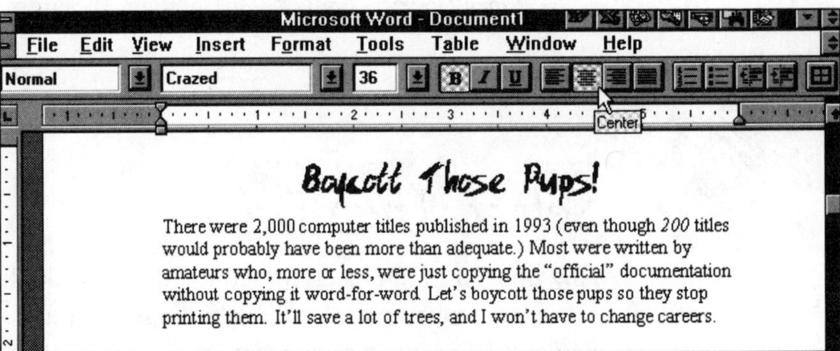

Of course this is just one simple example. You can select *any* amount of text in *any* document, using *any* of the techniques described in this section.

Selecting Text with a Mouse

Selecting text with a mouse is easy:

1. Click wherever you want to start the selection.
2. Hold down the mouse button, and drag the mouse in whatever direction you want to extend the selection.
3. When all the text you want is selected, release the mouse button.

TIP: *Word generally extends the selection area on a word-by-word basis. If you need to extend or shrink the selection area just slightly, hold down the Shift key and press the ← or → keys.*

Now you can choose menu commands or toolbar buttons to operate on that selected text.

Important Warnings!

A couple of important points to keep in mind when there's text selected on your screen:

- If you start typing while text is selected, your new text *completely replaces* the selected text. If you do this by accident (and you probably will—it's really easy to do), choose Edit ➢ Undo right away to bring back the deleted text.
- If you position the insertion point elsewhere in the document, using either mouse or keyboard, the selected text is immediately deselected (though not deleted). Once you've selected text, choose commands from the menus or toolbars unless you specifically want to deselect the selected text. If you need to scroll around without extending the selection area, use the scroll bars on the document window.

Some Shortcuts for Selecting Text

Table AB.5 lists some handy shortcuts for selecting chunks of text in Microsoft Word.

Selecting Text with the Keyboard

You can also select text using the keyboard. This is especially handy when you're typing and just want to select a small chunk of text without taking your hands off the keyboard. To select using the keyboard:

1. Use the cursor positioning keys (e.g. ↑, ↓, →, ←, Page Up, Page Down, and so forth), or the mouse, to move the insertion point to where you want to start the selection.
2. Use any of the combination keystrokes listed in Table AB.6 to extend the selection through whatever text you want to select. (Be sure to hold down the Shift key at all times while selecting text.)
3. Release the Shift key when the text is selected.

After you've selected your text, use the menu commands, toolbars, and shortcut keys to format that text. Remember, if you type anything while text is selected, you'll *replace* the selected text! If you move the cursor without holding down the Shift key, you'll deselect the selected text.

Selecting in Rows and Columns

When you're working with text or data that's organized into rows and columns, like a Word table or an Excel worksheet or an Access table, you

TABLE AB.5

Shortcuts for selecting text in Microsoft Word.

TO SELECT...	DO THIS
A word	Double-click the word.
A line	Click in the left margin next to the line.
A sentence	Hold down the Ctrl key and click anywhere within the sentence.
A paragraph	Double-click in the left margin just to the left of the paragraph, or triple-click anywhere within the paragraph.
The entire document	Triple-click anywhere in the left margin or press Ctrl+A.

can still select things by dragging the mouse through them, or by using the keys listed in Table AB.6. However, there are some additional short-cuts, as illustrated in Figures AB.21, AB.22, and AB.23:

Selecting a Picture or Chart

To select a picture or chart, just click it once. You'll know it's selected when it has sizing handles (little squares) around the frame, as below:

TABLE AB.6

Keys you can use to select text

TO EXTEND THE SELECTION...	PRESS
One character to the right	Shift+ →
One character to the left	Shift+ ←
To the end of the word	Ctrl+Shift+ →
To the start of a word	Ctrl+Shift+ ←
To the end of the line	Shift+End
To the start of the line	Shift+Home
Down one line	Shift+ ↓
Up one line	Shift+ ↑
To the end of the paragraph	Ctrl+Shift+ ↓
To the start of the paragraph	Ctrl+Shift+ ↑
To the end of the document	Ctrl+Shift+End
To the start of the document	Ctrl+Shift+Home
The entire document	Ctrl+A

FIGURE AB.21

To select entire rows and columns when working with a Microsoft Word table, place the mouse pointer just outside the row or column you want to select (the mouse pointer turns to a small arrow). Then click to select the current row or column, or drag the mouse pointer across columns or down through rows.

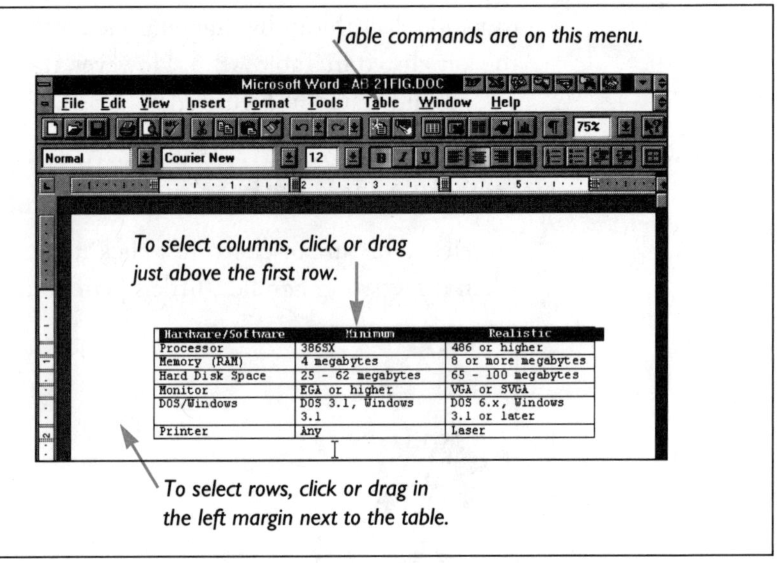

FIGURE AB.22

To select entire rows and columns when using an Excel worksheet, click, or drag through, the column and row headings.

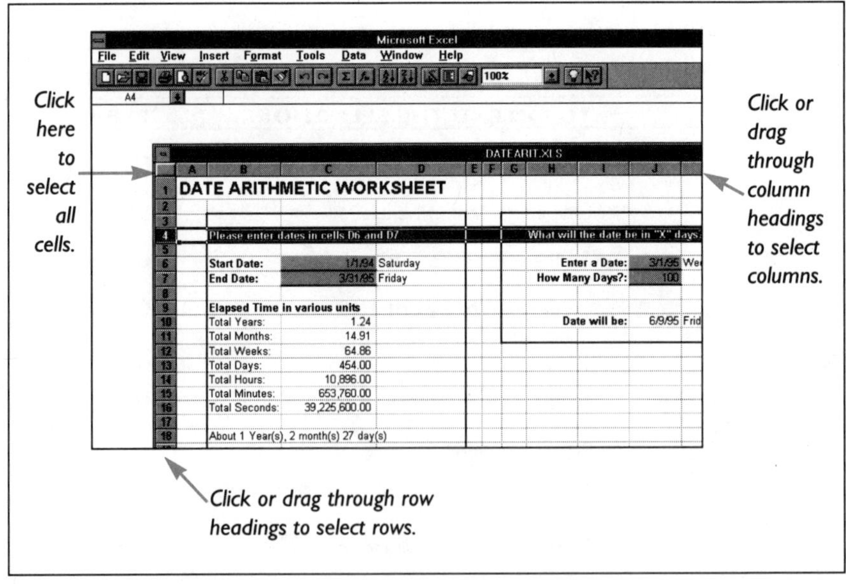

FIGURE AB.23

To select entire rows and columns when using an Access table, click, or drag through, the field names or record selectors.

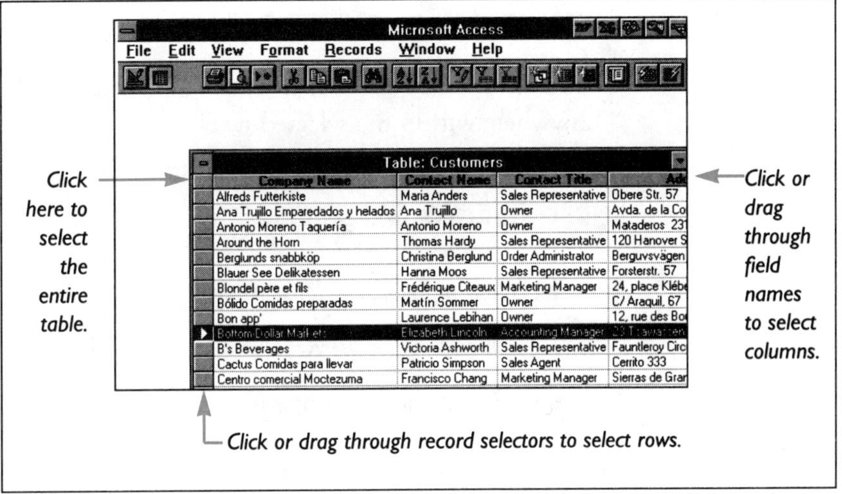

Once the picture is selected, you can (usually):

- Drag any sizing handle to resize the picture
- Drag the picture's frame to move the picture
- Cut or copy the picture to the Clipboard by using Edit ➢ Cut or Edit ➢ Copy.
- Press Delete (Del) to delete the picture. (If you do this accidentally, choose Edit ➢ Undo to bring the picture back.)
- In Word, you can frame the picture so text wraps around it. Right-click the picture and choose Frame Picture from the menu that appears. You can also drag the framed picture to any place in your document.

Some Things You Can Do with Selected Text

There are countless things you can do with text or a picture once its selected. (Only some of these things will apply to selected rows and columns.) Table AB.7 summarizes the most common things you'll want to do with selected text. Shortcuts for most of those features are available on the Formatting toolbar in most Office applications.

To Deselect Selected Text

To deselect selected text, press any arrow key (↑, ↓, → or ←), or click anywhere within the selected text.

Related Topics

- *How to Work a Mouse* in Appendix A
- *How to Work the Keyboard* in Appendix A
- *Toolbars* here in Appendix B.

TABLE AB.7:

Just a few of the things you can do with selected text in most Office applications. (If in doubt, try it out!)

IF YOU WANT TO...	DO THIS...
Apply **boldface**, *italics*, underline	Choose the appropriate button from the Formatting toolbar, or press Ctrl+B for Boldface, Ctrl+I for Italics, or Ctrl+U for underline.
Center, Right-Align, Justify (stretch), or Left-align	Choose the appropriate button from the Formatting toolbar, or press Ctrl+E to center, Ctrl+J to justify, Ctrl+L to left-align, Ctrl+R to right-align.
Copy selection to another application	Choose Edit ➢ Copy, move the insertion point to the destination, then choose Edit ➢ Paste.
Copy the selection	Hold down the Ctrl key and drag the selection to a new location.
Indent (Microsoft Word)	Press Ctrl+M to indent, press Ctrl+Shift+M to unindent.
Delete the selection	Press Delete (Del).
Double- or single-space (in Microsoft Word)	Press Ctrl+2 to double-space, Ctrl+1 to single-space
Font (Change)	Choose Format ➢ Font or make a selection from the Formatting toolbar.
Move the selection	Drag it to a new location.
Print the selected text	Choose File ➢ Print. Specify "Selection" as the amount to print, then choose OK
Replace the selected text	Type the new text.

Shortcuts

A shortcut is a keystroke (or in some cases, a combination keystroke) that you can use as an alternative to the menus or toolbars. They're handy when you're typing because you don't have to take your hands off the keyboard.

There's a shortcut for many of the commands in every application. You can see what the shortcut for a particular command is, just by looking at the shortcut key next to the command in the menu, as shown below (Ctrl+Z, Ctrl+Y, and so forth).

Edit View Insert For	
Undo Typing	Ctrl+Z
Repeat Typing	Ctrl+Y
Cut	Ctrl+X
Copy	Ctrl+C
Paste	Ctrl+V
Paste Special...	
Clear	Delete
Select All	Ctrl+A
Find...	Ctrl+F
Replace...	Ctrl+H
Go To...	Ctrl+G
AutoText...	
Bookmark...	

Some fairly universal shortcut keys are listed in Table AB.8. (I say they're *fairly* universal, because I can't be sure that every single one of the thousands of Windows applications out there follow these standards. If in doubt, just look for shortcuts in the menus, or search the application's help for *Shortcut.*)

Shortcuts for Moving through a Document

You can also move the cursor (or insertion point) using shortcut keys. These are handy when you don't want to take your hands off the keyboard to use the mouse and scroll bars. Table AB.9 lists some of the more commonly used cursor-positioning keys. But you might want to search your application's Help for *Shortcut* to see if it offers these same shortcuts, and also to see if it offers any others.

Related Topics

- *How to Work the Keyboard* in Appendix A.
- *Select, Then Do* here in Appendix B.
- *Shortcuts* in your application's help system.

TABLE AB.8

Some (fairly) universal shortcut keys.

TASK	COMMON SHORTCUT
Back out	Esc
Copy (to Clipboard)	Ctrl+C
Create new document	Ctrl+N
Cut (to Clipboard)	Ctrl+X
Exit	Alt+F4
Help	F1
Open a document	Ctrl+O
Paste (from Clipboard)	Ctrl+V
Print	Ctrl+P
Switch (to another open application)	Alt+Tab or Ctrl+Esc
Undo	Ctrl+Z

TABLE AB.9:

Shortcut keys you can use to move around a document, instead of using the mouse and scroll bars.

TO MOVE TO...	PRESS
Left one character	←
Right one character	→
Up one line	↑
Down one line	↓
Next word	Ctrl+→
Previous word	Ctrl+←
End of line	End
Start of line	Home
Up one screen	Page Up (PgUp)
Down one screen	Page Down (PgDn)
The top of a document	Ctrl+Home
The end of a document	Ctrl+End
Right one column (tables)	Tab
Left one column (tables)	Shift+Tab

Start an Application

Before you can start a Windows application, you must install it on your computer. But you need only install the application once. So if you or somebody else has already installed the application, you don't need to concern yourself with that. (All Windows applications come with their own installation instructions.)

Once an application is installed on your hard disk, you can use either of the techniques that follow to start that application.

Starting an App from Office Manager

If the Office Manager toolbar is visible on your screen, and you want to start one of the applications in that toolbar, just click the appropriate button in that toolbar.

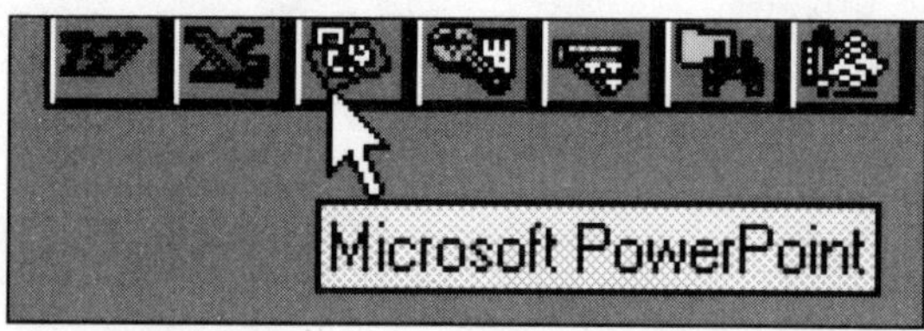

Starting an App from Program Manager

To start an application from Program Manager:

1. If Program Manager is readily visible on your screen, skip to Step 4.
2. If you're in DOS (the **C:\>** prompt), you'll need to get to Windows first. Type win then press ↵ at the DOS command prompt.
3. If you're in Windows, but can't see Program Manager anywhere on your screen, hold down the Alt key and press Tab until you see the box below. Then release the Alt key to bring Program Manager to the forefront.

TIP: *If your Program Manager screen is such a mess that you can't even find the icon you're looking for, you need to get a handle on keeping your screen organized! See Take Control of Windows in Appendix A.*

4. Double-click the group icon that contains the application you want to start (Figure AB.24).

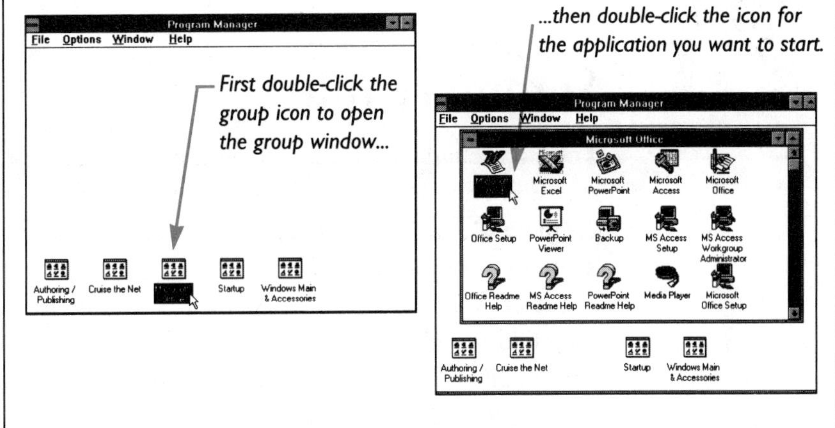

FIGURE AB.24

To start an application from the Windows Program Manager, first double-click the appropriate group icon to see its contents. Then double-click the icon for the application that you want to run.

5. Within the group window, double-click the icon for whatever application you want to run, as illustrated in Figure AB.24.

The application will start up, either in full-screen mode (thereby covering everything else on the screen), or in a partial window. To switch between full- and partial views, double-click the application's title at the top of the application's window.

When you've finished using the application, *remember to exit and save your work* (if you did any work with saving) before turning off the computer or exiting Windows.

Related Topics

- *Exit an Application* here in Appendix B.
- *Take Control of Windows* in Appendix A.
- *Instant Office* section

Summary Info

The eight-character maximum length of a file name, imposed by DOS and Windows 3.*x*, doesn't let you store a whole lot of information about a document. The latest versions of Word, Excel, and PowerPoint, however, let you store *summary information* along with your file.

Better yet, Microsoft Office (version 4.2) includes a small utility called Find File, which lets you search for a file based on its summary information. So, if you forget the little eight-character file name you gave a document, you can use Find File to search for the file based on its summary info.

Adding Summary Info to a Document

To add summary information to the Word, Excel, or PowerPoint document that's currently on your screen:

1. Choose File ➤ Summary Info from the application's menu bar. You'll see a Summary Info dialog box like the one below.

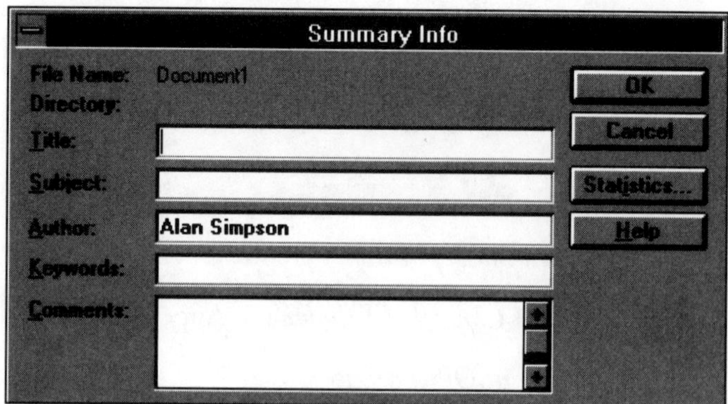

2. Fill in the blanks as you wish. But be sure to use meaningful information that will help you find the file later in case you forget its file name.

3. Choose OK.

When you save the document, the summary information will be saved along with the document.

Making the Summary Info Box Appear Automatically

If you want to get *always* create summary info for every new document you save, you can have the Summary Info dialog box appear automatically whenever you save a document. Or, if you don't want that box to appear automatically, you can follow these same steps to "de-automate" Summary Info:

1. If you have not already done so, start the application for which you want to automate (or "de-automate") the Summary Info dialog box.
2. From the application's menu bar, choose Tools ➢ Options. Then:
   - If you're in Microsoft Word, click on the Save Tab
   - If you're in Excel, click on the General tab.
3. To automate Summary Info, select Prompt for Summary Info so that option is marked with an X. To "de-automate" summary info, clear that same check box (by clicking it).
4. Choose OK.

If you automated summary information, the Summary Info dialog box will appear automatically whenever you save a document.

Related Topics

- *Find a Lost File* here in Appendix B.
- *Save Your Work* here in Appendix B.

Toolbars

Toolbars offer instant "one-click" access to application features. Each of the applications in Microsoft Office (i.e., Word, Excel, PowerPoint, and Access) has its own set of handy toolbars. Each toolbar is designed to help you with a particular type of work.

For example, the Standard toolbar in most applications offers buttons for saving, printing, and opening documents (among other things). The Formatting toolbar provides quick options for changing a font, adding boldface or italics, centering and aligning text. In the example below, the Standard and Formatting tools are docked just under Word's menu bar.

To Display or Hide Toolbars

You can easily hide and display toolbars at your own convenience. For example, when you're formatting text, you might want to have the Formatting toolbar on the screen. When you're not formatting text anymore, you can hide that toolbar so it's not taking up space on the screen.

1. To hide or display a toolbar, first do one of the following:
   - If there is any toolbar currently visible on your screen, right-click that toolbar, then choose Toolbars from the shortcut menu that appears.
   - Or, if there is no toolbar, or you just prefer to use the menus, choose View ➢ Toolbars from the application's menu bar. (If you can't find View in the menu bar, try choosing File ➢ Toolbars.)
2. You'll see a dialog box similar to the one below.

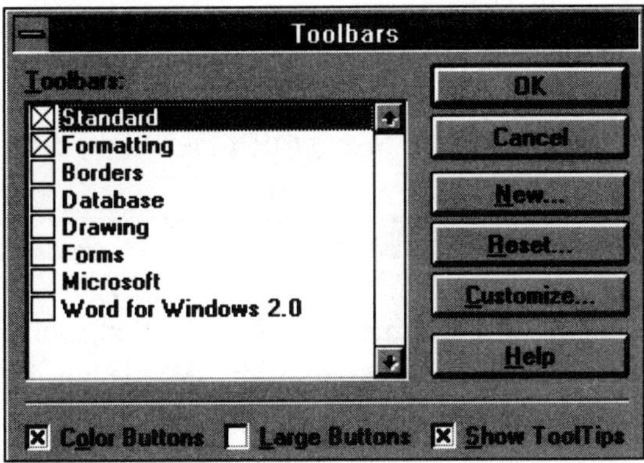

3. To display a toolbar, click its checkbox so it contains an X. To hide a toolbar, click its check box to clear the X. (In the example above, I've opted to display the Standard and Formatting toolbars.)

4. Choose OK.

That's it, you're done. The toolbars you marked with an X will now be visible on your screen.

What Does That Button Do?

It's not always easy to tell what a toolbar button will do simply from looking at its icon (the little picture). If you want a little plain-English description of a button *before* you click it, just rest the mouse pointer somewhere on the button for a couple of seconds. A tiny ToolTip appears below the mouse pointer, as in the example below.

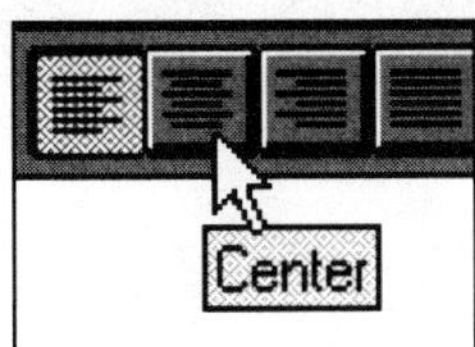

"Where's My ToolTip?"

ToolTips are a relatively new phenomenon in the PC world, and they are not available in all Windows applications. If the ToolTip doesn't appear in an Office application, however, perhaps that feature is just turned off. Right-click any toolbar, choose Toolbars, and then make sure the Show ToolTips checkbox is selected (marked with an X). If that checkbox is not selected, click it once. Choose OK to return to your document.

Positioning a Toolbar

Just about any toolbar can be *docked* to an edge of the screen or *free-floating* so that you can drag it around by its title bar. Figure AB.25 shows some examples.

FIGURE AB.25

A toolbar can be docked to any edge of the screen or it can be free-floating.

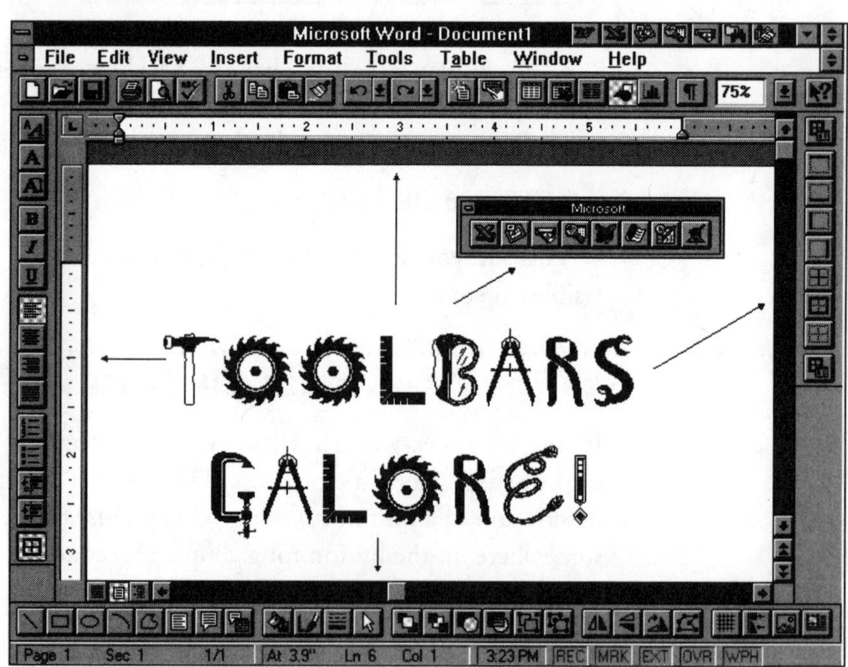

NOTE: *The techniques described here work with the toolbars inside an application, such as Word or Excel. To position or customize the Office Manager toolbar, right-click that toolbar and choose Small Buttons to dock it. Choose Regular Buttons or Large Buttons (if you have a small screen) to float it.*

The trick to positioning a toolbar is a simple one:

1. Carefully move the top of the mouse pointer to some "neutral part"

of the toolbar, either between two buttons or above or below a button, as shown here.

2. Gently press down the mouse button without moving the mouse pointer, and then drag the ghost-image that appears to its new location:

   - To make the toolbar free-floating, drag it near the center of the screen, so it's not near any edge. You can then drag it by its title bar to wherever you wish.

   - To dock the toolbar to the edge of the application's window, drag the ghost image to whatever side you want, until it takes on the shape of the edge.

3. Release the mouse button.

Piece of cake! And here are a couple of other pointers. When the toolbar is free-floating, you can move it simply by dragging its title bar. You can also switch between the most recent free-floating and docked positions by double-clicking the toolbar's title bar.

Customizing a Toolbar

After you become proficient with an application, you might want to change some of the built-in toolbars to give yourself quick access to the features that you use most. The exact steps for customizing a toolbar vary slightly from one Office application to the next. But here's how you can get started:

1. Bring the toolbar that you want to customize to the screen (take it out of hiding if it's hidden).

2. Right-click that toolbar and choose Customize. If there is no visible toolbar, choose View ➢ Toolbars ➢ Customize from the application's menu bar.

3. If you're in Microsoft Word, click the Toolbars tab near the top of the Customize dialog box.

4. Follow the instructions that appear on the screen to select a category of buttons. Then drag any button from the dialog box onto the actual toolbar. (For additional help while doing this, just press F1.)

5. When you're done customizing or creating your toolbar, choose the Close button.

Creating Your Own Toolbar

You can also create your own custom toolbars. Again, the exact procedure might vary slightly from one application to the next, but the general procedure is as follows:

1. If you have not already done so, start the application for which you want to create a toolbar.

2. Right-click any visible toolbar and choose Toolbars from the quick menu. Or choose View ➢ Toolbars from the application's menu bar. You'll come to a dialog box that resembles this one (from Microsoft Word).

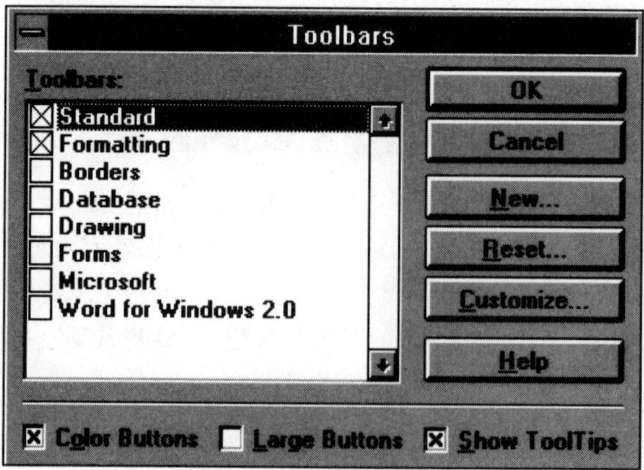

3. Choose New from the dialog box, then follow the instructions and respond to the prompts as they appear. As always, you can press F1 for additional help as you go along.

Related Topics

- *Menus* here in Appendix B.

Type Text and Numbers

Typing on a computer is pretty much the same as typing on a regular typewriter, with a few exceptions:

- To type on a computer, you must first have some kind of *document* window on the screen to type into. Typically, when you first start an application, it automatically presents a blank document window, so you can start typing right away.
- If you're in an application, and there is no document to type on, choose File ➢ New from that application's menu bar to bring up a new document window.
- Anything you type appears wherever the blinking insertion point is at the moment. To make a change or correction to existing text, first click the area where you want to type, or use the cursor-positioning keys, to move the insertion point to where you want to type.
- When typing numbers, never use the letter *l* for the number one, nor the letter O for the number 0. Always use the numbers along the top of the keyboard instead, or the numbers on the numeric keypad (when the Num Lock key is on).
- When you're typing at the end of a Word document and need to move down a line or need to insert a blank line, press ↵. To indent, press Tab.
- To press a combination keystroke (i.e., *key+key*), hold down the first key, tap the second key, then release the first key. See *Using the Keyboard* in Appendix A for more information on that.

Inserting versus Overwriting Text

Whenever you're typing within existing text, you have the option of either *inserting* the new text, or *overwriting* the existing text. Here's the difference: Suppose I type this sentence, and then move the insertion point to where the | character is:

```
My |is Alan
```

If I type the word "name" and press the spacebar while in Insert mode, that new word and space are inserted into the existing text, like this:

```
My name is Alan
```

If, however, I type the word "name" and press the spacebar while in Overwrite mode, the new text (and space) will replace the existing text, like this:

```
My namelan
```

If you want to know which mode you're in, before you type anything, glance down at the indicators near the bottom of your application window. If you don't see an OVR indicator, or you see OVR but it's dimmed, that means you're in Insert mode, and any text you type will be inserted into the existing text.

If, on the other hand, OVR is visible, and not dimmed, then you're in Overwrite mode, and any new text you type will replace existing text.

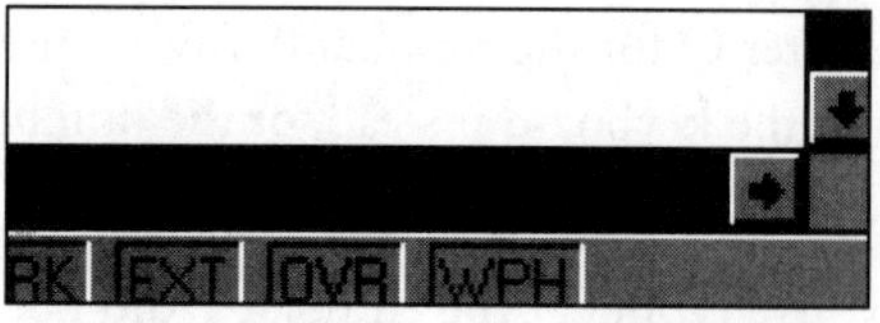

To switch between the Insert and Overwrite modes, just press the Insert (Ins) key. The OVR indicator appears, or disappears immediately. (If it doesn't work, someone else who uses your computer might have changed the role of the INS key to Paste. To return to normal insertion key behavior, you need to deselect *Use the INS Key for Paste* in Options. In Microsoft Word, choose Tools ➢ Options, click the Edit tab, and clear that option. Then choose OK.)

WARNING: *If text is selected when you start typing new text, your new text immediately replaces the selected text. This is a bummer when it happens by accident (I know, because I do it by accident all the time). To bring back that accidentally deleted text, choose Edit ➢ Undo from the application's menu bar or press Ctrl+Z.*

Related Topics

- *Start an Application* here in Appendix B
- *Create a Document* here in Appendix B
- *How to Work the Keyboard* in Appendix A
- *Select, Then Do* here in Appendix B.

Undo

Every time you complete some action with your keyboard or mouse, you see the results on your screen. In some cases, the result might not be exactly what you had in mind. If that happens, you can easily "undo" that action using any of these techniques:

- Choose Edit ➢ Undo from the application's menu bar.
- Or press Ctrl+Z.
- Or click the Undo button in the toolbar (if it's available).

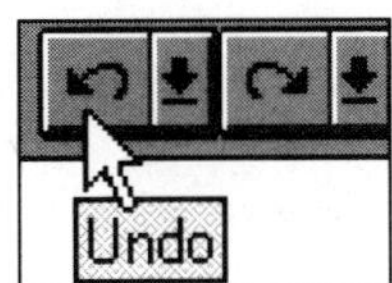

Related Topics

- *Menus* here in Appendix B.
- *Shortcuts* here in Appendix B.
- *Toolbars* here in Appendix B.

Version (Determine)

There are several ways to determine which version of an application you're using:

- When you first start an application, its version number generally appears on the startup screen for a few seconds.
- If you miss the startup screen, choose Help ➢ About... from the application's menu bar. You'll see a dialog box that includes the version number and other general information. (Choose OK to leave the dialog box).
- To determine which version of Windows you're using, choose Help ➢ About Program Manager from Program Manager's menu bar. (Choose OK to leave the dialog box).
- To determine which version of DOS you're using, get to the DOS command prompt (that C:\> thing). Then type **ver** and press ↵. The version number appears on the screen.

Related Topics

- *Menus* here in Appendix B
- The Introduction for information on versions described in this book.

Wizards

For the novice and casual computer users, Wizards are definitely the quickest and easiest way to get from point A (nothing useful on your screen), to point B (something you can print or use).

Wizards are so simple and self-explanatory, there's really hardly any need for me to explain how to use them. However, just so you're aware, here's the basic procedure for using a Wizard:

1. Start an Office application, such as Word, PowerPoint, Excel, or Access.
2. Within that application, start whatever Wizard you want to use, as described in the sections after this one. A Wizard window will appear, like the example in Figure AB.26.
3. Answers all questions in the Wizard window by clicking on the options of your choice. In most cases, the Wizard window will display a preview of your current selection, in a small sample document.

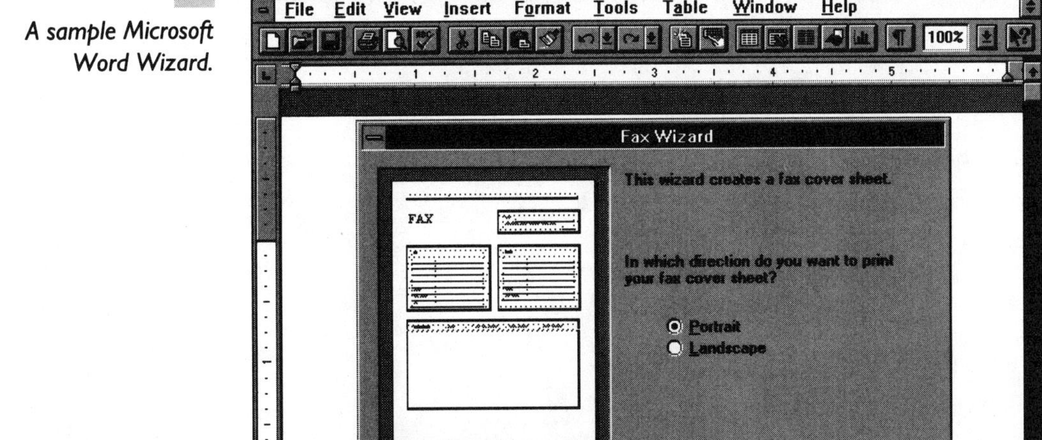

FIGURE AB.26: *A sample Microsoft Word Wizard.*

4. When you've completed the questions in the Wizard window, click the Next button to move onto the next set of questions.
5. Repeat Steps 3 and 4 until the Next button is dimmed and unavailable. At that point, you can choose Back if you want to go back and change a previous selection. Or click on Finish to complete the job.

Once you choose Finish, you can't back up to a previous Wizard screen. You need to make changes and corrections using the standard "non-Wizard" techniques, and perhaps the Cue Cards and Help screens. If you *really* don't like what the Wizard created, and you want to start over, first choose File ➢ Close ➢ No to close the current document without saving it. Then start over at Step 2 above.

Word Wizards

To try a wizard in Microsoft Word, start Word and choose File ➢ New from Word's menu bar. Then double-click on any template that has the word Wizard in its title.

Optionally, try some of these documents in the *Do-It Now Encyclopedia*:

- Agenda
- Award
- Calendar
- Fax Cover Sheet
- Letter
- Memo
- Table

Excel Wizards

The two main Wizards in Excel are the *Function Wizard* and the *Chart Wizard.* You need to learn the basics of using Excel before you use either Wizard (see *Microsoft Excel* in the *Instant Office* section). But once you learn the basics, here's how you can use Excel's function wizard:

1. In your Excel worksheet, position the cursor to wherever you want to type a formula.
2. Choose Insert ➢ Function from Excel's menu bar to start the Function Wizard, then follow the instructions in the Wizard window.

To use Excel's Chart Wizard:

1. Type the data you want to chart into any contiguous cells in the worksheet. Then select those cells (Figure AB.27).

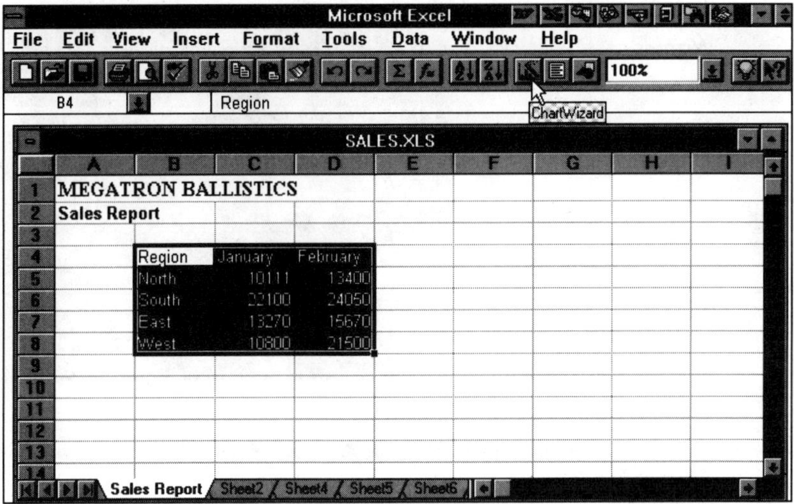

FIGURE AB.27

Cells to plot on a graph selected in an Excel worksheet by dragging the mouse pointer through the numbers.

2. Click the ChartWizard button in Excel's Standard toolbar (look for the tiny ToolTip near the top of Figure AB.27).

3. Click wherever you want the upper-left corner of the chart to appear in your worksheet. Then drag the mouse pointer down and to the right, to indicate how large you want the chart to be.

4. When you release the mouse button, you'll be at the first Chart Wizard window. Just follow the instructions, as usual.

If you want to see some live examples, choose Help ➢ Examples and Demos from Excel's menu bar. Then click on the button next to *Creating a Chart* in the window that appears.

PowerPoint Wizards

Typically, when you first start PowerPoint, you're automatically taken to the New Presentation dialog box shown in Figure AB.28. If you don't see that dialog box, choose File ➢ New from PowerPoint's menu bar.

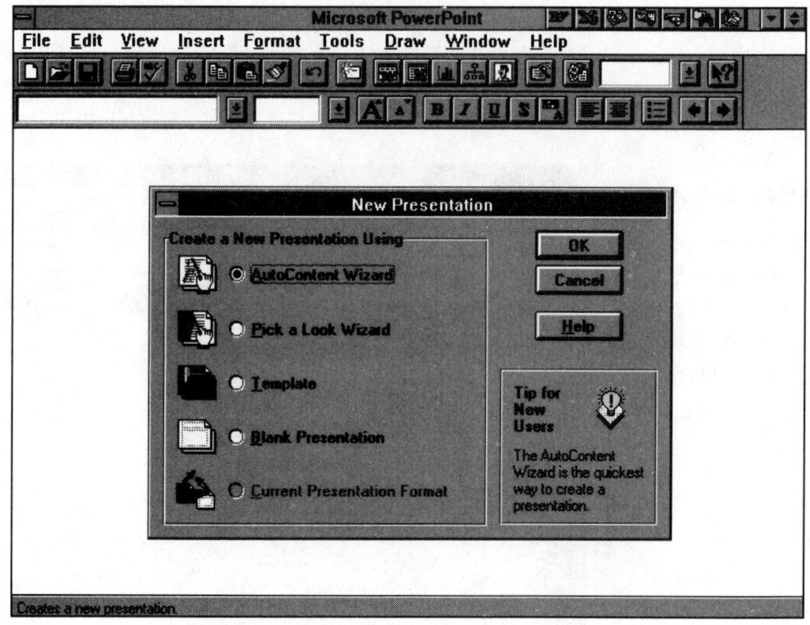

FIGURE AB.28

This PowerPoint dialog box gives you immediate access to two of PowerPoint's main Wizards.

To try out the AutoContent Wizard, just click that option, then choose OK, and follow the instructions that appear on the screen.

Access Wizards

Access Version 2.0 offers a very impressive "Tables Wizard."

To try it out, see *Database (Create)* in the *Do-It-Now Encyclopedia.*

Related Topics

- *Start an Application* here in Appendix B
- *Help* here in Appendix B
- *Cue Cards* here in Appendix B

APPENDIX C
Sources

Product Index

The product list in Table AC.1 lists specific products mentioned in this book, as well as general product categories. Publishers are listed alphabetically after the product index.

Publisher Names and Addresses

Adobe Systems Incorporated
1585 Charleston Road, P.O. Box 7900
Mountain View, CA 94039-7900
Voice: (800) 833-6687 or (408) 986-7555
Fax: (408) 986-6587 or (408) 562-6775
Product Type: Fonts and software

TABLE AC.1

Product Index by Category

PRODUCT	PUBLISHER
CLIP ART	
Art Parts	Art Parts
Clip Art collections	Software of the Month Club
DigitArt collection	Image Club Graphics, Inc.
Megatoons	Creative Media Services
Oswego Archives	Oswego Company
Presentation Task Force	New Vision Technologies
FONTS	
Font collections	Adobe Systems Incorporated
Kid fonts	ds design
Font collections	Emigre Graphics
Keycaps and Windows	RoadRunner Computing
Font collections	Software of the Month Club
Typecase fonts	Swfte International, Ltd.
PAPER/MEDIA: (LABELS, CARDS, TAGS, TRANSPARENCIES)	
Brochures	NEBS Brochure Express
Laser printer papers	Paper Direct, Inc.
Laser printer papers	Premier Papers, Inc.
Laser printer papers	Queblo
Slides (printed)	Genigraphics Corporation
Transparencies (printed)	Genigraphics Corporation
SOFTWARE	
Office	Microsoft Corporation
Windows	Microsoft Corporation
DOS	Microsoft Corporation

Art Parts
P.O. Box 2926
Orange, CA 92669-0926
Fax: (714) 633-9617
Product Type: Clip art and fonts

Creative Media Services
2936 Domingo Avenue
Berkeley, CA 94705-0955
Voice: (800) 358-2278 or (510) 843-3408
Fax: (510) 549-2490
Product Type: Megatoons Clip Art Library

ds design
2440 SW Cary Parkway
Suite 210
Cary, NC 27513
Voice: (800) 745-4037
Fax: (919) 460-5983
Product Type: Fonts and clip art by kids

Electronic Clipper
Dynamic Graphics, Inc.
6000 N. Forest Park Dr., P.O. Box 1901
Peoria, IL 61656-1901
Voice: (309) 688-8800
Fax: (309) 688-5873 or (309) 688-3075
Product Type: Clip art

Emigre Graphics
4475 D Street
Sacramento, CA 95819
Voice: (916)451-4344
Fax: (916)451-4351
Product Type: Fonts

Genigraphics Corporation
Two Enterprise Drive, Suite 305
Shelton, CT 06484
Voice: (800) 638-7348
Fax: (203) 925-3028
Product Type: Printed 35mm slides and overhead transparencies

Image Club Graphics, Inc.
729 24th Ave. Southeast
Calgary, Alberta
Canada T2G 5K8
Voice: (403) 262-8008
Fax: (403) 261-7013
Orders: (800) 661-9410
Product Type: Fonts and clip art

Microsoft Corporation
One Microsoft Way
Redmond, WA 98052-6399
Voice: (800) 426-9400
Technical Support: (206) 635-7056
Products: DOS, Windows, Office, others

NEBS Brochure Express
P.O. Box 643
Townsend, MA 01469
Voice: (800) 444-3977
Fax: (800) 444-3988
Product Type: Color brochures from your PC

New Vision Technologies, Inc.
38 Auriga Drive, Unit 13
Nepean, Ontario
Canada K2E 8A5
Phone: (613) 727-8184
Fax: (613) 727-8190
Product Type: Clip art

Oswego Company
610 SW Alder #609
Portland, OR 97205
Voice: (503) 274-9338
Fax: (503) 274-9326
Product Type: Clip art

Paper Direct, Inc.
205 Chubb Ave.
Lyndhurst, NJ 07071
Voice: (800)-A-PAPERS
Fax: (201) 507-0817
Product Type: Specialty papers for laser printers

Premier Papers, Inc.
P.O. Box 64785
St. Paul, MN 55164
Voice: (800) 843-0414
Fax: (800) 526-3029
Product Type: Specialty papers for laser printers

Queblo
1000 Florida Ave.
Hagerstown, MD 21740
Voice: (800) 523-9080
Fax: (800) 554-8779
Product Type: Specialty papers for laser printers

RoadRunner Computing
P.O. Box 21635
Baton Rouge, LA 70894
Voice: (504) 346-0019
Product Type: Keycap and Windows symbols fonts

Software of the Month Club

Software of the Month Club
5816 Dryden Place
Carlsbad, CA 92009
Voice: (619) 931-8111
Fax: (619) 931-8383 or (619) 929-1163
Product Type: Fonts and clip art

Swfte International, Ltd.
P.O. Box 219
Rockland, DE 19732
Voice: (800) 237-9383
Fax: (302) 234-1760
Product Type: Fonts

APPENDIX D

Dictionaries

FOR SOME PEOPLE, THE BIGGEST problem in using a computer is simply knowing how to phrase the question they want to ask. My favorite example is from an attorney friend of mine who had a little problem while writing some kind of legal paper on his home PC. He called late at night and in a panicky voice fired the following technical question at me:

"How do I get the thing back on the thing?"

Now I'm not saying that a lawyer is *supposed* to be any more computer literate than that. But you have to admit, that's a pretty tough question for *anyone* to answer.

As it turns out, he was trying to get the paper he was working on back on the screen. Or, in computer parlance, he was trying to *open a document.*

English–Computerese Dictionary

Well, anyway, I've been collecting the various terms people often use when trying to phrase their technical questions. I've put them in Table AD.1, along with the computerese translation. I hope this list helps you to phrase your own questions better, so you know what words to look for when looking through the index to this book or when searching Help on your screen.

Visual Dictionary

The Visual Dictionary that follows offers another way to get a crash course in computer terminology. Just flip through and look at the pictures to find out the real name of the gadgets and the various doohickeys you see on your screen from time to time.

TABLE AD.1

English–Computerese Dictionary

ENGLISH	COMPUTERESE TERM(S)
Add	*Insert*
Alphabetize	*Sort*
C:\>_	*DOS command prompt* followed by the blinking *cursor*
Cancel	*Undo*
Change	*Edit*
Cross out	*Strikethrough*
Disappear	If things seem to *disappear* from your screen, read *Take Control of Windows* in Appendix A.
Erase	*Delete*
Fancy print	*Font*
Get back to	*Open* or *Switch to*
Get into	*Start* an application, or *Open* a document
Get out of	*Exit* an application, or *close* a document, or *Cancel* (*Escape*) a dialog box
Gray box	*Window* or *dialog box*
Keep	*Save*
Kill	*Delete*
Little picture	*Icon*
Magnify	*Zoom* or *Maximize*
Modify	*Edit*
Order (put into order)	*Sort*
Put on the screen	*Start* an application or *Open* a document
Remove	*Delete*
Shrink	*Zoom* or *Minimize*
Squeeze in	*Insert*
Stuff, Thing	Anything that you create on the computer is generally called a *document*.
Undo	*Undo*

Visual Dictionary

Browse through for:

- A crash course in computer terminology
- Names of things you'll see often on your screen
- Tips on how to work things

Computer System

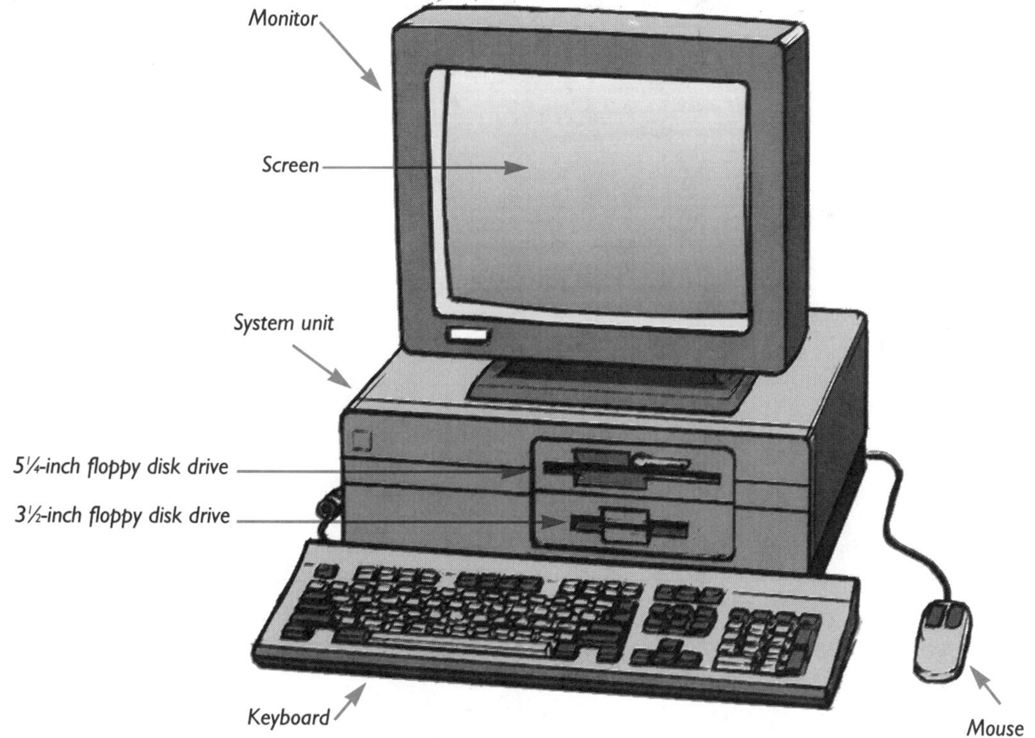

Computer System Configurations

Desktop configuration

Notebook (or laptop) configuration

Tower configuration

DOS Screen

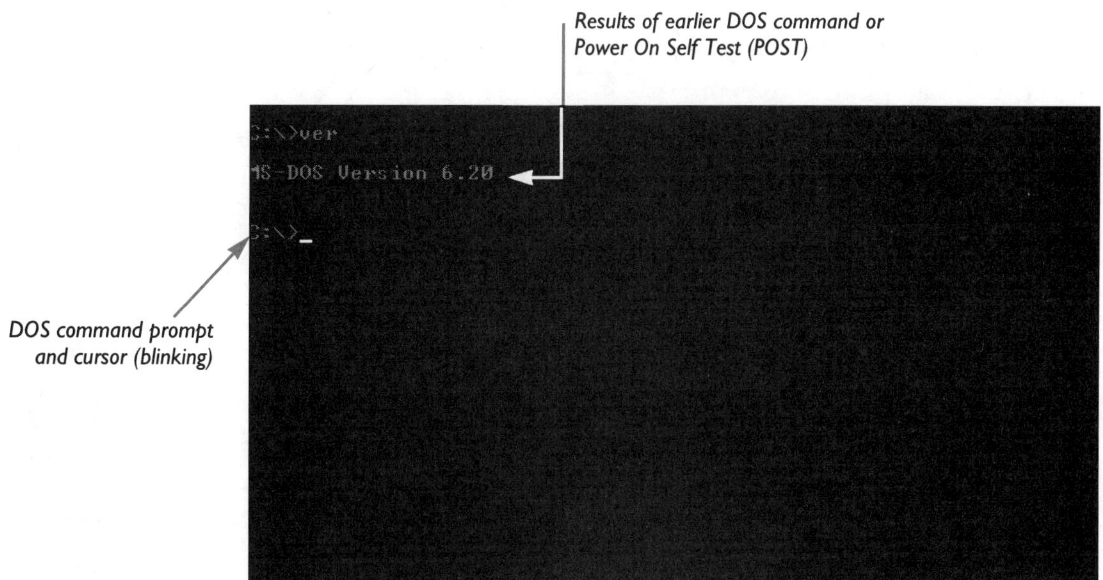

To switch from DOS to Windows, type ***win*** *and press Enter (↵).*

Microsoft Windows

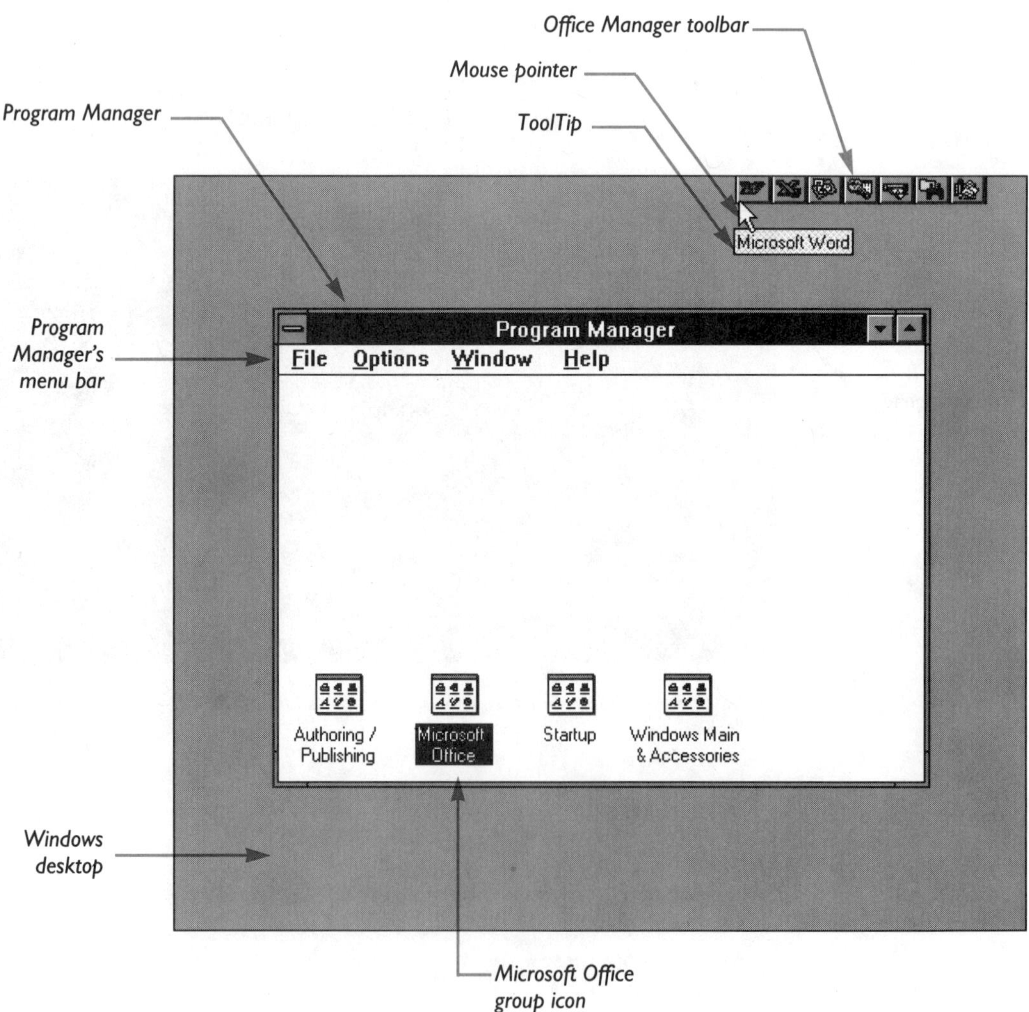

Office Manager toolbar
Mouse pointer
ToolTip
Program Manager
Microsoft Word
Program Manager
File Options Window Help
Program Manager's menu bar
Authoring / Publishing
Microsoft Office
Startup
Windows Main & Accessories
Windows desktop
Microsoft Office group icon

Windows Controls

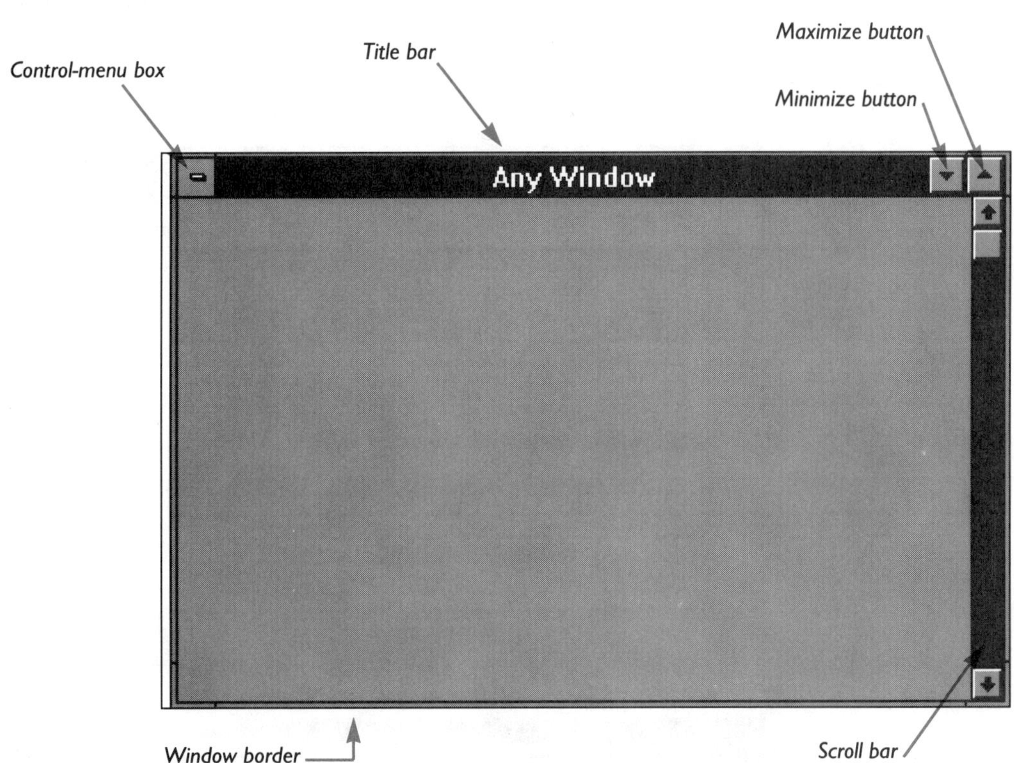

Control-menu box: *Click it to open the menu. Double-click it to close the window.*

Title bar: *Describes the contents of the window. Drag the title bar to move the window; double-click the title bar to enlarge the window or restore it to its previous size.*

Maximize button: *Click it to expand the window to full-screen size.*

Minimize button: *Click it to reduce the window to its smallest possible size.*

Scroll bar: *Scroll to display hidden contents of the window (if there are any).*

Window border: *Drag any edge or corner of a window to size the window.*

Windows and Icons

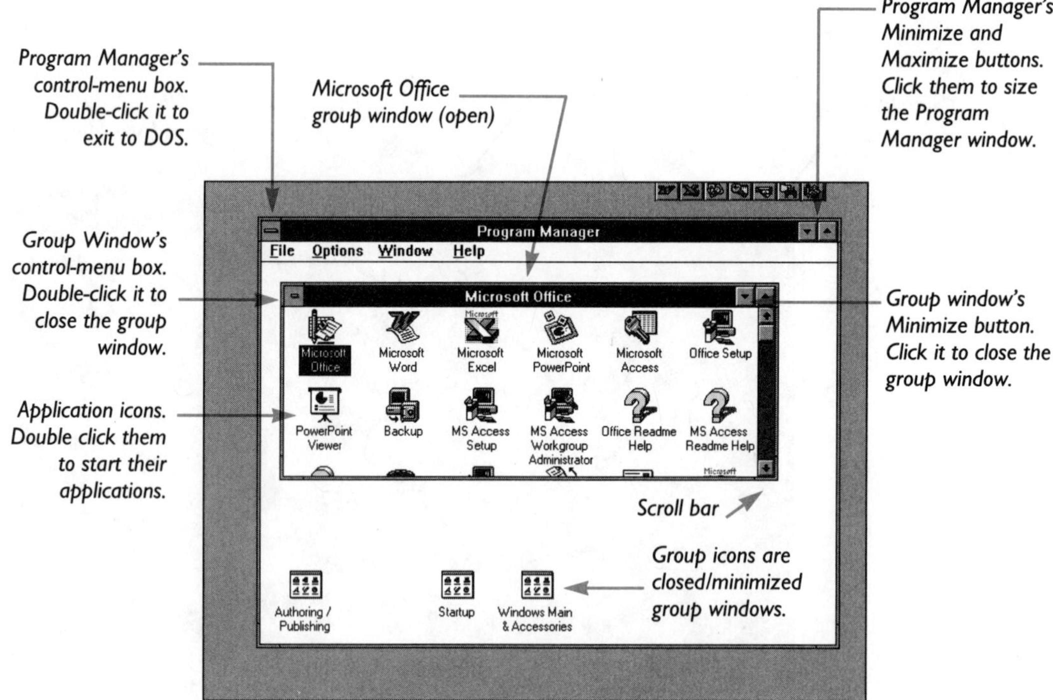

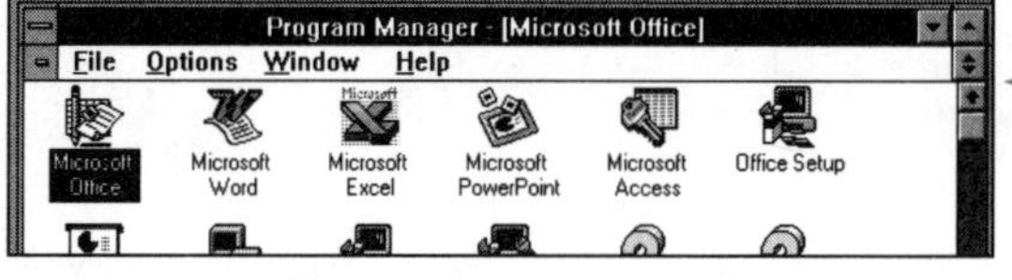

When a group window or document window is maximized, its title appears in the application window's title bar (next to Program Manager in this example). To shrink the group window, click the two-headed Restore button.

Dialog Box

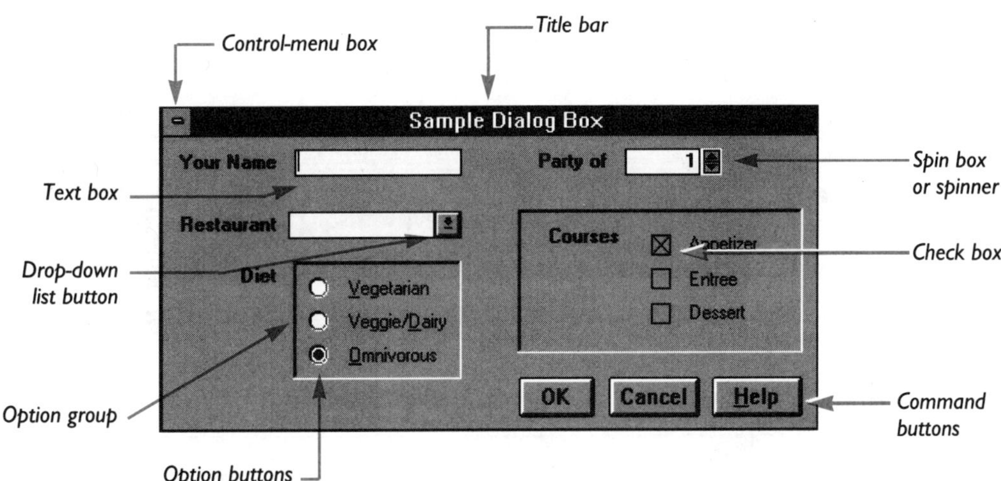

Title bar: *Drag it to move the dialog box.*

Text box: *Click in it and type in the contents.*

Drop-down list: *Click the button to view the list.*

Option group: *Click any one option button to choose it.*

Spin box: *Click the arrows to increase or decrease the number.*

Check box: *Click to select it or clear it.*

OK: *Click this button to accept the entries in the dialog box and proceed.*

Cancel: *Click this button to bail out without saving any selections made in the dialog box.*

Help: *Click this button for a description of the options in the dialog box.*

Microsoft Word

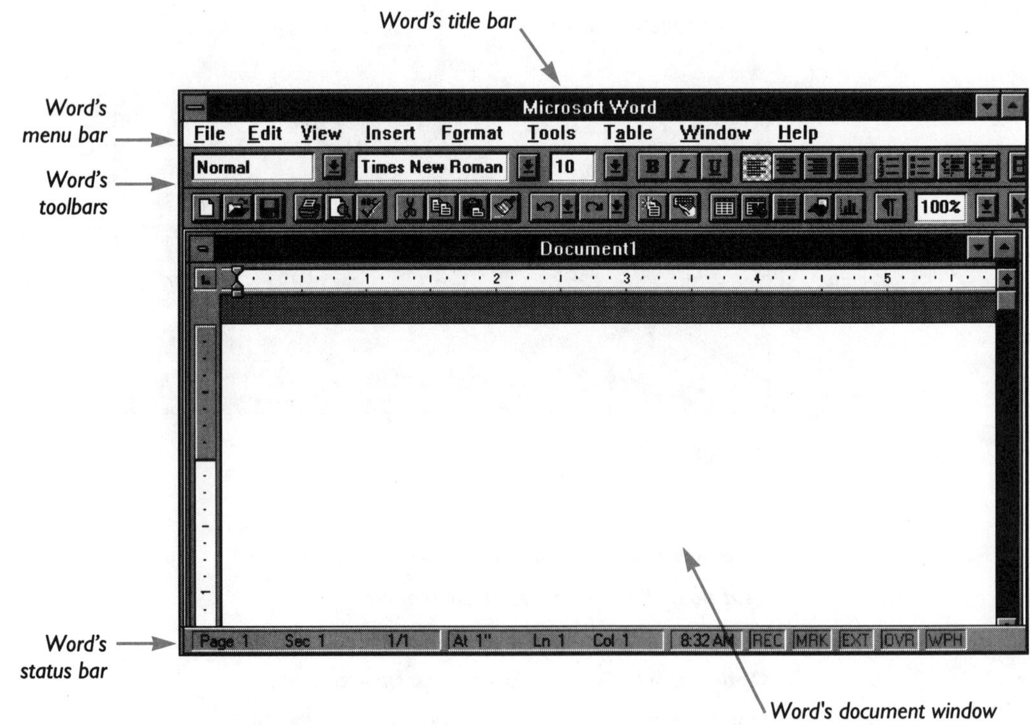

Word's title bar: *Drag it to move the window; double-click it to size the window.*

Word's menu bar: *Your selections affect only Microsoft Word.*

Word's toolbars: *Right-click in any toolbar to hide or display toolbars, or choose View ➢ Toolbars.*

Word document window: *Choose File ➢ New ➢ OK to start a new document. Choose Window ➢ Arrange All to arrange multiple windows.*

To exit Word: *Choose File ➢ Exit from Word's menu bar.*

Word Document

You can search Word's help for information on any feature shown here.

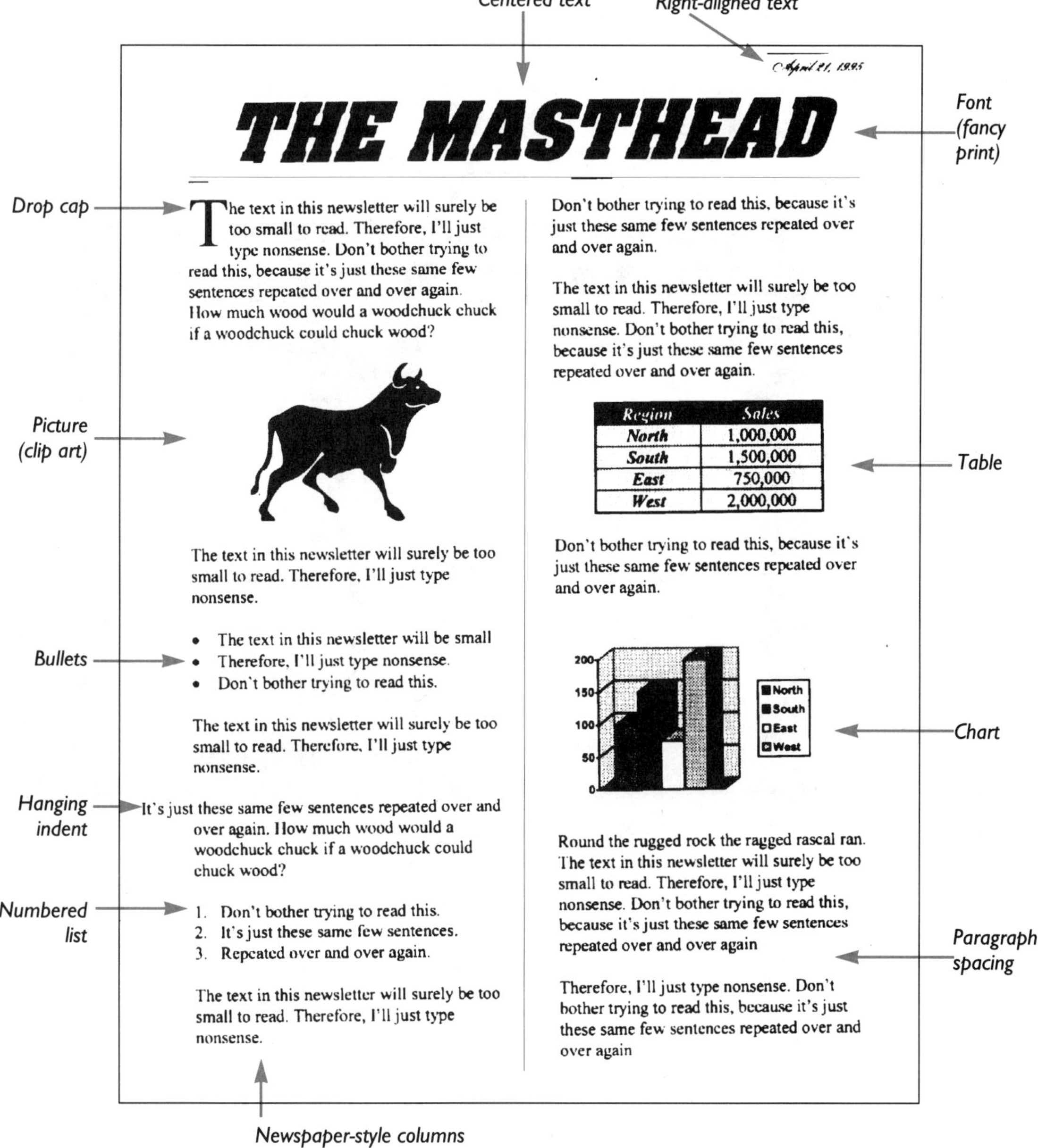

April 21, 1995

THE MASTHEAD

The text in this newsletter will surely be too small to read. Therefore, I'll just type nonsense. Don't bother trying to read this, because it's just these same few sentences repeated over and over again. How much wood would a woodchuck chuck if a woodchuck could chuck wood?

The text in this newsletter will surely be too small to read. Therefore, I'll just type nonsense.

- The text in this newsletter will be small
- Therefore, I'll just type nonsense.
- Don't bother trying to read this.

The text in this newsletter will surely be too small to read. Therefore, I'll just type nonsense.

It's just these same few sentences repeated over and over again. How much wood would a woodchuck chuck if a woodchuck could chuck wood?

1. Don't bother trying to read this.
2. It's just these same few sentences.
3. Repeated over and over again.

The text in this newsletter will surely be too small to read. Therefore, I'll just type nonsense.

Don't bother trying to read this, because it's just these same few sentences repeated over and over again.

The text in this newsletter will surely be too small to read. Therefore, I'll just type nonsense. Don't bother trying to read this, because it's just these same few sentences repeated over and over again.

Region	Sales
North	1,000,000
South	1,500,000
East	750,000
West	2,000,000

Don't bother trying to read this, because it's just these same few sentences repeated over and over again.

Round the rugged rock the ragged rascal ran. The text in this newsletter will surely be too small to read. Therefore, I'll just type nonsense. Don't bother trying to read this, because it's just these same few sentences repeated over and over again

Therefore, I'll just type nonsense. Don't bother trying to read this, because it's just these same few sentences repeated over and over again

Microsoft Excel

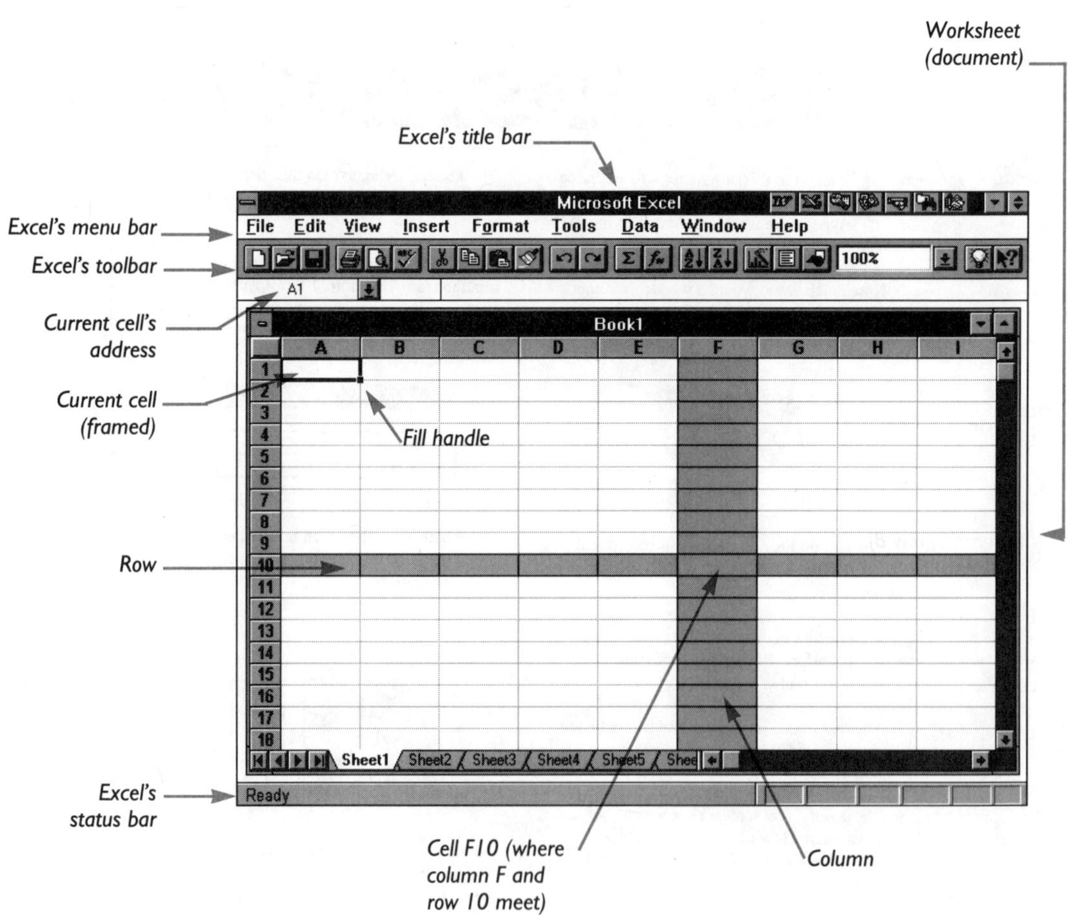

Excel Worksheet

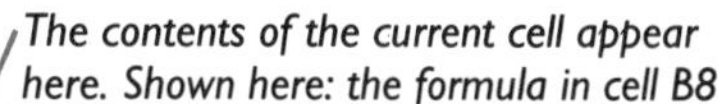

The contents of the current cell appear here. Shown here: the formula in cell B8

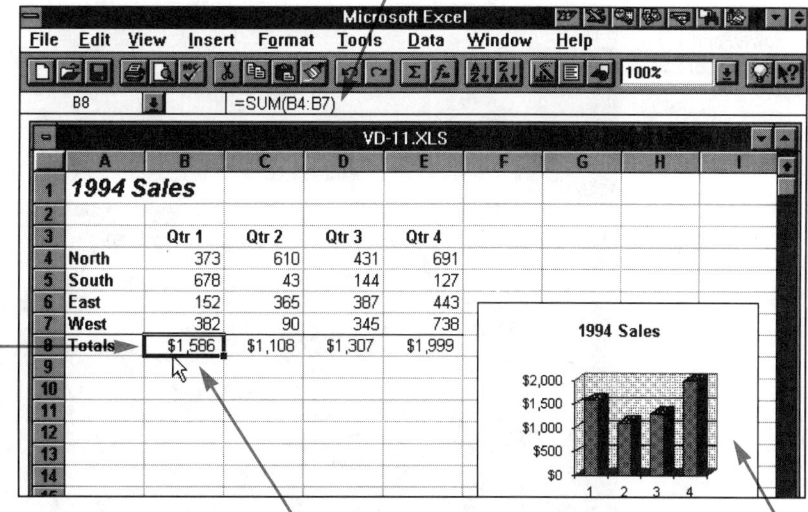

The current cell is framed. In this example, it's cell B8 (column B, row 8).

When a cell contains a formula, the results of the calculated formula appear in the cell. In this example, cell B8 contains the formula =SUM(B4:B7), which sums the numbers in cells B4, B5, B6, and B7.

Chart

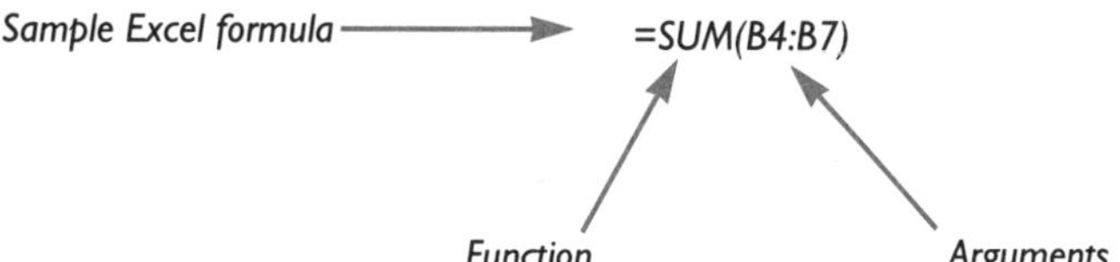

Microsoft PowerPoint

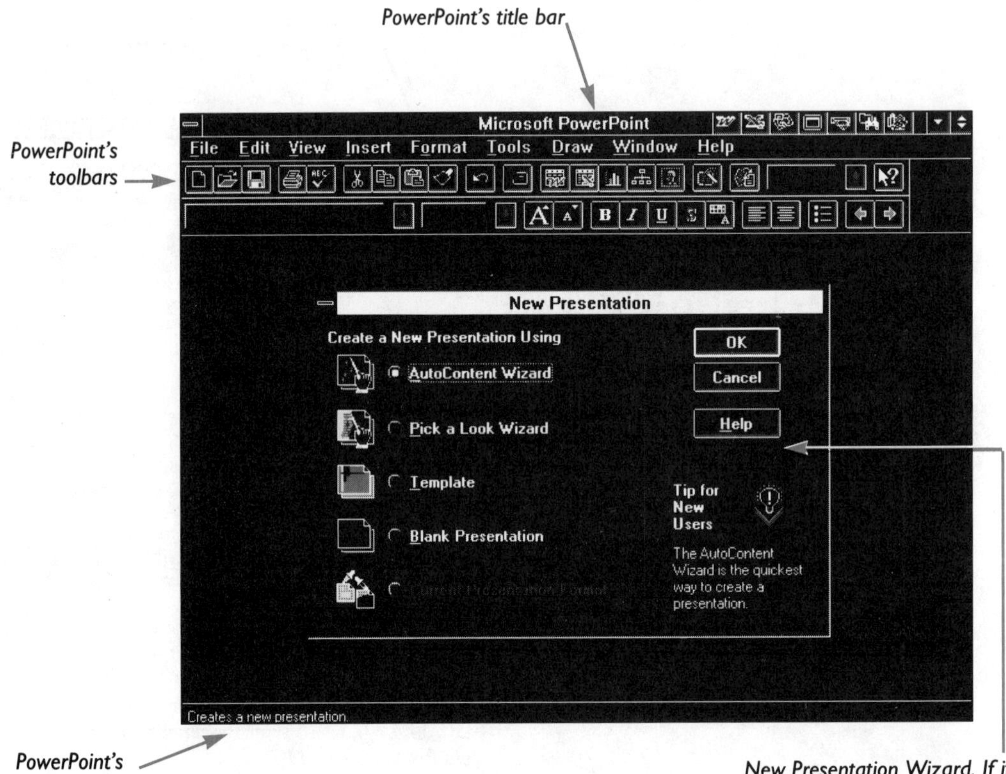

Microsoft Access

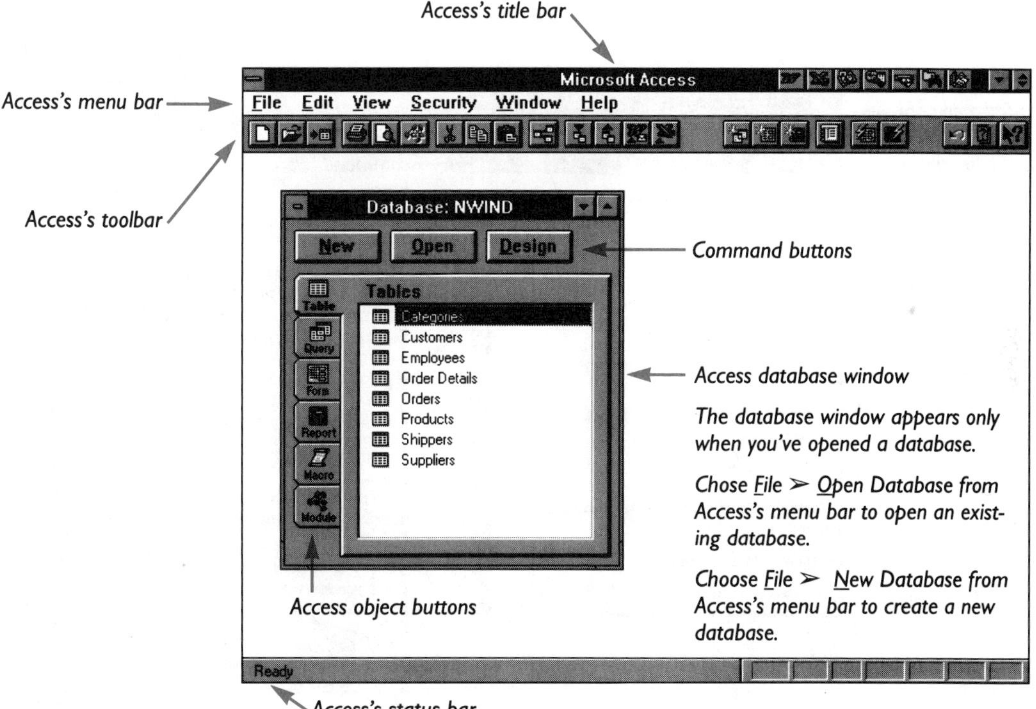
Access's title bar
Access's menu bar
Access's toolbar
Microsoft Access
File Edit View Security Window Help
Database: NWIND
New Open Design
Command buttons
Tables
Categories
Customers
Employees
Order Details
Orders
Products
Shippers
Suppliers
Table
Query
Form
Report
Macro
Module
Access database window
The database window appears only when you've opened a database.
Chose File ➢ Open Database from Access's menu bar to open an existing database.
Choose File ➢ New Database from Access's menu bar to create a new database.
Access object buttons
Ready
Access's status bar

Help

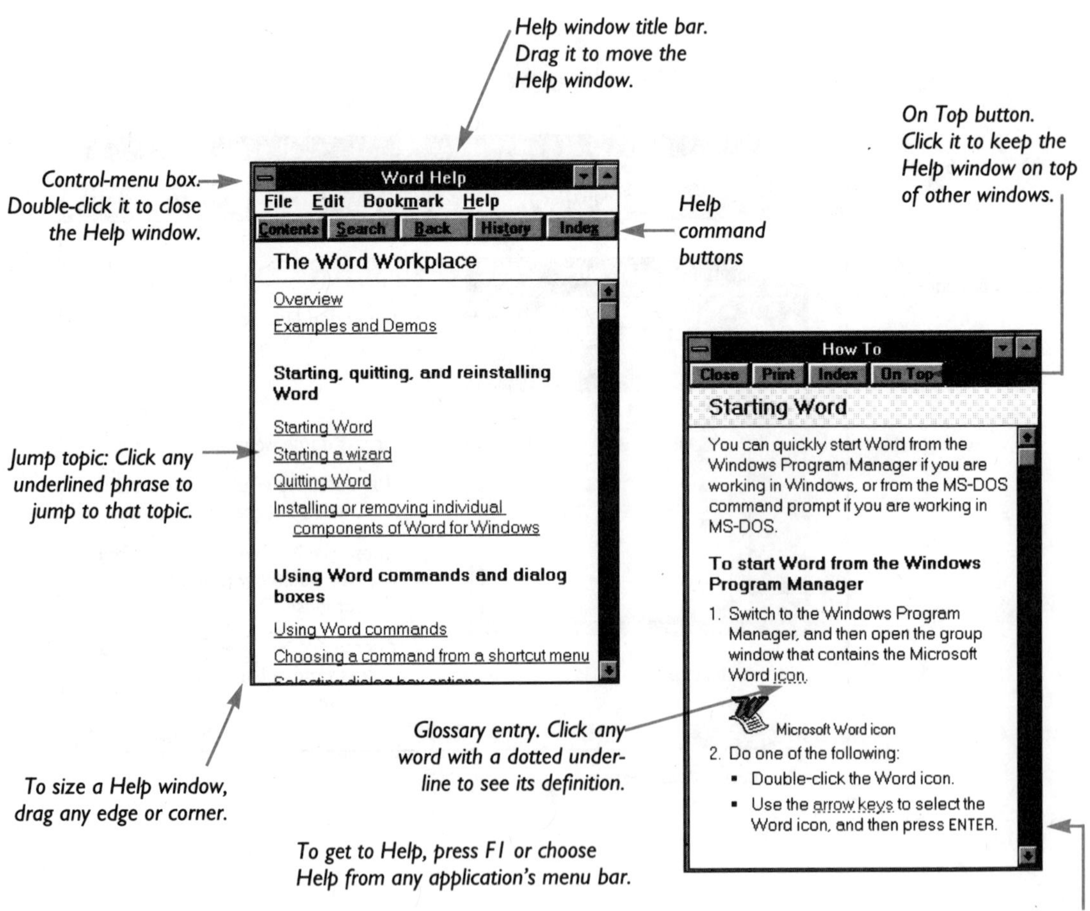

To get to Help, press F1 or choose Help from any application's menu bar.

Cue Card

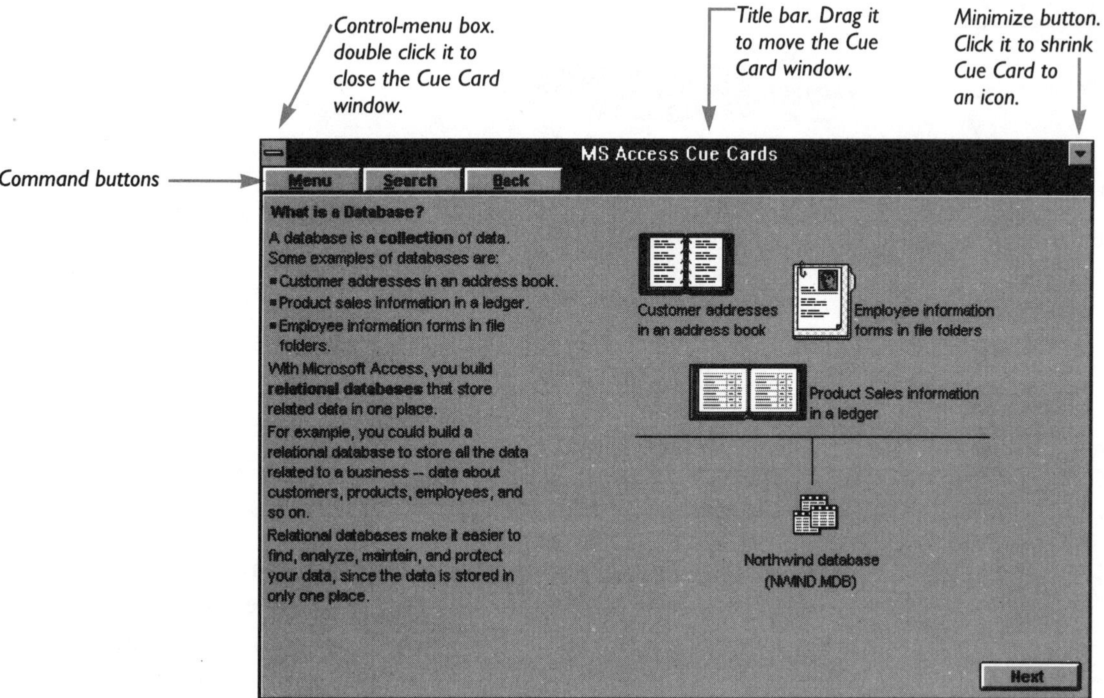

Click the Next button to move on to the next window.

Minimized Cue Card. Double-click the icon to reopen the Cue Card.

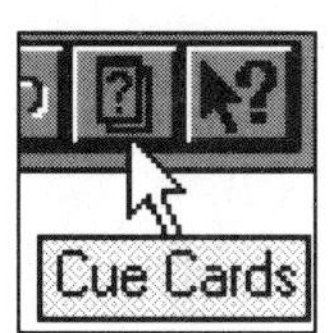

If an application offers Cue Cards, choose Help ➢ Cue Cards from the application's menu bar to get to the cards or click the Cue Cards button in the toolbar.

Glossary

Your Electronic Glossary

In this Glossary, I'll define some of the technical terms you might come across frequently. If you need to look up a term while you're actually using your computer, or don't find the term you're looking for here, consider using your more comprehensive, built-in glossary. To do so, in just about any Windows application, follow these simple steps:

1. Press F1 and wait for the Help window to appear.
2. Press F1 a second time.
3. Click the Glossary command button near the top of the Help window.

While you're in any Help window, you can also click any word that has a dotted underline beneath it to instantly see its definition. For more information, please see *Help* in Appendix B.

Glossary

Access: The database-management application that comes with Microsoft Office Professional Edition. Access can also be purchased independently from any computer store or mail-order house. This book discusses Microsoft Access 2.0.

App: Slang for *application.*

Applet: A small, simple application like the Calculator (see the *Calculator* entry in the *Do-It-Now Encyclopedia*) that comes with Windows.

Application: A software program that you purchase and install on your computer to help with certain types of work. For example, you use a word-processing application to help with typing and writing.

Boot/boot up: To make the computer start responding to your requests. First you turn on the computer, then it "boots itself up."

Cell: The place where a row and column meet in a worksheet or table.

Chart: General term used to describe a business graph, such as a pie chart or bar chart.

Choose: Click with the mouse. See *Choose* in Appendix B.

Click: To move the mouse pointer to something on the screen, then press and release the left mouse button. See Appendix A.

Clip art: Small drawings and cartoons you can purchase and put into your own documents to add some pizzazz. Many of the pictures in this book are clip art.

Clipboard: A general storage area for temporarily storing text and/or pictures when you're using Windows. To cut and paste, you select something and press Ctrl+C to copy it. Then you move the cursor to wherever you want to place the copy, and press Ctrl+V to paste. See your Windows documentation for more information.

Close: To remove a document or an application from the screen and from the computer's memory, most likely because you're not using it at the moment. For example, if you've just typed and printed a letter, and don't need it on your screen any more, you could *close* that document.

Control: An item in a dialog box or form that lets you make a choice. See *Dialog Boxes* in Appendix B.

Control menu: The tiny box in the upper-left corner of a window.

Database: A collection of all the information (data) and other objects (queries, forms, reports) pertaining to a particular topic. To create and manage a database, use Microsoft Access.

Directory: A section of a disk where files are stored, sort of like a drawer in a file cabinet.

Doc: Slang for *document.*

Document: Anything that you create using an application. For example, letters, memos, envelopes, mailing labels, and newsletters are a few examples of the types of document you can create using a word-processing application.

DOS: An acronym for Disk Operating System, the program that gets your computer started after you turn on the switch. DOS rhymes with *floss.*

Double-click: To point to an object on the screen, then press and release the mouse button twice in rapid succession (see Appendix A).

Drag: To point to an object on the screen, then press and hold down the mouse button while moving the mouse. (See Appendix A.)

Drive: Short for *disk drive*; refers to the thing in the computer where applications and documents are stored. Each drive has a one-letter name, such as C: (your hard disk).

Exit: To remove an application from the screen and from the computer's memory, most likely because you're not using it at the moment.

Field: One column in an Access table. Also refers to one "blank" on a form.

File: Any document you create and save is stored in a *file* on disk. Your applications are also stored in files.

Floppy drive: A disk drive that can read from, and write to, floppy disks. Floppy drives are named A: and B:.

Font: A print style.

Form: Like a fill-in-the-blanks paper form, except that it appears on your computer screen. You can use Microsoft Access to create forms.

Group/Group Icon: One of the icons inside Program Manager's window. When you open it (by double-clicking), you'll see application icons. To start an application, double-click its icon.

I-Beam: Another name for *insertion point.*

Icon: A little picture on your screen.

Insertion Point: The blinking vertical bar on the screen that indicates where any characters you type will appear. Also called the *cursor.*

Install: To set up an application (program) so you can use it on your computer. Any application that you buy will come with instructions telling you how to install it.

Microsoft: The company in Redmond, WA, that makes DOS, Windows, and Microsoft Office, as well as many other products for the PC.

Memory: The place where the application you're using at the moment, and the document or documents you're working on, are stored within the computer. Anything you're not using at the moment is stored on the disk.

Menu: A set of commands that you can choose from to make the computer do something. See *Menus* in Appendix B.

Monitor: That TV-like thing that you interact with to use the computer.

Mouse button: The button on the left-hand side of your mouse, where your right index finger would normally rest. See Appendix A.

Mouse pointer: The thing on the screen that moves when you move the mouse (see Appendix A).

OLE: An acronym for Object Linking and Embedding—a technique that allows Windows applications (e.g. Access, Excel, Word) to share objects (e.g., pictures, sounds, graphs). OLE 2.0 is the latest and easiest version of Object Linking and Embedding.

Operator: A character (or characters) used to perform an operation or comparison. For example, + is the operator used for addition.

Point: In typography, a height of approximately 1/72".

Point to: To move the mouse pointer so that it's touching something on the screen. See Appendix A.

Property: A characteristic of an item. For example, the color property of an item might be "blue."

RAM: An acronym for Random Access Memory. See *Memory.*

Report: General term used to describe information that's printed from a database. For example, a computer-generated invoice or receipt is a type of *report.*

Right-click: To point to an object on the screen, then click the mouse button on the right-hand side of the mouse. (See Appendix A.)

Select: To highlight by dragging the mouse pointer through it. See *Select, Then Do* in Appendix B.

Status bar: The bar along the bottom of an application window that occasionally displays messages and instructions, and also the status of various special keys like Num Lock and Insert.

String: A computer buzzword for "a chunk of text." For example, "Hello there" is a string. As opposed to 123.45, which is a number.

Table: Information that's organized into rows and columns. You can create small tables in Microsoft Word. Use Access for large tables (tables with several hundred rows or more).

Title bar: The bar across the top of a window that describes what's in the window.

Toggle: A menu command or setting that can have only one of two possible values: On or Off (or Yes or No).

Toolbar: A bar or box that offers buttons as shortcuts to specific features. See Appendix B.

VGA: The most modern of computer screens, capable of showing both text and highly detailed pictures. VGA is an acronym for Video Graphics Array.

Window: A section of the screen that displays a single application or document. See *Take Control of Windows* in Appendix A.

Windows: As a proper noun, with the first letter capitalized, refers to Microsoft Windows, the operating environment you must install on your computer before you can use Microsoft Office or any other Windows application.

Word processing: Using the computer to create and manage written text and pictures, as opposed to *data processing*, which focuses on numbers and math.

Index

About this index: Boldfaced page numbers indicate primary discussions of a topic. *Italicized* page numbers indicate illustrations.

A

G

J

K

L

M

N

O

Q

R

S

U

V

W

X

Z

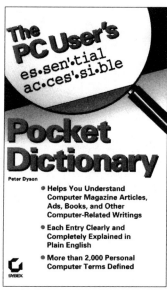

(Almost) Free Companion Disk

Stop! You don't need this optional disk to use this book. Most of the templates and Wizards described in the *Do-It-Now Encyclopedia* are built right into Microsoft Office.

But if you have problems creating complex spreadsheets, databases, and documents, or if you're *really* in a hurry, you may find the disk useful.

Freebie Download

If you have a CompuServe account, you can download the files free of charge. Follow the instructions on the back of this page, and don't bother to send in the coupon.

By Mail or Fax

If you don't have a modem or CompuServe account, we can send you a copy of the disk. But I'll need to tack on a $15 shipping/handling charge to cover my costs.

To get the disk by mail, complete the form below. Then mail or fax the completed form to us at the address or fax number shown.

Yes! I want the optional companion disk for *Instant Office for Microsoft Office.* I understand that there will be a $15.00 shipping/handling charge. Ship the disk to:

Fax or mail the completed form to:
Alan Simpson
P.O. Box 630
Rancho Santa Fe, CA 92067
Fax: (619)756-0159

Name: ______________________________

Company: ______________________________

Address: ______________________________

City, State, Zip (Country): ______________________________

Phone (required for credit card): (____)______________ Fax: (____)______________

Disk Size (choose one): ❑ **3.5"** ❑ **5.25"**

Payment ($10.00) (choose one):

❑ Enclosed (make check payable to *Alan Simpson Computing*) ❑ Master Card ❑ Visa

Account #______________________________ Exp. Date: _______

Signature:____ ______________________________

Downloading the Optional Files

If you have a CompuServe account, and enough experience with modems to download a file, you can download the optional files free of charge. (Well, "free," excluding your CompuServe charges and whatever Ma Bell charges for the call.). Here's how:

1. Get onto CompuServe and go to the SYBEX forum (GO SYBEX from the ! prompt, or Services ➢ Go ➢ type **sybex** from DOS CIM or WinCim).

   - To download sample Word documents, retrieve INSTWD.EXE from the Word Processing library to whatever directory you normally put your Word documents (e.g., C:\MSOFFICE \WINWORD).

   - To download spreadsheets, retrieve INSTXL.EXE from the Spreadsheets library to your Excel spreadsheets directory (e.g., C:\MSOFFICE\EXCEL).

   - To download a fancier, more user-friendly version of the PEOPLE.MDB database described in this book, retrieve INSTAC.EXE to your Access databases directory (e.g., C:\ACCESS).

2. Log off from CompuServe.

Each file is a self-extracting compressed file. To decompress, just go to the appropriate directory and execute the file. For example, to decompress spreadsheet files, go to your Excel spreadsheets directory, then choose File ➢ Run from Program Manager's menu bar. Then type INSTXL as the command and choose OK. From DOS, you'd go to the appropriate directory and just type the name of the file to decompress, then press ↵. For example, you could type **cd\msoffice\excel** ↵ to get to that directory, then type **INSTXL** ↵ to decompress.

Be sure to delete the compressed version of the file after decompressing it, so you don't waste disk space and so that you don't accidentally overwrite a decompressed, modified version of a file with the originally compressed version!

After the files have been decompressed, open (in Word) the file named INSTREAD.DOC in each directory that you downloaded files to for more information about those files.

Logo, Photo, Signature

We can digitize your signature, photo, or logo, so that you can put them in any Microsoft Office document that you create. Cost: $25.00 per item. Digitized images are guaranteed to work with any Microsoft Office application.

To complete this form:

- Follow the instructions on the back of this form and calculate your payment.
- Fill in your shipping address, amount owed, and preferred method of payment.
- Send this completed form and originals of the items to be digitized to:

Alan Simpson Computing
P.O. Box 630
Rancho Santa Fe, CA 92067
Fax: (619) 756-0159

Name: ______________________________

Company: ______________________________

Address: ______________________________

City, State, Zip (Country): ______________________________

Phone (required for credit card): (____)______________________

Fax: (____) ______________________________

Disk Size (choose one): ❑ 3.5" ❑ 5.25"

Amount owed (from other side): $______.____

Payment method (choose one)

❑ Enclosed (make check payable to *Alan Simpson Computing*) ❑ Master Card ❑ Visa

Account #______________________ Exp. Date: _______

Signature ______________________________

For credit card, *not* for scanning

INSTRUCTIONS FOR SUBMITTING ITEMS TO BE SCANNED

Signature: Send us your signature on a separate, clean white sheet of paper. *Use a black felt-tip pen.*

Photo: Submit only well-lit, well-focused photos: The quality of the *photo* determines the quality of the scanned image. No negatives or slides, please. If you want us to crop the photo, please make a photocopy of the photo and indicate *on the photocopy* how you want the photo cropped. If you know at what size you'll print the photo, fill in that measurement (*length width*) on the *Approx Size* column. If you don't know, just leave the Approx Size column empty.

Logo: Black and white is best, but we can do color as well. Send us a clean copy of your logo on clean white paper.

Disclaimer: Your originals will be returned along with your order. However, we are *not* liable for originals that get lost or damaged in transit. We do not recommend mailing rare or valuable photographs.

ITEMS TO BE SCANNED	APPROX. SIZE (IF KNOWN)	QTY	X $25.00	TOTAL
Signature(s)				
Photo(s)				
Logo(s)				
Other(s)				
		TOTAL	Please pay this amount::	

Thanks!